Women with Adult ADHD 10-in-1

The Complete Roadmap to Mastering Your Mind, Body, and Home, Evidence-Based Tools to Thrive with ADHD

Claim Your Free Bonus

As a thank you for reading, I've put together a powerful digital bonus pack to help you apply what you've learned — even if you only have a few minutes a day.

Inside you'll find:

- ✓ Quick-access emotional reset tools
- ✓ A printable clarity map for focus and purpose
- ✓ 30 powerful journaling prompts
- ✓ Daily progress & reflection trackers
- ✓ A mini affirmation deck for calm and confidence

Access below to download your full bonus pack:

https://livetolearn.lpages.co/vivian-withmore-women-with-adult-adhd-10-in-1-paperback/

Or, scan the QR code

CONTENTS

PART 1: WOMEN WITH ADHD 5-IN-1

INTRODUCTION 5

BOOK ONE - ORGANIZE YOUR LIFE: AN EASY GUIDE FOR WOMEN WITH ADHD 13

Introduction - The Cognitive Cost of Disorganization 15

Chapter 1 - Understanding the Organizational Brain 19

Chapter 2 - Creating Intuitive Physical Systems 24

Chapter 3 - Taming the Digital Deluge 30

Chapter 4 - From Idea to Action: Systems for Consistent Follow-Through 38

Chapter 5 - The Organized Mind: Habit Building and Maintenance 44

BOOK TWO - SHARPEN YOUR FOCUS: MASTERING YOUR ADHD BRAIN 53

Introduction - The Paradox of Focus 55

Chapter 1 - The Science of Focus 60

Chapter 2 - Designing Your Environment for Deeper Concentration 66

Chapter 3 - Mindfulness and Self-Compassion for Attentional Control 72

Chapter 4 - Single-Tasking and Deep Work Strategies 79

Chapter 5 - Sustaining Focus and Preventing Mental Fatigue 85

BOOK THREE - BALANCE YOUR HORMONES: A GUIDE FOR WOMEN WITH ADHD 97

Introduction - The Hormonal Connection 99

Chapter 1 - The Neurochemical Link 105

Chapter 2 - Navigating the Menstrual Cycle 111

Chapter 3: The Transition Years: Perimenopause, Menopause, and Cognitive Change ... 117
Chapter 4 - Hormones, Medication Efficacy, and Tailored Treatment ... 120
Chapter 5 - Hormonal Self-Care ... 126
BOOK FOUR - MASTER YOUR EMOTIONS: A PRACTICAL TOOLKIT FOR THE ADHD WOMAN ... 137
Introduction - The Emotional Rollercoaster and the Quest for Regulation ... 139
Chapter 1 - Emotional Dysregulation ... 145
Chapter 2 - Rejection Sensitive Dysphoria (RSD) ... 151
Chapter 3: CBT Tools: Identifying and Challenging Unhelpful Thoughts ... 157
Chapter 4: Behavioral Strategies for Emotional Regulation ... 164
Chapter 5 - Building Emotional Resilience and Self-Compassion ... 171
BOOK FIVE - MANAGE YOUR MONEY & RELATIONSHIPS: ESSENTIAL SKILLS FOR THE ADHD WOMAN ... 181
Introduction - The Adulting Challenge ... 183
Chapter 1 - Money and the ADHD Brain ... 188
Chapter 2 - Communication in Relationships ... 194
Chapter 3 - Navigating Shared Responsibilities and Social Dynamics ... 199
Chapter 4 - The Social Cost: Masking, Rejection, and Finding Your Community ... 206
Chapter 5 - Redefining Balance: Integrating Life Areas with ADHD ... 212
OVERALL CONCLUSION: THE EMPOWERED WOMAN WITH ADHD ... 222

PART 2: ADHD WORKBOOK FOR WOMEN 5-IN-1

INTRODUCTION: WELCOME TO YOUR EMPOWERED BRAIN 227

BOOK ONE - DECLUTTER YOUR SPACE AND BEAT OVERWHELM FOR THE ADHD WOMAN 237

- Introduction- The Cognitive Cost of Disorganization 239
- Chapter 1 - Conquer Paralysis: Break Down Overwhelming Tasks into Micro-Steps 245
- Chapter 2 - Design Your Sanctuary: Implement Visible, ADHD-Friendly Storage Systems 251
- Chapter 3 - Establish Predictability: Give Every Item a Designated "Home" 260
- Chapter 4 - Sustain Momentum: Use Body Doubling and Timers to Start Tasks 269
- Chapter 5 - Stop the Snowball: Implement Daily 15-Minute "Reset" Routines 278
- Chapter 6 - Reflect and Integrate: Your Decluttering Journey So Far 289
- Chapter 7 - Practice and Apply: Your Decluttering Action Toolkit 298
- Conclusion - Summary: Your Foundational Systems 308

BOOK TWO - BEAT OVERWHELM FOR THE ADHD WOMAN 315

- Introduction - The Paradox of Focus and the Mastering of Time 317
- Chapter 1 - Visualize Time: Banish Time Blindness with Concrete Scheduling Tools 324
- Chapter 2 - Schedule Success: Switch from Endless To-Do Lists to Time Blocking 337
- Chapter 3 - Customize Your Focus: Apply the Pomodoro Technique to Your Attention Span 349
- Chapter 4 - Future-Proof Your Brain: Strengthen Working Memory with Planning Routines 360
- Chapter 5 - Protect Your Energy: Reduce Cognitive Load by Eliminating Digital Noise 371

Chapter 6 - Reflect and Integrate: Your Focus Journey So Far..... 382
Chapter 7 - Practice and Apply: Your Executive Function Action Toolkit 394
Conclusion: Summary: Your Empowered Attention 398
BOOK THREE - SHARPEN EXECUTIVE FUNCTION IN WOMEN WITH ADHD 405
Introduction 407
Chapter 1 - Master Your Schedule: Transform Deadlines into Manageable Milestones 413
Chapter 2 - Prioritize Like a Pro: Techniques to Identify What Truly Matters 421
Chapter 3 - Harness Your Attention: Strategies to Build Lasting Focus 431
Chapter 4 - Strengthen Your Memory: Tools to Boost Working Memory Power 439
Chapter 5 - Simplify Decisions: Reduce Overwhelm with Clear Mental Frameworks 448
Chapter 6 - Reflect and Integrate: Insights and Growth in Your Executive Function Journey 457
Chapter 7 - Practice and Apply: Your Executive Function Action Toolkit 466
Conclusion: Summary: Your Empowered Attention 473
BOOK FOUR - SYNC HORMONES AND OPTIMIZE TREATMENT FOR THE ADHD WOMAN 479
Introduction 481
Chapter 1 - Map Your Cycle: Track Symptoms to Pinpoint Hormonal High-Risk Days 489
Chapter 2 - Optimize Your Flow: Strategically Schedule Tasks Around Energy Peaks 499
Chapter 3 - Advocate for Adjustment: Discuss Cycle Dosing of Stimulants with Your Doctor 510
Chapter 4 - Manage the Transition: Navigate Perimenopause and Menopausal Brain Fog 519

Chapter 5 - Build Your Buffer: Prioritize Sleep and Nutrition to Stabilize Mood 528
Chapter 6 - Reflect and Integrate: Your Hormonal Harmony Journey So Far 536
Chapter 7 - Practice and Apply: Your Hormonal Harmony Action Toolkit 544
Conclusion- Summary: A Holistic Approach to Hormonal Harmony 551
BOOK FIVE - TAME EMOTIONS AND STRENGTHEN RELATIONSHIPS IN WOMEN WITH ADHD 555
Introduction 557
Chapter 1 - Ground Yourself: Apply Sensory Techniques to Interrupt Acute Distress 562
Chapter 2 - Challenge the Critic: Identify and Reframe Unhelpful, Shame-Based Thoughts 571
Chapter 3 - Change the Script: Use "Opposite Action" to Interrupt Emotional Impulses 581
Chapter 4 - Connect Through Listening: Employ Mirroring and Validation for Deeper Communication 590
Chapter 5 - Fight Fair: Use 'I' Statements and Repair Attempts to Resolve Conflict 598
Chapter 6 - Reflect and Integrate: Your Emotional Mastery Journey So Far 607
Chapter 7 - Practice and Apply: Your Emotional Mastery Action Toolkit 615
Conclusion - Summary: Your Emotional Strength 621
OVERALL CONCLUSION - THE EMPOWERED WOMAN WITH ADHD 625
HERE'S ANOTHER BOOK BY VIVIAN WHITMORE THAT YOU MIGHT LIKE 630
CLAIM YOUR FREE BONUS 631
REFERENCES 632

PART 1: WOMEN WITH ADHD 5-IN-1

The Evidence-Based Guide to Organize Your Life, Sharpen Focus, Balance Hormones, and Master Emotions, Money and Relationships

Women with ADHD 5-in-1: The Evidence-Based Guide to Organize Your Life, Sharpen Focus, Balance Hormones, and Master Emotions, Money and Relationships

As a psychologist, I have worked with many women with ADHD, and I am familiar with the many challenges they face in daily life. I found this book to be a comprehensive and empowering resource for women navigating the unique challenges of a disorder that is often underdiagnosed or endured in silence among many women. The author integrates current research with practical strategies, offering readers an evidence-based roadmap to better understand themselves and develop skills that enhance daily functioning.

What distinguishes this work is its holistic perspective. Many ADHD guides focus narrowly on time management or productivity, but this book expands the lens to include hormones, emotional regulation, finances, and relationships—domains that are particularly relevant to women. The author underscores the interplay between fluctuating hormone levels and ADHD symptoms, an area often overlooked in traditional texts, and provides realistic coping tools for these cyclical changes.

The sections on organization and focus are pragmatic, with step-by-step approaches for managing clutter, prioritizing tasks, and creating sustainable systems that align with an individual's strengths rather than forcing rigid external models. Equally valuable are the chapters on mastering emotions and communication, which normalize the struggles women often experience in regulating affect and maintaining interpersonal balance. The financial guidance is another strength, addressing impulsive spending and decision fatigue with concrete, research-informed interventions.

Clinically, I appreciate the balance between validation and empowerment. The author avoids pathologizing, instead framing ADHD as a neurological difference that requires intentional management strategies. The content is relatable, and the evidence cited reassures both clinicians and readers that the recommendations are grounded in science.

Overall, this book is a valuable addition to the ADHD literature. It provides women with practical tools while acknowledging the layered experiences of gender, biology, and environment. I would confidently recommend it to clients and colleagues alike as both a guide on managing ADHD and a source of encouragement.

Carolina Estevez, Psy.D.

Licensed Psychologist

INTRODUCTION

Attention-Deficit/Hyperactivity Disorder (ADHD) has long been misunderstood, predominantly viewed through a lens shaped by the stereotypical image of a hyperactive young boy. This outdated narrative has created a significant and often devastating gap in understanding, leading to a profound, lifelong struggle for countless women.

For many, ADHD is an unseen battle, a condition that frequently goes under-diagnosed or is misdiagnosed entirely. This diagnostic disparity is largely due to the differences in how ADHD manifests between genders. While men are more likely to exhibit externalized, hyperactive symptoms, such as physical restlessness, excessive talking, and impulsive behaviors, that are easier to notice and lead to an earlier diagnosis, women and girls are more prone to the predominantly inattentive presentation of the disorder.

This inattentive subtype is characterized by internalized struggles, including disorganization, poor time management, forgetfulness, and a pervasive sense of internal restlessness.

The conventional diagnostic criteria, which were largely developed from studies on boys, often fail to capture the nuances of female symptom presentation. Early ADHD research predominantly focused on males, with one study noting that only 21% of participants in the field trials for the DSM-5 diagnostic criteria were girls.

As a result, many diagnostic tools were not designed with women and girls in mind, leading to a limited understanding of female ADHD. Women tend to be diagnosed much later than men, with some studies finding the mean age of diagnosis for females to be up to 28.6 years, compared to 22.7 years for males.

This delayed diagnosis means women often spend years, or even decades, struggling in secret before they receive the proper support. The lack of a diagnosis leaves them without a framework to understand their challenges, leading them to internalize their struggles and blame themselves for their difficulties, a pattern that fuels anxiety, depression, and low self-esteem.

This difference in symptom manifestation, combined with powerful societal expectations for women to be organized, emotionally mature, and calm, creates a pressure to conform that directly conflicts with the core symptoms of ADHD.

This conflict forces many women to engage in a practice known as "masking," where they develop sophisticated compensatory behaviors to hide their struggles and appear "neurotypical" to the outside world.

For instance, a woman might meticulously maintain a façade of punctuality by building in extra time for everything, a strategy she developed to combat her innate time blindness and avoid the social consequences of being late. Another might learn to pretend to take notes in a meeting to hide the fact that she is "zoning out" or has a "thousand-yard stare".

This constant, exhausting effort to appear "non-ADHD" is an invisible burden that leads to a lifetime of internalized shame, anxiety, depression, and a shattered sense of self-worth. This ongoing struggle often means that women are only diagnosed in adulthood, after years of self-blame and the accumulation of co-occurring mental health conditions that were fueled by their untreated and hidden ADHD. Studies confirm that girls are more likely to mask their symptoms than boys , and this can lead to significant negative consequences on their mental health, social functioning, and academic achievement.

The challenges of living with ADHD for women are not a series of isolated issues; rather, they form a complex, interconnected web. The struggle to maintain organization in Book 1, for example, is not merely about a messy living space, but about the profound mental and emotional toll that mess takes, leading a woman to feel such shame that she may avoid having people over.

Similarly, the difficulties with focus and productivity discussed in Book 2 are not just about getting things done, but about the overwhelming mental fatigue they create and the pervasive sense of being "frenzied" and "frazzled" that so many women with ADHD report.

This emotional and mental exhaustion then directly impacts a woman's ability to manage her hormones in Book 3, which in turn can exacerbate all of her other symptoms. The emotional dysregulation explored in Book 4 and the financial and relational challenges in Book 5 also feed into this cycle.

This guide will provide a comprehensive roadmap to navigate this complex landscape, offering evidence-based strategies to address the five core pillars of living a balanced and fulfilling life with ADHD. By providing a holistic approach, it aims to empower women to not just manage their symptoms but to truly thrive, transforming their unique neurobiology into a source of strength.

The Unique Neurobiology of ADHD in Women

The narrative that ADHD is a less problematic condition in women is outdated and inaccurate. While the core symptoms are similar in both genders, the way they manifest and the long-term impact on women's lives are dramatically different due to a "perfect storm" of internalized symptoms, hormonal fluctuations, and societal pressure. Research is only now beginning to fully explore why ADHD exacts a far greater toll on women.

A key difference is that hyperactivity in women often presents as an internal, rather than external, experience. Instead of fidgeting or running in circles, a woman's mind may be a "L.A. highway with high-speed cars zooming here, there, and everywhere". This internal restlessness and "flight of thoughts" can be just as disruptive as physical hyperactivity, but it is invisible to others and therefore less likely to be noticed or lead to a diagnosis. This can lead to a constant sense of being "frenzied, frazzled, and overwhelmed".

The ADHD brain is also wired differently due to variations in brain structure and neurotransmitter activity, particularly concerning dopamine and norepinephrine. Dopamine is a key neurotransmitter involved in motivation, reward, and executive functions like attention. For individuals with ADHD, the regulation of dopamine is thought to differ, leading to lower levels in the brain's synapses. This can make tasks that are not inherently stimulating or rewarding feel incredibly difficult to initiate and sustain.

The Emotional and Social Toll

For many women, the most debilitating aspect of their ADHD is not inattention, but emotional dysregulation. Research consistently shows that a significant percentage of adults with ADHD struggle to regulate their emotions, and women with the disorder are more likely than men to internalize these struggles, leading to self-blame.

This heightened emotional intensity is a hallmark of the female ADHD experience. A woman may experience emotions that feel "all or nothing" , with a rapid-fire succession of intense emotional states that can lead to being "overwhelmed by even minor hiccups and inconveniences".

This is because the frontal cortex of the ADHD brain, which is responsible for inhibiting big reactions, is often less activated. This can cause a woman to lash out, cry, or spiral into sadness with little warning, a pattern that is often misdiagnosed as a mood disorder.

A particularly painful and pervasive manifestation of this emotional dysregulation is Rejection Sensitive Dysphoria (RSD). While not a formal diagnosis, RSD is a descriptive term for an "extreme emotional responsiveness and anxiety in anticipation of, or in response to, perceived rejection or criticism from others".

For women with ADHD, who have often endured a lifetime of "chronic negative feedback" and a fear of their "perceived failures" being discovered , this can be an immediate, overwhelming emotional pain that feels physically agonizing. This hypersensitivity can make them people-pleasers or perfectionists, but it also makes them more susceptible to suicidal thoughts and self-harm than their male counterparts.

The combination of inattention and emotional dysregulation also takes a significant toll on relationships and friendships. Women with ADHD may struggle to form and maintain friendships, feeling a painful sense of "never fitting in". They may find it difficult to show up on time for social commitments, or to suppress the urge to interrupt in conversation because they fear they will forget what they wanted to say. This can lead to social rejection , and for women who have a greater need for social acceptance and connection than men, this can be particularly devastating.

The Interplay of Hormones and ADHD

A critical and often under-researched factor in the female ADHD experience is the profound impact of hormonal fluctuations throughout a woman's life. While this link has been an anecdotal reality for decades, many women feel their experiences are not "believed" by healthcare professionals.

Research confirms that sex hormones, like estrogen and progesterone, directly influence neurotransmitters like dopamine. Estrogen, in particular, is linked to an increase in dopamine levels. This connection explains why a woman's ADHD symptoms can feel different at various life stages, such as during puberty, the menstrual cycle, perimenopause, and menopause.

For women who menstruate, for example, studies suggest that attention and executive function can worsen in the low-estrogen luteal phase, which is the period leading up to menstruation. This hormonal environment can lead to more pronounced inattention, anxiety, and stress, and can even make a woman’s ADHD medication feel less effective.

The intersection of ADHD and Premenstrual Dysphoric Disorder (PMDD), a more severe form of PMS, is also significant, with a high percentage of women with ADHD also experiencing PMDD. The combination of these two conditions can make emotional regulation even more challenging, leading to more pronounced mood swings, irritability, and anger. This understanding of the hormonal link is crucial for developing personalized and effective treatment plans.

For women in midlife, the hormonal shifts of perimenopause and menopause can present a major and often unexpected challenge. As estrogen and progesterone levels decline, underlying ADHD symptoms that a woman has compensated for throughout her life can become unmanageable. Some experts refer to this as an "ADHD squared" effect: the compounding of low estrogen and low dopamine.

The symptoms of menopause, such as "brain fog," memory lapses, and difficulty with concentration, often mirror the symptoms of ADHD, making it difficult to differentiate between the two conditions and leading to a confusing and frustrating experience.

The Daily Cost of Unmanaged ADHD

The collective toll of these unmanaged symptoms can feel like a daily race to avoid disaster. This is often referred to as the "ADHD tax," a measurable cost that living with the condition can impose over a lifetime.

In the realm of personal finances, ADHD symptoms directly contribute to challenges. Studies show that people with ADHD have lower savings and higher debt, often remaining financially dependent on their families well into adulthood. The impulsivity that can drive spontaneous purchases and the time blindness that leads to late payments are direct consequences of ADHD-related executive function challenges. A woman with ADHD may also struggle to set and stick to a budget or to consistently organize bills and other financial paperwork.

Daily life can feel overwhelming, with even simple chores becoming a source of stress. A woman may find that unwashed dishes and laundry pile up, and she may dislike having people over due to the mess. The pervasive sense of disorganization can lead her to waste time looking for everyday items or to feel so overwhelmed that she struggles to make even small decisions.

This persistent feeling of being overwhelmed, of having to work "10 times harder than others to complete simple tasks" , and the constant fear of being seen as "incapable" contributes to a profound sense of inadequacy.

This guide is designed to address this complex, interconnected reality. By providing a holistic approach that validates the lived experience of women with ADHD, it aims to empower them to move beyond a lifetime of self-blame and shame. The following books will provide evidence-based strategies to address the five core pillars of living a balanced and fulfilling life with ADHD. By providing a comprehensive roadmap, it aims to empower women to not just manage their symptoms but to truly thrive, transforming their unique neurobiology into a source of strength.

BOOK ONE

ORGANIZE YOUR LIFE:

AN EASY GUIDE FOR WOMEN WITH ADHD

INTRODUCTION

THE COGNITIVE COST OF DISORGANIZATION

For women with ADHD, organization is not a simple matter of tidiness or a character trait; it is a profound struggle that drains mental energy and fuels a persistent sense of overwhelm. The inability to maintain order in one's physical and digital environments is a direct symptom of the disorder, a consequence of inherent difficulties with executive functions like working memory, planning, and task initiation.

This chronic disorganization is not merely inconvenient; it carries a significant cognitive and emotional cost. Valuable time is lost in frantic searches for misplaced items, crucial opportunities are missed due to forgotten deadlines or buried documents, and the constant visual and mental clutter creates a pervasive background hum of anxiety. This struggle is often compounded by societal expectations for women to be the caretakers of an organized home, leading to a deep sense of shame that can manifest in painful ways, such as avoiding having people over due to the mess.

Therefore, this guide approaches organization not as a rigid, perfectionistic ideal, but as a form of self-care. The goal is to establish "functional organization," a system that reduces cognitive load, minimizes friction, and works for the unique wiring of the ADHD brain, rather than against it.

For many women, the struggle with disorganization is a relentless and often invisible battle. Research indicates that executive function (EF) skills, which are essential for managing daily tasks and responsibilities, are significantly challenged in adults with ADHD. These deficits can lead to difficulty staying focused, disorganization, and missed details, all of which directly contribute to a messy physical and digital environment.

For instance, a woman with ADHD might find herself wasting time looking for everyday items, with her home being so cluttered that she dislikes having people over. The symptoms that define ADHD, such as inattention, can manifest as a disorganized workstation, poor time management, and an inability to work in noisy or busy environments.

This chronic disorganization creates a constant, low-grade stress that permeates daily life. The mind, much like the physical space it inhabits, is cluttered, making it difficult to find mental clarity. The brain's working memory, which functions as a "mental scratchpad," can feel like a sieve, making it nearly impossible to remember where an item was placed just moments ago or to hold a multi-step organizational plan in mind.

It’s a challenge so common that it's often described as the "out of sight, out of mind" phenomenon, where if something is put away in an opaque container or a cluttered drawer, it ceases to exist for the ADHD brain.

This struggle with disorganization is not a personal failing; it is a direct result of a neurobiological difference. For the ADHD brain, the very act of trying to start an organizing task can trigger a feeling of paralysis, a "can't get started" syndrome often referred to as a deficit in "task activation". The sheer scope of organizing a messy room or cleaning a cluttered inbox can trigger a feeling of overwhelm that makes task initiation nearly impossible.

The solution, as this guide will explore, is to break down these overwhelming tasks into smaller, more manageable steps. For example, instead of "Organize the entire bedroom," a more approachable task might be "Make the bed and place dirty clothes in the hamper". This systematic breakdown reduces the cognitive load and makes the first step feel psychologically approachable, transforming a daunting project into a series of achievable, low-friction steps.

The emotional toll of this disorganization is profound and often underestimated. Living with chronic disorganization and the constant effort to manage its consequences can lead to low self-esteem, self-blame, and feelings of inadequacy. Many women with undiagnosed ADHD endure childhoods filled with misunderstanding and self-blame, with a deep-seated feeling that there is something personally wrong with them.

Without a diagnosis, they may lack a better explanation for their struggles, attributing their challenges to personal flaws and developing a negative self-image. These women may also experience shame and frustration when they compare themselves to their peers and feel they are not living up to societal expectations. This constant inner critic and a repeated pattern of frustrations due to ADHD can contribute to or worsen co-occurring conditions like anxiety and depression.

This emotional burden is compounded by pervasive societal gender norms and roles. Society has long held the expectation for women to "do it all": to excel in both their public and private lives. While women have increasingly entered the workforce, they are still expected to shoulder the majority of household and domestic work.

It creates a "double burden" where women are under pressure to be perfect multitaskers, managing careers, households, and social lives simultaneously. Disorganization and messiness are often seen as violations of these traditional feminine norms, making women with ADHD particularly vulnerable to social judgment and internalizing feelings of inadequacy. When a woman with ADHD struggles to maintain an organized home, she may feel a deep sense of shame because her symptoms conflict with the unrealistic standards imposed on her.

This pressure can lead to feelings of overwhelm, anxiety, and a sense of inadequacy when they inevitably fail to meet these impossible standards. This guide rejects the notion of a rigid, perfectionistic ideal.

Instead, it champions a more compassionate and strategic approach to organization.

The goal is to establish "functional organization," a system that is intentionally designed to work with the unique wiring of the ADHD brain rather than against it. Functional organization is not about a perfect, magazine-ready home, but about creating external systems that reduce cognitive load, minimize friction, and create predictability. This includes using visual cues like clear storage bins and labels to combat the "out of sight, out of mind" problem and giving every item a designated "home" to eliminate constant decision-making about where to put things away.

It also involves adopting digital systems, such as a planner that is checked multiple times a day, to externalize crucial information and combat working memory issues. The foundation of this approach is self-compassion, acknowledging that a woman's struggle with organization is a neurobiological reality, not a personal failing. It is about building a supportive environment that frees up mental energy, which can then be redirected towards more fulfilling and productive endeavors.

By mastering these foundational systems, a woman can create a stable and predictable base for the more complex skills of focus, emotion management, and relationship nurturing that will be explored in the following books. A truly organized external life creates a sense of calm and clarity that allows the internal chaos to subside, paving the way for sustained growth and well-being.

CHAPTER 1

UNDERSTANDING THE ORGANIZATIONAL BRAIN

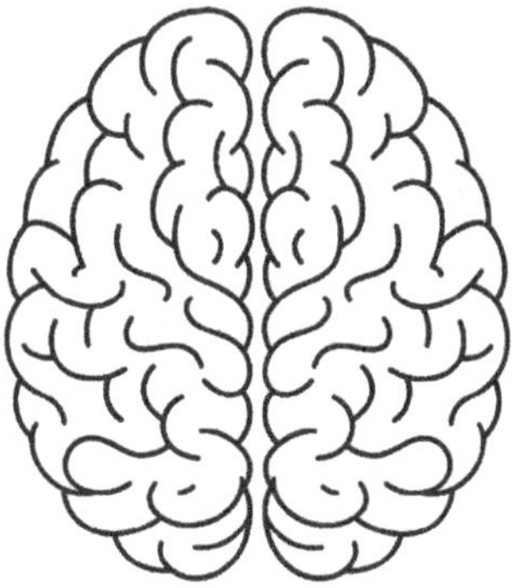

A foundational understanding of how the ADHD brain operates is essential to building an effective organizational system. The challenges with organization and planning are not a result of laziness or a lack of motivation; they are rooted in specific executive function differences.

Executive dysfunction is a range of behavioral symptoms that affect how a person regulates their emotions, thoughts, and actions, and it is a key symptom of ADHD. In fact, research indicates that the parts of the brain responsible for executive functions tend to be smaller, less developed, or less active in people with ADHD, which is why the disorder is nearly always associated with these symptoms.

Working memory, the brain's "mental scratchpad," can feel like a sieve, making it difficult to remember where an item was placed just moments ago or to hold a multi-step organizational plan in mind. Without a robust internal system for managing tasks and information, it is easy to become overwhelmed by the sheer number of things that need to be done.

The very act of trying to start an organizing task can trigger a feeling of paralysis, leading to procrastination. This is why a new approach is needed, one that validates the struggle and offers a compassionate, strategic way forward. The approach here is to externalize the cognitive load by building physical and digital structures that compensate for internal inconsistencies.

The Neurobiology of Executive Function Deficits

The organizational brain for a woman with ADHD operates on a different, and often more demanding, set of rules. Executive function (EF) is not a single skill, but a set of mental processes that allow a person to focus, plan, remember important details, and control impulses.

For the 40-60% of adults with ADHD who experience significant EF deficits, these challenges profoundly disrupt their personal and professional lives. They often score 10-15 points lower on EF measures than those without the condition, highlighting a measurable difference in cognitive ability.

This is not a matter of willpower, but rather a direct result of how the brain is wired. Research on memory and ADHD has found that these challenges are likely due to differences in the activation of various parts of the brain, including a reduced activation in the prefrontal cortex and cerebellum.

The prefrontal cortex is the brain's "command center" and is responsible for a variety of higher-level cognitive functions, such as planning, working memory, and impulse control. This reduced activity makes it more challenging to remember task goals, instructions, or rules. For example, the ADHD brain may process information in a disorganized manner, making it difficult to successfully move new information from short-term to long-term memory. This means that while the core machinery for memory is present, the process of encoding and retrieving information is often impaired.

This deficit can manifest as "brain fog," a temporary sluggishness and slowdown of your thinking abilities, leading to mental exhaustion, poor focus, carelessness, and forgetfulness. The cumulative effect of constantly fighting against this neurobiological reality is a profound sense of fatigue and being perpetually "frenzied, frazzled, and overwhelmed".

The Concept of Cognitive Load

A key factor in understanding the organizational struggles of the ADHD brain is the concept of cognitive load. Cognitive load refers to the total amount of mental effort being used in working memory. For a neurotypical person, the brain is able to efficiently filter out irrelevant stimuli and prioritize information, thus managing the cognitive load effectively.

For an individual with ADHD, this filtering mechanism is often less efficient, causing the brain to take in and process a disproportionate amount of incoming information, both internal and external. A single open browser tab, an unread email, a stray object on a desk, or an intrusive thought can all compete for attention with the same intensity as the main task at hand.

Research indicates that a high cognitive load can have a disproportionately negative impact on performance for people with ADHD. Studies have shown that as cognitive load increases, individuals with ADHD experience reduced performance, greater reaction time variability, and reduced brain network efficiency compared to those without the condition. This means that a cluttered physical or digital space isn't just an inconvenience; it is a direct contributor to reduced cognitive function and task performance, as each piece of clutter represents a subtle, but persistent, demand on a brain already struggling to filter and prioritize.

This is why the phrase "out of sight, out of mind" is so prevalent for people with ADHD. The sheer cognitive burden of managing multiple opaque containers, a cluttered desk, or a chaotic calendar can lead to tasks, items, and appointments ceasing to exist for the ADHD brain once they are no longer in the immediate visual field. The result is a constant drain on mental energy and a pervasive feeling of being overwhelmed by even minor daily inconveniences.

The Task Activation Deficit

A foundational hurdle for many women with ADHD is the "task activation deficit," a difficulty in initiating tasks without excessive procrastination. You may know exactly what needs to be done, but the gap between intention and action can feel immense, like a vast chasm you can't cross. This isn't laziness, but a neurological hurdle rooted in the brain's reward and motivation system. The very act of trying to start an organizing task, especially one that is perceived as boring or overwhelming, can trigger a feeling of paralysis, leading to what some refer to as "ADHD paralysis".

This paralysis is often a direct result of the overwhelming nature of a multi-step task. For instance, a woman might know she needs to clean her room, but the thought of organizing toys, putting away clothes, and making her bed feels so daunting that she can't figure out where to start. The sheer volume of an undifferentiated task can trigger an immediate shutdown response, as the brain's executive functions struggle to find a clear entry point. This is why breaking a to-do down into smaller, more manageable chunks is a highly effective strategy for the ADHD brain. It reduces the cognitive load and makes the initial step psychologically approachable, transforming a formidable project into a series of small, achievable steps.

The challenge with organization is also exacerbated by other related executive function deficits, such as difficulties with planning, prioritizing, and time management. The ADHD brain may struggle to create a step-by-step plan to achieve a goal, or to sort out which tasks are most important and which can wait. This combination of challenges makes it difficult to even begin the process of getting organized, creating a vicious cycle of disorganization leading to overwhelm, which in turn leads to procrastination.

The Emotional and Social Toll

This constant, daily struggle with organization and executive function deficits takes a significant emotional toll on women with ADHD, who often internalize their difficulties and blame themselves for their struggles. Research suggests that women with undiagnosed ADHD often endure childhoods filled with misunderstanding, self-blame, and rejection, with a persistent feeling that there is something personally wrong with them.

Without a clear explanation for their functional impairments, they may attribute their struggles to personal flaws, resulting in low self-esteem, shame, and a negative self-image. One woman with undiagnosed ADHD reported feeling "what I felt was I was actually a bad person... I was not an adequate human being".

This inner critic is often amplified by societal expectations for women to be the caretakers of an organized home and to perform as perfect multitaskers. When a woman with ADHD struggles to maintain order, her symptoms conflict with these unrealistic gender norms, leading to a profound sense of shame that can manifest in painful ways, such as avoiding having people over due to the mess. This constant pressure to meet impossible standards can lead to mental health struggles, including anxiety, depression, and feelings of inadequacy.

The emotional distress that arises from these challenges can be so severe that it contributes to or worsens co-occurring conditions, and it can be a source of significant distress and self-loathing.

Therefore, this guide approaches organization not as a rigid, perfectionistic ideal, but as a form of self-care. The goal is to establish "functional organization," a system that reduces cognitive load, minimizes friction, and works for the unique wiring of the ADHD brain, rather than against it. This compassionate, strategic approach is designed to free a woman from the debilitating cycle of self-blame and overwhelm, allowing her to build external systems that compensate for internal inconsistencies and create a sense of calm and clarity in her life. It is about understanding that your brain is not broken; it is simply wired differently and requires a tailored approach to thrive.

CHAPTER 2

CREATING INTUITIVE PHYSICAL SYSTEMS

Your physical environment can be either a source of stress or a powerful ally in your pursuit of a more organized life. The first step in creating a supportive space is to recognize the common challenge known as "out of sight, out of mind". For an ADHD brain, if something is tucked away in an opaque container or a cluttered drawer, it ceases to exist. This can be directly combated by using clear storage bins and labels to keep everything visible and easily identifiable. The key is to create intuitive systems that minimize the mental effort required to maintain them.

A foundational principle is to give every single item a designated "home". By assigning a specific place for everything, you eliminate the constant decision-making about where to put something away, a process that drains executive function and leads to clutter. For frequently lost items, such as keys, wallets, and phones, the use of a "landing strip" near the front door is a highly effective strategy that ensures these crucial items are always in a predictable and easily accessible location.

To manage the inevitable accumulation of new items, consider implementing a "one-in, one-out" rule, which forces a conscious decision and prevents your home from becoming overwhelmed.

Maintaining these systems does not require constant, perfectionistic tidying. For the ADHD brain, a more sustainable approach is to schedule regular "resets" or "start-of-day/end-of-day clean-ups". These short, dedicated periods allow you to put things back in their homes and prevent small messes from spiraling into overwhelming chaos. This approach transforms organization from a source of frustration into a manageable, routine practice.

The Emotional and Cognitive Cost of Clutter

The relationship between your physical environment and your brain is a two-way street. For a neurotypical individual, a cluttered space might be a minor inconvenience, but for a woman with ADHD, it can be a significant source of cognitive and emotional distress. Research has consistently shown that cluttered environments can increase stress and anxiety and reduce productivity. A study in the *Personality and Social Psychology Bulletin* found that cluttered spaces can raise cortisol levels, which is a stress hormone that can exacerbate ADHD symptoms.

This constant, low-grade stress is not just a feeling; it is a measurable cognitive drain. Each item in a cluttered space represents a potential point of distraction, demanding a fraction of your attention and consuming valuable working memory and executive function resources. Your brain, already working harder to filter out irrelevant stimuli, becomes overloaded by the sheer volume of visual and sensory information.

The result is a pervasive background hum of anxiety, mental exhaustion, and a feeling of being overwhelmed that can lead to procrastination and a complete shutdown, or what is often referred to as "ADHD paralysis."

This struggle is often compounded by powerful societal expectations for women to be the caretakers of an organized home. When a woman with ADHD struggles to maintain order, her symptoms conflict with these unrealistic gender norms, leading to a profound sense of shame that can manifest in painful ways, such as avoiding having people over due to the mess.

Research shows that women with undiagnosed ADHD often endure childhoods filled with misunderstanding, self-blame, and a persistent feeling that there is something personally wrong with them, a feeling that is exacerbated by the internal and external pressures related to organization.

The "Out of Sight, Out of Mind" Phenomenon: A Deeper Look

The idea that "if something is out of sight, it's out of mind" is a widely recognized experience for people with ADHD and is directly tied to challenges with working memory. Working memory is the brain's "mental scratchpad," and for a woman with ADHD, that scratchpad can feel like a sieve, making it difficult to hold information in mind for a short period of time.

As a result, if an item is not in your immediate visual field, your brain may fail to register its existence, location, or importance, leading to frantic searches for misplaced items and a constant feeling of being disorganized.

This is why traditional organizational advice, such as "tuck everything away neatly in opaque boxes," can be completely counterproductive for the ADHD brain. Instead of creating a sense of order, it creates a system of unreliability where items are lost the moment they are hidden. To counteract this, the organizational system must be intentionally designed to be visual and to externalize the cognitive load. By making everything visible and easily identifiable, you bypass the need for your working memory to constantly recall where an item is, allowing you to use that precious mental energy for other, more demanding tasks.

Strategies to combat this challenge include:

- **Clear Storage Bins:** Using clear bins or containers allows you to see the contents without having to open them, providing a constant visual cue of what is inside. This is a simple but powerful way to ensure that your items remain "in mind."
- **Labels, Labels, Labels:** For items that must be stored in opaque containers or drawers, clear, bold labels are essential. A label for "Office Supplies" or "First Aid Kit" serves as a crucial external reminder of the contents, eliminating the mental effort of guessing or having to search through every drawer.
- **Vertical Organization:** Piles of papers or objects on a flat surface can be a source of overwhelm and mental friction. Using clipboards to display current projects as a visual reminder or vertical file folders to keep important paperwork in sight can help manage this. This approach transforms an overwhelming pile into a manageable, visual system of organization.

The Power of a Designated "Home"

A foundational principle of intuitive physical systems is to give every single item a designated "home". This is not about being rigid or a perfectionist; it is a strategic approach to reduce decision fatigue, which is a major drain on executive function. Each time you pick up an item, your brain is faced with a micro-decision: "Where does this go?" When you don't have a clear, pre-determined "home" for an item, that micro-decision process can lead to an endless loop of deliberation that often ends with the item being placed on a random surface, contributing to clutter and chaos.

By assigning a specific and predictable place for every item, you eliminate this decision-making process. Putting an item away becomes a simple, automatic, and low-friction action. For frequently lost items, such as keys, wallets, phones, and glasses, a "landing strip" near the front door or a designated bowl on a counter is a highly effective, research-backed strategy that ensures these crucial items are always in a predictable and easily accessible location. By creating a system of predictability, you free up your mental resources and reduce the frantic, time-consuming searches that so often accompany ADHD.

This principle extends to all areas of your life, from the keys on the landing strip to the remote control on the coffee table to the notebooks on your desk. By making the "home" for an item obvious and intuitive, you build a system that works with your brain's unique wiring, not against it.

Maintenance Made Manageable: The Role of Routines

For the ADHD brain, the idea of "constant tidying" can feel like an impossible and overwhelming ideal that is destined for failure. This is why a perfectionistic approach to organization is often a fast track to burnout and abandonment of the system altogether. A more sustainable approach is to create and implement simple, non-negotiable routines and maintenance rituals.

One of the most effective strategies is to schedule regular "resets" or "start-of-day/end-of-day clean-ups". This involves dedicating a short, consistent period of time, for instance, 15 minutes in the morning or evening, to tidying up your physical and digital workspaces. This prevents small messes from snowballing into overwhelming mountains of clutter that seem impossible to tackle. The goal is not a pristine space, but a functional one. For example, instead of trying to keep an entire bedroom clean all the time, you could commit to simply making your bed and placing dirty clothes in a hamper at the start of each day. This small, manageable commitment provides a sense of accomplishment and prevents a small mess from spiraling into overwhelming chaos.

The "one-in, one-out" rule also plays a vital role in maintaining the system over time. This simple principle is a powerful preventative measure against the inevitable accumulation of new items that can quickly overwhelm a space. By forcing a conscious decision to remove an item every time a new one is introduced, you actively prevent your home from becoming a source of cognitive and physical clutter.

These maintenance routines are crucial because they transform organization from a source of frustration and anxiety into a manageable, routine practice that is integrated into your daily life. It acknowledges the reality that things will get messy and builds in a compassionate, strategic way to address it without succumbing to overwhelm or self-criticism.

Conclusion: Your External Sanctuary

This chapter has provided a roadmap for creating a physical environment that is not just organized, but is a sanctuary for your ADHD brain. By understanding the profound cognitive and emotional costs of disorganization, a woman can move beyond self-blame and begin to work with her brain, not against it. She has learned to combat the "out of sight, out of mind" phenomenon with visual cues and clear labels, to give every item a "home" to reduce decision fatigue, and to maintain her systems with realistic, non-perfectionistic routines.

The mastery of these strategies transforms your physical space from a source of friction and stress into a powerful ally for focus, clarity, and peace. It frees up immense mental energy that was once consumed by searching for misplaced items, navigating clutter, and feeling overwhelmed.

This newly available cognitive bandwidth can then be redirected toward more fulfilling and productive endeavors. A truly organized external life creates a sense of calm and clarity that allows the internal chaos to subside, paving the way for sustained growth and well-being.

CHAPTER 3

TAMING THE DIGITAL DELUGE

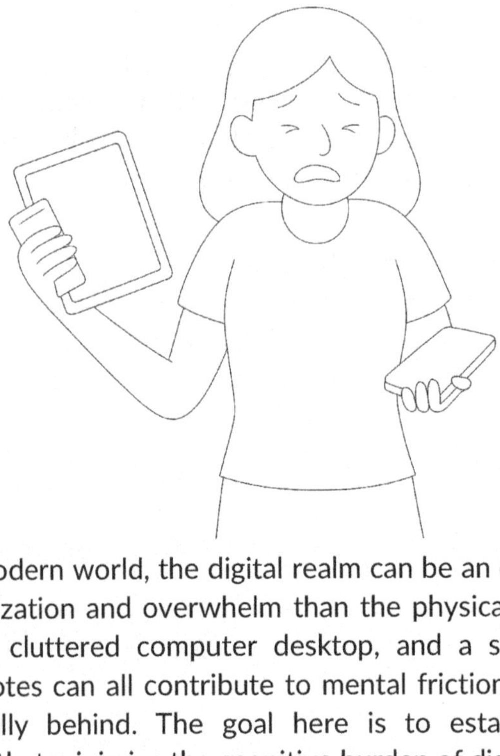

In the modern world, the digital realm can be an even greater source of disorganization and overwhelm than the physical one. A chaotic email inbox, a cluttered computer desktop, and a scattered collection of digital notes can all contribute to mental friction and a sense of being perpetually behind. The goal here is to establish simple, intuitive systems that minimize the cognitive burden of digital management.

For the ADHD brain, the digital world is a double-edged sword. On one hand, it offers a wealth of tools and external reminders that can be invaluable for compensating for working memory deficits. A digital planner with automatic alerts can provide the crucial structure needed to remember appointments and deadlines.

On the other hand, the digital environment is a hyper-stimulating landscape of endless distractions, notifications, and open loops that are perfectly designed to hijack an already scattered attention span. A single open browser tab can be a subtle demand on your attention, a pending notification can trigger an impulsive check, and a cluttered desktop can create a visual and cognitive drain that is as potent as a messy physical space.

This relentless barrage of digital stimuli exacerbates the struggle with executive functions like working memory and attention regulation, leading to what research refers to as high "cognitive load". Studies have shown that for individuals with ADHD, increasing cognitive load disproportionately reduces performance, increases reaction time variability, and decreases brain network efficiency compared to those without the condition . Therefore, just as you learned to intentionally design your physical space, mastering your digital environment is a non-negotiable step toward a more organized and peaceful life.

The Email Onslaught: Taming the Inbox

The email inbox is often a primary source of digital overwhelm, quickly transforming from a communication tool into a chaotic, constantly-updating to-do list that triggers a persistent sense of anxiety and defeat. The constant stream of messages demands attention and decision-making, a process that is particularly draining for the ADHD brain.

An effective strategy is to implement a triage system that reduces the cognitive load and turns email management into a predictable, low-friction process.

A core strategy for email is the "Inbox Zero" concept, but viewed through the lens of a clear, actionable system rather than a stressful ideal. This involves a four-step triage process for every email: delete it if it's junk, do it if it takes less than two minutes, delegate it to someone else, or defer it by moving it to a specific "To Do" folder in your email client.

By consistently processing your inbox this way, you prevent it from becoming a cluttered to-do list that drains your attention and provides a sense of overwhelming defeat. This process is not about achieving an empty inbox at all costs, but about consciously deciding the fate of each email and preventing the mental clutter that comes from having an open-ended list of pending tasks.

The "two-minute rule" is especially powerful for the ADHD brain because it leverages the psychological power of quick wins. By immediately tackling small, manageable tasks, you get a satisfying hit of dopamine, which reinforces productive behavior and builds momentum for the more demanding tasks that require a deferred response. This triage system also externalizes decision-making, so your brain is no longer constantly asking, "What should I do with this?"

This intentional processing reduces the mental friction of an unmanaged inbox and creates a sense of control over a traditionally chaotic digital space.

For managing the inflow of emails, consider creating dedicated email blocks in your daily schedule. Instead of leaving your email client open all day and reacting to each incoming message, which constantly fragments your attention, dedicate two or three specific 20-minute periods to process your inbox. This practice turns email from a persistent distraction into a manageable, time-bound task.

You can also create simple rules or filters to automatically send newsletters, notifications, or less important messages to a designated folder, ensuring that your main inbox remains a clear space for high-priority communication.

The Digital Planner: Your External Working Memory

For a woman with ADHD, relying solely on internal working memory to keep track of deadlines, appointments, and tasks is a recipe for anxiety and forgetfulness. As research has shown, working memory deficits are a core feature of the disorder, and these challenges are linked to a reduced activation in the prefrontal cortex, which is the brain's command center for planning and memory. This is why externalizing your memory is a crucial compensatory strategy.

The use of a simple, digital planner is also crucial for combating the working memory issues inherent in ADHD by externalizing important deadlines and tasks. By checking this planner at least twice a day, once in the morning and once at night, a woman can eliminate the fear of forgetting a crucial deadline or appointment. Digital planners, calendars, and apps with reminders and alerts are particularly effective because they provide a reliable, automated system that doesn't rely on inconsistent internal memory.

When setting up your digital planner, be intentional:

- **Color-Code:** Use a color-coding system to visually represent different areas of your life, such as work, personal appointments, family events, and self-care. Visual cues make your schedule easier for the ADHD brain to process and understand at a glance.
- **Time Block:** Don't just list tasks; block out specific time slots for them. Time blocking helps make time more tangible by assigning a finite duration to a task, which is a powerful antidote to "time blindness".
- **Set Multiple Reminders:** For important deadlines or appointments, set multiple alarms or alerts. Set one for a week before, one for a day before, and one for an hour before. This redundancy provides crucial support for a brain that can easily be derailed by last-minute distractions.

By consistently relying on an external planner, you offload the immense cognitive burden of remembering everything, freeing up your mental energy for focused work and creative thinking.

Digital Filing: The "Less is More" Approach

A cluttered digital workspace—a desktop covered in files, a downloads folder with hundreds of unsorted documents, and a complex hierarchy of folders—is a significant drain on cognitive resources. The ADHD brain, already struggling to filter out irrelevant information, can become quickly overwhelmed by digital disorganization. The mental effort required to navigate a chaotic digital environment, remember where files are, and make decisions about where to save new documents creates unnecessary mental friction.

To combat this, the most effective strategy is to adopt a "less is more" approach to digital filing by creating a few broad, consistently used folders and relying on powerful search functions. This approach is not about a rigid, perfectionistic system but about creating a simple, intuitive structure that is easy to maintain.

- **Create a Flat Hierarchy:** Instead of creating a deeply nested folder structure (e.g., Documents > Work > Client A > Project X > Research > Q1), create a flat hierarchy with a few main folders that are easy to navigate (e.g., Projects, Clients, Reference, Archive). The ADHD brain can easily get lost in a complex folder structure.
- **Use Consistent Naming Conventions:** Implement a simple naming convention for your files (e.g., ProjectName_DocumentType_Date). This makes it easier to find files using the search bar, which should be your primary tool for locating information.
- **Leverage Search:** Modern operating systems and cloud storage platforms have incredibly powerful search functions. By relying on a consistent naming system, you can use search as your main tool for finding documents, eliminating the need to remember complex folder paths. This is an external solution that bypasses your working memory deficits.
- **Desktop Decluttering:** Treat your computer desktop as a temporary holding space, not a permanent storage solution. Move all files from your desktop to a single, designated "To Sort" folder at the end of each day or week. This prevents visual clutter from accumulating and reduces the cognitive load of a messy digital space.

Taming Digital Noise and Distractions

The digital world is a constant source of interruptions that can derail focus and fragment attention for the ADHD brain. Each notification, pop-up, or email chime is a "ping" that pulls your mental spotlight away from your current task. The brain's tendency to struggle with filtering out irrelevant stimuli means that these digital pings are given disproportionate weight, making it incredibly difficult to achieve a state of "deep work."

A powerful strategy is to create a digital "attention zone" by proactively minimizing distractions:

- **Notification Annihilation:** This is paramount. Turn off all non-essential notifications on your phone, tablet, and computer. Be ruthless. Turn off alerts for social media, news apps, and email clients. The fewer pings your devices make, the easier it is for your brain to stay on task.
- **App Management:** Regularly review the apps on your phone and computer. Delete those you don't use. For apps you find distracting, consider grouping them into a folder on your phone's last screen to create a deliberate moment of friction before you can access them.
- **Browser Management:** Commit to having only 1-3 tabs open at any given time. Each additional tab is an open loop that demands a piece of your working memory. Use browser extensions like "StayFocusd" or "Freedom" to block distracting websites during your work periods.
- **Digital Self-Care:** Recognize that digital clutter and noise are a source of stress. Schedule intentional periods of "digital detox" where you completely unplug from screens. This allows your brain to reset, reducing the mental fatigue that comes from constant digital stimulation.

By implementing these digital hygiene practices, you'll create a calmer, more focused digital environment that supports your attention rather than constantly fighting for it.

Leveraging Technology for Automation and Externalization

Beyond simple organization, modern technology offers powerful tools that can be leveraged to create automated systems that work for the ADHD brain, further reducing the need for conscious effort and decision-making.

- **Automate Everything:** Wherever possible, automate tasks that are repetitive or easy to forget. This is a highly effective way to combat the challenges of working memory and time blindness. Set up automatic bill payments, so you no longer have to worry about late fees. Use recurring calendar reminders for habits you want to build or tasks that need to be done regularly.

- **Use Visual Tools:** Many people with ADHD are visual thinkers. Use budgeting apps with charts and graphs, or project management tools with Kanban boards (like Trello) that allow you to see the entire flow of a project. These visual systems make abstract concepts more tangible and easier for the ADHD brain to process, reducing overwhelm and increasing task initiation.
- **Digital Backups:** Prevent the emotional distress and wasted time that comes with losing important files by regularly backing up your data. Use automated cloud backups or external hard drives. The emotional and cognitive cost of losing a critical document is immense, and this simple system provides a reliable safety net.

By embracing technology in these strategic ways, you're not just managing your digital life; you're building a sophisticated external support system that compensates for your internal challenges, allowing you to operate with greater efficiency, less stress, and more confidence.

Your Roadmap to Becoming Digital Savvy

This chapter has provided a roadmap for creating a digital environment that is not a source of constant stress and distraction, but a powerful ally in your pursuit of a more organized life. By understanding how digital clutter and noise contribute to cognitive overload for the ADHD brain, you can move beyond a reactive, frantic approach to a proactive, strategic one.

You have learned to:

- **Tame your email** with a low-friction triage system that reduces decision fatigue.
- **Externalize your working memory** with a digital planner that provides a reliable, visual anchor for your schedule and tasks.
- **Simplify your digital filing** with a "less is more" approach that leverages powerful search functions.
- **Build a digital sanctuary** by proactively managing notifications, browser tabs, and apps to protect your focus.
- **Leverage technology** for automation, visual support, and reliable backups that compensate for your internal challenges.

The mastery of these digital systems transforms your online world from a source of friction and overwhelm into a clean, intuitive, and supportive extension of your mind. This newly available cognitive bandwidth, once consumed by fighting digital chaos, can now be redirected towards more fulfilling and productive endeavors. A truly organized digital life creates a sense of calm and clarity that allows the internal chaos to subside, paving the way for sustained growth and well-being.

CHAPTER 4

FROM IDEA TO ACTION: SYSTEMS FOR CONSISTENT FOLLOW-THROUGH

A solid organizational system is invaluable, but it's only truly powerful when it bridges the gap between intention and action. The immense, amorphous nature of large projects can trigger a feeling of overwhelm that paralyzes the ADHD brain and makes task initiation nearly impossible. The solution to this is to systematically break down every large, intimidating task into smaller, more manageable chunks.

For example, instead of "Organize the Garage," a task could be broken down into "Clear one shelf" or "Sort tools into a basket." This reduces the cognitive burden and makes the first step feel psychologically approachable, transforming a daunting project into a series of achievable, low-friction steps.

The Chasm Between Intention and Action

For women with ADHD, the journey from a brilliant idea to a completed project is often fraught with a unique and frustrating barrier: the gap between intention and action. You may have a clear vision and a strong desire to accomplish a goal, but an invisible wall seems to prevent you from taking that crucial first step. This isn't a sign of laziness or a lack of motivation; it is a neurological hurdle, a symptom of a task activation deficit that is deeply intertwined with the brain's executive function challenges.

Research on the ADHD brain's executive functions, such as working memory, planning, and prioritization, has found that these skills are often less efficient, which can make getting started on tasks feel overwhelming, especially when there are multiple steps involved.

The sheer scale of a large, undifferentiated project, like "Write a business plan" or "Organize the entire closet", can trigger a state of mental paralysis known as "ADHD paralysis." For an ADHD brain, which already struggles with filtering and prioritizing, the cognitive load of holding a multi-step plan in mind can feel immense.

The brain's prefrontal cortex, which is responsible for these higher-level cognitive functions, can become overwhelmed, leading to a shutdown response rather than initiation. The solution, therefore, is not to simply "try harder," but to create a strategic and compassionate system that bypasses this internal resistance by externalizing the cognitive load and making the initial step so small and non-intimidating that the activation energy required is minimal.

The Art and Science of Task Breakdown

The core strategy for bridging the gap between intention and action is to systematically break down every large, intimidating task into smaller, more manageable chunks. This process reduces cognitive overwhelm and makes the first step feel psychologically approachable, transforming a daunting project into a series of achievable, low-friction steps.

Research indicates that breaking tasks into smaller chunks reduces cognitive load and increases task initiation, which is crucial for a brain that struggles with executive function deficits.

This is not a purely theoretical exercise; it is a practical art with a scientific basis. The ADHD brain is constantly seeking a fresh hit of dopamine, the neurotransmitter associated with motivation and reward. By breaking down a large task into smaller steps, you create more opportunities for a sense of accomplishment and a satisfying burst of dopamine each time you complete one. This positive reinforcement loop builds momentum, making it easier to sustain your effort over time.

Here's how to apply a systematic approach to task breakdown:

- **The Brain Dump:** Before you can organize a project, you must first get everything out of your head. Write down every single thought, step, worry, and idea related to the large task onto a piece of paper, a whiteboard, or a digital note-taking app. Don't worry about order or logic; just get it all out. This externalizes the mental clutter and provides a raw inventory of the project, freeing up your working memory for a more organized approach.
- **Identify the "Next Action":** For every item on your list, ask yourself: "What is the very next physical action I need to take to move this forward?" The key is to make this step so small that it feels almost ridiculous not to do it. Instead of "Clean the kitchen," the next action might be "Put one dish in the dishwasher." Instead of "Write the report," it could be "Open a new document and type the title." This micro-commitment lowers the activation energy required to begin, making procrastination less likely.
- **Create a Visual Checklist:** Once you have a series of tiny, actionable steps, transfer them to a visual checklist. This could be a physical list on a clipboard, a visual calendar with color-coded blocks, or a digital task manager like a Kanban board in Trello. The visual satisfaction of physically or digitally checking off small items provides valuable, immediate dopamine hits. This consistent, visible progress combats the feelings of stagnation and overwhelm that so often accompany large projects.

The Pomodoro Technique: A Structured Solution for Sustained Focus

The Pomodoro Technique is an excellent tool to implement this strategy, as it breaks down the day into manageable, focused work sprints. It is particularly effective for the ADHD brain because it works

with its natural need for novelty and breaks, rather than fighting against it. The traditional technique involves committing to 25 minutes of uninterrupted, single-task focus, followed by a 5-minute break. After four of these cycles, you take a longer, more restorative break of 20-30 minutes.

The power of this technique for the ADHD brain lies in its built-in structure:

- **It Reduces Overwhelm:** The idea of working on a boring or difficult task for an undefined period can be paralyzing. Committing to a task for a short, manageable burst of 25 minutes makes it feel less intimidating and more approachable. This is a powerful antidote to "ADHD paralysis."
- **It Accommodates the Need for Breaks:** The scheduled 5-minute breaks provide regular, guilt-free opportunities for the brain to reset and seek novelty without derailing the entire work session. This prevents the mental fatigue and restlessness that can build up during prolonged, static focus. The breaks serve as a reward and a mental reset, accommodating the brain's natural rhythms.
- **It Builds Momentum:** The short, focused bursts help the ADHD brain get into a state of momentum. Once you're in motion, it's often easier to stay in motion. The consistent, rhythmic nature of the Pomodoro cycles helps to gradually train your brain to sustain attention for longer periods.

Research supports the efficacy of this approach. One study found that implementing the Pomodoro technique in a digital marketing company helped employees work more efficiently and improve their work-life balance. The discipline of single-tasking, enforced by a timer, is a powerful antidote to a scattered mind, allowing a woman to reduce feelings of overwhelm and achieve a higher quality of work with less mental effort.

Beyond Pomodoro: Additional Strategies for Consistent Follow-Through

While task breakdown and the Pomodoro Technique are foundational, there are other strategies that can be integrated to support consistent follow-through and counteract the ADHD brain's tendency to lose momentum.

- **Body Doubling:** Working alongside another person, either in person or virtually, can be a remarkably effective way to combat "activation energy" deficits and sustain focus. The mere presence of another person provides a subtle sense of accountability and structure, making it easier to start and remain on task without relying solely on willpower. The other person acts as an external executive function, providing a stable, non-distracting presence that helps anchor your attention.
- **Gamification and Rewards:** The ADHD brain thrives on immediate feedback and rewards. To maintain momentum on a long task, inject elements of a game into your work. Use a timer to "compete" against yourself, create a points system for completed sub-tasks, or build in small, intentional rewards for hitting a milestone. The promise of an immediate, enjoyable reward, like a 5-minute break, a favorite song, or a cup of tea, can provide the necessary dopamine hit to push through a tedious section of a project.
- **The "One-in, One-out" Rule (for Tasks):** Just as you might apply this rule to physical items to prevent clutter, you can apply it to your to-do list. Commit to finishing one task before you allow yourself to start a new one. This prevents the "half-finished pile" from accumulating and forces you to bring tasks to completion. It's a deliberate act of single-tasking that builds a habit of follow-through.
- **Embrace Imperfection:** For many women with ADHD, perfectionism is a subtle but powerful form of procrastination. The fear of not doing something perfectly can prevent you from starting or, more commonly, from finishing. Remind yourself constantly that "done is better than perfect." The goal

is completion and tangible progress, not flawlessness. A completed, even imperfect, project creates momentum and allows for iteration, while a "perfect" project that is perpetually stuck in the planning stage serves no one.

- **Public Accountability:** Tell a trusted friend, partner, or colleague what specific task you intend to accomplish by a certain time. Knowing someone else is aware of your commitment can provide a powerful external motivator to follow through, leveraging social pressure to push past resistance. This can be as simple as a quick text: "I'm going to finish the draft of that report by 3 PM."

This intentional, systematic approach to task management is fundamental to converting intentions into tangible accomplishments. By understanding the neurobiological hurdles of task initiation and follow-through, and by consistently implementing these evidence-based strategies, a woman can transform her relationship with productivity. She learns to build a bridge across the chasm of procrastination, creating a clear and reliable path from a brilliant idea to a tangible, satisfying reality.

CHAPTER 5

THE ORGANIZED MIND: HABIT BUILDING AND MAINTENANCE

Building a functional organizational system is not a one-time event; it is an ongoing practice that requires building and maintaining habits. The ADHD brain can find it particularly challenging to maintain organization consistently, but this can be addressed by implementing structured routines. A powerful strategy is to conduct regular "resets" or "start-of-day/end-of-day clean-ups".

This involves dedicating a short, consistent period of time, for instance, 15 minutes in the morning or evening, to tidying up your physical and digital workspaces. This prevents small messes from snowballing into overwhelming mountains of clutter that seem impossible to tackle.

Additionally, a key to maintaining momentum is to tackle small, manageable parts of a larger task. This approach provides frequent, small wins and a tangible sense of progress that fuels continued effort. For example, instead of committing to "Clean the entire kitchen," one could simply focus on "Washing the dishes".

This reduces the sense of being overwhelmed and provides a feeling of accomplishment that makes it easier to continue the work later. The ultimate goal is to create a rhythm of organization that becomes an intuitive, supportive part of your daily routine, rather than a frustrating chore.

The Neurobiology of Habit Formation in the ADHD Brain

For a woman with ADHD, the process of building and maintaining a habit can feel like trying to build a sandcastle against a relentless tide. While the intention is there, the follow-through often falters. This isn't a failure of willpower, but a direct result of how the ADHD brain's reward system and executive functions operate.

Habits are typically formed through a cycle of cue, routine, and reward, but for a brain with dysregulated dopamine, the reward from a mundane, long-term habit can feel too distant or too small to motivate consistent action. The brain craves immediate, satisfying hits of dopamine, which are often not provided by the repetitive, unglamorous tasks required to maintain organization.

Furthermore, the executive function deficits that make organization so difficult in the first place, such as challenges with working memory, task initiation, and prioritization, also make habit formation a significant hurdle. A woman might forget the steps of a new routine, find it impossible to start the habit without an external cue, or feel so overwhelmed by the sheer number of things to remember that the routine is abandoned before it even begins. This is why a traditional, rigid approach to habit formation is often counterproductive.

The key to success is to build a system that works with the ADHD brain's wiring, leveraging its need for novelty, external cues, and immediate rewards to make maintenance feel less like a chore and more like a game.

Creating a Routine-Based Framework for Maintenance

Instead of aiming for constant, perfectionistic tidiness, a more sustainable approach is to implement flexible, structured routines that provide stability without feeling restrictive. These routines reduce decision fatigue, a common challenge for the ADHD brain, by creating predictable pathways for action that don't require conscious thought or a sudden burst of motivation. Research from

Cognitive Development has shown that predictable environments can improve cognitive functioning, which is precisely what these routines aim to create.

A powerful strategy is to conduct regular "resets" or "start-of-day/end-of-day clean-ups". These aren't meant to be exhaustive deep cleans, but rather short, dedicated periods to tidy up and put things back in their designated homes. This prevents small messes from snowballing into overwhelming mountains of clutter that seem impossible to tackle, a state that often triggers "ADHD paralysis" or procrastination.

- **The End-of-Day Reset:** Dedicate 10-15 minutes at the end of each day to a quick reset of your physical and digital workspaces. This could involve putting away dishes, clearing a specific surface, or processing your email inbox. The purpose is to close out the day with a sense of order and to prevent tomorrow's self from being overwhelmed by today's mess.
- **The Start-of-Day Clean-Up:** Similarly, spend a few minutes each morning to tidy up. For many, simply making the bed and placing dirty clothes in a hamper can create a sense of order and accomplishment that sets a positive tone for the entire day. This micro-commitment lowers the activation energy required to engage with the day's tasks, which is a major hurdle for the ADHD brain.
- **The Weekly Review:** In addition to daily resets, schedule a 30-minute weekly review session to declutter a specific area and get back on track. This could be processing all the mail that has piled up, tackling a messy drawer, or organizing a downloads folder. This dedicated, time-bound session prevents a general

sense of chaos from accumulating and provides a fresh slate for the week ahead.

The Power of Small, Actionable Steps: The "Swiss Cheese" Method

Habit maintenance for a woman with ADHD often fails when a task feels too large or overwhelming. This is where the concept of breaking down tasks into small, manageable parts becomes a crucial, continuous strategy. This approach provides frequent, small wins and a tangible sense of progress that fuels continued effort. Research from

Neuropsychology Review confirms that breaking down tasks into smaller chunks reduces cognitive load and increases task initiation, both of which are core challenges for the ADHD brain.

The "Swiss Cheese" method is a useful metaphor for this approach. Instead of trying to tackle a solid block of a large, intimidating task, you simply "poke holes" in it by committing to completing a small, manageable part of it. For example, instead of committing to "Clean the entire kitchen," one could simply focus on "Washing the dishes" or "Wiping down the counters".

This reduces the sense of being overwhelmed and provides a feeling of accomplishment that makes it easier to continue the work later. The immediate, satisfying feeling of a completed micro-task provides a much-needed burst of dopamine that reinforces productive behavior and builds momentum for the next step. This strategy transforms a seemingly insurmountable task into a series of achievable, low-friction steps, and is particularly effective at overcoming the "all-or-nothing" thinking that often leads to procrastination and avoidance.

Leveraging Motivation and Positive Reinforcement

For the ADHD brain, motivation is often a product of immediate reward rather than a sense of long-term accomplishment. Therefore, a successful maintenance system must be intentionally designed with positive reinforcement in mind. After all, if the behavior isn't rewarding, the brain is far less likely to repeat it.

- **Gamify the Task:** Making an organizational task feel like a game can be an excellent way to boost motivation. Set a timer and see if you can beat your previous time. Give yourself points for each item you put away. The element of competition or play can provide the necessary stimulation to get through a boring or repetitive task.

- **Pair the Task with a Reward:** Intentionally pair a dreaded chore with something you genuinely enjoy. For example, "I will only listen to my favorite podcast while I'm doing the laundry," or "I'll allow myself to have a cup of tea and read a chapter of my book once the dishes are done." This strategy is a form of "temptation bundling," which makes the unpleasant task feel more palatable by linking it to an immediate, positive reward.
- **Focus on the "Now" and Celebrate the Win:** A woman with ADHD may experience a strong emotional response to the perception of failure or disapproval. To counteract this, it's crucial to focus on the present moment and the small, tangible wins of each day. Instead of dwelling on past mistakes or times when you felt disorganized, celebrate your successful efforts. The simple act of checking a task off a list or admiring a clean counter can provide a powerful sense of accomplishment that fuels continued effort.

The Organized Mind: A Continuous Cycle of Review and Adaptation

Ultimately, the goal is to create a rhythm of organization that becomes an intuitive, supportive part of your daily routine, rather than a frustrating chore. This process is not a linear journey, and there will be days when routines are missed, tasks are forgotten, and chaos creeps back in. The key to sustainable maintenance is not rigid adherence to a perfect system, but rather a compassionate, iterative process of review and adaptation.

Instead of engaging in harsh self-criticism when a system fails, a woman can use these moments as a form of valuable data collection. She can ask herself: "What happened here? What was the friction point? What made this system hard to maintain today?"

By approaching these moments with curiosity and compassion, she can learn from them and make small, strategic adjustments to her systems, making them more resilient and effective over time. This continuous cycle of review, adaptation, and refinement is the true foundation of a well-organized and peaceful life. It's about building a supportive, forgiving relationship with your brain, and creating a system that is as flexible and dynamic as your unique neurobiology requires.

Conclusion: Your Foundational Systems

This book has provided a blueprint for building foundational systems for organization. The core of this work has been about externalizing the burdens of your ADHD brain, creating physical and digital structures that compensate for internal challenges with working memory, planning, and task initiation. By giving everything a home, simplifying your digital world, and breaking down overwhelming tasks into manageable steps, a woman can free up immense mental energy. This newly available cognitive bandwidth can then be redirected towards more fulfilling and productive endeavors.

The mastery of these foundational systems provides a stable and predictable base for the more complex skills of focus, emotion management, and relationship nurturing that will be explored in the following books. A truly organized external life creates a sense of calm and clarity that allows the internal chaos to subside, paving the way for sustained growth and well-being.

The Liberation of Externalizing the Mind

For many women with ADHD, the internal experience is one of a mind that is perpetually "frenzied, frazzled, and overwhelmed". This internal chaos is not an emotional state in isolation; it is a direct consequence of a brain that struggles with its core executive functions, such as working memory, planning, and prioritization.

Research shows that people with ADHD score significantly lower on executive function measures, highlighting a measurable difference in cognitive ability that is not related to intelligence. This neurobiological reality means that a woman's brain is constantly expending mental energy on tasks that neurotypical individuals do unconsciously, such as filtering out irrelevant stimuli or holding a multi-step plan in mind. This constant, conscious effort to manage internal inconsistencies creates a significant "ADHD tax," a measurable cognitive cost that leaves a woman mentally exhausted and with a diminished capacity for deep work or meaningful connection.

The strategies outlined in this book, such as giving every item a designated "home," using visual systems, and breaking down tasks, are all designed to externalize this immense cognitive burden. When a woman with ADHD can trust that her external systems (a planner, a calendar, a designated key hook) are reliable, she no longer has to use her inconsistent internal working memory to hold onto a mountain of information.

This act of offloading, of creating an "external brain," is profoundly liberating. It frees up immense mental bandwidth that was once consumed by the frantic, low-level anxiety of remembering where things are or what needs to be done. This is why a cluttered environment isn't just an inconvenience; it's a significant drain on executive function, as each piece of clutter represents a subtle demand on a brain already struggling to filter and prioritize. By consciously creating systems that work with the ADHD brain's wiring, a woman can transform her relationship with productivity from one of perpetual struggle to one of intentional action.

From Chaos to Calm: The Emotional Impact of Order

The impact of this foundational work on organization extends far beyond a tidy home or a clear inbox; it directly addresses the emotional toll that chronic disorganization takes on women with ADHD. For many, the constant struggle with organization is a source of profound shame, anxiety, and a shattered sense of self-worth. This struggle is often compounded by deeply ingrained societal expectations for women to be the caretakers of an organized and harmonious home. When a woman's ADHD symptoms, such as disorganization and messiness, violate these traditional feminine norms, she becomes particularly vulnerable to social judgment and feelings of inadequacy. Research shows that women with undiagnosed ADHD often endure childhoods filled with misunderstanding and self-blame, with a deep-seated feeling that they are "not an adequate human being" or that something is inherently "wrong" with them.

This cycle of shame, self-blame, and frustration is a direct contributor to co-occurring mental health conditions that are so prevalent in women with ADHD, such as anxiety and depression. The relentless pressure to perform, to "do it all," creates a "double burden" that leaves a woman feeling overwhelmed and undervalued . She might internalize her struggles and engage in the practice of "masking," where she develops sophisticated compensatory behaviors to hide her chaos and appear "neurotypical" to the outside world. This constant, exhausting effort to appear organized is an invisible burden that leads to a lifetime of internal shame and a sense of being an impostor.

By building a functional organizational system, a woman is not just tidying up her space; she is actively engaging in a powerful form of self-care. She is creating an external sanctuary that reduces the persistent background hum of anxiety and the internal chaos that so many women with ADHD report feeling. She is transforming her home from a source of stress into a supportive ally, a place where she no longer has to feel shame for the mess and can finally feel a sense of calm and clarity.

This mastery of her physical and digital worlds provides a tangible sense of control and self-efficacy, which is a powerful antidote to the feelings of helplessness and inadequacy that have so often accompanied her struggle with organization.

The Bridge to the Future: Paving the Way for Deeper Work

The work of organization is foundational because it is the prerequisite for all the more complex work that follows. A brain that is constantly consumed by the low-level noise of disorganization, the search for lost keys, the overwhelming email inbox, the mental energy spent on planning a simple task, is a brain that is unable to engage in the kind of deep work that is required for sustained focus, emotional regulation, and meaningful relationships.

The mastery of these foundational systems provides a stable and predictable base for the more complex skills of focus, emotion management, and relationship nurturing that will be explored in the following books. A woman who has a system for taming her digital world (Book 1) is better equipped to manage the digital distractions that derail her focus (Book 2).

A woman who has reduced her daily stressors through functional organization (Book 1) has more mental and emotional bandwidth to manage the intense feelings and emotional dysregulation that are so prevalent in ADHD (Book 4), and she is less likely to feel overwhelmed by the minor inconveniences that can trigger a disproportionate emotional storm. Similarly, a woman who has a system for managing her responsibilities (Book 1) can reduce the friction in her relationships (Book 5) that so often arises from her neurotypical partner feeling they are taking care of everything on their own.

She can move from a place of reactive chaos to one of intentional, proactive planning, allowing her to build a life that is not just manageable but truly fulfilling.

This book has empowered a woman to recognize that her struggle with organization is not a character flaw, but a neurobiological reality that can be addressed with the right tools and a compassionate, strategic approach. She has learned to break down overwhelming projects into manageable steps, to leverage routines to make maintenance feel less like a chore, and to externalize the cognitive burdens that have left her feeling mentally exhausted for a lifetime. This is a crucial step in her journey toward self-mastery.

A truly organized external life creates a sense of calm and clarity that allows the internal chaos to subside, paving the way for sustained growth, self-acceptance, and genuine well-being.

Reflection questions

- What is the primary emotional cost of disorganization for you (e.g., anxiety, shame, stress)? How can you use "functional organization" as a form of self-care?
- The book discusses the "out of sight, out of mind" phenomenon. What is one area of your physical or digital life where this applies, and what is one visual system you can create to combat it?
- The text suggests breaking down overwhelming tasks into smaller, more manageable steps. Think of one task you've been putting off. What is the single, low-friction first step you can take right now?

BOOK TWO

SHARPEN YOUR FOCUS: MASTERING YOUR ADHD BRAIN

INTRODUCTION

THE PARADOX OF FOCUS

For many women with ADHD, the concept of "focus" is a paradox, a double-edged sword that can feel both like a superpower and a cruel burden. On one hand, a woman's attention can be so scattered that she experiences a "thousand-yard stare," daydreaming or zoning out in conversations or meetings. This can lead to forgetfulness, missed information, and a pervasive sense of being in a fog.

When a topic is intensely stimulating or novel, the ADHD brain can lock into a state of intense, almost obsessive hyperfocus. While this state can lead to incredible bursts of productivity, it is often a source of frustration for partners who feel neglected, as the woman becomes so engrossed in a task that she loses track of time and fails to attend to other responsibilities.

The challenge is not a lack of ability to pay attention, but rather a profound difficulty in regulating it. The issue lies in the brain's struggle to control its "on/off" switch, preventing it from consistently directing its mental spotlight where it needs to be.

The Neurobiological Underpinnings of Attention Dysregulation

The ADHD brain's relationship with attention is distinct and deeply rooted in its neurobiology. This is not a personal failing but a reality of how the brain is wired and how it processes information. Research indicates a significant link between the brain's focus and its dopamine system. Dopamine, a key neurotransmitter involved in motivation, reward, and attention, is often dysregulated in the ADHD brain.

This dysregulation is at the heart of the "on/off" switch of attention. When a task is under-stimulating, the brain struggles to produce enough dopamine to sustain engagement, leading to a desperate search for internal or external novelty.

This is what causes mind-wandering and distractibility. Conversely, a task that provides a constant flow of stimulation, such as a new project or a deeply engaging hobby, can cause a dopamine surge, leading to the state of intense hyperfocus.

The challenge, therefore, is to manage this neurochemical ebb and flow, creating systems that provide the necessary external structure to sustain attention on mundane tasks and prevent hyperfocus from becoming a form of avoidance.

The brain's inability to filter out irrelevant stimuli is a central component of this dysregulation. While a neurotypical brain can effortlessly tune out background noise or visual clutter, the ADHD brain often registers all incoming stimuli with almost equal importance, which is a significant drain on cognitive resources. This struggle with cognitive control, which allows us to regulate attention and ignore distractions, is particularly evident when working memory demands are high.

As a result, the ADHD brain can be easily pulled off course by a phone notification, a colleague walking by, or a fleeting internal thought, making it incredibly difficult to maintain a state of "deep work." This constant battle against a barrage of stimuli creates a significant and measurable cognitive load, which research has shown disproportionately reduces task performance and brain network efficiency in individuals with ADHD compared to their peers without the condition. This constant effort to maintain focus against a brain that is fighting against it leads to a profound sense of "mental fatigue" and being perpetually "frenzied, frazzled, and overwhelmed."

The Dual Edges of Focus: Hyperfocus vs. Inattention

For many women with ADHD, this struggle with focus manifests as two distinct, and often paradoxical, states: a fragmented, scattered inattention and a powerful, almost obsessive hyperfocus. While the world often labels the inattention as a "deficit," it's more accurately a dysregulation of attention, a difficulty in directing and sustaining one's mental spotlight.

Inattention and a Fragmented Mind: The inattentive subtype of ADHD, which is more common in women, is characterized by internalized struggles like daydreaming, a "thousand-yard stare," and a pervasive sense of being in a fog. This can lead to a woman appearing to be disengaged or inattentive in conversations, even when she is genuinely trying to listen, leading her partner or colleagues to feel unheard or unprioritized. This fragmented attention makes it difficult to remember instructions, organize a schedule, or stay on task, all of which are essential for daily functioning. This is not an intellectual deficit, but a difference in how the brain processes and retains transient information, often due to a reduced activation in the prefrontal cortex, which is responsible for remembering task goals and rules.

Hyperfocus: The Superpower with a Catch: Conversely, the ADHD brain can also lock into a state of intense, almost obsessive hyperfocus when a task is intensely stimulating or novel. While this state can lead to incredible bursts of productivity, where a woman might work for hours without noticing the time, it is often a source of frustration for partners and family members who feel neglected.

This is because the hyperfocus is often uncontrolled, leading a woman to become so engrossed in a task that she loses track of time and fails to attend to other responsibilities, such as preparing meals, doing household chores, or engaging in a scheduled activity with her children.

The challenge is that hyperfocus is not a conscious decision to focus, but a reactive state of deep absorption that the brain finds so rewarding it struggles to disengage from it. It's a form of attention dysregulation, not controlled focus, and it can create significant imbalances in a woman's life.

The Cognitive and Emotional Toll of a Fragmented Mind

The daily struggle with attention dysregulation takes a significant toll on a woman's cognitive and emotional well-being. This isn't just about lost productivity; it's about the pervasive feeling of inadequacy, anxiety, and shame that so many women with ADHD report feeling.

Cognitive Load and Mental Fatigue: For a woman with ADHD, the constant effort to filter distractions and sustain focus on mundane tasks is a profound drain on her mental energy. The brain is constantly running on high alert, trying to manage an immense amount of internal and external information without a robust filtering system. This creates a state of chronic mental fatigue, a temporary sluggishness and slowdown of your thinking abilities, which leads to poor focus, carelessness, and forgetfulness. This continuous cognitive effort is often described as the "ADHD tax," a measurable cost that depletes mental energy reserves and makes a woman more susceptible to burnout.

The Emotional Impact on Self-Worth: The persistent difficulties with focus, organization, and follow-through often lead a woman with ADHD to internalize her struggles and blame herself. She may have grown up with a persistent feeling that she is "not an adequate human being" or that there is something personally wrong with her.

She may feel a deep sense of shame when she compares herself to her peers and feels she is not living up to societal expectations of being organized, put-together, and in control. This internalized self-blame, combined with chronic frustrations and a repeated pattern of failures, can contribute to or worsen co-occurring conditions like anxiety and depression.

Focus and the Female Experience: Internalization and Masking

The challenges of attention dysregulation for women are often exacerbated by societal expectations and a greater tendency to internalize their symptoms, rather than externalize them like men. While men are more likely to exhibit the hyperactive and impulsive symptoms that are easier to notice, women often present with the predominantly inattentive subtype, characterized by internalized restlessness and daydreaming that is less obvious to outside observers. This diagnostic disparity is a major reason why women are often underdiagnosed or misdiagnosed in childhood and adulthood.

This internalization of symptoms is directly linked to a practice known as "masking," where women develop sophisticated compensatory behaviors to hide their struggles and appear "neurotypical" to the outside world.

A woman might pretend to take notes in a meeting to hide the fact that she is "zoning out," or she might meticulously maintain a façade of punctuality by building in extra time for everything, a strategy she developed to combat her innate time blindness. This constant, exhausting effort to appear "non-ADHD" is an invisible burden that leads to a lifetime of internalized shame, anxiety, and a shattered sense of self-worth.

Studies confirm that girls are more likely to mask their symptoms than boys, and this can lead to significant negative consequences on their mental health, social functioning, and academic achievement. Masking is a coping mechanism that prevents a woman from feeling seen and understood, often leading to chronic loneliness and a sense of never "fitting in."

The path forward, therefore, is not to force yourself to conform to neurotypical norms, but to build strategies and systems that support your unique brain. It is about moving from a state of reactive distraction to one of proactive, intentional attention. The goal is to stop fighting your brain and to start working with it. This involves recognizing the unique triggers that derail your focus, designing your environment to support deep work, and building an internal toolkit that helps you to anchor your attention in the present moment, even amidst the chaos of a racing mind.

This is how you reclaim control over your mental spotlight and transform your relationship with focus from a source of frustration to a powerful, cultivated skill.

CHAPTER 1

THE SCIENCE OF FOCUS

The ADHD attentional system is distinct and operates in a way that is profoundly influenced by neurobiology. This is not a personal failing but a reality of how the brain is wired. Research indicates a significant link between the brain's focus and its dopamine system. Dopamine, a key neurotransmitter involved in motivation and reward, is often dysregulated in the ADHD brain.

This dysregulation is at the root of the "on/off" switch of attention. When a task is under-stimulating, the brain struggles to produce enough dopamine to sustain engagement, leading to a desperate search for internal or external novelty. This is what causes mind-wandering and distractibility.

On the other hand, a task that provides a constant flow of stimulation, such as a favorite hobby or a new project, can cause a dopamine surge, leading to the state of intense hyperfocus.

The challenge, therefore, is to manage this neurochemical ebb and flow, creating systems that provide the necessary external structure to sustain attention on mundane tasks and prevent hyperfocus from becoming a form of avoidance.

The Neurobiology of the Attentional System

To truly master focus, it is essential to understand the intricate neurobiological systems at play. The ADHD brain's relationship with attention is distinct and deeply rooted in its neurochemistry. This is not a matter of willpower, but rather a direct result of how the brain processes and prioritizes information.

At the center of this mechanism is dopamine. Often called the brain's "reward" or "motivation" chemical, dopamine is a key neurotransmitter that plays a crucial role in regulating attention and motivation.

Research indicates that individuals with ADHD often have low dopamine levels or a dysregulation in how dopamine is processed, a phenomenon known as the "low dopamine hypothesis". This reduced dopamine signaling can make it exceptionally difficult for the brain to sustain engagement on tasks that are not inherently stimulating or rewarding.

When a task is boring, repetitive, or requires sustained effort, the ADHD brain struggles to produce enough dopamine to find it interesting, leading to a desperate search for internal or external novelty to get that much-needed hit of stimulation.

This is the neurochemical basis for mind-wandering, distractibility, and the constant pull of the "shiny object" syndrome.

This dysregulation also explains the paradox of hyperfocus. When a task is intensely stimulating, novel, or provides immediate and satisfying feedback, it can cause a surge of dopamine. This release of dopamine is so rewarding that the brain locks into a state of intense, almost obsessive hyperfocus, making it difficult to disengage.

While this state can be highly productive, it is often uncontrolled and can lead to the neglect of other responsibilities, as the brain struggles to activate the "off" switch of its mental spotlight. This is why women with ADHD might become so engrossed in a task that they lose track of time and fail to attend to critical duties, leading to frustration for partners who feel neglected. The challenge, therefore, is to manage this neurochemical ebb and flow, creating systems that provide the necessary external structure to sustain attention on mundane tasks and prevent hyperfocus from becoming a form of avoidance.

The neurobiology of ADHD focus also involves other key neurotransmitters and brain networks. Norepinephrine, a close cousin of dopamine, is vital for alertness and arousal, and its dysregulation can impact the brain's ability to maintain an optimal state of readiness for focused work.

Furthermore, the brain's filtering mechanism is often impaired, making it struggle to differentiate between relevant and irrelevant stimuli. This means a phone notification, a fleeting internal thought, or a colleague walking by can all compete for attention with the same intensity as the main task at hand, creating significant cognitive noise and fragmentation.

The Brain's Competing Networks: DMN vs. TPN

Beyond individual neurotransmitters, the ADHD focus challenge can also be understood through the lens of specific brain networks that are responsible for attention and rest. Research has identified two primary networks that play a critical role in our ability to focus: the Default Mode Network (DMN) and the Task Positive Network (TPN).

- **The Default Mode Network (DMN)** is a network of brain regions that is active when the mind is at rest, engaged in daydreaming, mind-wandering, introspection, or thinking about the past and future. It's essentially the brain's "idle" state.
- **The Task Positive Network (TPN)** is the network that becomes active when we engage in focused, goal-directed tasks that require conscious attention and effort.

In a neurotypical brain, these two networks have a reciprocal relationship: when one is active, it suppresses the activity of the other. When you're focusing on a task, your TPN is on, and your DMN is off. This reciprocal balance allows for the efficient allocation of cognitive resources and helps maintain focus on the task at hand.

However, in the ADHD brain, this balance is often disrupted. The DMN can remain active even when the TPN is supposed to be engaged, leading to a constant internal turmoil of intrusive thoughts, mind-wandering, and a struggle to stay on task. This constant internal "chatter" and the inability to effectively suppress the DMN is a significant source of distraction and cognitive drain for a woman with ADHD.

Another network, the Salience Network (SN), acts as a kind of "switch" between the DMN and TPN, analyzing internal and external information to determine what is most important and requires attention. In the ADHD brain, the connections between these networks can be weaker, which can make it more difficult for the brain to effectively switch from one mode to another.

This explains why it can be hard to initiate a new task (switching from DMN to TPN) or to stop focusing on an engaging task (switching from TPN to DMN) and a brief distraction can often lead to a lengthy derailment, as the brain "sticks" to the new stimulus.

The Cognitive Cost of Attention Dysregulation

The daily struggle with attention dysregulation takes a significant toll on a woman's cognitive and emotional well-being. This is not just about lost productivity; it's about the pervasive feeling of inadequacy, anxiety, and shame that so many women with ADHD report feeling. The constant effort to filter distractions and sustain focus on mundane tasks is a profound drain on mental energy, a phenomenon known as "high cognitive load".

Research confirms that as cognitive load increases, individuals with ADHD experience reduced performance, greater reaction time variability, and reduced brain network efficiency compared to those without the condition.

The brain, already working harder to filter out irrelevant stimuli, becomes overloaded by the sheer volume of visual and sensory information, a significant drain on executive function. This constant battle against a barrage of stimuli creates a profound sense of "mental fatigue" and being perpetually "frenzied, frazzled, and overwhelmed".

This continuous cognitive effort is the "ADHD tax" that depletes mental energy reserves and makes a woman more susceptible to burnout, a phenomenon that research shows is significantly higher in employees with ADHD due to executive function difficulties.

The persistent difficulties with focus, organization, and follow-through often lead a woman with ADHD to internalize her struggles and blame herself. She may have grown up with a persistent feeling that she is "not an adequate human being" or that something is personally wrong with her.

She may feel a deep sense of shame when she compares herself to her peers and feels she is not living up to societal expectations of being organized, put-together, and in control. This internalized self-blame, combined with chronic frustrations and a repeated pattern of failures, can contribute to or worsen co-occurring conditions like anxiety and depression.

The Genetic and Neurobiological Basis

The differences in brain function and chemistry that contribute to ADHD are not a matter of choice, but are rooted in genetics and neurobiology. Research has focused on specific genes that are involved in the regulation of dopamine and other neurotransmitters.

- **Dopamine Transporter Gene (DAT1):** This gene codes for the dopamine transporter protein, which is responsible for the reuptake of dopamine from the synaptic cleft back into the presynaptic neuron. Variations in this gene have been shown to influence the effectiveness of dopamine reuptake, directly impacting the availability of dopamine in the brain and contributing to symptoms of inattention and impulsivity.
- **Dopamine Receptor D4 (DRD4):** This gene is involved in the function of dopamine receptors. Some studies suggest that certain variations of this gene may be associated with learning and working memory disabilities in children with ADHD.

Furthermore, brain imaging studies have found that individuals with impaired focus and memory tend to have reduced activation in specific brain regions, including the prefrontal cortex and cerebellum. The prefrontal cortex, often called the brain's "command center," is responsible for higher-level cognitive functions like attention, working memory, and impulse control. This reduced activity makes it more challenging to remember task goals, instructions, or rules, and contributes to the experience of "brain fog," a temporary sluggishness of thinking abilities that leads to mental exhaustion and poor focus.

This growing body of evidence makes it clear that the ADHD focus challenge is a genuine, neurobiological reality. Understanding this science is the first step toward self-compassion and building effective strategies. It shifts the perspective from a moral failing to a recognition of a genuine neurological difference, paving the way for a more intentional and supportive approach to managing attention.

CHAPTER 2

DESIGNING YOUR ENVIRONMENT FOR DEEPER CONCENTRATION

Just as a physical environment can be a source of disorganization, it can also be a significant cause of distraction and attention fragmentation for a woman with ADHD. The ADHD brain struggles with filtering out irrelevant stimuli, making it highly susceptible to sensory and visual overload.

The constant hum of a noisy office, a cluttered desk, or a busy view can all pull the mental spotlight off course. To combat this, creating a supportive environment is essential. This involves minimizing visual noise by decluttering and arranging a workspace to face a wall or a serene view. Using tools like noise-cancelling headphones can create a crucial "sound bubble" that helps block out distracting external noise and provides a cue for deep work.

Also, leveraging external accountability can be a powerful tool to initiate and sustain focus. The strategy of "body doubling," where one works alongside another person (either in person or virtually) on their own tasks, has been found to be a highly effective way to combat "activation energy" deficiency. The mere presence of another person provides a subtle sense of accountability and structure, making it easier to start and remain on task without having to rely on willpower alone.

These proactive environmental and social designs reduce the constant mental effort required to fight against distractions, allowing a woman to save her executive function for the actual work.

The Science of Sensory Overload: Why Your Brain Can't Tune Out

For a neurotypical individual, a noisy or cluttered space might be a minor inconvenience, but for a woman with ADHD, it can be a significant source of cognitive and emotional distress. The ADHD brain's neurobiology makes it exquisitely sensitive to sensory input, as it often struggles to filter out irrelevant stimuli with the same efficiency as a neurotypical brain.

This reduced filtering capacity means that a constant barrage of sensory information, be it a flickering light, the hum of an appliance, or a distracting visual, is registered with nearly equal importance as the task at hand. This constant battle against a flood of stimuli creates a significant cognitive load, which research has shown can have a disproportionately negative impact on performance, increase reaction time variability, and reduce brain network efficiency in individuals with ADHD.

This is why a cluttered space or a noisy environment isn't just an inconvenience; it's a direct contributor to reduced cognitive function and task performance.

This struggle with sensory processing can manifest in several key ways, impacting both your ability to focus and your overall emotional state:

- **Auditory Hypersensitivity:** Many individuals with ADHD experience auditory hypersensitivity, clinically known as hyperacusis or misophonia, where routine environmental sounds are not just distracting but can be genuinely distressing or painful. Sounds like a ticking clock, people chewing, or a colleague's tapping keyboard can feel almost unbearable, making it nearly impossible to tune them out and focus on a task. This heightened sensitivity can lead to distress, anxiety, and a constant feeling of being on edge. Using tools like noise-cancelling headphones is a highly effective and evidence-based strategy to create a "sound bubble" that blocks out these triggering noises, allowing your brain to enter a state of deep work without the constant assault of auditory stimuli.

- **Visual Distractions:** Cluttered environments, a messy desk, or a busy view from a window are all powerful visual distractors for the ADHD brain. Each item in your line of sight is a potential mental "ping," demanding a fraction of your attention and consuming valuable working memory resources. This visual noise can increase stress hormones like cortisol, which can in turn exacerbate ADHD symptoms. To combat this, it is essential to minimize visual clutter by clearing your desk of everything not directly related to your current task. Positioning your workspace to face a blank wall can also be an effective strategy to reduce the visual inputs that can pull your mental spotlight off course.
- **The Impact of Temperature and Lighting:** Environmental factors like temperature and lighting can also have a profound impact on focus and cognitive performance for a woman with ADHD. Studies show that being too hot or too cold can significantly impair a person's ability to think and learn, with cognitive ability performing optimally in a temperature range of 20°C to 22°C (68°F to 72°F). Heat exposure, in particular, can worsen ADHD symptoms, increasing irritability, anxiety, and reducing focus by disrupting the brain's delicate balance of neurotransmitters. Similarly, lighting plays a significant role. Natural light is ideal for maintaining focus and promoting a sense of calm, while harsh, flickering fluorescent lights can be overstimulating and contribute to fatigue. Creating a workspace with soft, adjustable lighting can reduce visual strain and create a more soothing atmosphere that supports sustained attention.

Creating Your "Attention Zone": Practical Design Strategies

Your workspace is not just where you do your work; it's a powerful psychological cue for your brain. By intentionally designing a specific "attention zone," you create a clear signal that it's time to focus, reducing the mental friction of constantly having to decide when and where to engage in deep work.

- **Declutter Ruthlessly:** A cluttered physical environment leads to a cluttered mind. The presence of multiple items on a desk, each demanding a fraction of your attention, increases cognitive load and makes it harder to focus. To counteract this, commit to clearing your desk or workspace of everything not directly related to your current task. Implement a "one-touch" rule: if you pick up an item, either take immediate action on it, file it away, or give it a designated "home". This practice frees up cognitive bandwidth by reducing the constant visual scanning and mental processing required to filter out irrelevant items.
- **The Power of a Designated "Home":** A foundational principle of intuitive physical systems is to give every single item a designated "home". This is not about being rigid or a perfectionist; it is a strategic approach to reduce decision fatigue, which is a major drain on executive function. Each time you pick up an item, your brain is faced with a micro-decision: "Where does this go?" By assigning a specific and predictable place for every item, you eliminate this decision-making process. For frequently lost items, such as keys, wallets, and phones, the use of a "landing strip" near the front door is a highly effective strategy that ensures these crucial items are always in a predictable and easily accessible location. This system of predictability reduces the frantic, time-consuming searches that so often accompany ADHD.
- **The "Out of Sight, Out of Mind" Principle:** As mentioned, the ADHD brain can struggle with working memory, a deficit that often leads to the "out of sight, out of mind" phenomenon. This is why traditional organizational advice, such as tucking everything away in opaque boxes, can be completely

counterproductive. To counteract this, the organizational system must be intentionally designed to be visual. Using clear storage bins and bold labels allows you to see the contents without having to open them, providing a constant visual cue of what is inside and ensuring your items remain "in mind".

- **Dedicated Work Zones:** If possible, designate a specific area in your home only for deep work. This could be a desk in a corner, a specific chair, or even just a table used only for work during certain hours. The principle here is strong environmental association: your brain learns to associate a certain place with a certain activity. By dedicating a "work zone," you train your brain to enter a focused state merely by being in that area, creating a consistent and reliable cue for focus.

Leveraging External Accountability: The Power of "Body Doubling"

While a well-designed physical environment is critical, some tasks, especially those that are boring, tedious, or require a high degree of sustained effort, can still be incredibly difficult to initiate and complete. For these moments, a powerful strategy for the ADHD brain is to leverage external accountability.

The concept of "body doubling" is a productivity strategy where one works alongside another person on their own tasks. The body double's role is not to help with the work itself, but to serve as a supportive presence that helps the individual with ADHD stay focused and reduce distractions. This strategy is highly effective because it acts as a form of "external executive functioning," providing a stable, non-judgmental anchor for your attention.

Here's a deeper look into why it works and how to implement it:

- **It Provides a Sense of Accountability:** The mere presence of another person, even if they are silent and working on their own task, creates a subtle sense of accountability and pressure. The perception of being "watched" can be a powerful external motivator, making you more likely to follow through on your intended actions without having to rely on willpower alone. The feeling of "I can't waste this gift of time" can be enough to get you started and keep you going.

- **It Models Focused Behavior:** Watching someone else stay focused on a task can naturally encourage the person with ADHD to do the same. The body double becomes a quiet model of control, confidently reflecting the message: "I can concentrate. I am working. I am focused." This modeled behavior is a potent psychological cue that helps you enter a similar state of mind.
- **It Reduces Procrastination and Increases Motivation:** By scheduling a body doubling session, you're proactively setting aside time to work alongside someone else, which makes you more likely to get started when the time comes. This can combat the "activation energy" deficiency that makes task initiation so difficult for the ADHD brain. The novelty of having someone else in the workspace, even virtually, can also add a sense of freshness to a boring routine, which can be helpful since the ADHD brain craves novelty.
- **Virtual Body Doubling:** Body doubling sessions don't have to be in person. Virtual sessions, where you and a partner work together on a video call with your cameras on, have become a popular and effective way to leverage this strategy. This is especially helpful if you're not ready to meet with someone in person or if your schedules don't align. You can each do your own work but keep the call on for accountability and a shared sense of focus.
- **Beyond Body Doubling:** Sometimes, even being in a public space where others are working quietly, like a library or a coffee shop, can create a focused environment. The quiet, productive energy of others can be motivating and act as a passive form of body doubling, helping to anchor your attention.

These proactive environmental and social designs reduce the constant mental effort required to fight against distractions, allowing a woman to save her executive function for the actual work. By intentionally designing your physical and digital environments, and by strategically leveraging external accountability, you are building a system that supports your brain's natural tendencies rather than fighting against them. This is how you create a sustainable, focused, and ultimately more peaceful life.

CHAPTER 3

MINDFULNESS AND SELF-COMPASSION FOR ATTENTIONAL CONTROL

While external environmental design is crucial, true mastery of focus also requires cultivating an internal toolkit. This is where mindfulness and self-compassion become powerful allies for the ADHD brain. Mindfulness is the practice of paying attention to the present moment without judgment.

For a brain that is prone to racing thoughts, internal restlessness, and a constant stream of new ideas, mindfulness provides a much-needed anchor. It helps a woman become more aware of her thoughts and emotions without becoming entangled in them, providing a crucial pause before she acts on an impulse or gets lost in a mental spiral.

By consistently practicing mindfulness, a woman can learn to gently guide her attention back to her intended focus each time it wanders, which acts as a form of exercise for her attentional muscle.

This practice is deeply intertwined with emotional regulation and distress tolerance. The ability to observe a racing mind or an intense emotion without judgment is the first step toward managing it effectively.

This is particularly important for women with ADHD who often internalize their struggles and feel a deep sense of shame or a lack of self-worth. By approaching her mind with curiosity and compassion, a woman can begin to let go of the rigid expectation that she "should" be able to focus effortlessly. This compassionate stance reduces the anxiety and self-criticism that often accompanies inattentive symptoms, making it easier to re-engage with a task, even after a period of distraction.

The Neurobiological Basis of Mindfulness and the ADHD Brain

Mindfulness for the ADHD brain is not about achieving a perfectly empty, still mind. The ADHD brain is an often overactive, engine of thought, and trying to force it into absolute stillness is often a recipe for frustration and self-criticism. Instead, mindfulness is a form of cognitive training, a practice that builds the brain's capacity for sustained attention and self-regulation over time.

Neuroscientific research supports the efficacy of mindfulness for ADHD by highlighting its ability to influence key brain functions. The ADHD brain is often characterized by a dysregulation in its two primary attentional networks: the Default Mode Network (DMN), which is active during mind-wandering and daydreaming, and the Task Positive Network (TPN), which is active during focused, goal-directed tasks.

In a neurotypical brain, these two networks have a reciprocal relationship, meaning one quiets down when the other is active. However, in the ADHD brain, this balance is disrupted, and the DMN can remain overly active even when the TPN is supposed to be engaged, leading to a constant internal turmoil of intrusive thoughts and mind-wandering.

Mindfulness practice, particularly focused meditation, helps to strengthen the brain's ability to regulate these networks. By repeatedly bringing your attention back to an anchor, such as your breath or a physical sensation, each time it wanders, you are strengthening the neural pathways that are responsible for attentional control and the ability to switch between the DMN and TPN.

This consistent, gentle redirection of focus acts as a form of exercise for the prefrontal cortex, the brain's "command center" for executive functions like attention and impulse control, which is often less active in individuals with ADHD. Over time, this training can make it easier to initiate tasks, sustain attention, and recover from a period of distraction. The practice helps a woman become the observer of her thoughts and emotions, rather than being solely subject to their whims, which is the first step towards self-mastery.

Mindfulness and the Regulation of Emotional Dysregulation

For many women with ADHD, the most debilitating aspect of their condition isn't inattention, but emotional dysregulation. This is a core, significant, and often misunderstood aspect of ADHD, characterized by a heightened emotional intensity and a surprising lack of an internal "buffer" to modulate feelings.

Research suggests that this is due to differences in brain function, particularly in the frontal cortex, which is less likely to inhibit big reactions. This can lead to emotions that feel all-or-nothing, where a woman might hold back her feelings to fit in, but a small trigger can unleash an overwhelming emotional response.

This is where mindfulness becomes a profound ally. The ability to simply observe a racing mind or an intense emotion without judgment is the first step toward managing it effectively. Mindfulness creates a crucial pause between stimulus and response, a space where a woman can recognize the emotion and choose a deliberate action rather than reacting impulsively.

This practice is deeply intertwined with Dialectical Behavioral Therapy (DBT), a highly effective therapeutic approach that combines elements of Cognitive Behavioral Therapy (CBT) with mindfulness techniques to help individuals develop coping skills for managing impulsivity and regulating emotions.

The skills taught in DBT for ADHD are particularly well-suited for women, and mindfulness is the foundational skill upon which the others are built. It helps a woman become more aware of her thoughts and emotions, which can decrease distress and improve her ability to respond effectively to difficult situations. The ability to observe a racing mind or a surge of intense emotion without getting entangled in it is the first step toward gaining a sense of control over it.

Self-Compassion: The Antidote to Shame and the Inner Critic

The journey of living with ADHD for women is often defined by a profound and pervasive sense of shame. This shame is not a symptom of ADHD itself, but a consequence of a lifetime of internalizing struggles and feeling a deep sense of inadequacy. Societal expectations for women to be organized, emotionally mature, and calm create a pressure to conform that directly conflicts with the core symptoms of ADHD.

When a woman with ADHD struggles to maintain order or regulate her emotions, she often internalizes her difficulties and blames herself, a pattern that fuels anxiety, depression, and low self-esteem.

Research suggests that women with undiagnosed ADHD often endure childhoods filled with misunderstanding, self-blame, and a persistent feeling that there is something personally wrong with them, a feeling that is exacerbated by the internal and external pressures they face.

This painful internal dialogue, the "inner critic," becomes a source of stress that can significantly deplete the emotional resources needed for resilience and self-regulation.

Self-compassion is the powerful antidote to this shame. It's the practice of treating yourself with the same kindness, understanding, and support you would offer a good friend in a similar situation. It's acknowledging that your suffering is real and offering comfort, rather than judgment.

For a woman with ADHD, this means letting go of the rigid expectation that she "should" be able to focus effortlessly or get everything done perfectly. It means recognizing that her struggles are a neurobiological reality, not a character flaw.

Practicing self-compassion reduces the anxiety and self-criticism that often accompanies inattentive symptoms, making it easier to re-engage with a task, even after a period of distraction. For example, instead of saying, "I'm so useless for forgetting that," she can rephrase it as, "It's okay to forget things; my brain works differently. What can I do to help myself remember next time?"

This practice of actively cultivating a supportive inner dialogue builds an inner ally who champions her efforts and provides the psychological safety needed to learn from mistakes without being crippled by them. Self-compassion is not self-indulgence; it is the essential fuel that allows for sustainable growth and emotional resilience.

Practical Mindfulness and Self-Compassion Techniques

The power of mindfulness and self-compassion lies in their accessibility. You don't need a dedicated meditation cushion or hours of free time. You can integrate these practices into your daily life in small, manageable ways that work for the ADHD brain.

1. The Breath Anchor: Your breath is always with you and is a constant, subtle sensation. It is perhaps the most fundamental and universally accessible anchor because it is always present, it is neutral, and its rhythm can be both observed and subtly influenced. When you notice your mind wandering, gently bring your attention to the sensation of your breath. Notice the rise and fall of your chest or the feeling of air at your nostrils.

The key is the gentle return of your attention, without judgment, each time it wanders.

Each return is a strengthening of your attentional muscle. A simple practice is to count your breaths, inhaling on "one" and exhaling on "two," up to "ten," and then starting over. This provides just enough mental engagement to keep the ADHD brain from getting bored while still directing attention to the breath.

2. The 5-4-3-2-1 Sensory Grounding Method: This technique is a rapid, powerful circuit-breaker for an overactive mind. When your mind is racing, you feel overwhelmed by internal chatter, or you're stuck in a thought loop, this exercise can quickly ground you in the present by bringing your awareness to external reality.

- **5 things you can see:** Look around and name five distinct things you can see, focusing on details like color, texture, or shape.
- **4 things you can feel:** Notice four things you can feel (e.g., your feet on the floor, the texture of your clothes against your skin, the air temperature, the pressure of your chair).
- **3 things you can hear:** Listen for three distinct sounds (e.g., distant traffic, your own breathing, the hum of a computer).
- **2 things you can smell:** Notice two distinct smells (even if faint).
- **1 thing you can taste:** Notice one taste in your mouth.

This exercise forces your attention outwards, providing a quick reset for your attention and interrupting the emotional spiral.

3. Mindful Movement: For the ADHD brain, which often has physical restlessness, combining mindfulness with movement is an excellent strategy. Instead of seeing fidgeting or restlessness as a sign of failure, you can use it as an anchor for attention.

- **Mindful Walking:** As you walk, shift your attention from your thoughts to the physical sensations of walking. Pay attention to the sensation of your feet touching the ground, the heel-to-toe roll, and the swing of your arms.
- **Mindful Stretching:** Focus intensely on the sensations in your body as you stretch. Notice the stretch, the release, the tension, and the relaxation. This is a great way to combine physical activity with mental anchoring.

4. Compassionate Rephrasing: Actively challenge your inner critic by rephrasing harsh, judgmental thoughts into compassionate and realistic ones.

- **Harsh thought:** "I can't believe I missed that deadline. I'm so useless."
- **Self-compassionate rephrasing:** "It's okay. I missed the deadline. That's a common ADHD challenge. What was the friction point here? What can I learn from this for next time?"
- **Harsh thought:** "I am so lazy; I can't even get started on this chore."

- **Self-compassionate rephrasing:** "This chore feels hard right now. My brain is seeking stimulation. What is one tiny, manageable step I can take right now to get started?"

This is not about ignoring the problem but about approaching it from a place of understanding and solution-oriented thinking rather than self-blame.

Cultivating mindfulness and self-compassion is a lifelong practice, not a quick fix or a destination. It's a journey of continuous learning and gentle redirection. By consistently training your internal toolkit, you'll find it easier to direct your focus where you intend, even in a world clamoring for your attention and a mind prone to wandering.

This internal mastery is a vital complement to designing your external environment, creating a holistic approach that empowers you to truly take command of your attention and, by extension, your emotional well-being and life.

CHAPTER 4

SINGLE-TASKING AND DEEP WORK STRATEGIES

In a world that praises the illusion of multitasking, a highly effective strategy for the ADHD brain is to embrace single-tasking and cultivate a capacity for "deep work." Multitasking is a myth; what it actually involves is rapid task-switching, a process that is incredibly inefficient and mentally exhausting for the ADHD brain.

The cognitive cost of switching from one task to another is a significant drain on executive function, as the brain must reorient itself and load new information into its working memory each time. To counteract this, a woman can train her brain to focus on one thing at a time.

The Myth of Multitasking and the Science of Task-Switching

For decades, multitasking has been celebrated as a hallmark of efficiency and competence, but neuroscientific and psychological research has decisively debunked this myth. The human brain is simply not built to handle multiple conscious, cognitively demanding tasks simultaneously. Instead, what we perceive as multitasking is actually a process of rapid task-switching, where the brain rapidly shifts its attention between two or more different activities.

For the ADHD brain, which already struggles with attention regulation and executive function, this process of task-switching is inefficient and detrimental. Each time you switch from one task to another, your brain incurs a measurable "task switch cost". This cost involves the mental energy required to disengage from the previous task, reorient your focus, and load new information and rules into your working memory.

This process is incredibly draining and can be a major source of mental fatigue for a woman with ADHD. A 2021 study highlighted that individuals with ADHD experience a reduced amount of cognitive resources available for task-switching, making it far more challenging for them to switch between tasks and complete them efficiently. The frontal lobe, which is responsible for executive functions like working memory and inhibitory control, struggles to disengage from one task and engage with another, leading to a diminished ability to maintain focus and control.

Furthermore, task-switching compromises working memory, sustained focus, and even long-term memory consolidation, and it often leads to a higher rate of errors and a slower working pace. For a woman with ADHD, who may already be prone to careless mistakes and difficulties with memory, this process of constant toggling can become a significant source of frustration, shame, and a sense of being perpetually behind.

Over time, this constant task-switching can overload the brain's attention control system, reducing performance even on single tasks and contributing to a state of chronic mental fatigue. It also puts a significant strain on the prefrontal cortex, which relies on optimal levels of dopamine and norepinephrine to function. When multitasking, the brain may become overstimulated, allowing the amygdala to become more reactive and inhibiting logical reasoning, which further degrades cognitive processing.

The Power of Deep Work: A Counter-Cultural Approach

The antidote to this chaotic, fragmented mode of working is to embrace single-tasking and cultivate a capacity for "deep work." Deep work, a concept coined by author Cal Newport, is the ability to focus without distraction on a cognitively demanding task. It is the kind of work that creates new value, improves your skills, and is difficult to replicate, requiring sustained intellectual effort at the highest level.

For the ADHD brain, deep work is not always easy, but it is profoundly rewarding. The moments of true deep work are where innovation happens, where complex problems are solved, and where significant personal and professional growth occurs. The challenge lies in the ADHD brain's natural inclination towards novelty and immediate stimulation.

A single, demanding task, especially if it involves sustained effort and lacks immediate gratification, can quickly feel boring or difficult, prompting the mind to seek out distractions to get a quick dopamine hit. However, by deliberately engaging in single-tasking and structuring your environment and time for deep work, you can train your brain to embrace sustained effort and achieve higher levels of productivity and satisfaction. You are not fighting your brain but rather teaching it to find reward in sustained, focused effort through structured practice and strategic reinforcement.

This intentional approach to work, which prioritizes impact over "busywork," is a powerful way to move beyond the frustration of a scattered mind and achieve a new level of self-efficacy and accomplishment.

The Pomodoro Technique: Your Anchor for Deep Work

The Pomodoro Technique, developed by Francesco Cirillo in the late 1980s, is one of the most effective and research-backed tools for achieving and sustaining single-task focus for the ADHD brain. It provides a clear, external structure that bypasses the internal difficulties with task initiation and follow-through. The technique involves breaking down a task into short, focused work intervals, traditionally 25 minutes long, followed by a mandatory short break of 5 minutes. After four of these cycles, you take a longer, more restorative break.

The power of this technique for the ADHD brain is multifaceted:

- **It Reduces Overwhelm and Lowers Activation Energy:** The idea of working on a boring or difficult task for an undefined period can be paralyzing, a phenomenon often referred to as "ADHD paralysis." Committing to a task for a short, manageable burst of 25 minutes makes it feel less intimidating and more approachable, making it easier to initiate. This strategic approach reduces the cognitive load of the entire task and provides a clear starting point.
- **It Accommodates the Brain's Need for Breaks:** The scheduled 5-minute breaks provide regular, guilt-free opportunities for the brain to reset and seek novelty without derailing the entire work session. This prevents the mental fatigue and restlessness that can build up during prolonged, static focus. The breaks serve as a reward and a mental reset, accommodating the brain's natural rhythms without allowing them to hijack progress.
- **It Builds Momentum and Provides Rewards:** For the ADHD brain, which is driven by a craving for immediate reward, the Pomodoro Technique provides a satisfying and tangible sense of progress with each completed work interval. This positive reinforcement loop, fueled by small bursts of dopamine from each "win," builds momentum and makes it easier to sustain effort over time. The discipline of single-tasking, enforced by a timer, is a powerful antidote to a scattered mind, allowing a woman to reduce feelings of overwhelm and achieve a higher quality of work with less mental effort. A study found that implementing the Pomodoro technique in a digital marketing company helped employees work more efficiently and improve their work-life balance.

Beyond the Pomodoro: Advanced Strategies for Sustained Focus

While the Pomodoro Technique is a foundational tool, there are other strategies that can be integrated to support consistent follow-through and a capacity for deep work.

- **Batch Similar Tasks:** While the goal is single-tasking within a work session, you can still improve efficiency by batching similar tasks together across your day or week. For example, dedicate a specific block of time solely to answering emails, another block for making phone calls, and yet another for administrative paperwork. This minimizes the "context switching" cost that is so draining for the ADHD brain. By grouping similar activities, you allow your brain to stay in a particular "mode," reducing the friction and cognitive load associated with frequent transitions.
- **The "Pre-Flight Checklist":** Before starting a deep work session, develop a brief, consistent ritual or "pre-flight checklist." This ritual cues your brain that it's time to engage in sustained focus and helps you smoothly transition into deep work. This could include: reviewing your single, specific task for the session, gathering all necessary materials, getting a fresh drink of water, closing all unnecessary programs and tabs, and silencing all notifications. This consistent ritual acts as a psychological trigger, preparing your mind and body for intense concentration and reducing the mental load of having to make these decisions in the moment.
- **Embrace the "Messy Middle":** All projects, especially large ones, have a point where the initial excitement and novelty wear off, and the end isn't yet in sight. This "messy middle" is where many with ADHD abandon projects, as the dopamine hit from novelty fades. Recognize this phase as a normal, predictable part of the creative or productive process. Remind yourself that it's normal to feel less engaged, bored, or frustrated here, and double down on your tiny, actionable steps and leverage your accountability and reward systems to push through this phase.

- **Gamification and Rewards:** The ADHD brain thrives on immediate feedback and rewards. To maintain momentum on a long task, inject elements of a game into your work. Use a timer to "compete" against yourself, create a points system for completed sub-tasks, or build in small, intentional rewards for hitting a milestone. The promise of an immediate, enjoyable reward, like a 5-minute break, a favorite song, or a cup of tea, can provide the necessary dopamine hit to push through a tedious section of a project.
- **Automate and Systemize:** Wherever possible, create systems that reduce the need for conscious effort in follow-through. Set recurring reminders, use templates, or automate routine steps. The less you have to think about it, the more likely you are to do it. The ADHD brain thrives on automation and consistent systems because they reduce decision fatigue and the reliance on inconsistent executive functions. By setting up recurring calendar reminders for tasks that need to be done regularly, for example, you can offload as much routine cognitive load as possible, freeing up your mental energy for deep work.

The commitment to single-tasking and deep work is a powerful counter-cultural act, and it's especially transformative for a woman with ADHD. By deliberately creating mental and environmental space for sustained focus on one thing at a time, you'll not only complete more meaningful work but also experience a profound sense of accomplishment and clarity, moving beyond the chaos of constant distraction.

This intentional approach allows you to harness your considerable potential, achieving a level of productivity and satisfaction that might have previously seemed out of reach.

CHAPTER 5

SUSTAINING FOCUS AND PREVENTING MENTAL FATIGUE

Sustaining focus is not just about the moment of concentration; it is about intelligently managing one's energy to prevent burnout over the long term. A prominent, but often overlooked, challenge for women with ADHD is a profound sense of "mental fatigue" and being perpetually "frenzied, frazzled, and overwhelmed".

This is not simply a feeling of being tired; it is the result of the constant, conscious effort to manage internalized symptoms, such as a racing mind and emotional dysregulation, that neurotypical individuals do unconsciously. This constant cognitive effort is the "ADHD tax" that depletes mental energy reserves and makes a woman more susceptible to burnout.

For women, this experience is particularly daunting as the demands of work, relationships, and self-care, along with the relentless storm of ADHD symptoms, can pose serious challenges to their mental well-being. Studies show that 58% of employees with ADHD report high burnout levels, a statistic largely attributed to difficulties with executive functions, like attention regulation and emotional control.

Burnout in women with ADHD is a significant cause of stress, frustration, and overwhelm, often caused by trying to mask symptoms and function within systems that are not accommodating to the ADHD brain. This chapter will provide proactive strategies for energy management, ensuring your newfound capacity for concentration is not only powerful but also sustainable.

The Cycle of ADHD Burnout: Understanding the Warning Signs

Burnout is a state of chronic physical, emotional, and mental exhaustion caused by prolonged or excessive stress. It is not just about being tired; it's a deep state of depletion that can leave a woman feeling mentally drained, emotionally numb, and lacking motivation to complete even the simplest of tasks.

For women with ADHD, this can follow a cyclical pattern of intense productivity followed by extreme exhaustion. A woman might hyperfocus on a project for days, neglecting basic needs like food or sleep, which leads to a significant energy debt. This exhaustion then prompts a period of task paralysis and procrastination, which creates an even more urgent need for intense productivity later on, leading to more fatigue and restarting the cycle.

The emotional toll of this cycle is significant. A woman may begin to feel as though her best is not good enough and lose belief in her ability to complete simple tasks. When the cycle sets in, it's common to experience heightened irritability, frustration, mood swings, and an inability to control emotions, sometimes leading to crying spells, yelling, or emotional breakdowns.

Other common signs of burnout include a lack of motivation, emotional detachment, chronic fatigue, headaches, muscle tension, and sleep issues. This cycle is particularly difficult to break because the same ADHD symptoms that contribute to burnout, such as the difficulty with stress regulation, also make it hard to recover. Recognizing these red flags early is the first step toward intervention, allowing you to prioritize rest and self-care before full burnout sets in.

Prioritizing Sleep Hygiene: The Foundation of Focus

For anyone, quality sleep is non-negotiable for cognitive function, but for a woman with ADHD, it is the bedrock of sustained focus, emotional control, and working memory. Research indicates that an estimated 50-75% of adults with ADHD experience sleeping problems, with studies showing that sleep deprivation in ADHD can be as impairing as other adult symptoms combined.

Sleep problems often differ depending on the ADHD subtype: women with predominantly inattentive symptoms are more likely to have a later bedtime, while those with hyperactive-impulsive symptoms are more likely to experience insomnia.

To combat this, a woman must prioritize consistent and healthy sleep hygiene practices.

- **Establish a Consistent Routine:** The human body thrives on regularity, and the ADHD brain is no exception. A consistent bedtime and wake-up time, even on weekends, helps regulate your natural sleep rhythm.
- **Create a Relaxing Ritual:** Your bedtime routine should signal to your body that it's time to wind down. This could include listening to a relaxing audiobook, reading a physical book, taking a warm bath or shower, or practicing deep breathing exercises.
- **Avoid Stimulating Activities:** In the hours before bed, avoid screens, caffeine, sugar, and stimulating work projects that can trigger hyperfocus. The blue light from screens can interfere with melatonin production, while engaging in a highly stimulating task can make it difficult for the ADHD brain to wind down.
- **Clear Your Mental Clutter:** Ruminating on a to-do list or worrying about unfinished tasks can keep you awake. Take time before bed to write out your "to-do" list for the next day, which helps to offload these worries from your mind, allowing you to relax and fall asleep more easily.

The Proactive Power of Physical Activity

Exercise is not just for physical health; it's a powerful tool for managing ADHD symptoms, regulating mood, and combating mental fatigue. Research has shown that physical activity has a positive effect on inhibitory control in adults with ADHD, and it can also improve cognitive function, emotional state, and mental health. The mechanism behind this is linked to exercise-induced dopamine release, which is associated with improved attention and can help regulate the brain's reward system.

- **Find Your Joyful Movement:** For the ADHD brain, which craves novelty and can struggle with boring, repetitive tasks, finding an activity you genuinely enjoy is key to maintaining a consistent routine. This could be dancing, lifting weights, cycling, hiking, or a team sport.
- **Leverage Both Acute and Chronic Exercise:** Research indicates that both short, intense bursts of exercise (acute) and long-term, consistent physical activity (chronic) have a beneficial effect on inhibitory control. A brisk walk or a short burst of jumping jacks can serve as a powerful "brain break" to combat restlessness and re-energize your focus.
- **Use Exercise to Manage Emotional States:** Physical activity is a direct and healthy way to discharge pent-up emotional energy, which is especially useful for a brain prone to emotional dysregulation. When you feel anger, anxiety, or frustration building, a quick burst of intense movement can act as a physiological "reset button," preventing the emotion from spiraling out of control.

Nourishing Your Brain: Diet and Hydration

What you consume directly impacts your brain's ability to function. Consistent, high-quality fuel is crucial for maintaining stable energy levels, which in turn supports sustained focus and emotional regulation. Dehydration and erratic blood sugar levels can mimic or exacerbate ADHD symptoms, making it even more challenging to stay on track.

- **Mindful Eating:** Focus on balanced meals with lean protein, healthy fats, and complex carbohydrates to maintain steady energy levels. Avoid an excess of sugars and processed foods, which can cause rapid energy spikes followed by a crash that leaves you feeling sluggish and unfocused.
- **The Power of Omega-3s:** Several studies have linked low omega-3 fatty acid levels to common ADHD symptoms like learning difficulties, hyperactivity, and problems with emotional regulation. The brain uses omega-3s as a building block for cell membranes and as a tool to help neurotransmitters carry signals more effectively. Supplementing with omega-3s has been shown to improve mood, reduce hyperactivity, and even enhance working memory.
- **Consistent Hydration:** Being properly hydrated is essential for optimal brain function. Keep a water bottle with you and aim for consistent intake throughout the day rather than large, infrequent amounts. This simple habit can have a significant impact on your focus and mental clarity.

Mindful Breaks and Strategic Pacing

The ADHD brain is not built for sustained, static effort. Pacing yourself and taking mindful breaks is a proactive strategy to prevent overwhelm and cognitive overload before it happens.

- **Build in "Micro-Breaks":** Every 15-20 minutes, take a 30-second to 1-minute brain break. Look away from your screen, stretch, take a few deep breaths, or simply close your eyes. These micro-pauses prevent overstimulation and allow your prefrontal cortex a brief moment of rest.
- **The "ADHD Tax" on Time:** Acknowledge your tendency to underestimate how long tasks will take, a phenomenon known as "time blindness," and add a time buffer of 25-50% to your schedule. This gives you crucial breathing room, reducing the stress that comes from constant rushing and providing a more realistic view of your day.

- **Set Boundaries and Avoid Overcommitment:** Overcommitting is a fast track to overwhelm and burnout for the ADHD brain, as it stretches your executive function resources too thin. Learn to identify your capacity and politely decline requests that will overwhelm you. By protecting your time and energy, you create a buffer against the constant demands of a busy life.

By recognizing that sustained focus is a product of overall well-being, a woman can learn to protect her energy and maintain her newfound capacity for concentration without succumbing to burnout. Proactive self-care is not a luxury but a fundamental necessity for sustainable productivity and emotional well-being. This integrated approach ensures that your sharpened focus becomes a consistent, reliable asset, helping you thrive in a world that constantly vies for your attention, rather than merely survive it.

Conclusion: Your Empowered Attention

This guide has provided a comprehensive framework for sharpening focus, moving from a paradoxical and frustrating experience to a cultivated skill. By understanding the neurobiological underpinnings of inattention and hyperfocus, a woman can stop blaming herself and begin to work with her brain, not against it.

She has learned to design her environment to support deep work, to use mindfulness to anchor her attention internally, and to embrace single-tasking as a more efficient way to work. She also recognizes that true, sustained focus is a product of careful energy management and self-care.

The mastery of these skills empowers a woman to direct her mental spotlight where she wants it to go, rather than being pulled by every fleeting impulse or demand. This provides a profound sense of self-efficacy and a foundation for achieving her goals with greater clarity and control.

From Internal Chaos to Intentional Action: The Foundational Shift

The journey through this book has been a process of profound re-education and self-discovery. For so long, the struggle with attention for a woman with ADHD may have felt like an internal battle, a chaotic torrent of racing thoughts and unyielding distractions. The prevailing narrative, often shaped by societal expectations and a historical lack of research on female ADHD, taught her that her difficulties with focus were a personal failing, a sign of laziness or inadequacy.

This belief system is often at the root of a woman's tendency to internalize her struggles, which, as studies show, can lead to lower self-esteem, self-blame, and a shattered sense of self-worth that is significantly more prevalent in women with ADHD than in their male counterparts.

This book has provided a crucial, liberating shift in perspective by illuminating the neurobiological realities behind these struggles. You have learned that your brain's attentional system is not "broken" but is simply wired differently, a reality deeply rooted in the dysregulation of neurotransmitters like dopamine and the unique interplay of your brain's attentional networks.

You have come to understand that the two sides of your focus, the scattered mind and the state of intense hyperfocus, are not a paradox, but two manifestations of the same core challenge: a difficulty in regulating the brain's "on/off" switch for attention.

This understanding is the bedrock of compassionate self-management. It allows a woman to move past a lifetime of self-recrimination and begin to approach her focus challenges with curiosity and a strategic, problem-solving mindset, rather than with shame and frustration.

The Toolkit of an Empowered Attentional System

This book has not just offered a new perspective; it has provided a concrete, actionable toolkit for transforming this understanding into a cultivated skill. You are now equipped with strategies that work *with* your brain's unique wiring, not against it. The core of this mastery lies in a three-pronged approach: designing your external world to support focus, cultivating an internal toolkit for self-regulation, and building a sustainable foundation of energy management.

1. The Sanctuary of an Optimized Environment: You've learned that your physical and digital environments are not just passive backdrops but active participants in your ability to concentrate. For the ADHD brain, which struggles with filtering out irrelevant stimuli, a cluttered desk, a noisy office, or a constantly pinging phone is not a minor inconvenience—it is a significant source of cognitive overload that reduces performance and efficiency. By learning to design an "attention zone," you have created an external sanctuary that signals to your brain that it is time for deep work. This includes:

- **Minimizing Visual Noise:** Clearing your desk of clutter, facing a blank wall, and using clear storage to combat the "out of sight, out of mind" phenomenon reduces the number of competing stimuli for your mental spotlight.
- **Controlling Sensory Input:** Using tools like noise-cancelling headphones to create a crucial "sound bubble" for the brain that is exquisitely sensitive to auditory input.
- **Leveraging External Accountability:** The simple but powerful strategy of "body doubling," where you work alongside someone else, acts as an external executive function, providing a sense of accountability and a model of focused behavior that helps you initiate and sustain tasks.

2. The Anchor of an Internal Toolkit: The greatest distractions for the ADHD brain often come from within: a racing mind, a flood of new ideas, or an intense emotional surge. This book has provided a framework for cultivating an internal anchor through mindfulness and self-compassion.

- **Mindfulness for Attentional Control:** You have learned that mindfulness is a form of cognitive training that strengthens your ability to gently guide your attention back to your intended focus, acting as a form of exercise for your attentional muscle. This practice helps to regulate the overactive Default Mode Network (DMN), which is responsible for mind-wandering, allowing the brain to more effectively engage its Task Positive Network (TPN) for focused work.
- **Mindfulness for Emotional Regulation:** This practice is deeply intertwined with emotional regulation and distress tolerance, two core challenges for women with ADHD. The ability to observe a racing mind or an intense emotion without judgment creates a crucial pause between stimulus and response,

allowing you to choose a deliberate action rather than reacting impulsively. This is a foundational step toward managing the intense emotions that so many women with ADHD report feeling.

- **Self-Compassion as an Antidote to Shame:** For a woman who has internalized her struggles and feels a deep sense of shame, self-compassion is the powerful antidote. By learning to approach her mind with curiosity and kindness, she can begin to let go of the rigid expectation that she "should" be able to focus effortlessly. This compassionate stance reduces the anxiety and self-criticism that so often accompanies inattentive symptoms, making it easier to re-engage with a task after a period of distraction.

3. The Structure for Sustainable Effort: You've learned to abandon the myth of multitasking, recognizing it as a detrimental form of rapid task-switching that is incredibly inefficient and mentally exhausting for the ADHD brain. The discipline of single-tasking is a powerful antidote to a scattered mind, allowing you to achieve a higher quality of work with less mental effort.

- **Deep Work and Single-Tasking:** You have learned to embrace single-tasking and to proactively carve out "deep work" blocks for your most demanding tasks, using a timer to create external structure that reduces overwhelm and makes initiation easier. The Pomodoro Technique provides a clear, manageable structure that makes it easier to initiate and sustain a single task, and its short, scheduled breaks serve as a reward and a mental reset, accommodating the brain's need for novelty without allowing it to derail progress.
- **Energy Management and Preventing Burnout:** You have recognized that true, sustained focus is a product of overall well-being, not just a burst of willpower. A prominent, but often overlooked, challenge for women with ADHD is a profound sense of "mental fatigue" and being perpetually "frenzied, frazzled, and overwhelmed." This constant cognitive effort is the "ADHD tax" that depletes mental energy reserves and makes a woman more susceptible to burnout, a state of

chronic exhaustion that research shows is significantly higher in employees with ADHD. To combat this, you have learned to prioritize good sleep hygiene, as quality sleep is critical for attention, emotional control, and working memory. You also recognize that regular exercise serves as a powerful antidote to mental fatigue, as it helps regulate dopamine levels, reduce restlessness, and improve mood.

The Future of Your Focused Edge

The mastery of these skills empowers a woman to direct her mental spotlight where she wants it to go, rather than being pulled by every fleeting impulse or demand. This provides a profound sense of self-efficacy and a foundation for achieving her goals with greater clarity and control.

She is no longer merely coping with her ADHD symptoms but is actively crafting a life that is aligned with her unique strengths and values. This newfound capacity for sustained, intentional focus is a powerful catalyst for growth and achievement, providing a stable and predictable base for the more complex skills of emotion management and relationship nurturing that will be explored in the following books.

- **A Bridge to Emotional Regulation:** The ability to direct your attention is a foundational skill for emotional regulation. The next book, "Master Emotions," will explore how the skills of mindfulness and self-awareness you have cultivated here can be leveraged to create a crucial pause between feeling an intense emotion and reacting to it. You will learn to use your attentional skills to identify and challenge the distorted thoughts that often fuel emotional dysregulation, transforming your relationship with your feelings.
- **A Catalyst for Connection:** The inability to sustain focus in conversations is a common challenge for women with ADHD that can strain relationships. By cultivating a more stable and reliable attentional system, you are better equipped to engage in active, mindful listening, which is the bedrock of meaningful connection. The final book will explore how this sharpened focus can enhance your communication and nurture the deeper bonds that are central to a fulfilling life.

The journey of mastering focus is a continuous practice, not a one-time event. There will be days when the strategies feel effortless and days when the internal chaos feels overwhelming. The true strength lies not in achieving perfection, but in your ability to consistently return to your toolkit, re-engage with your strategies, and approach each challenge with self-compassion. You now have the blueprint to navigate a distracting world with a sharper, more sustained focus, giving you a distinct advantage in all your endeavors. This is the moment you reclaim control over your mental spotlight, and with it, your journey toward a more empowered and intentional life truly begins.

Reflection questions

- This part explores how the ADHD brain's attentional system is not "broken" but is "wired differently". How has this reframing helped you move past self-blame and approach your focus challenges with self-compassion?
- The book discusses the two sides of focus for the ADHD brain: the scattered mind and intense hyperfocus. How can you leverage your capacity for hyperfocus as a strength in your work or hobbies, while also creating systems to manage its challenges?
- The text suggests that proactive self-care is not a luxury but a necessity for sustainable focus. What is one self-care practice you can prioritize this week to protect your mental energy?

BOOK THREE

BALANCE YOUR HORMONES: A GUIDE FOR WOMEN WITH ADHD

INTRODUCTION

THE HORMONAL CONNECTION

For many women with ADHD, living with the condition is not a linear experience; rather, it is a journey profoundly influenced by the natural ebbs and flows of their hormonal cycles throughout their lives.

While this link has been a significant lived experience for countless women for decades, it remains an under-researched topic in the medical community. This lack of understanding can be deeply frustrating, leading to a feeling of not being "believed" when a woman reports that her symptoms worsen during certain times of the month.

This book will address this critical gap, providing an evidence-based discussion that validates a woman's anecdotal experience with scientific research, empowering her to understand and manage this often-ignored aspect of her ADHD. The goal is to move beyond the traditional, male-normed view of ADHD treatment and provide a holistic perspective that accounts for the powerful and dynamic role of hormones.

The Research Gap: Acknowledging the Lived Experience

For too long, the scientific and medical communities have operated under the assumption that ADHD manifests similarly across genders, a misconception rooted in a history of male-centric research. This has created a significant gap in our understanding of the nuances of female ADHD, particularly concerning the powerful influence of hormones. While women have anecdotally reported for years that their symptoms of inattention, anxiety, and emotional dysregulation are exacerbated by hormonal fluctuations, they have often been met with skepticism from healthcare professionals who claim to have "never heard of anything like that."

This lack of belief is not only invalidating but also has tangible, negative consequences. When a woman's hormonal shifts intensify her inattentive symptoms, such as forgetfulness, disorganization, and poor time management, these struggles are often misdiagnosed as anxiety or a mood disorder, leading to ineffective treatment plans and a delayed, or missed, ADHD diagnosis.

A rigorous retrospective study found that the mean age of ADHD diagnosis for females ranged from 16.3 to 28.6 years, compared to 11.2 to 22.7 years for males, underscoring the reality of this diagnostic disparity.

The journey for many women is a lifetime of undiagnosed struggles, fueled by a profound sense of shame and self-blame, before a diagnosis in adulthood finally provides a framework to understand their experience. A key factor in this delay is that women's symptoms are often internalized, such as a "flight of thoughts" or a pervasive sense of internal restlessness, making them less obvious to external observers than the externalized hyperactivity more common in men.

This book provides a critical intervention by shifting the focus from simply validating the symptoms to exploring the neurobiological mechanisms that cause them. It serves as a necessary bridge between a woman's lived experience and the emerging scientific research that is finally beginning to confirm the profound link between hormones and ADHD.

The Neurochemical Link: Estrogen, Dopamine, and the Brain

To understand the profound impact of hormones on ADHD, one must first grasp the intricate link between key sex hormones and the brain's neurochemical systems, particularly dopamine. Research has shown that estrogen, a primary female sex hormone, plays a crucial role in regulating neurotransmitters like dopamine and serotonin.

For individuals with ADHD, dopamine regulation is thought to be different, with lower levels of dopamine in the brain's synapses contributing to symptoms like poor motivation, inattention, and executive dysfunction. Because estrogen can directly influence dopamine levels, fluctuations in this hormone throughout a woman's life can significantly impact the severity of her ADHD symptoms.

For example, lower levels of estrogen are linked to lower levels of dopamine, which can exacerbate core ADHD challenges. This scientific connection provides a powerful explanation for why ADHD can look so different in women at various life stages and why symptoms may feel more severe at certain times.

The relationship is complex, but the key takeaway is that estrogen, in many ways, can be a supportive ally for the ADHD brain. When estrogen levels are high, they can enhance cognitive function and improve mood, often providing a natural boost to a woman's executive functions. However, when estrogen levels drop, this supportive effect diminishes, which can feel like a sudden, and often bewildering, worsening of her symptoms. This understanding is critical because it moves the discussion from a feeling of being "moody" or "overly emotional" to a clear, neurobiological reality that can be observed, tracked, and managed with intention.

The Hormonal Lifespan: From Puberty to Menopause

ADHD in women is not a static condition; it is a dynamic experience that changes across her lifespan in concert with her hormonal journey.

1. Puberty and the Teenage Years: The onset of puberty is a pivotal time when many girls who have previously managed their subtle ADHD symptoms begin to struggle. As sex hormones begin to surge, particularly progesterone and a form of estrogen called estradiol, the balance of the brain's neurochemistry can be significantly disrupted. This hormonal shift, particularly high levels of progesterone, can prime the brain's emotional center, the amygdala, for a greater reaction. This can lead to increased irritability, impulsivity, anxiety, and depression, making a girl's ADHD symptoms harder to manage and often leading to misdiagnosis as a mood disorder. It can also make stimulant medication less effective, as the fluctuating hormones interfere with the medication's ability to regulate the dopamine system. During this time, boys, in contrast, experience a surge in testosterone that can lead to more externalized, hyperactive symptoms, which are more easily noticed and lead to an earlier diagnosis, further widening the diagnostic gap between genders.

2. The Menstrual Cycle: The natural hormonal fluctuations of the menstrual cycle can have a direct and powerful impact on a woman's ADHD symptoms. Research suggests that attention and executive function can worsen in the low-estrogen, high-progesterone luteal phase of the cycle, which occurs in the days leading up to menstruation. This hormonal environment can lead to increased inattention, anxiety, and stress, and can even make a woman's ADHD medication feel less effective. This experience is so common that it aligns with what many women with ADHD have anecdotally reported for years: that their attention is better before ovulation and can worsen after. The intersection of ADHD and premenstrual symptoms is also significant. A high percentage of women with ADHD also experience Premenstrual Dysphoric Disorder (PMDD), a more severe form of PMS, and the combination of the two conditions can make emotional regulation even more challenging, leading to more pronounced mood swings, irritability, and anger. For women with ADHD, PMDD can heighten feelings of depression, anxiety, and hopelessness, and can lead to more pronounced mood swings and increased anger and irritability, making it even harder to manage emotions. PMDD is also linked to chronic fatigue and sleep issues, both of which can further exacerbate ADHD-related challenges with motivation and concentration.

3. Perimenopause and Menopause: For women in midlife, the hormonal shifts of perimenopause and menopause can present a major and often unexpected challenge. As estrogen and progesterone levels begin to decline, the underlying ADHD symptoms that a woman may have compensated for throughout her life can become unmanageable. Research suggests that this hormonal decline can "unmask" a previously undiagnosed ADHD condition or significantly worsen the symptoms of a diagnosed one, creating what some experts refer to as an "ADHD squared" effect—the compounding of low estrogen and low dopamine. The symptoms of menopause, such as "brain fog," memory lapses, and difficulty with concentration, often mirror the symptoms of ADHD, making it difficult to differentiate between the two conditions and leading to a confusing and frustrating experience. For women with undiagnosed ADHD, perimenopause may be the tipping point when symptoms become too difficult to ignore, leading to increased frustration and self-doubt. It is critical for a woman to understand that the cognitive changes she experiences at this life stage may be directly related to her underlying neurobiology, as this understanding is a vital step toward seeking effective support.

Implications for a Holistic, Personalized Treatment

The link between hormones and ADHD has profound implications for a woman's treatment plan, particularly regarding medication. Many individuals with ADHD who menstruate anecdotally report that the effectiveness of their stimulant medication changes across their menstrual cycle. This aligns with the hypothesis that fluctuating hormonal status can directly influence the effectiveness of ADHD medication, as hormones like estrogen can impact the dopamine system that these medications target.

This growing body of evidence has led to the development of potential new approaches to treatment, such as "cycle dosing," where medication dosages are tailored to a woman's hormonal status. While research in this area is still in its early stages, it empowers a woman to take control of her treatment by tracking her own symptoms and their relationship to her cycle.

By keeping a detailed log of her symptoms, she can gather concrete data to present to her doctor, validating her experience and advocating for a more personalized, effective treatment plan that addresses her unique neurobiological needs across her lifespan. This holistic approach ensures that her treatment is not a static prescription but a dynamic, lifelong process that accounts for her unique and fluctuating hormonal profile.

Beyond medication, a woman can also implement proactive lifestyle strategies to help manage the cognitive and emotional symptoms that arise from hormonal fluctuations. A holistic approach that supports both the brain and the body is essential for building resilience. Regular physical exercise is a powerful tool, as it helps regulate mood and brain function, reduces stress, and improves sleep quality.

Good sleep hygiene is also a critical component, as sleep is vital for attention, emotional control, and working memory, and a lack of it can exacerbate hormonal imbalances and ADHD symptoms. Nutrition plays a significant role in brain health and mood stability. The consumption of foods rich in omega-3 fatty acids, antioxidants, and protein can help support brain function and stabilize mood and energy levels. A conscious effort to reduce sugars and processed foods can also help to prevent the energy crashes that exacerbate ADHD symptoms.

Finally, managing stress through mindfulness and other techniques is crucial, as high stress levels can further disrupt hormonal balance and cognitive function. By consistently engaging in these self-care strategies, a woman can build a buffer against the hormonal ebbs and flows and create a more stable and supportive internal environment for her ADHD brain.

This book will provide a groundbreaking discussion on the critical, yet understudied, link between hormones and ADHD in women. It has validated the lived experience of countless women who have anecdotally reported that their symptoms are profoundly impacted by their hormonal cycles. By understanding the neurochemical connection, navigating the challenges of the menstrual cycle and menopause, and exploring tailored treatment and self-care strategies, a woman can move from feeling powerless against her symptoms to a place of informed action.

This holistic approach ensures that her treatment plan is not a static prescription but a dynamic, lifelong process that accounts for her unique neurobiological needs. This understanding is a crucial step towards achieving genuine balance and well-being.

CHAPTER 1

THE NEUROCHEMICAL LINK

To understand the profound impact of hormones on ADHD, one must first grasp the intricate link between key sex hormones and the brain's neurochemical systems, particularly dopamine. Research has shown that estrogen, a primary female sex hormone, plays a crucial role in regulating neurotransmitters like dopamine.

For individuals with ADHD, dopamine regulation is thought to be different, with lower levels of dopamine in the brain's synapses contributing to symptoms like poor motivation, inattention, and executive dysfunction. Because estrogen can directly influence dopamine levels, fluctuations in this hormone throughout a woman's life can significantly impact the severity of her ADHD symptoms.

For example, lower levels of estrogen are linked to lower levels of dopamine, which can exacerbate core ADHD challenges. This scientific connection provides a powerful explanation for why ADHD can look so different in women at various life stages and why symptoms may feel more severe at certain times.

The Role of Dopamine: The Brain's Fuel for Focus and Motivation

At the very core of the ADHD experience lies a distinct neurochemical reality, and dopamine is at its center. Often called the brain's "reward" or "motivation" chemical, dopamine is a key neurotransmitter that plays a crucial role in regulating attention, motivation, and executive functions like planning and focus.

Research indicates that individuals with ADHD often have low dopamine levels or a dysregulation in how dopamine is processed within the brain, a phenomenon known as the "low dopamine hypothesis". This reduced dopamine signaling makes it exceptionally difficult for the brain to sustain engagement on tasks that are not inherently stimulating or rewarding. When a task is boring, repetitive, or requires sustained effort, the ADHD brain struggles to produce enough dopamine to find it interesting, leading to a desperate search for internal or external novelty to get that much-needed hit of stimulation.

This is the neurochemical basis for mind-wandering, distractibility, and the constant pull of the "shiny object" syndrome that so many women with ADHD report feeling.

The brain's ability to focus is also directly tied to the efficiency of its neurotransmitter systems. When these systems are dysregulated, the brain's filtering mechanism can be impaired, making it struggle to differentiate between relevant and irrelevant stimuli. This means that a constant barrage of sensory information, be it a flickering light, the hum of an appliance, or a distracting visual, is registered with nearly equal importance as the task at hand.

This persistent battle against a flood of stimuli creates a significant cognitive load, which research has shown can have a disproportionately negative impact on performance, increase reaction time variability, and reduce brain network efficiency in individuals with ADHD. The constant effort to maintain focus against a brain that is fighting against it leads to a profound sense of "mental fatigue" and being perpetually "frenzied, frazzled, and overwhelmed".

Estrogen and its Influence on the Dopamine System

The female hormonal cycle introduces a powerful, dynamic variable into this neurochemical equation. Estrogen, a primary female sex hormone, plays a crucial role in regulating dopamine and other key neurotransmitters like serotonin and norepinephrine. Research has consistently shown that higher levels of estrogen are linked to increased levels of dopamine, which can have a supportive effect on the brain's attentional and emotional systems. This can feel like a natural cognitive and emotional boost, where a woman's executive functions are slightly more robust, and her mood is more stable.

Conversely, when estrogen levels drop, this supportive effect diminishes, which can feel like a sudden, and often bewildering, worsening of her ADHD symptoms. Lower levels of estrogen are linked to lower levels of dopamine, which can exacerbate core ADHD challenges like poor motivation, inattention, and executive dysfunction. This relationship provides a powerful, scientific explanation for what countless women have anecdotally reported for years: that their ability to focus, their energy levels, and their emotional stability are directly tied to the ebb and flow of their hormonal cycles.

The influence of hormones is so profound that it can even impact the effectiveness of ADHD medication. Many individuals with ADHD who menstruate anecdotally report that the effectiveness of their stimulant medication changes across their menstrual cycle. This aligns with the hypothesis that fluctuating hormonal status can directly influence the effectiveness of ADHD medication, as hormones like estrogen can impact the dopamine system that these medications target.

By understanding this, a woman can begin to track her symptoms and their relationship to her cycle, gathering concrete data to have a more informed conversation with her doctor about potential new approaches, such as "cycle dosing," where medication dosages are tailored to her hormonal status.

The Complicating Factor: The Role of Progesterone

While estrogen is often the star player in this hormonal conversation, progesterone, the other major female sex hormone, also plays a significant and often complicating role. Progesterone levels are typically low during the follicular phase of the menstrual cycle but rise significantly during the luteal phase, which occurs in the days leading up to menstruation.

Research suggests that high levels of progesterone can moderate or even negate some of estrogen's positive emotional and cognitive benefits. This is because high progesterone can prime the amygdala, the brain's emotional center, for a greater reaction, which can lead to increased irritability, impulsivity, anxiety, and depression.

The combination of low estrogen and high progesterone that occurs during the luteal phase can create a particularly challenging environment for the ADHD brain, exacerbating symptoms and making a woman more susceptible to emotional dysregulation, anxiety, and stress.

This complex hormonal interplay provides a clear neurobiological basis for why many women feel that their symptoms worsen in the days leading up to their period. The intersection of ADHD and Premenstrual Dysphoric Disorder (PMDD) is also significant, with a high percentage of women with ADHD also experiencing PMDD, a more severe form of PMS that is characterized by intense emotional symptoms like depression, anxiety, and anger.

The combination of these two conditions can make emotional regulation even more challenging, leading to more pronounced mood swings, irritability, and anger.

Genetic Influences on Dopamine and Hormonal Sensitivity

The interplay between hormones and neurochemistry is further complicated by genetics. Research has focused on specific genes that are involved in the regulation of dopamine and other neurotransmitters. The Dopamine Transporter Gene (DAT1) and the Dopamine Receptor D4 (DRD4) genes are two of the most well-studied candidates. The DAT1 gene codes for the dopamine transporter protein, which is responsible for the reuptake of dopamine from the synaptic cleft back into the presynaptic neuron. Variations in this gene have been shown to influence the effectiveness of dopamine reuptake, directly impacting the availability of dopamine in the brain and contributing to symptoms of inattention and impulsivity.

Similarly, certain variations of the DRD4 gene, which is involved in the function of dopamine receptors, have been associated with difficulties in working memory and other cognitive functions in children with ADHD.

This intricate genetic basis means that a woman's sensitivity to hormonal fluctuations may not be uniform. Some women may be more genetically predisposed to experiencing significant symptom exacerbation during periods of low estrogen due to a particular genetic variation, while others may be less affected. This is a complex interplay of genetics, hormones, and environmental factors that creates a unique neurobiological profile for each woman.

The "ADHD Squared" Effect: Perimenopause and Menopause

The hormonal influence on ADHD culminates in midlife, during the transition into perimenopause and menopause, presenting a major and often unexpected challenge. As estrogen and progesterone levels begin to decline, the underlying ADHD symptoms that a woman may have compensated for throughout her life can become unmanageable.

Research suggests that this hormonal decline can "unmask" a previously undiagnosed ADHD condition or significantly worsen the symptoms of a diagnosed one, creating what some experts refer to as an "ADHD squared" effect, the compounding of low estrogen and low dopamine.

The symptoms of perimenopause, such as "brain fog," memory lapses, and difficulty with concentration, often mirror the symptoms of ADHD, making it difficult to differentiate between the two conditions and leading to a confusing and frustrating experience.

A woman might wonder if she is developing early-onset dementia or if her struggles are a normal part of aging, when in fact, they may be directly related to her underlying neurobiology. This is why it is critical for a woman to understand this link, as it provides a clear, actionable pathway toward seeking effective support.

This growing body of evidence makes it clear that the ADHD focus challenge is a genuine, neurobiological reality. Understanding this science is the first step toward self-compassion and building effective strategies. It shifts the perspective from a moral failing to a recognition of a genuine neurological difference, paving the way for a more intentional and supportive approach to managing attention.

The Path Forward: From Anecdote to Action

The journey of living with ADHD for women has long been marked by a feeling of not being believed, with their experiences dismissed as a character flaw or a mood disorder. This lack of understanding is a direct result of a research gap that has historically focused on a male-normed view of ADHD. However, the emerging research on the neurochemical link between hormones and ADHD provides a powerful framework for change.

It validates a woman's anecdotal experience with scientific evidence, empowering her to take control of her health and advocate for a more personalized, holistic approach to treatment that accounts for her unique and dynamic neurobiological needs.

This knowledge is not just for healthcare providers; it is a vital tool for every woman with ADHD. By understanding the neurochemical and hormonal interplay, a woman can become an expert on her own body and mind.

She can begin to track her symptoms in relation to her cycle, her sleep, and her stress levels, gathering the data needed to make informed decisions about her well-being. This is how she can move from feeling powerless against her symptoms to a place of informed action and genuine self-mastery.

This chapter has provided the foundational scientific context for this journey, and the following chapters will build on this understanding, offering a practical roadmap for navigating the hormonal fluctuations of the menstrual cycle and menopause, and for exploring tailored, evidence-based strategies for a more balanced and fulfilling life.

CHAPTER 2

NAVIGATING THE MENSTRUAL CYCLE

The natural hormonal fluctuations of the menstrual cycle can have a direct and powerful impact on a woman's ADHD symptoms. Research suggests that attention and executive function can worsen in the low-estrogen, high-progesterone luteal phase of the cycle, which occurs in the days leading up to menstruation. This hormonal environment can lead to increased inattention, anxiety, and stress, and can even make a woman's ADHD medication feel less effective. This experience is so common that it aligns with what many women with ADHD have anecdotally reported for years: that their attention is better before ovulation and can worsen after.

The intersection of ADHD and premenstrual symptoms is also significant. A high percentage of women with ADHD also experience Premenstrual Dysphoric Disorder (PMDD), and the combination of the two conditions can make emotional regulation even more challenging, leading to more pronounced mood swings, irritability, and anger. By learning to track her menstrual cycle and its impact on her symptoms, a woman can gain valuable insights to help her proactively manage her energy, plan her schedule, and have a more informed conversation with her doctor.

The Hormonal Landscape of the Menstrual Cycle

To effectively navigate the impact of the menstrual cycle on ADHD symptoms, it is crucial to understand the two main phases and the hormones that dominate them. The two primary hormones at play are estrogen and progesterone, both of which fluctuate in a predictable pattern each month and have a direct line to the brain's emotional and cognitive centers. The brain is filled with receptors for these hormones, and their levels directly influence the brain's neurotransmitter systems, particularly dopamine, which is heavily implicated in ADHD.

The menstrual cycle can be broadly divided into two main phases:

- **The Follicular Phase:** This phase begins on the first day of menstruation and lasts until ovulation, around day 14 of a typical cycle. During this time, estrogen levels gradually rise. For many women with ADHD, this can be a period of relative calm and improved functioning. Because higher levels of estrogen are linked to increased levels of dopamine, this phase can offer a welcome boost of energy, a better mood, and greater cognitive clarity. Women may feel more focused, motivated, and emotionally stable, which can make it a productive and positive time of the month.
- **The Luteal Phase:** This phase begins after ovulation and lasts until menstruation. Progesterone levels are low during the follicular phase but rise significantly in the luteal phase, while estrogen levels drop after ovulation and then decrease again in the days leading up to menstruation. This low-estrogen, high-progesterone environment can be particularly challenging for the ADHD brain. As the supportive effects of estrogen diminish, symptoms of inattention, poor planning, and executive dysfunction can become more pronounced. This is often the time when women feel a noticeable worsening of their ADHD symptoms, making it harder to focus, manage daily

tasks, and regulate their emotions. This aligns with what many women anecdotally report: their attention is better before ovulation and can worsen after.

The relationship between these hormones is so powerful that a woman's hormonal status can influence her ADHD symptoms, medication effectiveness, and overall functioning across her entire lifespan, from puberty through to menopause.

The Intersection of ADHD and Premenstrual Dysphoric Disorder (PMDD)

The premenstrual or late luteal phase is not just a time of poor attention and increased anxiety; for a significant number of women with ADHD, it is a period of profound emotional and physical distress. Research indicates that over 40% of women with ADHD also experience Premenstrual Dysphoric Disorder (PMDD), a more severe form of premenstrual syndrome (PMS). This high rate of co-occurrence highlights how closely these two conditions are connected and how powerfully they can overlap.

PMDD is characterized by at least one significant emotional symptom, which can include strong feelings of depression and hopelessness, significant anxiety or tension, and persistent anger or irritability that can cause conflicts in relationships. Both ADHD and PMDD are linked to changes in brain function and hormones, and their combination can create a perfect storm of emotional dysregulation.

For a woman with ADHD who already struggles with emotional intensity and a lack of an internal "buffer" to modulate feelings, the added burden of PMDD can make emotional regulation even more challenging. This can lead to more pronounced mood swings, irritability, and anger, making it difficult to manage emotions and maintain a sense of control.

PMDD also brings a host of other symptoms that directly compound the challenges of ADHD:

- **Exhaustion and Low Energy:** PMDD is linked to sleep disturbances, fatigue, and low energy, which can further lower motivation and make it even harder for a woman with ADHD to get things done.

- **Cognitive Difficulties:** The brain fog and forgetfulness associated with PMDD can become even more pronounced when combined with the working memory and inattention issues of ADHD. This compounds the typical focus-related challenges a woman faces, making it harder to stay focused, organize tasks, and follow through on instructions.
- **Physical Symptoms:** PMDD symptoms can also be physical, including headaches, muscle or joint pain, and bloating, all of which can increase a woman's discomfort and make it more challenging to manage her daily responsibilities.

The combination of these conditions can make the emotional and physical toll of the premenstrual phase feel unbearable. By understanding this link, a woman can stop blaming herself for what feels like a "meltdown" and start developing proactive strategies to manage this difficult period with greater self-compassion and support.

Hormones and Medication Efficacy: A Personalized Approach

The intricate link between hormones and ADHD has profound implications for a woman's treatment plan, particularly regarding medication. Many individuals with ADHD who menstruate anecdotally report that the effectiveness of their stimulant medication changes across their menstrual cycle. This aligns with the hypothesis that fluctuating hormonal status can directly influence the effectiveness of ADHD medication, as hormones like estrogen can impact the dopamine system that these medications target.

Research on this front is limited, but a rigorous study that is pioneering a new stage of work has been designed to directly examine the role of circulating estrogen in relation to ADHD symptoms in young women.

Preliminary data from this study suggests that for women with greater ADHD symptoms, within-person declines in estrogen, particularly in the context of rising progesterone levels just after ovulation, are associated with clinically significant increases in ADHD symptoms. The results of such work have the potential to change clinical practice by indicating the need to account for cycle phase in ADHD evaluations and to suggest personalized approaches to treatment targeted to a woman's unique hormone levels.

This emerging body of evidence has led to the development of potential new approaches, such as "cycle dosing," where medication dosages are tailored to a woman's hormonal status. While this is still an area of active research, it empowers a woman to take control of her treatment by tracking her own symptoms and their relationship to her cycle.

By keeping a detailed log of her symptoms, she can gather concrete data to present to her doctor, validating her experience and advocating for a more personalized, effective treatment plan that addresses her unique neurobiological needs across her lifespan.

Proactive Strategies for Managing Your Cycle

The knowledge of how your hormones impact your ADHD is only truly powerful when it is paired with a proactive plan of action. The goal is not to fight against your cycle but to work with it, creating systems that provide support when you need it most.

- **Track Your Symptoms:** The first step is to become a detective of your own body and mind. Use a simple journal or a dedicated tracking app to record your ADHD symptoms each day. Note your energy levels, focus, motivation, emotional state, and the effectiveness of your medication. Be sure to also track your menstrual cycle, marking the days of your period and when you ovulate. Over two to three months, you will begin to see clear patterns emerge, providing you with invaluable data to anticipate your more challenging days and plan accordingly.
- **Plan Your Schedule with Your Cycle in Mind:** Once you have a clear understanding of your patterns, you can begin to strategically plan your schedule. For instance, if you know that the luteal phase is particularly challenging for you, avoid scheduling major projects, difficult conversations, or demanding social events during that time. Instead, front-load your more cognitively demanding tasks in the follicular phase and save more routine, low-energy tasks for the days leading up to your period. This approach reduces frustration and guilt by working with your natural rhythms.

- **Prioritize Proactive Self-Care:** Your self-care routine should be a non-negotiable part of your monthly cycle, especially during the more challenging phases. Regular physical activity, even just a brisk walk, can serve as a powerful antidote to mental fatigue, help regulate dopamine levels, reduce restlessness, and improve mood. Consistent and high-quality sleep is critical for attention, emotional control, and working memory, and a lack of it can exacerbate hormonal imbalances and ADHD symptoms. Nutrition also plays a significant role. Focusing on a diet rich in omega-3 fatty acids, antioxidants, and protein can help support brain function and stabilize mood and energy levels, while a conscious effort to reduce sugars and processed foods can help prevent the energy crashes that exacerbate ADHD symptoms.
- **Communicate and Set Boundaries:** Openly and gently communicate with your partner, family, and close friends about the impact your cycle has on you. This isn't about making excuses, but about fostering empathy and understanding. You can say, "The week before my period is often difficult for me, so I may be more irritable or forgetful. It's not personal, but I'll need a little more space and support during that time." This proactive communication can reduce conflict and resentment by setting clear expectations.
- **Have a Crisis Plan for Intense Days:** On days when you feel an emotional storm brewing, have a plan of action ready to go. This could include a pre-planned calming activity, like a hot bath or listening to a specific playlist, a list of people you can reach out to, or an "exit strategy" for social situations that feel overwhelming. Having a pre-defined plan reduces the need for difficult decision-making in the moment of crisis.

By consistently applying these proactive, evidence-based strategies, a woman can move from feeling powerless against her symptoms to a place of informed action. This holistic approach ensures that her treatment plan is not a static prescription but a dynamic, lifelong process that accounts for her unique neurobiological needs. This understanding is a crucial step towards achieving genuine balance and well-being.

CHAPTER 3:

THE TRANSITION YEARS: PERIMENOPAUSE, MENOPAUSE, AND COGNITIVE CHANGE

For women in midlife, the hormonal shifts of perimenopause and menopause can present a major and often unexpected challenge. As estrogen and progesterone levels begin to decline, the underlying ADHD symptoms that a woman may have compensated for throughout her life can become unmanageable.

Research suggests that this hormonal decline can "unmask" a previously undiagnosed ADHD condition or significantly worsen the symptoms of a diagnosed one, creating what some experts refer to as an "ADHD squared" effect: the compounding of low estrogen and low dopamine.

The symptoms of menopause, such as "brain fog," memory lapses, and difficulty with concentration, often mirror the symptoms of ADHD, making it difficult to differentiate between the two conditions and leading to a confusing and frustrating experience. This is why it is critical for a woman to understand that the cognitive changes she experiences at this life stage may be directly related to her underlying neurobiology.

Table: The Impact of Hormones on ADHD Symptoms Across the Female Lifespan

Phase of Life	Key Hormonal Changes	Corresponding ADHD Symptom Changes	Neurochemical Link
Childhood	Hormone levels are low and consistent	Symptoms are often more consistent, which can make treatment easier	Stable hormones lead to more predictable brain chemistry.
Puberty	Sharp increase in progesterone and estrogen	Symptoms can become harder to manage, with increased irritability and impulsivity	High progesterone can impact brain regions related to emotion, while testosterone in boys may lead to externalized symptoms.
Menstrual Cycle	Estrogen and progesterone fluctuate monthly	Symptoms may worsen during the low-estrogen luteal phase, leading to more inattention, anxiety, and mood swings.	Lower estrogen is linked to lower dopamine levels, which can exacerbate ADHD symptoms.

Phase of Life	Key Hormonal Changes	Corresponding ADHD Symptom Changes	Neurochemical Link
Perimenopause & Menopause	Gradual decline in estrogen and progesterone	Symptoms may become unmanageable, including worsening inattention, poor time management, and emotional dysregulation. Previously subthreshold symptoms can become highly apparent.	The combination of declining estrogen and low dopamine creates a compounding effect, or "ADHD squared".

CHAPTER 4

HORMONES, MEDICATION EFFICACY, AND TAILORED TREATMENT

The link between hormones and ADHD has profound implications for a woman's treatment plan, particularly regarding medication. Many individuals with ADHD who menstruate anecdotally report that the effectiveness of their stimulant medication changes across their menstrual cycle. This aligns with the hypothesis that fluctuating hormonal status can directly influence the effectiveness of ADHD medication, as hormones like estrogen can impact the dopamine system that these medications target.

This growing body of evidence has led to the development of potential new approaches to treatment, such as "cycle dosing," where medication dosages are tailored to a woman's hormonal status.

While research in this area is still limited and in its early stages, it empowers a woman to take control of her treatment by tracking her own symptoms and their relationship to her cycle. By keeping a detailed log of her symptoms, she can gather concrete data to present to her doctor, validating her experience and advocating for a more personalized, effective treatment plan that addresses her unique neurobiological needs across her lifespan.

The Neurochemical Basis for Medication Efficacy Fluctuations

For a woman with ADHD, the journey of finding an effective medication and a stable dose is often a long and arduous one. But even after finding a regimen that seems to work, many women anecdotally report that their medication's efficacy fluctuates throughout the month. This isn't an imagined experience; it has a clear neurochemical basis. As discussed, estrogen plays a crucial role in regulating dopamine, the key neurotransmitter targeted by stimulant medications used to treat ADHD.

The effectiveness of stimulant medication is tied to its ability to increase dopamine availability in the brain's synapses, thereby improving attention, motivation, and executive function. When estrogen levels are high, they can enhance dopamine levels, which can have a supportive effect on the brain's attentional systems and may potentiate the effects of medication.

When estrogen levels drop, particularly in the low-estrogen luteal phase that precedes menstruation, this supportive effect diminishes. The drop in estrogen can be linked to lower levels of dopamine, which can exacerbate core ADHD challenges and make the medication feel less effective.

This biological shift can feel like hitting a wall, where a woman's medication suddenly stops working as it should, leading to a frustrating return of her inattentive symptoms, anxiety, and a feeling of being out of control. It's a common experience that a woman's attention is better before ovulation and can worsen after.

This link is so profound that some women with ADHD who have predominantly inattentive symptoms report a significant worsening of their symptoms during the luteal phase. They may experience more pronounced difficulties with planning, organizing, and focusing, while also feeling a greater sense of anxiety and stress. This is further complicated for women with ADHD who also experience Premenstrual Dysphoric Disorder (PMDD), as the combination of the two conditions can make emotional regulation even more challenging, leading to more pronounced mood swings, irritability, and anger.

This is why it is so critical for a woman to recognize that her struggles during this time are not a personal failing but a neurobiological reality that can be managed with a tailored approach.

The Call for Personalized Treatment: The Rise of "Cycle Dosing"

The traditional, male-normed approach to ADHD treatment often involves a static medication dose that is expected to be effective every day of the month. However, a woman's brain chemistry is not static; it is a dynamic landscape that changes with her hormonal cycle. This disconnect between a static treatment plan and a dynamic reality is at the heart of many women's struggles.

A growing body of anecdotal evidence from women, combined with emerging research, is leading to the development of potential new approaches to treatment, such as "cycle dosing." This approach involves tailoring medication dosages to a woman's hormonal status, for example, by slightly increasing her dose during the low-estrogen luteal phase when her symptoms are most pronounced. While research in this area is still limited and in its early stages, it empowers a woman to take control of her treatment by tracking her own symptoms and their relationship to her cycle.

The results of studies pioneering this new work have the potential to change clinical practice by indicating the need to account for a woman's cycle phase in ADHD evaluations, and to suggest personalized approaches to treatment targeted to her unique hormone levels.

The need for personalized treatment extends beyond the menstrual cycle. For women in midlife, the hormonal shifts of perimenopause and menopause can present a major and often unexpected challenge. As estrogen and progesterone levels decline, underlying ADHD symptoms that a woman may have compensated for throughout her life can become unmanageable.

This hormonal decline can "unmask" a previously undiagnosed ADHD condition or significantly worsen the symptoms of a diagnosed one, creating what some experts refer to as an "ADHD squared" effect: the compounding of low estrogen and low dopamine. A woman may feel that her stimulant medication, which once worked well, is now much less effective at a time in her life when she is dealing with significant cognitive changes like "brain fog" and memory lapses. This is why an informed discussion with a doctor about medication and dosage is critical at this life stage.

Empowering Your Voice: Tracking Symptoms to Advocate for Yourself

For years, women who reported a link between their menstrual cycle and ADHD symptoms were often told by doctors that they "had never heard of anything like that." This profound lack of understanding and belief from the medical community can leave a woman feeling invalidated, hopeless, and alone. To move past this, a woman must become an expert on her own body and mind, gathering concrete, objective data to back up her subjective experience.

The most powerful tool for this is a detailed symptom log. By diligently tracking her symptoms, a woman can transform her experience from a collection of vague feelings into a clear, visual, and measurable pattern that can be presented to a doctor.

This process turns a subjective report of "I'm more tired and irritable" into an objective report of "My inattention, anxiety, and fatigue scores were consistently 40% higher during the five days leading up to my period for the last three months, and my medication's effectiveness was reduced by 50% during that time."

By keeping a detailed log of her symptoms, she can:

- **Identify Her Unique Patterns:** She will begin to see clear, consistent patterns in how her symptoms, emotional regulation, energy levels, and medication efficacy are influenced by her cycle. This self-knowledge is the first step toward a proactive, rather than reactive, approach to her well-being.

- **Validate Her Experience:** The data she collects provides undeniable evidence of a correlation between her hormonal status and her ADHD symptoms, which can be crucial for an informed discussion with a healthcare provider who may be unaware of this link.
- **Advocate for a Personalized Plan:** With this data in hand, a woman is in a powerful position to advocate for a more personalized treatment plan, whether that involves a discussion about cycle dosing, a conversation about non-medication strategies to implement during her more challenging days, or a comprehensive review of her overall well-being.

This process of tracking is a vital step toward an empowered and informed approach to treatment. It is about moving from a place of feeling powerless against her symptoms to a place of informed action, ensuring that her treatment plan is not a static prescription but a dynamic, lifelong process that accounts for her unique and fluctuating neurobiological needs. This understanding is a crucial step toward achieving genuine balance and well-being.

A Holistic Approach: The Synergy of Medication and Self-Care

The conversation around medication efficacy and hormones is not just about dosage adjustments; it's about a holistic approach that recognizes the synergy between medical treatment and self-care. Even with a perfectly tailored medication regimen, lifestyle factors like sleep, nutrition, and exercise play a crucial role in regulating the brain's neurochemistry and building resilience against hormonal ebbs and flows.

For example, a woman may find that during the low-estrogen luteal phase, when her medication feels less effective, she needs to double down on her self-care practices. This could include:

- **Prioritizing Sleep Hygiene:** As quality sleep is critical for attention, emotional control, and working memory, she might need to be even more diligent about her sleep routine during this time, creating a relaxing ritual and avoiding stimulating activities that can trigger insomnia or restlessness.

- **Increasing Physical Activity:** Regular physical exercise can serve as a powerful antidote to mental fatigue, helping to regulate dopamine levels, reduce restlessness, and improve mood, all of which are a significant challenge during the luteal phase.
- **Focusing on Brain-Supporting Nutrition:** A diet rich in omega-3 fatty acids, antioxidants, and protein can help support brain function and stabilize mood and energy levels, providing a buffer against the cognitive and emotional rollercoasters that accompany hormonal shifts.

Furthermore, many women with ADHD have a tendency to internalize their struggles and blame themselves for their difficulties, which can lead to a significant lack of confidence and a sense of being perpetually overwhelmed. It is important to note that stimulant medications enhance the dopamine system and improve executive function.

For this reason, stimulants can be effective in menopausal women, but combining them with non-medication strategies like cognitive-behavioral therapy, coaching, stress management, and exercise can help support executive function, mood, and cognitive health. This integrated approach acknowledges that a woman's well-being is a complex interplay of biology, lifestyle, and psychology.

The link between hormones and ADHD has provided a groundbreaking discussion that validates the lived experience of countless women who have anecdotally reported that their symptoms are profoundly impacted by their hormonal cycles.

By understanding the neurochemical connection, navigating the challenges of the menstrual cycle and menopause, and exploring tailored treatment and self-care strategies, a woman can move from feeling powerless against her symptoms to a place of informed action. This holistic approach ensures that her treatment plan is not a static prescription but a dynamic, lifelong process that accounts for her unique neurobiological needs. This understanding is a crucial step towards achieving genuine balance and well-being.

CHAPTER 5

HORMONAL SELF-CARE

Beyond medication, a woman can also implement proactive lifestyle strategies to help manage the cognitive and emotional symptoms that arise from hormonal fluctuations. A holistic approach that supports both the brain and the body is essential for building resilience. Regular physical exercise is a powerful tool, as it helps regulate mood and brain function, reduces stress, and improves sleep quality. Good sleep hygiene is also a critical component, as sleep is vital for attention, emotional control, and working memory, and a lack of it can exacerbate hormonal imbalances and ADHD symptoms.

Nutrition plays a significant role in brain health and mood stability. The consumption of foods rich in omega-3 fatty acids, antioxidants, and protein can help support brain function and stabilize mood and energy levels.

A conscious effort to reduce sugars and processed foods can also help to prevent the energy crashes that exacerbate ADHD symptoms. Finally, managing stress through mindfulness and other techniques is crucial, as high stress levels can further disrupt hormonal balance and cognitive function.

By consistently engaging in these self-care strategies, a woman can build a buffer against the hormonal ebbs and flows and create a more stable and supportive internal environment for her ADHD brain.

The Proactive Power of Physical Activity

For a woman with ADHD, regular physical exercise is not just a tool for physical health; it is a profound and proactive strategy for managing the neurochemical and hormonal imbalances that fuel her symptoms.

Research has shown that physical activity has a beneficial effect on inhibitory control in adults with ADHD, a core executive function that helps with impulse control and emotional regulation. It can also improve cognitive function, emotional state, mental health, and physical fitness indicators.

The mechanism behind this is linked to exercise-induced dopamine release, which is associated with improved attention and can help regulate the brain's reward system, which is often dysregulated in individuals with ADHD. Furthermore, exercise can enhance brain plasticity and improve blood flow to the brain, which supports memory and learning.

To make exercise a consistent part of your routine, it's essential to find an activity that is genuinely enjoyable, as the ADHD brain craves novelty and can struggle with boring, repetitive tasks.

This could be dancing, running, swimming, lifting weights, or a team sport. Research suggests that while all forms of physical activity can be beneficial, interventions that involve higher levels of cognitive engagement and motor skill development, such as cognitively enriched aerobic exercise (combining physical activity with simultaneous cognitive tasks), may lead to greater improvements in working memory performance.

Beyond long-term, consistent activity, acute, intense bursts of exercise can also serve as a powerful "brain break" to combat restlessness and re-energize your focus. A brisk walk, a short jog, or a burst of jumping jacks can help to discharge pent-up emotional energy, which is especially useful for a brain prone to emotional dysregulation. This physical "reset button" can prevent an emotional storm from spiraling out of control, as it provides a direct, healthy outlet for intense feelings like anger, anxiety, or frustration.

Prioritizing Sleep Hygiene: The Foundation of Well-Being

Quality sleep is non-negotiable for anyone seeking to maintain optimal cognitive and emotional health, but for a woman with ADHD, it is the bedrock of sustained focus, emotional control, and working memory. Research indicates that an estimated 50-75% of adults with ADHD experience sleeping problems, with studies showing that sleep deprivation in ADHD can be as impairing as other adult symptoms combined.

These sleep challenges often vary by ADHD subtype, with women who have predominantly inattentive symptoms being more likely to have a later bedtime, and those with hyperactive-impulsive symptoms more likely to experience insomnia.

To combat this, a woman must prioritize consistent and healthy sleep hygiene practices. The human body thrives on regularity, and the ADHD brain is no exception. A consistent bedtime and wake-up time, even on weekends, helps regulate your natural sleep rhythm and reinforces the connection between bed and sleep.

- **Create a Relaxing Ritual:** Your bedtime routine should signal to your body that it's time to wind down. This could include listening to a relaxing audiobook, reading a physical book (as opposed to an overstimulating screen), taking a warm bath or shower, or practicing deep breathing exercises. This ritual helps to transition the ADHD brain from its "on the go" state to a calmer state, preparing it for rest.
- **Avoid Stimulating Activities:** In the hours before bed, it is crucial to avoid screens, caffeine, sugar, and stimulating work projects that can trigger hyperfocus. The blue light from screens can interfere with melatonin production, while engaging in a highly stimulating task can make it difficult for the ADHD brain to wind down.

- **Clear Your Mental Clutter:** A racing mind and ruminating on a to-do list or worrying about unfinished tasks can keep you awake. A simple but effective strategy is to take time before bed to write out your "to-do" list for the next day, which helps to offload these worries from your mind, allowing you to relax and fall asleep more easily.

Nourishing Your Brain: Diet and Hydration

What you consume directly impacts your brain's ability to function. Consistent, high-quality fuel is crucial for maintaining stable energy levels, which in turn supports sustained focus and emotional regulation. Dehydration and erratic blood sugar levels can mimic or exacerbate ADHD symptoms, making it even more challenging to stay on track.

- **Mindful Eating:** Focusing on balanced meals with lean protein, healthy fats, and complex carbohydrates is key to maintaining steady energy levels throughout the day. Conversely, a conscious effort to reduce sugars and processed foods can help to prevent the rapid energy spikes followed by a crash that leaves you feeling sluggish and unfocused, which can exacerbate ADHD symptoms.
- **The Power of Omega-3s:** The brain uses omega-3 fatty acids as a building block for cell membranes and as a tool to help neurotransmitters carry signals more effectively. Several studies have linked low omega-3 fatty acid levels to common ADHD symptoms like learning difficulties, hyperactivity, and problems with emotional regulation. Research has shown that supplementing with omega-3s can improve mood, reduce hyperactivity, and even enhance working memory. Fish high in omega-3 fatty acids include mackerel, lake trout, herring, sardines, and salmon.
- **Consistent Hydration:** Staying properly hydrated is essential for optimal brain function and mental clarity. Keeping a water bottle with you and aiming for consistent intake throughout the day can have a significant impact on your focus and mental energy.

Managing Stress: Building a Buffer Against Hormonal Chaos

For a woman with ADHD, the constant effort to manage symptoms, navigate societal expectations, and deal with the relentless demands of daily life can be a source of chronic, low-grade stress.

This prolonged stress can further disrupt hormonal balance and cognitive function. Research shows that high stress levels can worsen working memory deficits and emotional regulation, creating a vicious cycle where ADHD symptoms lead to stress, and stress, in turn, exacerbates ADHD symptoms.

Managing stress is crucial for building resilience against the hormonal ebbs and flows of a woman's life. Mindfulness and other stress-reduction techniques provide the internal toolkit to manage the physiological arousal that comes with stress.

- **Mindfulness Practices:** Mindfulness, such as meditation, journaling, or yoga, can help to support emotional regulation, improve focus, and reduce stress by providing a much-needed anchor for a racing mind. By consistently practicing mindfulness, a woman can learn to become a curious observer of her thoughts and emotions rather than being solely subject to their whims.
- **Deep Breathing Exercises:** When stress levels are high, deep breathing exercises can directly impact your nervous system, promoting a sense of calm and control amidst the chaos. By slowing your breath, you can calm your body's "fight or flight" response and engage its more relaxed, parasympathetic state.
- **Creative Outlets:** Engaging in creative activities such as painting, drawing, or writing can provide a positive outlet for expression and help channel any overwhelming thoughts or emotions, a key skill taught in Dialectical Behavior Therapy (DBT).

By consistently engaging in these self-care strategies, a woman can build a buffer against the hormonal ebbs and flows and create a more stable and supportive internal environment for her ADHD brain. This integrated approach ensures that your newfound capacity for concentration is not only powerful but also sustainable, helping you thrive in a world that constantly vies for your attention, rather than merely survive it.

Conclusion: A Holistic Approach to Hormonal Harmony

This book has provided a groundbreaking discussion on the critical, yet understudied, link between hormones and ADHD in women. It has validated the lived experience of countless women who have anecdotally reported that their symptoms are profoundly impacted by their hormonal cycles.

By understanding the neurochemical connection, navigating the challenges of the menstrual cycle and menopause, and exploring tailored treatment and self-care strategies, a woman can move from feeling powerless against her symptoms to a place of informed action. This holistic approach ensures that her treatment plan is not a static prescription but a dynamic, lifelong process that accounts for her unique neurobiological needs. This understanding is a crucial step towards achieving genuine balance and well-being.

The Liberation of a Scientific Explanation

For too long, the unique challenges of ADHD in women have been overlooked, a reality underscored by a history of male-centric research and diagnostic criteria that fail to capture the nuances of female symptom presentation.

A woman's emotional and cognitive struggles, which are often exacerbated by hormonal shifts, have been dismissed as anxiety, depression, or a mood disorder, leading to misdiagnosis, ineffective treatment, and a profound sense of not being "believed" by the medical community. For many, this lack of validation has fueled a deep and pervasive sense of shame, a feeling that their struggles are a personal failing rather than a neurobiological reality.

This book provides a critical intervention by shining a light on the science behind these struggles. The knowledge that the ebb and flow of estrogen and progesterone are directly linked to the brain's dopamine system is profoundly liberating. It transforms a vague, frustrating feeling of being out of control into a clear, scientific understanding.

You now know that when your symptoms worsen in the days leading up to your period, it's not because you're "moody" or "overly emotional" but because lower levels of estrogen are linked to lower levels of dopamine, which can exacerbate core ADHD challenges. This understanding allows for a powerful shift in perspective, moving from a place of self-blame and frustration to a place of self-compassion and informed action.

The Three Pillars of Hormonal Self-Mastery

The holistic approach to hormonal harmony presented in this book is built on three core pillars: understanding the neurobiology, tracking your unique patterns, and implementing tailored, proactive strategies. This is a dynamic process that recognizes a woman's hormonal journey as a constant, ever-changing landscape, not a static condition.

1. Understanding the Neurobiological Landscape: You have learned that ADHD is not a static condition but a dynamic experience that changes across a woman's lifespan in concert with her hormonal journey.

- **The Menstrual Cycle:** You now understand that the low-estrogen, high-progesterone environment of the luteal phase, which precedes menstruation, can intensify symptoms of inattention, anxiety, and emotional dysregulation. This is why many women anecdotally report that their attention is better before ovulation and can worsen after. This insight is a powerful tool for self-compassion, as it provides a clear, non-judgmental explanation for a woman's fluctuating capacity for focus and emotional control throughout the month. The knowledge of this link is a crucial step toward managing the intense mood swings, irritability, and anger associated with the co-occurrence of ADHD and Premenstrual Dysphoric Disorder (PMDD) that many women report.
- **Perimenopause and Menopause:** You have also gained a deeper understanding of the significant and often unexpected challenge that the hormonal shifts of midlife can present. As estrogen and progesterone levels decline, underlying ADHD symptoms that a woman may have compensated for

throughout her life can become unmanageable. This hormonal decline can "unmask" a previously undiagnosed ADHD condition or significantly worsen the symptoms of a diagnosed one, creating what some experts refer to as an "ADHD squared" effect—the compounding of low estrogen and low dopamine. This understanding is crucial for a woman to be able to differentiate between menopausal "brain fog" and a worsening of her ADHD symptoms, providing a clear pathway toward seeking effective support.

2. Becoming a Self-Advocate Through Symptom Tracking: The most powerful tool for navigating this journey is becoming an expert on your own body and mind. For years, women who reported a link between their menstrual cycle and ADHD symptoms were often told by doctors that they "had never heard of anything like that". This profound lack of understanding and belief from the medical community can leave a woman feeling invalidated and hopeless. To move past this, a woman must become an expert on her own body and mind, gathering concrete, objective data to back up her subjective experience.

By diligently tracking her symptoms, a woman can transform her experience from a collection of vague feelings into a clear, visual, and measurable pattern that can be presented to a doctor.

This process turns a subjective report of "I'm more tired and irritable" into an objective report of "My inattention, anxiety, and fatigue scores were consistently 40% higher during the five days leading up to my period for the last three months, and my medication's effectiveness was reduced by 50% during that time." With this data in hand, a woman is in a powerful position to advocate for a more personalized treatment plan, validating her experience and empowering her to take control of her health.

3. Implementing a Tailored, Holistic Treatment Plan: The conversation around medication efficacy and hormones is not just about dosage adjustments; it's about a holistic approach that recognizes the synergy between medical treatment and self-care.

- **Medication and "Cycle Dosing":** The link between hormones and ADHD has led to the development of potential new approaches to treatment, such as "cycle dosing," where medication dosages are tailored to a woman's hormonal status. While research in this area is still limited and in its early stages, it empowers a woman to have a more informed discussion with her doctor about how medication can be a dynamic, rather than static, part of her treatment plan.

- **Proactive Lifestyle Strategies:** Even with a perfectly tailored medication regimen, lifestyle factors like sleep, nutrition, and exercise play a crucial role in regulating the brain's neurochemistry and building resilience against hormonal ebbs and flows. A woman may find that during the low-estrogen luteal phase, when her medication feels less effective, she needs to double down on her self-care practices. This could include prioritizing good sleep hygiene, as quality sleep is critical for attention, emotional control, and working memory. Regular physical exercise can serve as a powerful antidote to mental fatigue, helping to regulate dopamine levels, reduce restlessness, and improve mood. A diet rich in omega-3 fatty acids, antioxidants, and protein can also help support brain function and stabilize mood and energy levels, providing a buffer against the cognitive and emotional rollercoasters that accompany hormonal shifts. Finally, managing stress through mindfulness and other techniques is crucial, as high stress levels can further disrupt hormonal balance and cognitive function.

The Bridge to Your Balanced Life

The work you have done in this book is foundational. A brain that is constantly battling the unpredictable shifts of a hormonal cycle is a brain that has less mental and emotional bandwidth for all the other challenges of living with ADHD. The harmony you have cultivated here is the prerequisite for the more complex work that follows.

- **A Foundation for Emotional Mastery (Book 4):** Emotional dysregulation is a core challenge for women with ADHD, and it is profoundly impacted by hormonal fluctuations. The knowledge you have gained in this book empowers you to recognize that your intense emotional reactions are often a neurobiological reality, not a personal failing. A more stable hormonal baseline provides a woman with more emotional resilience and greater capacity to apply the CBT and DBT tools for emotional regulation that will be explored in the next book. You will be better equipped to manage the intense feelings and emotional dysregulation that are so prevalent in ADHD, and less likely to feel overwhelmed by the minor inconveniences that can trigger a disproportionate emotional storm.

- **A Catalyst for Nurturing Relationships (Book 5):** The unpredictable emotional and cognitive challenges that accompany hormonal shifts can be a significant source of friction in relationships, as a woman's partner may struggle to understand her fluctuating moods or energy levels. By understanding her unique neurobiological needs, a woman is better equipped to communicate them to her loved ones, fostering empathy and understanding. A more stable internal environment, achieved through hormonal harmony, provides a more predictable and reliable emotional base for building and sustaining meaningful relationships.

By consistently engaging in these self-care strategies, a woman can build a buffer against the hormonal ebbs and flows and create a more stable and supportive internal environment for her ADHD brain. This integrated approach ensures that her treatment plan is not a static prescription but a dynamic, lifelong process that accounts for her unique neurobiological needs. This understanding is a crucial step towards achieving genuine balance and well-being, and is the essential foundation for the rest of your journey.

Reflection questions

- The book validates the link between hormonal fluctuations and ADHD symptoms. How has understanding this connection helped you to be more compassionate with yourself during different phases of your hormonal cycle?
- What is one lifestyle strategy (e.g., exercise, nutrition, sleep) that you can implement to support your brain's neurochemistry and build resilience against hormonal shifts?

- The text discusses a “holistic approach” to treatment. What is one new piece of information you can share with your healthcare professional to advocate for a more personalized treatment plan?

BOOK FOUR

MASTER YOUR EMOTIONS:

A PRACTICAL TOOLKIT FOR THE ADHD WOMAN

INTRODUCTION

THE EMOTIONAL ROLLERCOASTER AND THE QUEST FOR REGULATION

For many women with ADHD, the journey of self-mastery is often defined by the profound challenge of emotional regulation. While a woman may be highly capable and intelligent, an intense emotional surge, a flash of anger, a wave of anxiety, or the crushing sting of a perceived criticism, can feel impossible to control, derailing her best intentions and leaving a wake of regret.

This isn't a character flaw or a sign of being overly sensitive; it is a core, significant, and often misunderstood aspect of ADHD. Research consistently shows that emotional dysregulation, or the difficulty in managing and appropriately expressing emotions, is a prominent feature of the disorder.

For women, this can manifest differently than in men, often leading to a greater tendency to internalize feelings and blame themselves for their struggles, a pattern that fuels anxiety, depression, and a shattered sense of self-worth. This book will provide a compassionate, evidence-based roadmap to help a woman navigate this inner emotional landscape.

The Neurobiological Underpinnings of Emotional Dysregulation

The emotional dysregulation experienced by women with ADHD is a genuine, neurobiological reality, not a personal failing. Research suggests that a key factor is the distinct functioning and structure of the ADHD brain, particularly in areas responsible for emotional processing and regulation. While the traditional narrative of ADHD has focused on inattention and hyperactivity, the experience of intense, unpredictable emotions is one of the most debilitating and pervasive symptoms for many women.

At the center of this challenge is a disconnect between the brain's emotional center and its "command center" for self-control. The amygdala, a small, almond-shaped region deep within the brain, is the brain's alarm system, responsible for detecting and responding to threats, and it often has an overactive response in individuals with ADHD, leading to a quick trigger for strong emotions like anger, fear, and frustration.

The frontal cortex, which is responsible for higher-level executive functions, acts as the brain's "brakes," allowing you to pause, think, and inhibit an automatic reaction before it takes over. Studies have shown a decreased activation of the frontal cortex in the ADHD brain, making it less likely to inhibit big reactions as it's supposed to. This means there is a disconnect between the emotional accelerator and the emotional brakes, leading to a profound difficulty in controlling and regulating the intensity and duration of feelings.

This struggle is further complicated by the dysregulation of key neurotransmitters, such as dopamine, which is heavily involved in the brain's motivation, reward, and mood systems. When dopamine levels are inconsistent, a woman may struggle with emotional regulation and experience mood swings that are hard to predict, leaving her feeling frenzied, frazzled, and overwhelmed. The combination of a less active frontal cortex and a dysregulated neurochemical system creates a perfect storm for emotional dysregulation, where emotions can feel "all or nothing," and even minor inconveniences can trigger an overwhelming emotional response.

The Nuances of Emotional Dysregulation in Women

While emotional dysregulation is a prominent feature of ADHD regardless of gender, its manifestation and consequences can be dramatically different for women. The pressure of societal expectations for women to be emotionally mature, nurturing, and calm creates a direct conflict with the core symptoms of ADHD, forcing many women to internalize their struggles and blame themselves for their difficulties. This internalization is often a stark contrast to men, who are more likely to externalize their frustration through anger and defensiveness.

For a woman with ADHD, this internalization can take several forms:

- **Intense Emotional Surges:** Emotions can flare up with startling speed and intensity. A minor inconvenience can lead to a disproportionate outburst, or a small disappointment can trigger a deep, overwhelming wave of sadness. This isn't simply about being moody; it's a genuine difficulty in modulating the intensity, duration, and even the type of emotional response.
- **A Low Tolerance for Frustration:** A hallmark of this dysregulation is a low tolerance for frustrating situations. The immense, amorphous nature of tasks, coupled with the internal restlessness of the ADHD brain, can lead a woman to feel so overwhelmed that she gives up on a project before she even starts, leading to a cycle of self-blame and avoidance.
- **Pervasive Feelings of Overwhelm and Fatigue:** The constant, conscious effort to manage internalized symptoms—such as a racing mind and emotional dysregulation—that neurotypical individuals do unconsciously is a significant drain on mental energy. This constant cognitive effort is the "ADHD tax" that depletes mental energy reserves and makes a woman more susceptible to burnout, leading to a chronic sense of being "frenzied, frazzled, and overwhelmed".

Rejection Sensitive Dysphoria (RSD): A Deeper Look

A particularly painful and debilitating manifestation of emotional dysregulation that is highly common in women with ADHD is Rejection Sensitive Dysphoria (RSD). While not a formal medical diagnosis, RSD is a descriptive term for an "extreme emotional responsiveness and anxiety in anticipation of, or in response to, perceived rejection or criticism from others". For a woman with ADHD, this is more than just feeling hurt; it is an immediate, overwhelming emotional pain that can feel physically agonizing, sometimes described as akin to being punched in the gut or stabbed in the heart.

This profound hypersensitivity is fueled by a lifetime of internalizing struggles and the fear that their "perceived failures" will be discovered. For many women, their resilience was chipped away by early traumatic experiences of chronic negative feedback, bullying, exclusion, and humiliation from family, peers, and teachers. This repeated threat of rejection can trigger primitive survival mechanisms, often causing a woman to "freeze up" or become unable to act. This sets the stage for a learned expectation of future social adversity and a deep-seated fear that they are, in fact, unworthy of love and acceptance.

The pain of RSD is often amplified by the fact that women with ADHD are more prone to internalizing their struggles, interpreting this painful experience as a personal failing that confirms a deeply held belief of inadequacy. A woman's emotional volatility may be seen as a "melodramatic overreaction" by others, which further invalidates her pain and reinforces her sense of being unworthy.

This painful feedback loop, where emotional dysregulation leads to RSD, and RSD feeds a deep sense of shame, creates a devastating barrier to authentic connection and self-acceptance. This shame, when left unaddressed, can lead to dangerous behaviors, including self-harm and suicidal thoughts, at a much greater rate than in their male counterparts. To cope, a woman may become a people-pleaser or a perfectionist to avoid any potential criticism, a strategy that is both exhausting and unsustainable.

The Impact on Mental Health and Relationships

The collective toll of this emotional rollercoaster is significant and often leads to a variety of co-occurring conditions and challenges that further destabilize a woman's life. Research confirms that a repeated pattern of failures and frustrations due to ADHD can contribute to or worsen other mental health conditions, such as depression and anxiety, which are highly prevalent in women with ADHD.

In fact, many women are initially diagnosed with anxiety or a mood disorder before the underlying ADHD is identified, leading to a long and frustrating journey of ineffective treatment. The sadness and shame that arise from the feelings of "never fitting in" to social groups is a major part of the lived experience of women with ADHD.

These emotional struggles also have a profound impact on relationships. For a woman with ADHD, difficulty with emotional regulation can make it hard to respond to a partner's frustrations calmly, leading to disagreements that spiral out of control. Her impulsive emotional reactions can lead to her saying things she later regrets, which can cause significant friction and misunderstanding. Furthermore, a woman with ADHD may struggle to read social cues, and her tendency to over-talk or interrupt in conversation can make it difficult for her to form and maintain friendships, leading to feelings of loneliness and isolation.

The emotional volatility, combined with the other challenges of ADHD, often leads to a sense of inadequacy and self-blame, a pattern that is significantly more prevalent in women with ADHD than in men. This book provides a much-needed roadmap for navigating this inner landscape, moving a woman from a place of emotional reactivity to one of thoughtful, intentional response.

A Compassionate, Evidence-Based Roadmap for Emotional Mastery

The journey to emotional mastery for a woman with ADHD is not about suppressing your emotions or pretending they don't exist; it is about developing a guiding hand to lead you through your inner world with greater awareness and control. The solution lies in building a robust, evidence-based toolkit that acknowledges your neurobiological reality while providing a strategic pathway toward self-regulation.

This book will provide a comprehensive roadmap to navigate this inner emotional landscape, drawing on the principles of Cognitive Behavioral Therapy (CBT) and Dialectical Behavioral Therapy (DBT), which are highly effective therapeutic approaches for managing the emotional dysregulation, anxiety, and stress that frequently co-occur with ADHD. These tools will empower a woman to develop a keen awareness of her emotional triggers, understand the intricate connection between her thoughts, feelings, and actions, and build a robust toolkit to respond to emotions more effectively and constructively.

We will begin by providing a framework for identifying and challenging the distorted thoughts that often fuel intense emotional reactions, which is a cornerstone of CBT. We will then delve into practical behavioral strategies from DBT, such as mindful movement, sensory grounding, and the "STOP" skill, which provide direct, actionable steps to either reduce the immediate intensity of an emotion or shift your physiological and psychological state to a more regulated one.

This will be followed by a discussion on how to build emotional resilience and distress tolerance, equipping you with the capacity to endure and cope with uncomfortable emotional states without resorting to impulsive, unhelpful behaviors. Finally, we will explore the critical role of compassionate self-talk in transforming your inner critic into an inner ally who supports your growth, resilience, and emotional well-being, which is an essential antidote to the shame that so many women with ADHD feel.

This compassionate, evidence-based roadmap is designed to empower a woman to transform her relationship with her emotions, moving from a place of chronic emotional turbulence to one of intentional, thoughtful response. This mastery of her inner world is the bedrock upon which all other areas of her life, from relationships to productivity, are built, and it is a crucial step towards achieving genuine balance and well-being.

CHAPTER 1

EMOTIONAL DYSREGULATION

Emotional dysregulation in women with ADHD is a nuanced and pervasive struggle. It is marked by a heightened emotional intensity and a surprising lack of an internal "buffer" or "brakes" to modulate feelings. This can lead to emotions that feel all-or-nothing, where a woman might hold back her feelings to fit in, but a small trigger can unleash an overwhelming emotional response.

Research suggests that this is due to differences in brain function, particularly in the frontal cortex, which is less likely to inhibit big reactions. This often manifests as rapidly shifting moods and a low tolerance for frustration, where minor inconveniences can trigger a disproportionate emotional storm.

A woman may go from calm to intensely frustrated or angry in moments, followed by feelings of deep sadness or shame over her reaction. Unlike their male counterparts who may be more likely to externalize their frustration through anger, women are more prone to internalizing their struggles, leading to self-blame, anxiety, depression, and low self-esteem.

The Neurobiology of the Emotional Brain

The emotional dysregulation experienced by women with ADHD is not a character flaw or a sign of being overly sensitive; it is a core, significant, and often misunderstood aspect of ADHD that is rooted in neurobiological differences. While the traditional narrative of ADHD has focused on inattention and hyperactivity, a growing body of contemporary research highlights that emotional dysregulation is a pervasive and often debilitating aspect of the disorder.

At the center of this challenge is a disconnect between the brain's emotional centers and its "command center" for self-control. The amygdala, a small, almond-shaped region deep within the brain, is the brain’s alarm system, responsible for detecting and responding to threats. In individuals with ADHD, this alarm system can be overactive, leading to a quick trigger for strong emotions like anger, fear, and frustration.

The frontal cortex, which is responsible for higher-level executive functions, acts as the brain's "brakes," allowing you to pause, think, and inhibit an automatic reaction before it takes over. Research has found that there is a decreased activation of the frontal cortex in the ADHD brain, making it less likely to inhibit these big reactions as it's supposed to. This means there is a disconnect between the emotional accelerator and the emotional brakes, leading to a profound difficulty in controlling and regulating the intensity and duration of feelings.

This struggle is further complicated by the dysregulation of key neurotransmitters, such as dopamine, which is heavily involved in the brain's motivation, reward, and mood systems. When dopamine levels are inconsistent, a woman may struggle with emotional regulation and experience mood swings that are hard to predict, leaving her feeling "frenzied, frazzled, and overwhelmed".

The combination of a less active frontal cortex and a dysregulated neurochemical system creates a perfect storm for emotional dysregulation, where emotions can feel "all or nothing," and even minor inconveniences can trigger an overwhelming emotional response.

The Nuances of Emotional Dysregulation in Women

While emotional dysregulation is a prominent feature of ADHD regardless of gender, its manifestation and consequences can be dramatically different for women. The pressure of societal expectations for women to be emotionally mature, nurturing, and calm creates a direct conflict with the core symptoms of ADHD, forcing many women to internalize their struggles and blame themselves for their difficulties.

This internalization is often in stark contrast to men, who are more likely to externalize their frustration through anger and defensiveness, leading to a diagnostic disparity where girls' and women's symptoms are often overlooked or misdiagnosed as a mood disorder.

For a woman with ADHD, internalization can take several forms:

- **Intense Emotional Surges:** Emotions can flare up with startling speed and intensity. A minor inconvenience can lead to a disproportionate outburst, or a small disappointment can trigger a deep, overwhelming wave of sadness that feels all-consuming. This is not simply about being moody; it's a genuine difficulty in modulating the intensity, duration, and even the type of emotional response.
- **Low Tolerance for Frustration:** A hallmark of this dysregulation is a low tolerance for frustrating situations. The immense, amorphous nature of tasks, coupled with the internal restlessness of the ADHD brain, can lead a woman to feel so overwhelmed that she gives up on a project before she even starts, leading to a cycle of self-blame and avoidance. The emotional distress that arises from these challenges can be so severe that it contributes to or worsens co-occurring mental health conditions like anxiety and depression.
- **Pervasive Feelings of Overwhelm and Fatigue:** The constant, conscious effort to manage internalized symptoms, such as a racing mind and emotional dysregulation, that neurotypical individuals do unconsciously is a significant drain on mental energy. This constant cognitive effort is the "ADHD tax" that

depletes mental energy reserves and makes a woman more susceptible to burnout, a state of chronic exhaustion that research shows is significantly higher in employees with ADHD due to executive function difficulties. A woman might report feeling perpetually "frenzied, frazzled, and overwhelmed".

The Pervasive Toll of Internalization and Masking

A particularly painful and debilitating manifestation of emotional dysregulation is Rejection Sensitive Dysphoria (RSD), a common experience among women with ADHD that involves an extreme emotional responsiveness to perceived rejection or criticism. For a woman with ADHD, this is more than just feeling hurt; it is an immediate, overwhelming emotional pain that can feel physically agonizing, sometimes described as akin to being punched in the gut.

This hypersensitivity is fueled by a lifetime of internalizing struggles and the fear that their "perceived failures" will be discovered and provoke rejection.

For many women, their resilience was chipped away by early traumatic experiences of chronic negative feedback, bullying, and humiliation from family, peers, and teachers. This painful experience is often interpreted as a personal failing, confirming a deeply held belief of inadequacy that can be a major part of the lived experience of women with ADHD.

This cycle of emotional dysregulation leading to RSD, and RSD feeding shame, creates a devastating barrier to authentic connection and self-acceptance. This shame, when left unaddressed, can lead to dangerous behaviors, including self-harm and suicidal thoughts, at a much greater rate than in their male counterparts.

Emotional volatility is often made worse by the practice of "masking," where women develop sophisticated compensatory behaviors to hide their struggles and appear "neurotypical" to the outside world. While this may be a survival strategy developed to avoid social rejection, it can also lead to chronic loneliness and a debilitating sense of not being able to be one's authentic self. A woman might meticulously maintain a façade of punctuality, or she might learn to pretend to take notes in a meeting to hide the fact that she is "zoning out" or has a "thousand-yard stare".

The stress of this constant, exhausting effort to appear "non-ADHD" is an invisible burden that leads to a lifetime of internalized shame, anxiety, depression, and a shattered sense of self-worth. Studies confirm that girls are more likely to mask their symptoms than boys, and this can lead to significant negative consequences on their mental health, social functioning, and academic achievement.

The Cycle of Emotional Dysregulation and Mental Health

The collective toll of this emotional rollercoaster is significant and often leads to a variety of co-occurring conditions that further destabilize a woman's life. Research confirms that a repeated pattern of failures and frustrations due to ADHD can contribute to or worsen other mental health conditions, such as depression and anxiety, which are highly prevalent in women with ADHD.

In fact, a woman may be diagnosed with anxiety, depression, or a mood disorder before the underlying ADHD is identified, leading to a long and frustrating journey of ineffective treatment. A new assessment, BRIEF2A, even divides executive function deficits into behavioral regulation, emotional regulation, and cognitive regulation, highlighting the importance of understanding this interplay in a clinical setting.

Furthermore, the intersection of ADHD and Premenstrual Dysphoric Disorder (PMDD) is highly significant, with over 40% of women with ADHD also experiencing PMDD, a more severe form of PMS. The combination of these two conditions can make emotional regulation even more challenging, leading to more pronounced mood swings, irritability, and anger.

This is because PMDD, like ADHD, is linked to changes in the brain and hormones, and the combination can create a perfect storm of emotional dysregulation that is difficult to manage without a holistic approach.

The path forward, therefore, is not to simply suppress these emotions or pretend they don't exist. It's about developing a guiding hand to lead you through your inner world with greater awareness and control. The solution lies in building a robust, evidence-based toolkit that acknowledges your neurobiological reality while providing a strategic pathway toward self-regulation.

This book will provide a compassionate, evidence-based roadmap to help a woman navigate this inner emotional landscape, drawing on the principles of Cognitive Behavioral Therapy (CBT) and Dialectical Behavioral Therapy (DBT), which are highly effective therapeutic approaches for managing the emotional dysregulation, anxiety, and stress that frequently co-occur with ADHD. These tools will empower a woman to develop a keen awareness of her emotional triggers, understand the intricate connection between her thoughts, feelings, and actions, and build a robust toolkit to respond to emotions more effectively and constructively.

The journey to emotional mastery for a woman with ADHD is not about becoming emotionless or suppressing who you are, but about developing the capacity to respond to life's inevitable challenges with greater intention, resilience, and effectiveness. This mastery of her inner world is the bedrock upon which all other areas of her life, from relationships to productivity, are built, and it is a crucial step towards achieving genuine balance and well-being.

CHAPTER 2

REJECTION SENSITIVE DYSPHORIA (RSD)

A particularly painful and debilitating manifestation of emotional dysregulation is Rejection Sensitive Dysphoria (RSD), a common experience among women with ADHD that involves an extreme emotional responsiveness to perceived rejection or criticism. For a woman with ADHD, this is more than just feeling hurt; it is an immediate, overwhelming emotional pain that can feel physically agonizing. This pain is often triggered not by actual rejection, but by a perceived snub, a tone of voice, or a hint of disapproval.

This hypersensitivity is fueled by a lifetime of internalizing struggles and the fear that their "perceived failures" will be discovered, a fear that can lead a woman to become a perfectionist or a people-pleaser to avoid any potential criticism.

Such a painful feedback loop is amplified by the fact that women are more likely to internalize their struggles. This painful experience is often interpreted as a personal failing, confirming a deeply held belief of inadequacy. A woman's emotional volatility may be seen as a "melodramatic overreaction" by others, which further invalidates her pain and reinforces her sense of being unworthy. This cycle of emotional dysregulation leading to RSD, and RSD feeding shame, creates a devastating barrier to authentic connection and self-acceptance.

The Neurobiology of Rejection Pain

While RSD is not a formal diagnosis or disorder in official medical manuals, its profound impact on a woman's quality of life is undeniable, and research is beginning to uncover the neurobiological roots of this intense experience. Experts believe that the extreme emotional pain that defines RSD, the feeling of being punched in the gut or stabbed in the heart, is a real, physiological response in the ADHD brain. This intense, overwhelming pain is what separates RSD from basic emotional dysregulation.

The underlying mechanism is thought to involve a distinct functioning of brain regions responsible for emotional processing and regulation, particularly the amygdala and the prefrontal cortex. The amygdala acts as the brain's alarm system, and in individuals with ADHD, this system can be overactive, leading to a quick trigger for strong emotions like anger, fear, and frustration. When a person with ADHD experiences a perceived rejection, the amygdala's alarm bells may ring with a disproportionate intensity, leading to an immediate and overwhelming emotional response.

At the same time, the prefrontal cortex, which is responsible for the brain's "brakes" and allows for a thoughtful, inhibited response, may be less active in the ADHD brain. This creates a disconnect between the emotional accelerator and the emotional brakes, leading to a profound difficulty in controlling and modulating the intensity of the rejection-based feelings.

This neurological difference explains why a woman may go from calm to intensely frustrated or angry in moments, followed by feelings of deep sadness or shame over her reaction, as the emotional wave hits with little warning and overwhelms her ability to self-regulate.

The Origins of Hypersensitivity: A Lifetime of Negative Feedback

The hypersensitivity of RSD is not a random occurrence; it is often a direct result of a lifetime of chronic negative feedback and a learned expectation of rejection. Research shows that girls and women with ADHD are often met with a lack of understanding from a young age, as their symptoms of disorganization, inattention, and emotional over-reactivity are inconsistent with societal expectations for girls. This can lead to a childhood filled with misunderstanding, self-blame, and rejection from family, peers, and teachers. For example, girls with ADHD may be bullied or ostracized for being overly sensitive or for missing social cues, which sets the stage for a deep-seated fear of social adversity later in life.

A constant stream of criticism and humiliation chips away at a girl's resilience, altering her brain chemistry and increasing her vulnerability to emotional pain. These early traumatic experiences, which are often unpredictable, inescapable, and repeated, can trigger primitive survival mechanisms in the brain. When faced with a threat of rejection, a woman's brain, too vulnerable for a "fight or flight" response, may instead "freeze up," leaving her unable to act.

These episodes of learned helplessness in the face of perceived rejection create a painful feedback loop that reinforces her belief that her behavior merits rejection and that she is, indeed, unworthy. A new assessment, BRIEF2A, even divides executive function deficits into emotional, behavioral, and cognitive regulation, highlighting the importance of understanding this interplay in a clinical setting.

The Social Cost: People-Pleasing and the Impostor Syndrome

This profound hypersensitivity to rejection often drives a woman with ADHD to develop sophisticated compensatory behaviors to avoid any potential criticism. She may become a perfectionist in her work, believing that a flawless performance is the only way to shield herself from judgment.

She may also become a people-pleaser, constantly trying to accommodate the needs of others while neglecting her own, as a way to curry favor and prevent others from seeing her "perceived failures".

This strategy, while it may provide temporary emotional safety, is both exhausting and unsustainable.

A constant effort to avoid rejection is often rooted in a deep-seated fear of being discovered as a fraud. For women with ADHD who have successfully "masked" their symptoms for a lifetime, a sense of impostor syndrome is a common companion. They fear that their well-guarded secret, the constant struggle with focus, disorganization, and emotional dysregulation, will be revealed, and that they will finally be rejected for who they truly are. This fear of exposure creates a constant, low-grade anxiety that makes it incredibly difficult to form authentic connections and truly feel accepted.

This painful feedback loop is amplified by the fact that women are more likely to internalize their struggles, a pattern that is often a stark contrast to men, who are more likely to externalize their responses with defensiveness, anger, and projecting blame on others. An internalized experience is often misinterpreted by others, as a woman's emotional volatility may be seen as a "melodramatic overreaction," which further invalidates her pain and reinforces her sense of being unworthy.

A woman's emotional volatility may be seen as a "melodramatic overreaction" by others, which further invalidates her pain and reinforces her sense of being unworthy. This cycle of emotional dysregulation leading to RSD, and RSD feeding shame, creates a devastating barrier to authentic connection and self-acceptance.

The Impact on Relationships and Mental Health

The consequences of unmanaged RSD can be severe and far-reaching, profoundly impacting a woman's mental health and relationships. In romantic relationships, RSD can make it incredibly difficult to navigate conflict and criticism. Even if a partner calmly expresses a concern, the "lens of ADHD" can color their statements as being overtly critical or micromanaging, which triggers an intense emotional reaction and can lead to a spiral of hurt and defensiveness.

It can create a dysfunctional "parent-child" dynamic, where the ADHD partner feels scolded and the neurotypical partner feels frustrated and unheard, leading to a breakdown in communication and a loss of intimacy.

The painful experience of RSD is also strongly linked to mental health struggles. Research shows a significant connection between RSD and feelings of depression, anxiety, and a shattered sense of self-worth. For women with ADHD, who already experience higher rates of anxiety and depression than the general population, the added burden of RSD can be debilitating. Studies reveal that the cumulative effect of a lifetime of negative feedback and a feeling of unworthiness can lead to a significant decline in a woman's mental health, and RSD can be a key factor in driving a woman to self-harm and even suicidal ideation at a much greater rate than her male counterparts. The despair that comes from a belief in their own unworthiness and the constant feeling that they "can do nothing right" can lead to dangerous behaviors, including substance abuse and self-harm.

The link between emotional dysregulation and ADHD is so central that a significant number of women are initially diagnosed with anxiety, depression, or a mood disorder before the underlying ADHD is identified, leading to a long and frustrating journey of ineffective treatment.

This is further complicated by the fact that the intense mood swings, irritability, and anger associated with RSD can overlap with symptoms of Premenstrual Dysphoric Disorder (PMDD), which is disproportionately common in women with ADHD, creating a perfect storm of emotional dysregulation that is difficult to manage without a holistic approach.

The profound impact of RSD is a call for a new approach, one that moves beyond simply validating the pain to providing a concrete roadmap for managing it. This is not about becoming less sensitive or trying to suppress who you are, but about developing a guiding hand to lead you through your inner world with greater awareness and control. The goal is to build a robust, evidence-based toolkit that acknowledges your neurobiological reality while providing a strategic pathway toward self-regulation.

By understanding the origins of your emotional pain, recognizing your triggers, and learning to create a crucial pause between stimulus and response, you can begin to transform your relationship with rejection from a source of profound emotional agony to a manageable, though still difficult, part of your life. This chapter sets the stage for the practical, CBT-based strategies that will empower you to break free from the cycle of shame, people-pleasing, and avoidance that RSD creates, and to build a life of genuine self-acceptance and authentic connection.

CHAPTER 3:

CBT TOOLS: IDENTIFYING AND CHALLENGING UNHELPFUL THOUGHTS

To gain mastery over emotional dysregulation, an essential task is understanding the connection between thoughts, feelings, and behaviors. Cognitive Behavioral Therapy (CBT) is a powerful, evidence-based approach that helps a person identify and challenge unhelpful or irrational thought patterns, which are often at the root of intense emotional reactions.

A crucial first step is recognizing common cognitive distortions that women with ADHD are prone to, such as "catastrophizing", blowing a small mistake into a major disaster, or "mind reading," which involves assuming a negative judgment from others without any evidence.

By learning to pause and question these automatic thoughts, a woman can break the cycle of emotional reactivity. She can ask herself:

"Is that thought 100% true? What is the evidence for it? What is a more balanced way to look at this?" Applied consistently, this process helps a woman reframe her inner narrative from one of self-blame to one of understanding and compassion.

The Foundational Principle of CBT: Thoughts Are Not Facts

The fundamental premise of Cognitive Behavioral Therapy (CBT) is elegantly simple yet profoundly impactful: your thoughts are not facts. Thoughts are interpretations of reality, often automatic and unexamined, and these interpretations directly and powerfully influence how you feel and how you act.

For a woman with ADHD, who may experience rapid shifts in mood and intense emotional responses, these quick, often automatic, and unhelpful thought patterns are particularly impactful, amplifying her emotional rollercoaster. Decades of rigorous research have demonstrated CBT's efficacy in helping individuals identify, evaluate, and ultimately change unhelpful thinking patterns, leading to significant and lasting improvements in mood, anxiety, and stress levels.

Consider a common scenario: receiving an email with critical feedback from a boss. The event itself is neutral; your interpretation of the event dictates your subsequent emotional and behavioral response. A distorted thought pattern, for instance, might be, "I'm a complete failure. I can never do anything right. This proves I'm incompetent, and they're definitely going to fire me for this small mistake".

Such a thought would likely lead to intense shame, crippling anxiety, and despair, causing a woman to procrastinate further on the task, avoid interacting with the boss, and ruminate endlessly on the negative thought, leading to reduced productivity and increased stress.

A balanced, helpful thought, on the other hand, would be, "This feedback is tough to hear. It points out an area where I can improve. What specifically can I learn from this? How can I implement this feedback and improve next time? Everyone makes mistakes." Such a thought would likely lead to feelings of concern and determination, but without the crushing weight of shame. The same external event can lead to vastly different emotional and behavioral outcomes based solely on your initial, often automatic, thought.

The ADHD Brain and its Susceptibility to Distorted Thoughts

Neurobiologically, a woman with ADHD is often more susceptible to these pervasive "thinking traps" or cognitive distortions. The emotional dysregulation so common in women with ADHD is rooted in the distinct functioning and structure of the ADHD brain, particularly in areas responsible for emotional processing and regulation.

The amygdala, the brain's alarm system, is often overactive, leading to a quick trigger for strong emotions like anger, fear, and frustration. Conversely, the frontal cortex, which is responsible for higher-level executive functions and acts as the brain's "brakes," is less likely to inhibit these big reactions, making it difficult to regulate the intensity and duration of feelings.

In this neurobiological context, thoughts can become powerful catalysts for emotional turmoil. A fleeting negative thought, unexamined and unchallenged, can quickly be amplified by an overactive amygdala and an underactive frontal cortex, leading to a full-blown emotional storm.

Furthermore, the challenges of ADHD, such as difficulties with planning, working memory, and consistent follow-through, can create a lifetime of frustrating experiences that reinforce negative self-talk. A woman may be prone to a harsh inner critic, which, as research shows, is a major contributor to shame and feelings of inadequacy in women with ADHD.

Unmasking Common Cognitive Distortions

Cognitive distortions are irrational or exaggerated thought patterns that reinforce negative thinking, undermine self-esteem, and exacerbate emotional distress. They are like mental shortcuts that, while sometimes quick, often lead you down a wrong path. Recognizing them is the first crucial step toward challenging them and reclaiming control over your emotional responses.

- **All-or-Nothing Thinking (Black-and-White Thinking):** Seeing things in extremes, with no middle ground. Everything is either perfect or a total disaster, a complete success or an utter failure. For instance, a woman might think, "I missed that deadline, so I'm a total failure and completely incompetent at my job," discounting all past successes and efforts. A woman might also think, "If I can't do it perfectly, there's no point in starting it at all," which fuels procrastination and perfectionism. This distortion often stems from the ADHD brain's tendency to struggle with nuance and moderation.

- **Catastrophizing:** Exaggerating the negative consequences of an event, jumping to the worst possible conclusion, even when it's highly unlikely. For example, a woman might think, "If I forget to pay this bill today, my credit will be ruined, I'll go bankrupt, and I'll lose everything I own." This distortion is heavily linked to Rejection Sensitive Dysphoria (RSD), where a perceived disapproval from a partner can escalate to thoughts of an impending catastrophe and a relationship ending, turning a minor oversight into an apocalyptic scenario.
- **Mind Reading:** Assuming you know what others are thinking or feeling, usually negatively, without any actual evidence. An example would be, "My boss didn't say hello to me this morning and walked past without a smile, so she must think I'm doing a terrible job and is disappointed in my performance." This distortion is extremely common and painful for women with RSD, as their hypersensitivity to perceived rejection makes them prone to jumping to negative conclusions about others' intentions and feelings towards them.
- **"Should" Statements:** Holding rigid, often unrealistic, expectations for yourself or others, often expressed with words like "should," "must," or "ought." When these expectations are not met, they lead to intense guilt, shame, and frustration. A woman might think, "I should be able to focus for hours without any distractions, just like everyone else," which ignores the neurobiological reality of ADHD. These "shoulds" are often internalized from societal expectations that do not account for neurodiversity and female symptom presentation, leaving women with ADHD particularly vulnerable to feelings of shame and inadequacy.

- **Emotional Reasoning:** Believing something is true solely because you feel it strongly, treating your feelings as definitive evidence of reality. For instance, a woman might think, "I feel like a lazy, unproductive person today, so I must be lazy and incapable," which discounts all her efforts and past accomplishments. The intensity of ADHD emotions can make this distortion particularly compelling and difficult to challenge.
- **Overgeneralization:** Drawing a sweeping negative conclusion based on a single event or piece of evidence, assuming that if something happened once, it will always happen, or that it applies to all situations. An example would be, "I messed up that presentation last week, so I'm terrible at public speaking and will never succeed in any leadership role." This distortion can exacerbate feelings of inadequacy.
- **Personalization:** Blaming yourself for external events or taking things personally that are not actually your fault, or over-attributing events to your own actions. An example would be, "Our team project failed because I didn't push hard enough on my part," even when multiple factors were involved. This distortion can tie into RSD, where any negative outcome is quickly internalized as a personal failing.
- **Disqualifying the Positive:** Ignoring, discounting, or dismissing positive experiences, compliments, or achievements, often by saying they "don't count" or were due to luck. For example, a woman might think, "I finished that tough project ahead of schedule, but anyone could have done it; it was just easy." This distortion sabotages efforts to build self-worth and recognize progress, a key motivator for the ADHD brain.

The Practice: Becoming a Thought Detective

The key to breaking free from the grip of distorted thoughts is to become a detective of your own mind. This is an active process of observation, questioning, and re-framing. When you notice a strong negative emotion, pause and investigate the thoughts that immediately preceded it.

Step 1: Catch the Thought (The "Pause and Observe") When you feel a sudden surge of a strong negative emotion, whether it's anger, shame, intense anxiety, crushing frustration, or deep sadness, use that emotion as a trigger. Ask yourself: "What thought just went through my mind right before I felt this way?" or "What am I telling myself right now about this situation or about myself?" Write the thought down immediately, even if it feels silly or fragmented. The act of externalizing the thought helps you gain some crucial distance from it, allowing you to view it as an object of analysis rather than an undeniable truth. This is the first, most vital step in breaking the automatic emotional reaction.

Step 2: Challenge the Thought (The "Courtroom Test") Once you have identified the thought, put it on trial. Imagine you are a neutral judge or a rigorous lawyer, meticulously examining the evidence for and against the thought.

- **Ask for the evidence:** What is the concrete, factual evidence that this thought is true? What is the evidence against it? Be specific and factual, not just general feelings or past assumptions.
- **Look for alternatives:** Are there other, more balanced ways to interpret the situation? What might a neutral observer see?
- **Name the distortion:** Am I falling into one of the thinking traps or cognitive distortions I just learned about? Naming the distortion helps you to depersonalize it.
- **Practice perspective-taking:** What would I tell a friend in this exact situation if they came to me with this thought? We are often far kinder and more rational with others than we are with ourselves.
- **Assess its helpfulness:** Is this thought helpful? Does it move me towards my goals or away from them? Does it help me feel better or worse? A thought can be partially true but still unhelpful and unproductive.

Step 3: Reframe and Replace (The "Constructive Alternative") Based on your rigorous questioning, formulate a more balanced, realistic, and ultimately more helpful thought. This is not about forced positive affirmations that feel untrue or saccharine; it is about finding a more accurate, nuanced, and empowering perspective that reflects reality more fully.

- **Original Distorted Thought (All-or-Nothing):** "I didn't finish everything on my to-do list today, so today was a complete waste and I'm a failure."
- **Reframed Thought:** "I didn't finish everything, but I did complete, and that's solid progress. It wasn't a perfect day, but it wasn't a total waste. I'll re-prioritize for tomorrow and continue my momentum."
- **Original Distorted Thought (Catastrophizing/RSD):** "My partner looked annoyed when I brought up the chore list; he must be mad at me, and our relationship is in trouble; he'll probably leave me."
- **Reframed Thought:** "My partner looked annoyed. I'm going to take a breath and assume he might be tired or thinking about something else, or I can gently ask him later if everything is okay without immediately assuming it's about me or a catastrophe."

The practice of identifying and challenging distorted thoughts takes consistent, compassionate effort. These unhelpful patterns are often deeply ingrained automatic shortcuts developed over a lifetime. With persistent practice, you will find yourself catching these thoughts earlier, questioning them more effectively, and ultimately choosing more balanced, realistic, and empowering interpretations of your experiences.

The direct intervention on your thought patterns is a cornerstone of emotional regulation, giving you profound control over your inner landscape and transforming it from a turbulent, reactive space to one of greater clarity and intentional response.

This is a crucial first step in your emotional mastery journey. When you learn to change your thoughts, you can begin to change your feelings, and ultimately, your actions. This internal work is the bedrock that will support the behavioral strategies for emotional regulation that you will explore in the following chapters, allowing you to not only navigate your emotional storms but also to build the resilience to weather them with greater strength and self-compassion.

CHAPTER 4:

BEHAVIORAL STRATEGIES FOR EMOTIONAL REGULATION

While challenging thoughts is crucial, it's only one part of the solution. When emotions run high, a woman's brain needs immediate, actionable steps to regain control. Dialectical Behavioral Therapy (DBT), a highly effective offshoot of CBT, provides a toolkit of such skills. DBT's four core skills are particularly well-suited for the challenges of ADHD in women: mindfulness, distress tolerance, emotion regulation, and interpersonal effectiveness.

Mindfulness helps a woman learn to observe her thoughts and emotions without judgment, grounding her in the present and reducing internal overwhelm. Distress tolerance is a "crisis survival" skill that teaches a woman how to cope with intense, painful emotions without resorting to unhelpful behaviors, a pattern sometimes observed in those with ADHD.

Emotion regulation teaches a woman how to manage and change intense, unwanted emotions. It involves understanding triggers and using proactive strategies to prevent emotional outbursts. Interpersonal effectiveness provides a woman with the tools to navigate relationships and communicate her needs effectively, reducing the emotional friction that can arise from misunderstandings and poor communication.

By learning and practicing these skills, a woman can gain greater control over her emotional reactions, transforming her emotional experience from an overwhelming rollercoaster into a more manageable journey.

The Role of Action in Emotional Mastery

A woman's brain needs immediate, actionable steps to regain control when emotions run high. While the cognitive work of identifying and challenging distorted thoughts is foundational, it's often not enough in the moment of an intense emotional surge. For the ADHD brain, which can have less effective inhibitory control from the prefrontal cortex, a profound emotional wave can sweep a woman away before her logical brain can fully engage. This is where behavioral strategies become a vital first line of defense.

The physical act of doing something, a movement, a sensory input, a grounding exercise, can create a crucial pause, a circuit-breaker that interrupts the emotional spiral and allows the nervous system to calm down.

DBT, which combines elements of cognitive behavioral therapy with mindfulness techniques, offers a comprehensive toolkit of these skills, empowering women to manage their impulsivity and emotional volatility. Rather than passively waiting for the overwhelming emotion to pass, these strategies encourage you to actively engage in behaviors that can calm your nervous system, strategically change your focus, or provide a healthy, constructive outlet for intense feelings, preventing them from spiraling out of control.

The skills are most effective when practiced regularly and integrated into your daily routine, as they become more readily available and effective when emotions become overwhelming.

The Foundational Skill: Mindfulness for Emotional Grounding

Mindfulness is a cornerstone of DBT and is often the first skill taught because it is a prerequisite for all the others. A practice of mindfulness helps you learn how to pay attention to the present moment without judgment, which is a powerful tool for a brain that is prone to racing thoughts, internal restlessness, and intense emotional surges.

A woman can use this tool to become more aware of her thoughts and emotions, which can decrease distress and improve her ability to respond effectively to difficult situations. The ability to simply observe a racing mind or an intense emotion without judgment is the first step toward managing it effectively. A moment of observation creates a crucial pause between stimulus and response, a space where a woman can recognize the emotion and choose a deliberate action rather than reacting impulsively.

This practice is a form of cognitive training that strengthens your brain's capacity for sustained attention and self-regulation over time, making you less likely to be derailed by a sudden emotional shift.

Riding the Wave: Distress Tolerance Skills

Distress tolerance skills are your "crisis survival" tools, designed for moments when emotions are so intense that you can't rationally process or change them. The goal is not to eliminate the distress but to endure it without resorting to impulsive, unhelpful, or harmful behaviors. For the ADHD brain, which often seeks immediate gratification or relief from discomfort, learning to "sit with" strong emotions is a powerful act of self-mastery.

- **The TIPP Skills:** TIPP is a powerful acronym that provides rapid physiological interventions to calm an activated nervous system. TIPP stands for:
    - **Temperature:** Splashing cold water on your face, or holding an ice pack on your wrists or neck, can activate the mammalian dive reflex, which naturally slows your heart rate and calms your nervous system.
    - **Intense Exercise:** Engaging in brief, intense physical activity, such as sprinting in place or a quick walk around the block, can help burn off excess emotional energy. A

burst of physical movement is a direct and healthy way to discharge pent-up emotional energy that might otherwise lead to an emotional outburst.

  - **Paced Breathing:** Slowing your breathing down to a slower, more deliberate pace can directly impact your nervous system, shifting it from a "fight or flight" stress response to a more relaxed state. A simple exercise is to inhale slowly for four counts and exhale slowly for six counts, which can calm your body and mind.
  - **Paired Muscle Relaxation:** By tensing a muscle group very tightly for a few seconds and then completely relaxing it, you can create a tangible sense of relaxation that is felt throughout your body.

- **Radical Acceptance:** Some situations and intense emotions simply are. Fighting reality or trying to force a different emotional response only increases suffering. Radical acceptance is acknowledging the reality of a situation or an emotion without judgment, even if you don't like it or wish it were different. It's letting go of the struggle against what is. When faced with an unchangeable situation or an intense, unwanted emotion, you can internally (or even aloud) say, "I accept that I feel angry right now," or "This is a painful moment." The act of radical acceptance is not approval of the situation or emotion, but a release of the mental and emotional fight against reality, which can paradoxically reduce distress and free up energy for more constructive actions.
- **Wise Distraction:** Sometimes, when emotions are too intense to process rationally, a temporary, healthy distraction can be incredibly helpful to prevent escalation and give your nervous system time to cool down. A quick, absorbing task, like a puzzle or a short video game, can provide a healthy outlet that pulls your attention away from the intense emotion for a few minutes, allowing the intensity to subside to a more manageable level.

Managing the Ebb and Flow: Emotion Regulation Skills

Emotion regulation skills are about proactively managing emotions before they become overwhelming and reducing their intensity once they arise. This set of skills moves beyond simply tolerating distress to actively shaping your emotional experience.

- **Understanding Triggers:** A crucial step in emotion regulation is to become an expert on your own triggers. A woman can track her symptoms and their emotional impacts to understand the patterns that lead to intense feelings. For example, a woman with ADHD who also has PMDD might notice that her emotions become more difficult to manage in the days leading up to her period, which is a powerful trigger for emotional dysregulation. Identifying these patterns allows you to either avoid the trigger or proactively prepare for it with a plan of action.
- **Opposite Action:** A core DBT skill, opposite action is about identifying the unhelpful emotional urge and then doing the opposite of what that urge tells you to do. For example, if you are experiencing deep sadness and the urge is to withdraw from friends, the opposite action would be to reach out to a supportive friend. If you feel intense anxiety and the urge is to avoid a social situation, the opposite action would be to go to the event. Doing the opposite of an unhelpful emotional urge can directly change your emotional trajectory and prevent a negative spiral.
- **Building Positive Emotions:** Proactively building positive experiences into your life can make you more resilient to negative emotional swings. A woman can schedule activities that bring her joy, competence, or a sense of accomplishment. Research shows that engaging in creative activities such as painting, drawing, or writing can provide a positive outlet for expression and help channel overwhelming thoughts or emotions. Regular physical exercise also helps regulate mood and can serve as a powerful antidote to mental fatigue, helping you stay grounded. These small, consistent wins create a

buffer of positive emotion that can help a woman weather the inevitable emotional storms with greater strength and stability.

Navigating Connections: Interpersonal Effectiveness Skills

Interpersonal effectiveness skills are a vital set of tools that help women with ADHD get their needs met, set boundaries, and maintain self-respect in relationships. A woman with ADHD often struggles with communication due to her tendency to interrupt, over-talk, or miss social cues, all of which can strain her relationships. These skills provide a structured way to navigate these challenges with greater clarity and effectiveness.

- **DEAR MAN:** The DEAR MAN acronym is a structured approach to assertive communication that is highly effective for women with ADHD who may struggle with being a people-pleaser to avoid rejection. The acronym stands for:
    - **Describe:** Describe the situation objectively, using facts, without judgment.
    - **Express:** Express your feelings using "I" statements.
    - **Assert:** Assert your needs or wishes clearly and respectfully.
    - **Reinforce:** Reinforce why they should help you by explaining the positive outcome.
    - **Mindful:** Stay mindful of your goals in the conversation.
    - **Appear Confident:** Appear confident and self-respecting.
    - **Negotiate:** Be willing to negotiate and offer a compromise.
- **"I" Statements:** Using "I" statements, which focus on your own feelings rather than the other person's actions, can de-escalate conflict and prevent the unhealthy "parent-child" dynamic that can develop in neurodiverse relationships. For example, instead of saying, "You never listen to me," a woman can say, "I feel unheard when I'm speaking and you're looking at your phone." By adopting these intentional communication strategies, a woman can build a stronger, more empathetic connection with her loved ones.

A Holistic and Integrated Approach

By learning and practicing these behavioral skills, a woman can gain greater control over her emotional reactions, transforming her emotional experience from an overwhelming rollercoaster into a more manageable journey. The power of DBT lies in its integrated approach. It acknowledges that a woman's emotional world is a complex interplay of thoughts, feelings, and actions.

Learning how to identify and challenge unhelpful thoughts provides the cognitive map, while mastering these behavioral skills gives you the practical tools to navigate your inner landscape when the terrain becomes turbulent.

The journey to emotional mastery is not a destination but a continuous practice of learning and adaptation. There will be days when the strategies feel effortless and days when emotional surges feel overwhelming. The true strength lies not in achieving perfection, but in a woman's ability to consistently return to her toolkit, re-engage with her strategies, and approach each challenge with self-compassion. This is how you reclaim control over your emotional responses and build a foundation of genuine self-worth, emotional resilience, and ultimately, a more fulfilling life.

CHAPTER 5

BUILDING EMOTIONAL RESILIENCE AND SELF-COMPASSION

Emotional resilience is a long-term goal that is built through a consistent practice of self-compassion. For women with ADHD who have internalized their struggles, a harsh inner critic is often a constant companion. That voice is a source of shame and a barrier to growth, often telling a woman that she is "not good enough" or that she will "fail anyway".

The antidote to this voice is to actively cultivate a supportive inner dialogue. A woman must consciously reframe her self-talk, replacing harsh judgments with understanding and encouragement. For instance, instead of saying, "I'm so useless for forgetting that," she can rephrase it as, "It's okay to forget things; my brain works differently. What can I do to help myself remember next time?"

Practicing compassionate self-talk is not about ignoring her challenges; it is about building a powerful inner ally who champions her efforts. By treating herself with the same kindness and empathy she would offer a close friend, a woman can begin to heal from a lifetime of self-blame and build a foundation of genuine self-worth. Inner kindness is a crucial catalyst for resilience, allowing her to learn from mistakes without being crippled by them and to navigate life's challenges with greater strength and self-acceptance.

The Science of Self-Criticism and Its Consequences

For many women with ADHD, the harsh inner critic is not a recent development but a voice that has been shaped by a lifetime of experiences. Undiagnosed ADHD can have profound impacts on self-esteem and feelings of self-worth. When referencing her childhood, one woman reported, "what I felt was I was actually a bad person... I was not an adequate human being."

The constant feeling that her struggles are personal flaws can lead to a pervasive sense of shame and self-blame, a pattern that research shows is significantly more common in women with ADHD than in men.

Neuroscience provides a clear explanation for why this internal dynamic is so damaging. Self-criticism and self-judgment trigger the brain's "threat-defense system." This automatic response releases stress hormones like cortisol and adrenaline, putting the body in a state of chronic stress and physiological arousal. Over time, this state of constant alert can lead to feelings of intense anxiety, fatigue, and even physical symptoms.

A continuous loop of self-blame and shame can deplete the emotional resources needed for resilience and self-regulation, making a woman more susceptible to burnout and emotional overwhelm. The pursuit of perfectionism is often a direct result of that intense self-criticism, as a woman tries to perform flawlessly to avoid any potential criticism from others or her inner voice.

The Three Pillars of Self-Compassion

Self-compassion, as defined by leading researcher Dr. Kristin Neff, is being warm and understanding toward yourself when you suffer, fail, or feel inadequate, rather than ignoring your pain or falling into self-criticism. It is not a sign of weakness or self-indulgence but a powerful physiological process that can fundamentally change the brain's structure and function. The practice is comprised of three core pillars that directly counteract the pain of the ADHD experience:

1. **Self-Kindness vs. Self-Judgment:** A woman with ADHD may habitually judge herself harshly for her symptoms, such as being late, forgetting an appointment, or struggling with a project. Self-kindness involves treating yourself gently instead of being critical and punitive. It means showing yourself patience and understanding, even when you stumble. Rather than falling into a spiral of self-criticism, a woman can respond to her own suffering with care and acceptance. This practice of self-kindness helps deactivate the brain's threat system and activates its care system, releasing feel-good hormones like oxytocin and endorphins.
2. **Common Humanity vs. Isolation:** When a woman with ADHD struggles with her symptoms, a common feeling is that she is alone in her suffering and that something is uniquely "wrong" with her. The struggle with organization, focus, and emotional regulation can feel like a private battle, leading to a deep sense of isolation. The principle of common humanity counters this by recognizing that all people experience difficulties and imperfections. A woman's struggles are part of the shared human experience. She is not alone in feeling this way. Recognizing that you are not unique in your difficulties helps to dismantle the shame and isolation that feeds the inner critic, fostering a sense of connection and belonging.
3. **Mindfulness vs. Over-identification:** The ADHD brain can struggle to find a middle ground between being completely disengaged from emotions and being entirely consumed by them. Over-identifying with an emotion means being so entangled in it that it feels all-consuming and unchangeable. Mindfulness is the practice of having a non-judgmental awareness of your thoughts and emotions. It means observing negative emotions as they arise without judgment or falling into a spiral of rumination. A woman can notice an emotion, such as shame, without believing that she is her shame. This mindful stance creates a crucial distance from the emotional storm, allowing you to observe it rather than be swept away by it, and to choose a more thoughtful response.

The Neurobiological Antidote: Self-Compassion in Action

The biological foundations of self-compassion prove it is more than just a psychological construct. It represents a powerful physiological process that can fundamentally change the brain's structure and function, which results in improved emotional regulation and greater psychological well-being. The physiological effects go beyond the brain to impact the nervous system. Research shows that practicing self-compassion activates the parasympathetic nervous system, also known as the "rest and digest" response.

This activation leads to increased heart rate variability, which indicates better emotional regulation and stress resilience. By deactivating the brain's threat response, self-compassion enables the care system to release oxytocin and endorphins, which create feelings of safety and security.

Imaging studies reveal generating self-compassion uses similar neural processes as showing compassion for others, suggesting that being kind to ourselves activates the same caregiving circuits that help us support and nurture others. For women with ADHD who have often spent their lives trying to care for and please others to avoid criticism, turning that same well-practiced kindness inward is a powerful, restorative act.

Practical Tools for Cultivating an Inner Ally

The journey of building self-compassion is a continuous practice, not a quick fix. You can integrate these strategies into your daily life to slowly but surely reframe your inner dialogue and build a stronger foundation of resilience.

1. Compassionate Rephrasing: Actively challenge your inner critic by rephrasing harsh, judgmental thoughts into compassionate and realistic ones.

- **Harsh thought:** "I'm so lazy, I can't believe I procrastinated on that project again."
- **Self-compassionate rephrasing:** "That project was hard for my brain to get started on. Procrastination is a common ADHD struggle. What made this task particularly hard? What small step can I take now, or what strategy can I try next time?"

- **Harsh thought:** "I totally screwed up that conversation. I must have said something wrong, and now they hate me."
- **Self-compassionate rephrasing:** "I felt awkward in that conversation. It's okay to feel disappointed. My brain sometimes struggles with social cues, and that's not a personal failing. What's one thing I can learn for the next time, or can I ask them if I misinterpreted something?"

2. Supportive Touch: Your body can be a powerful tool for self-soothing and deactivating the threat response. When you feel overwhelmed or are being hard on yourself, use a comforting physical gesture.

- Place a hand on your heart and feel the warmth of your skin. Feel the rise and fall of your chest with each breath.
- Gently cup your own face in your hands, or give yourself a warm hug. The physical act of holding yourself with kindness provides a direct, physiological signal of safety to your nervous system.
- A woman can even imagine that they are the hands of someone who cares deeply for her.

3. The Compassionate Anchor: A woman with ADHD can use a simple, repetitive phrase to ground her in self-compassion when her inner critic becomes loud or she feels overwhelmed by a negative emotion. She can close her eyes, place her hands on her heart, and breathe deeply while repeating a compassionate mantra.

- "I'm here for you."
- "It's okay to make mistakes. My best is enough."
- "I'm doing my best and that's enough."
- "May I find peace, or happiness, or relief from my stress and suffering."

This is not a quick fix but a continuous practice that slowly rewires your brain's default emotional responses. It builds a powerful internal resource for emotional resilience, allowing you to navigate the ups and downs of life with greater inner stability and self-acceptance. By transforming your inner dialogue, you transform your entire emotional landscape, becoming your own most reliable guiding hand.

Conclusion: Your Emotional Strength

A powerful roadmap for navigating the inner emotional landscape of ADHD has been provided in this book. Your emotional intensity and reactivity have been validated as a neurobiological reality and you have been equipped with the tools to manage it. By learning to identify and challenge unhelpful thought patterns, implementing practical behavioral strategies from DBT, and cultivating a foundation of self-compassion, a woman can transform her relationship with her emotions.

She is no longer a passive victim of her feelings but an empowered guide who can navigate her inner world with intention and control. Emotional strength is the bedrock upon which all other areas of her life, from relationships to productivity, are built.

The Liberation of a Validated Experience

The journey through this book has been a process of profound self-discovery. For so long, the emotional struggles of a woman with ADHD may have felt like a chaotic internal battle, a torrent of feelings that were impossible to contain and often led to a deep sense of shame and inadequacy.

A prevailing narrative, often shaped by societal expectations and a lack of understanding, taught a woman that her emotional difficulties were a personal failing, a sign of being "overly sensitive" or "dramatic" rather than a legitimate aspect of her neurobiology. Research has consistently shown that women with ADHD tend to internalize their struggles and blame themselves, a pattern that fuels anxiety, depression, and a shattered sense of self-worth that is significantly more prevalent in women than in their male counterparts.

A crucial, liberating shift in perspective has been provided by this book, which illuminates the neurobiological realities behind these struggles. You now understand that your emotional intensity is a direct result of distinct brain function, particularly in a disconnect between the brain's emotional alarm system, the amygdala, and its "brakes" in the frontal cortex. You have learned that your emotions can feel "all-or-nothing" not because of a character flaw, but because your brain is less likely to inhibit big reactions.

This understanding is the bedrock of compassionate self-management. It allows a woman to move past a lifetime of self-recrimination and begin to approach her emotional challenges with curiosity and a strategic, problem-solving mindset, rather than with shame and frustration. Recognizing that your emotional reactivity is a neurobiological reality, not a personal failing, is the first and most powerful step toward reclaiming control over your inner world.

The Integrated System of Emotional Mastery

Learning how to master your emotional landscape is not about a single technique or a one-time fix. It is about building a cohesive, integrated system that works together to support your emotional well-being. The core of this system is built on a three-tiered approach that addresses your inner world from different angles: the cognitive, the behavioral, and the physiological.

1. The Cognitive Foundation: Challenging Unhelpful Thoughts You have learned that your thoughts are not facts; they are interpretations of reality that directly influence how you feel and act. The ADHD brain is particularly susceptible to "thinking traps" or cognitive distortions, such as "catastrophizing", jumping to the worst possible conclusion, or "mind reading," which involves assuming a negative judgment from others without evidence. That kind of negative self-talk often fuels intense emotional reactions, especially the debilitating pain of Rejection Sensitive Dysphoria (RSD).

By learning to pause and question these automatic thoughts, a woman can break the cycle of emotional reactivity. She has learned to become a "thought detective," meticulously examining the evidence for and against her thoughts and reframing her inner narrative from one of self-blame to one of understanding and compassion. This cognitive work creates a crucial pause, allowing the logical brain to engage before an emotional reaction takes over.

2. The Behavioral Toolkit: Active Regulation in the Moment When an emotional surge hits, a woman's brain needs immediate, actionable steps to regain control. The DBT toolkit you have explored provides concrete strategies to either calm your nervous system or strategically change your emotional state in the moment. You now have a repertoire of skills to use when emotions run high, such as the TIPP skills (Temperature, Intense Exercise, Paced Breathing, Paired Muscle Relaxation) that provide rapid physiological interventions to calm an activated nervous system. You have also learned about "Radical Acceptance," the powerful skill of letting go of the struggle against a painful reality, and "Opposite Action," which involves doing the opposite of what an unhelpful emotional urge tells you to do. These behavioral strategies are your first line of defense, empowering you to actively intervene in an emotional spiral rather than being a passive victim of your feelings.

3. The Physiological and Psychological Anchor: Self-Compassion and Resilience The work of emotional mastery is only sustainable when it is rooted in self-compassion. For women with ADHD, who have often internalized their struggles, a harsh inner critic is a constant companion. That voice is a source of shame and a barrier to growth, often telling a woman that she is "not good enough" or that she will "fail anyway". The antidote to this voice is to actively cultivate a supportive inner dialogue. You have learned that self-compassion, as defined by Dr. Kristin Neff, is a practice that activates the brain's "care system," releasing feel-good hormones like oxytocin and endorphins, and deactivating the threat-defense system that is triggered by self-criticism and shame. The consistent practice of self-kindness, recognizing your common humanity, and mindfulness provides a physiological and psychological buffer against emotional distress, allowing a woman to build a foundation of genuine self-worth. This inner kindness is a crucial catalyst for resilience, allowing you to learn from mistakes without being crippled by them and to navigate life's challenges with greater strength and self-acceptance.

The Bedrock for a Balanced Life

Emotional strength is not a skill that operates in isolation. It is the bedrock upon which all other areas of a woman's life are built. Without emotional mastery, even the most robust organizational systems or the most diligent time management strategies can crumble under the weight of an overwhelming emotional surge or a period of intense mental fatigue.

- **A Bridge to Sharpened Focus (Book 2):** Emotional chaos fragments attention. A brain that is constantly in a state of emotional turmoil is a brain that has less mental bandwidth for sustained focus and deep work. The constant, conscious effort to manage internalized emotional symptoms depletes mental energy reserves, creating what is known as the "ADHD tax" that leaves a woman mentally exhausted and more susceptible to burnout. Emotional mastery provides a sense of calm and clarity that allows the internal chaos to subside, freeing up immense cognitive bandwidth that can be redirected toward purposeful focus.
- **A Catalyst for Nurturing Relationships (Book 5):** Emotional intensity and reactivity, especially RSD, are major sources of friction in relationships. By learning to identify and challenge unhelpful thought patterns and practicing the "STOP" skill before reacting, a woman is better equipped to navigate conflict with greater intentionality. She can use "I" statements to communicate her needs effectively without blaming her partner, which can de-escalate conflict and prevent the unhealthy "parent-child" dynamic that can sometimes develop in neurodiverse relationships. A more stable emotional baseline, achieved through the practice of these skills, provides a more predictable and reliable emotional base for building and sustaining meaningful relationships.
- **A Foundation for Productivity (Book 3):** Emotional dysregulation, low frustration tolerance, and the fear of failure can lead to task paralysis and procrastination. The intense shame and self-criticism that often accompany a woman's struggles with productivity can be so debilitating that she avoids tasks altogether rather than risking imperfection or criticism. Emotional resilience and self-compassion provide the mental fortitude to push through difficult projects and recover from setbacks. By developing a supportive inner ally, a woman is better able to learn from her mistakes, accept that progress is more important than perfection, and continue to engage with her goals, even when the initial novelty wears off. Emotional strength is the fuel for consistent action,

transforming a cycle of avoidance into a journey of accomplishment.

A woman is no longer merely coping with her emotional world; she is actively shaping it with intention and control. The journey to emotional mastery is not a destination but a continuous practice of learning and adaptation. There will be days when the strategies feel effortless and days when emotional surges feel overwhelming. The true strength lies not in achieving perfection but in a woman's ability to consistently return to her toolkit, re-engage with her strategies, and approach each challenge with self-compassion.

You now have the blueprint to navigate a challenging emotional landscape with greater inner stability, resilience, and strength, giving you a powerful foundation for building the extraordinary life you are capable of living.

Reflection Questions

- The book highlights how emotional dysregulation is a hallmark of the female ADHD experience. Can you identify a common trigger for an intense emotional reaction you experience? What CBT tool (e.g., challenging a thought) or DBT skill (e.g., Opposite Action) can you use the next time you feel this way?
- How has the practice of self-compassion changed your inner dialogue? What is one specific, kind thing you can tell yourself the next time you make a mistake or feel like a "failure?"The text talks about emotional strength as a foundation for other areas of life. How does managing your emotions affect your ability to stay organized or focused?

BOOK FIVE

MANAGE YOUR MONEY & RELATIONSHIPS: ESSENTIAL SKILLS FOR THE ADHD WOMAN

INTRODUCTION

THE ADULTING CHALLENGE

For many women with ADHD, the transition into adulthood brings a unique set of challenges related to money and relationships. These are two vital areas of life that require sophisticated executive functions, such as planning, organization, impulse control, and emotional regulation, which are often compromised by ADHD symptoms.

The result is a persistent feeling of being overwhelmed and a consistent struggle to manage finances and nurture relationships in a way that feels seamless to a neurotypical individual. The consequences of these struggles are not just financial or social; they create a pervasive feeling of inadequacy and amplify the shame that so many women with ADHD already feel. This book will provide an honest, evidence-based guide to navigating these challenges, empowering women to build systems that support their financial and social well-being.

The journey into adulthood is a period defined by an increasing need for independence and self-management, a reality that can be particularly daunting for a woman with ADHD. Executive functions, the brain's "command center" for planning, organizing, and controlling impulses, are crucial for navigating this transition successfully.

Difficulties with these core mental processes directly impact a woman's ability to manage her finances, build and maintain a career, and nurture healthy, stable relationships, all of which are benchmarks of a successful adult life. For many women, these struggles are invisible, a constant, private battle fought against a neurobiological reality that makes "adulting" feel like an impossible task. The gap between the societal expectation of a put-together, organized, and emotionally mature woman and her internal experience of chaos and overwhelm can lead to a profound and debilitating sense of shame and self-blame.

The Financial Toll: The "ADHD Tax" on Your Wallet and Well-Being

The financial challenges faced by women with ADHD are a direct result of core ADHD symptoms and are not a reflection of their intelligence or character. Research provides a clear picture of what can be called the "financial ADHD tax," a measurable cost that living with ADHD can impose over a lifetime.

A 2020 study found that between the ages of 25 and 30, adults with ADHD show considerably slower growth in income and savings and often remain financially dependent on their families. By age 30, they earn 37% less per month than their peers, and the projected retirement gap is staggering: 40% less net worth in the best-case scenario, potentially ballooning to 64% less, about $431,000, when accounting for inconsistent saving patterns.

These sobering statistics are a direct consequence of ADHD-related executive function challenges, particularly impulsivity, time blindness, and poor organization.

- **The Impulsivity of Spending:** A primary cause of financial instability is impulsivity, which can lead to spontaneous purchases that undermine budgeting and saving goals. The ADHD brain's love of novelty and search for stimulation often makes it susceptible to the allure of new hobbies or expensive gadgets, which can lead to significant financial and physical clutter. These are often not deliberate or malicious acts but a genuine difficulty in delaying gratification or considering the long-term consequences of a financial decision in the face of an immediate reward. A key strategy to combat this is creating a crucial pause before a purchase, perhaps by physically writing down an item before buying it.

- **The Cost of Time Blindness:** A significant factor contributing to financial distress is time blindness, a difficulty in accurately perceiving the passage of time that leads to rushed decisions, late payments, and the accumulation of late fees and fines. A woman may genuinely believe she has "plenty of time" to pay a bill, only to find the deadline has passed, leading to a financial penalty that could have easily been avoided. This isn't intentional negligence but a neurocognitive reality that makes it challenging to plan and prioritize based on future deadlines, as the future can often feel less "real" than the present.
- **Disorganization and Avoidance:** Poor planning and a struggle to stay organized make it difficult to manage paperwork, keep track of bills, and stick to a budget, which further contributes to financial instability. A woman might feel so overwhelmed by the thought of sitting down with a budget or sorting through a pile of bills that she avoids the task entirely, a pattern of spontaneous and avoidant decision-making that is common in individuals with ADHD. The avoidance of these tasks is not laziness but a coping mechanism for the immense cognitive load and feelings of overwhelm they can trigger.

The Relational Toll: The Intricacies of Neurodiverse Dynamics

Relationships, while a source of great joy, can also be a mirror for a woman's underlying ADHD symptoms. Communication, in particular, can be a major source of friction. One of the most common challenges is difficulty with active listening, where a woman's mind may wander or "zone out" during a conversation, leading her partner to feel unheard or unprioritized.

This is often compounded by impulsive interruptions, where a woman might blurt out her thoughts or finish a sentence because she fears she will forget what she wanted to say. A woman's communication style can be misinterpreted as disinterest, when in reality, she is battling a fragmented attention span.

The challenges of ADHD in relationships are further complicated by the inherent gender differences in symptom presentation and societal expectations. While men may exhibit externalized, hyperactive symptoms, women's inattentive symptoms are often internalized, leading to a greater tendency to self-blame and a shattered sense of self-worth.

These internalization tendencies are a direct conflict with societal expectations for women to be nurturing, emotionally available, and cooperative, particularly within their families and relationships.

A common dynamic that can emerge in neurodiverse couples is a "parent-child" relationship, where in an attempt to help the ADHD partner better organize their lives or remember tasks, the neurotypical partner may unwittingly leave the ADHD partner feeling like a scolded child. This can lead to avoidance or dishonesty from the ADHD partner and can trigger a symptom known as Rejection Sensitive Dysphoria (RSD), an extreme emotional responsiveness to perceived rejection or criticism.

For a woman with ADHD, a partner who calmly expresses a concern may be perceived through the "lens of ADHD" as being overly critical or micromanaging, which can lead to an intense emotional reaction and a breakdown in communication.

The challenges of living with ADHD in women extend beyond romantic relationships to friendships and social dynamics as well. Research indicates that women with ADHD have a harder time forming and maintaining friendships, which can lead to painful feelings of loneliness and a sense of never "fitting in".

This is often a consequence of being socially rejected in childhood and a struggle to meet the social expectations of others, such as suppressing the urge to interrupt or showing up on time. A lack of a well-developed social support network for women with ADHD is particularly damaging, as a strong social network can serve as a vital buffer against stress and emotional turmoil, a coping mechanism that women are more likely to rely on than men.

Shame and Inadequacy: The Amplifying Emotional Burden

The consequences of these financial and relational struggles are not just external; they create a pervasive and amplifying emotional burden. A lifetime of feeling misunderstood, coupled with a string of failures rooted in ADHD symptoms, can lead to a deep-seated belief that a woman is inadequate or "not good enough." The constant pressure to meet impossible standards and the perpetual cycle of feeling overwhelmed and behind can erode a woman's self-esteem and feed a pervasive sense of shame.

Without a diagnosis or a framework to understand her struggles, a woman may attribute her difficulties with organization, focus, and emotional regulation to personal flaws, a pattern that fuels anxiety, depression, and a shattering sense of self-worth. A woman with undiagnosed ADHD reported feeling "what I felt was I was actually a bad person... I was not an adequate human being."

These painful feelings are often made worse by the societal expectation for women to "do it all", to excel in a career, maintain an organized home, and be an emotionally available partner and mother, a "double burden" that directly conflicts with the core symptoms of ADHD. When a woman with ADHD inevitably falls short of these unrealistic standards, the shame can be immense and debilitating, leading to a self-loathing that can be a source of significant distress.

This book is a direct response to this reality. It acknowledges that a woman's struggles with money and relationships are not a sign of a character flaw but a neurobiological reality that requires a new set of tools. By providing an honest, evidence-based guide to navigating these challenges, it aims to empower women to build systems that support their financial and social well-being. A woman can move from a place of chronic overwhelm to a place of integrated success by confronting financial challenges with systems that work for her ADHD brain, strengthening her communication with loved ones, and actively building a community that validates her experience. She can then build a truly resilient and fulfilling life.

CHAPTER 1

MONEY AND THE ADHD BRAIN

The financial challenges faced by women with ADHD are a direct result of core ADHD symptoms and are not a reflection of their intelligence or character. Research provides a clear picture of what can be called the "financial ADHD tax," a measurable cost that living with ADHD can impose over a lifetime.

Studies have found that people with ADHD have lower savings, higher debt, and slower income growth than their peers. This is a direct consequence of ADHD-related executive function challenges.

A primary cause of this is impulsivity, which can lead to spontaneous purchases that undermine budgeting and saving goals. The ADHD brain's love of novelty and search for stimulation often makes it susceptible to the allure of new hobbies or expensive gadgets, which can lead to significant financial and physical clutter.

Another significant factor is time blindness, a difficulty in accurately perceiving the passage of time that leads to rushed decisions, late payments, and the accumulation of late fees and fines. Poor planning and organization make it difficult to manage paperwork, keep track of bills, and stick to a budget, which further contributes to financial instability.

The "Financial ADHD Tax": A Lifelong Cost

The financial struggles of women with ADHD are not merely isolated incidents of poor judgment; they are a pervasive and measurable phenomenon with long-term consequences. A 2020 study, which followed individuals from childhood into adulthood, painted a sobering picture of the "financial ADHD tax".

The research found that between the ages of 25 and 30, adults with ADHD show considerably slower growth in income and savings, and often remain financially dependent on their families. A projected retirement gap is staggering: a person with ADHD could have 40% less net worth in the best-case scenario, potentially ballooning to 64% less when accounting for inconsistent saving patterns, which is a hallmark of the condition.

These patterns persist regardless of education level or income, highlighting that the challenges are not rooted in a lack of knowledge but in the neurobiological difficulties that make traditional financial management so difficult.

The research is clear that even individuals who had only moderate ADHD symptoms in childhood, and may have never received a diagnosis, fared worse financially as adults compared to their peers without the condition. This suggests that the more severe the ADHD symptoms, the stronger the effect on financial distress.

A woman may not be aware that her financial difficulties are a symptom of her ADHD, leading her to internalize her struggles and blame herself, a pattern that can lead to feelings of confusion, anxiety, and depression that further demotivate her from making positive changes.

Impulsivity: The Dopamine-Driven Spending

The ADHD brain's natural inclination toward novelty and immediate gratification is a primary driver of financial instability. The dysregulated dopamine system, which is involved in motivation and reward, makes it difficult to delay gratification for a more distant reward, such as saving for retirement. A spontaneous purchase of a new gadget or a new hobby provides an immediate hit of stimulation and dopamine, which feels far more compelling to the ADHD brain than the abstract, long-term reward of financial security.

This impulsivity can lead to a cycle of overspending, acquiring significant debt, and investing valuable time and money into a hobby of the day, only to lose interest and move on to the next.

The modern retail environment is uniquely designed to trigger this impulsivity. Retail apps and online platforms often "gamify" shopping with points, streaks, flash sales, and "limited time" offers that can trigger impulsivity. To combat this, a woman can create a crucial "pause" between an impulse and a purchase.

Even if a perfect record isn't kept, the simple act of writing down a purchase before making it can be a powerful tool for preventing impulsive buys. This provides a moment for executive functions to intervene and reconsider the long-term impact of a purchase before it's made. Additionally, setting up a separate account for "spontaneous" or lifestyle purchases can create a boundary that prevents impulsive spending from derailing a budget.

Time Blindness: The Cost of Chronic Lateness

A significant and often misunderstood contributor to financial challenges is time blindness, a difficulty in accurately perceiving the passage of time that leads to rushed decisions, late payments, and the accumulation of late fees and fines. A woman with ADHD may genuinely believe she has "plenty of time" to pay a bill, only to find the deadline has passed, leading to a financial penalty that could have easily been avoided.

The future can often feel less "real" than the present, making it challenging to prioritize tasks based on their true time sensitivity. This isn't intentional negligence but a neurocognitive reality that requires external support systems to manage effectively.

The financial costs of time blindness can add up over a lifetime, from late fees on bills to a lack of emergency savings due to an inability to prioritize long-term benefits over short-term rewards. To counteract this, automation is a powerful strategy.

Setting up automatic bill payments, investment transfers, and savings contributions to happen immediately after payday eliminates the need for constant decision-making and manual follow-through. This system bypasses the cognitive challenges of time blindness and provides a reliable safety net for a woman's finances. Using multiple reminders or scheduling a specific day each month to pay bills can also serve as an external cue to manage these tasks proactively.

The Cognitive Hurdles of Planning and Organization

Traditional financial management advice often relies on the very executive functions that are compromised by ADHD: sustained focus, planning, and organization. For many women with ADHD, the symptoms make it harder to track expenses, remember due dates, stay organized with bills and documents, and focus on financial statements and budgets. The very act of trying to focus on setting a monthly budget or calculating expenses can feel overwhelming and is often put off or avoided entirely, a pattern of avoidant and spontaneous decision-making that is common in individuals with ADHD.

To overcome these hurdles, a woman can leverage a new set of tools and strategies:

- **Visual Systems:** Many people with ADHD are visual thinkers. Using budgeting apps with charts and graphs, creating simple visual budget boards, or using color-coded systems can be particularly helpful. These visual aids make abstract numbers more tangible and easier for the ADHD brain to process, reducing the feeling of being overwhelmed.
- **Technology to the Rescue:** Utilizing expense and money-tracking apps can help a woman stay on top of her spending in real time, rather than trying to revisit purchases later. Setting up automatic payments and transfers ensures that financial

tasks are completed reliably without the need for manual initiation.

- **External Support:** For tasks that require sustained focus, such as setting up a budget, the strategy of "body doubling" can be highly effective. A woman can work alongside a friend, either in person or virtually, to provide a subtle sense of accountability and structure that makes it easier to start and remain on task.

By confronting these financial challenges with systems that work for the ADHD brain, a woman can move from a place of chronic overwhelm to a place of integrated success. This is not about becoming a financial expert overnight but about building a supportive framework that mitigates the inherent challenges of ADHD. It's about understanding that financial well-being doesn't evolve from budgets, math, and spreadsheets alone; it evolves from a healthy financial mindset and a toolbox of strategies that empower you to take control of your financial life.

Table: Common Financial Pitfalls and Evidence-Based Solutions

Common Financial Pitfall	ADHD Symptom Connection	Evidence-Based Solution
Impulse spending	Impulsivity, novelty-seeking	Automate savings and bill payments; create a "pause" by physically writing down purchases.
Late bill payments	Time blindness, disorganization	Use automatic bill payments and set multiple reminders; schedule a specific day to pay bills.
Poor budgeting	Executive dysfunction, difficulty with sustained focus	Use visual budgeting apps with charts and graphs; use body doubling to get the task done.

Common Financial Pitfall	ADHD Symptom Connection	Evidence-Based Solution
Inconsistent saving	Preference for short-term rewards	Automate transfers to a separate savings account immediately after payday to make it a non-negotiable habit.

CHAPTER 2

COMMUNICATION IN RELATIONSHIPS

Relationships, while a source of great joy, can also be a mirror for a woman's underlying ADHD symptoms. Communication, in particular, can be a major source of friction. One of the most common challenges is difficulty with active listening, where a woman's mind may wander or "zone out" during a conversation, leading her partner to feel unheard or unprioritized.

Often, a woman might blurt out her thoughts or finish a sentence because she fears she will forget what she wanted to say, which further compounds this. To combat a fragmented attention span, practicing mindfulness and active listening is crucial. Consciously putting away distractions and paraphrasing what the other person is saying helps to ensure comprehension.

To navigate difficult conversations, a shift from blaming to understanding is essential. Using "I" statements, which focus on one's own feelings rather than the other person's actions, can de-escalate conflict and prevent the unhealthy "parent-child" dynamic that can develop in neurodiverse relationships.

For example, instead of saying, "You never listen to me," a woman can say, "I feel unheard when I'm speaking and you're looking at your phone." By adopting intentional communication strategies, a woman can build a stronger, more empathetic connection with her loved ones.

The Neurobiology of Relational Friction

The communication challenges that arise in relationships affected by ADHD are not a reflection of a woman's desire to be a good partner; they are a direct consequence of a brain that is wired differently. The ADHD brain often has a harder time concentrating than a neurotypical brain and a reduced ability to filter out irrelevant stimuli.

A woman's mind can either "hypofocus" (a daydream-like state) or "hyperfocus" (a state of intense focus on a single subject, and only that subject), both of which can create a powerful external appearance of not paying attention during conversations.

Her partner may believe she is not interested in what they have to say, which can lead to resentment over time, even though she is genuinely trying to listen.

A woman's tendency to impulsively interrupt or blurt out her thoughts is also rooted in this neurobiology. The brain's working memory can feel like a sieve, making it difficult to hold a thought for even a few moments. A woman may feel an intense urge to speak immediately, fearing that the thought will be lost forever if she waits for her turn in the conversation. While a neurotypical individual may interpret this as a lack of social graces, it is, in fact, a symptom of a neurocognitive reality.

A constant barrage of internal thoughts can also make it difficult for a woman with ADHD to pick up on social cues, read body language, or be attuned to the emotions of others, which can be a significant source of friction in social dynamics and lead to a painful sense of "never fitting in."

The Parent-Child Dynamic and the Pain of RSD

A particularly difficult dynamic can emerge in relationships where one partner has ADHD, often resembling a parent-child relationship. In an attempt to help their partner better organize their lives or remember tasks, a neurotypical partner may unintentionally take on the role of a taskmaster or a reminder, leaving the ADHD partner feeling like a scolded child.

This can lead to avoidance, dishonesty, or even resentment from the ADHD partner and can trigger a significant symptom of ADHD known as "rejection sensitivity."

Rejection Sensitive Dysphoria (RSD), while not a formal diagnosis in diagnostic manuals, is a term used to describe an "extreme emotional responsiveness and anxiety in anticipation of, or in response to, perceived rejection or criticism from others."

For a woman with ADHD, who may have spent a lifetime internalizing her struggles, a partner who calmly expresses a concern may be perceived through the "lens of ADHD" as being overly critical or micromanaging. This can trigger an immediate, overwhelming emotional pain that can feel physically agonizing and lead to a disproportionate emotional reaction that compromises the relationship and the well-being of both partners.

The behaviors and coping mechanisms that stem from this profound sensitivity can ironically lead to more rejection, creating a challenging and painful cycle in the relationship. To break free from this cycle, both partners must understand that RSD is a real and often debilitating experience for the ADHD partner and not a deliberate choice to be "difficult."

Building a Bridge: Strategies for Effective Communication

Communication is the bedrock of any healthy relationship. For couples navigating ADHD, being intentional and strategic about how they communicate can build a powerful bridge of empathy and understanding.

- **Practice Active and Mindful Listening:** Active listening is paramount to fostering trust and deepening understanding. To combat a fragmented attention span, a woman can consciously turn off distractions, such as putting down her phone and closing her laptop. Making eye contact and turning her body towards her partner shows she is fully engaged. Another powerful technique is to paraphrase or use reflective responses. After her partner speaks, she can say, "So, what you're saying is..." to confirm her understanding. This not only shows she is actively listening but also helps to clarify any misunderstandings before they can escalate into conflict. A woman can also ask open-ended questions to encourage her partner to share more about their thoughts and feelings, which shows genuine interest and creates space for deeper conversations.
- **Use "I" Statements to Express Needs:** When discussing difficult topics or expressing emotions, using "I" statements is essential to de-escalate conflict and prevent the other person from feeling blamed. Rather than saying, "You never help me with the chores," a woman can say, "I feel overwhelmed when I'm the only one taking care of the laundry." This approach shifts the focus from the other person's actions to your own feelings, which can prevent defensiveness and open the door for a more productive conversation.
- **Structured Conversations and "Relationship Roundtables":** Spontaneous, emotionally charged conversations are often difficult for the ADHD brain to navigate. A woman's emotional intensity can lead to impulsive reactions and regrettable words that she later regrets, which is why a more structured approach to important discussions is so effective. Setting aside a specific time each week for a "Relationship Roundtable" can be one of the single most useful strategies for improving communication and connection. This is a designated, distraction-free time to discuss logistics, plan for the week, and address any ongoing challenges. By tackling these issues in a structured, calm environment, both partners can feel heard and avoid the emotional friction that can arise from having a

difficult conversation in the heat of the moment.

- **Create a Shared Language and External Systems:** A powerful tool for managing emotionally charged conversations is to create a shared language or signal that both partners can use. A pre-agreed "safe word" or signal can be used when a conversation is becoming too overwhelming for one partner, providing a non-confrontational way to pause or exit a difficult situation without it feeling like a rejection. Furthermore, a woman can leverage external systems to offload the mental burden of remembering things. Using shared digital calendars, chore charts on a whiteboard, or reminder apps can shift the responsibility of remembering tasks off the non-ADHD partner, which can reduce resentment and prevent the parent-child dynamic from taking hold.
- **Education, Empathy, and a Shared Journey:** A foundational strategy is for both partners to educate themselves about ADHD. Understanding how ADHD works in the brain and how it uniquely impacts a woman's presentation of symptoms can help reduce blame and increase understanding. A woman can gently educate her partner about the neurobiological reasons for her struggles, helping them understand that her behaviors are not a reflection of a lack of care but a result of a different brain wiring. In a relationship with ADHD, both partners are equally responsible for the success of the relationship. Open communication and a shared commitment to building new structures and methods of communication that work for both partners are crucial.

Nurturing relationships and improving communication for women with ADHD is an ongoing process of self-awareness, intentional action, and open dialogue. By applying these strategies, a woman can build a more resilient, empathetic, and fulfilling connection with her loved ones, transforming her relationships from a source of frustration and misunderstanding into a wellspring of support and joy.

CHAPTER 3

NAVIGATING SHARED RESPONSIBILITIES AND SOCIAL DYNAMICS

Beyond communication, shared responsibilities and social interactions present a unique set of challenges for women with ADHD. A neurotypical partner can become frustrated by a woman's disorganization or her difficulty with task initiation on household chores.

The partner may feel that they are taking care of everything on their own, a situation that often leads to resentment. This is a direct result of the woman's struggle with executive function and is not a lack of caring.

One powerful solution is to externalize shared responsibilities with visual aids, such as a whiteboard chore chart, and to proactively break down larger tasks into smaller, manageable steps with scheduled reminders.

In broader social dynamics, women with ADHD often face significant barriers. Research indicates that they have a harder time forming and maintaining friendships, which can lead to feelings of loneliness and a sense of never "fitting in".

This is often a consequence of being socially rejected in childhood and a struggle to meet the social expectations of others, such as suppressing the urge to interrupt or showing up on time. It is important to acknowledge this struggle and actively seek out communities that are affirming and supportive, where a woman can feel seen and accepted for who she is.

The Mental Load of Shared Responsibilities

The challenges of managing shared responsibilities for a woman with ADHD go far beyond the physical act of doing a chore. Research from Gallup News shows that married or partnered women in the U.S. still shoulder the primary responsibility for the majority of household chores, including laundry, cleaning, and preparing meals.

Even in households where both partners work, women still perform the bulk of the domestic work and childcare planning. The expectation for women to "do it all", to excel in a career while also flawlessly managing the home, creates a "double burden" that directly conflicts with the core symptoms of ADHD. This immense, often invisible, mental burden is a significant drain on executive function, a set of cognitive skills that are essential for planning, prioritizing, and completing tasks.

For a woman with ADHD, a disorganized or neglected household is not a sign of laziness but a reflection of her brain's executive function challenges. She may struggle with task initiation, a "just can't start" syndrome where the thought of organizing a room or doing a pile of laundry feels so overwhelming that she is paralyzed.

Poor planning and organization make it difficult to keep track of a household schedule or to consistently follow through on chores, leading to a home environment that feels chaotic and unpredictable. When a neurotypical partner is forced to constantly remind their partner with ADHD about tasks, a difficult and unhealthy "parent-child" dynamic can emerge in the relationship. The neurotypical partner may unknowingly take on the role of a taskmaster, while the ADHD partner may feel like a scolded child, which can lead to resentment, avoidance, and a profound sense of shame for not being able to manage daily life like a competent adult.

Research shows that neurodiverse couples can develop this dynamic when one partner consistently feels underappreciated for the extra effort they take to manage the household and the other partner feels criticized and misunderstood for their struggles. This dynamic undermines the core sense of partnership and respect that is vital to a healthy relationship.

The Impact on Social Dynamics

The same executive function and emotional regulation challenges that affect a woman's home life also create significant barriers in her broader social dynamics and friendships. Research indicates that women with ADHD have a harder time forming and maintaining friendships, which can lead to painful feelings of loneliness and a profound sense of never "fitting in".

A study in girls with ADHD found that those who were hyperactive or impulsive were "socially rejected" by peers, while those with the quieter, inattentive subtype were "socially neglected," or simply left out of social groups. These patterns persist into adulthood, a reality that is particularly painful for women who have a greater need for social acceptance and connection than men.

A woman's struggles to meet neurotypical social expectations are often rooted in her ADHD symptoms. She may have difficulty with active listening, where her mind wanders or "zones out" during conversations, leading her partner or friends to feel unheard or unprioritized. A woman with ADHD may also struggle to suppress the urge to interrupt in conversation because she fears she will forget what she wanted to say. The inability to consistently meet these social expectations, such as showing up on time for social commitments or curbing the tendency to talk too much, can lead to social rejection or the perception of being rude, which can take a significant toll on a woman's self-esteem and feed her belief that she is unworthy of authentic connection.

This is further compounded by a woman's tendency to struggle with reading social cues or body language, a challenge that can make navigating complex social situations difficult and anxiety-inducing.

The Social Cost of Masking

The constant effort to mask ADHD symptoms carries a profound social cost for women. Masking is a coping mechanism where a woman develops sophisticated behaviors to hide her struggles and appear "neurotypical" to the outside world. For example, a woman might meticulously maintain a façade of punctuality by building in extra time for everything, a strategy she developed to combat her innate time blindness and avoid the social consequences of being late. Another might learn to pretend to take notes in a meeting to hide the fact that she is "zoning out" or has a "thousand-yard stare".

While masking may be a survival strategy developed to avoid social rejection, it can also lead to chronic loneliness and a debilitating sense of not being able to be one's authentic self. A woman may feel like an impostor, constantly fearing that her true self will be discovered and she will be rejected. This painful experience is particularly damaging and reinforces the low self-esteem and shame that are so prevalent in women with ADHD.

The stress of this constant, exhausting effort to appear "non-ADHD" is an invisible burden that can lead to a lifetime of internalized shame, anxiety, and depression, and can also prevent a woman from forming the robust social support network that is so vital for her well-being.

Building a Bridge: Strategies for Shared Responsibilities

Overcoming the challenges of shared responsibilities requires a shift from blame and frustration to a collaborative, solution-oriented mindset. The goal is to build external systems that compensate for internal inconsistencies and to work as a team to create a household that is supportive for everyone.

- **Externalize Shared Responsibilities:** Do not rely on one person's internal memory or emotional bandwidth to manage the household. Use visual aids, such as a whiteboard chore chart, a shared digital calendar, or a simple analog system to track all household responsibilities. This external system offloads the mental burden from the neurotypical partner, reduces the need for reminders, and provides a clear, objective record of what needs to be done.

- **Divide Tasks by Strengths, Not Fairness:** Rather than trying to divide all tasks equally, divide them in a way that leverages each partner's unique strengths. If one person thrives on spontaneity and the other on structure, split responsibilities accordingly. Perhaps one person handles tasks that are more fluid or require a quick burst of energy, while the other manages more routine or administrative tasks like paying bills.
- **Break Down Overwhelming Tasks:** Large household tasks can trigger "ADHD paralysis" or overwhelm. Break down larger tasks into smaller, more manageable steps with scheduled reminders. For instance, instead of "Clean the entire kitchen," a more manageable step would be "Load and start the dishwasher," or "Wipe down the countertops." A successful completion of a small task provides a small but satisfying burst of dopamine that builds momentum for the next step.
- **Have a Weekly "Relationship Roundtable":** Set aside a specific, non-distracting time each week to sit down with your partner and discuss logistics, shared responsibilities, and upcoming plans. Calling it a "Relationship Roundtable" can make the conversation feel less like a confrontational "chore meeting" and more like a collaborative team huddle. This dedicated time allows for a calm, structured discussion of issues before they can escalate into a reactive argument in the heat of the moment.

Building a Network: Strategies for Social Dynamics

Navigating social dynamics and building meaningful friendships for a woman with ADHD requires a proactive and compassionate approach that acknowledges her unique challenges while also seeking out supportive connections.

- **Gently Educate Your Loved Ones:** An important strategy is to gently educate your loved ones about ADHD, helping them to understand that your behaviors are not a reflection of a lack of care but a result of a different brain wiring. You can explain that your tendency to interrupt is because you fear you will forget your thought if you wait, or that your struggle with time is due to a neurocognitive difference called "time blindness". This fosters empathy and can help reduce the blame and misunderstanding that so often arise from these situations.
- **Seek Out Affirming Communities:** Actively seek out communities that are validating and affirming, where a woman can feel seen and accepted for who she is. This can be through online forums, support groups, or other channels where she can connect with others who share her experience. This practice of finding her community is an essential step towards healing from a lifetime of masking and building a foundation of genuine self-acceptance and belonging.
- **Create a Shared Language for Overwhelm:** For a woman who struggles with emotional and sensory overload in social situations, having a pre-agreed "safe word" or signal with a partner or close friend can be a non-confrontational way to pause or exit a challenging situation without it feeling like a rejection. For example, a woman could signal that she needs a few minutes to reset, and her partner would know to step outside with her for a moment or give her space to breathe without it feeling like an insult or a rejection.
- **Embrace Self-Compassion:** Acknowledging the social challenges of ADHD is not about excusing your behavior, but about building a foundation of self-compassion that allows you to approach your struggles with curiosity and kindness rather than shame and self-blame. Women with ADHD are more likely to internalize their struggles, leading to a deep sense of shame and feelings of worthlessness. By reframing her struggles as a neurobiological reality and celebrating her genuine efforts to connect, a woman can begin to heal from a lifetime of hurt and build the confidence to form authentic, lasting bonds.

Nurturing relationships and navigating social dynamics for women with ADHD is an ongoing process of self-awareness, intentional action, and open dialogue. By applying these strategies, a woman will not only reduce friction and misunderstanding but also build deeper, more resilient connections that enrich her life and provide invaluable support on her journey to a balanced existence.

CHAPTER 4

THE SOCIAL COST: MASKING, REJECTION, AND FINDING YOUR COMMUNITY

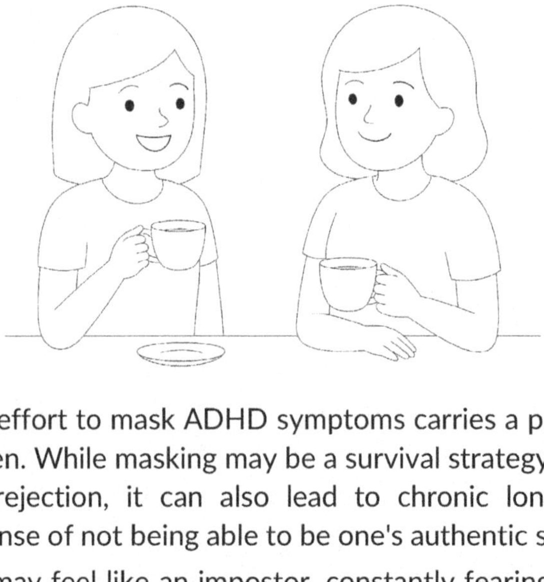

The constant effort to mask ADHD symptoms carries a profound social cost for women. While masking may be a survival strategy developed to avoid social rejection, it can also lead to chronic loneliness and a debilitating sense of not being able to be one's authentic self.

A woman may feel like an impostor, constantly fearing that her true self will be discovered and she will be rejected. An experience like this is particularly painful and reinforces the low self-esteem and shame that are so prevalent in women with ADHD. The struggle is further compounded by the fact that women with ADHD are often less successful at forming a robust social support network, which can serve as a vital buffer against stress and emotional turmoil.

To break free from this cycle, a woman must begin to cultivate a more compassionate and accepting relationship with her neurodiversity. She can start by gently educating her loved ones about her ADHD, helping them understand that her behaviors are not a reflection of a lack of care but a result of a different brain wiring. She must also actively seek out and find communities that are validating and affirming. Finding her community is an essential step towards healing from a lifetime of masking and building a foundation of genuine self-acceptance.

The Silent Burden of Masking

For women with ADHD, masking is not a conscious choice to deceive others; it is often a deeply ingrained, unconscious survival strategy developed over a lifetime to conform to neurotypical expectations and avoid social judgment.

The diagnostic disparity in ADHD, where males are more frequently diagnosed due to their external, hyperactive symptoms, is partly explained by the fact that girls and women are more likely to develop these compensatory behaviors that obscure their underlying struggles.

A woman may meticulously maintain a façade of punctuality by building in extra time for everything, a strategy she developed to combat her innate time blindness and avoid the social consequences of being late.

Another might learn to pretend to take notes in a meeting to hide the fact that she is "zoning out" or has a "thousand-yard stare." These are just a few examples of the sophisticated coping mechanisms developed to appear "non-ADHD".

While a woman may be successful in hiding her struggles, the emotional and psychological cost of this performance is immense. The constant, exhausting effort to appear neurotypical is an invisible burden that leads to a lifetime of internalized shame, anxiety, depression, and a shattered sense of self-worth. Research confirms that girls are more likely to mask their symptoms than boys, and this can lead to significant negative consequences on their mental health, social functioning, and academic achievement.

A woman may feel like a fraud or an impostor, constantly fearing that her "perceived failures" will be discovered and that she will be rejected for who she truly is. This fear of exposure can lead to chronic loneliness and a debilitating sense of not being able to be one's authentic self. The longer a woman masks her symptoms, the more difficult it can be to find out who she really is after a diagnosis.

The Neurobiological Pain of Rejection Sensitive Dysphoria (RSD)

A particularly painful and debilitating manifestation of emotional dysregulation that is highly common in women with ADHD is Rejection Sensitive Dysphoria (RSD). For a woman with ADHD, a perceived social snub, a critical tone of voice, or a hint of disapproval is not just hurtful; it is an immediate, overwhelming emotional pain that can feel physically agonizing. Experts believe that the extreme pain of RSD is a real, physiological response in the ADHD brain, rooted in a distinct functioning of brain regions responsible for emotional processing and regulation.

An overactive amygdala (the brain's alarm system) combined with a less active prefrontal cortex (the brain's emotional "brakes") can lead to an immediate and overwhelming emotional response with little time for a thoughtful, inhibited reaction.

The hypersensitivity of RSD is often a direct result of a lifetime of chronic negative feedback and a learned expectation of rejection. As girls, their ADHD symptoms of impulsivity, emotional over-reactivity, or disorganization were inconsistent with societal expectations, making them a target for criticism or social judgment from family, peers, and teachers. These early traumatic experiences, which are often unpredictable and repeated, can trigger primitive survival mechanisms in the brain, leaving a girl's resilience chipped away.

An expectation of future social adversity is created, and a woman may interpret a partner's neutral or ambiguous behavior as an intentional sign of rejection, which can trigger an overreaction that ironically can compromise the relationship.

To avoid the profound emotional pain of RSD, a woman may develop sophisticated compensatory behaviors like people-pleasing and perfectionism. A woman may constantly try to accommodate the needs of others while neglecting her own, a strategy that is both exhausting and unsustainable.

However, the painful feedback loop continues, as a woman's emotional volatility may be seen as a "melodramatic overreaction" by others, which further invalidates her pain and reinforces her sense of being unworthy. A combination of a lifetime of negative feedback and the belief that she can do "nothing right" can lead to despair, which is why studies suggest women with untreated ADHD are more likely to make suicide attempts and self-harm than their male counterparts.

The Erosion of Connection: Loneliness and the Social Toll

The same executive function and emotional regulation challenges that affect a woman's home life also create significant barriers in her broader social dynamics and friendships. For women, social connections are central to their well-being, and a lack of a well-developed support network can be a significant source of pain.

Research indicates that women with ADHD have a harder time forming and maintaining friendships, which can lead to feelings of loneliness and a painful sense of "never fitting in". A study on girls with ADHD found that those with hyperactive/impulsive symptoms were "socially rejected," while those with the quieter, inattentive subtype were "socially neglected," or simply left out of social groups altogether. These patterns, which are deeply painful for women who have a greater need for social acceptance than men, persist into adulthood.

A woman's struggles to meet neurotypical social expectations are often rooted in her ADHD symptoms. She may have difficulty with active listening, where her mind wanders or "zones out" during conversations, leading her friends to feel unheard or unprioritized.

A woman with ADHD may also struggle to suppress the urge to interrupt in conversation because she fears she will forget what she wanted to say. An inability to consistently meet these social expectations, such as showing up on time for social commitments or curbing her tendency to talk too much, can lead to social rejection or the perception of being rude, which can take a significant toll on a woman's self-esteem.

The stress of these social challenges is heightened for women with ADHD, as they are less likely to have a well-developed social support network, which serves as a vital buffer against stress and emotional turmoil for neurotypical women.

Healing from a Lifetime of Shame: The Path to Self-Acceptance

The social cost of living with ADHD, the shame, the loneliness, the pain of rejection sensitivity, is a heavy burden to carry, but it is not a permanent one. Healing from a lifetime of masking requires a fundamental shift in a woman's relationship with her neurodiversity. It is a journey of moving from a place of self-blame and self-loathing to a place of self-compassion and genuine self-acceptance.

A woman can begin to cultivate a more compassionate and accepting relationship with her neurodiversity by actively challenging the negative narrative she has internalized. She must learn to recognize that her struggles are not a reflection of her character but a result of her brain's unique wiring.

A woman can reframe her struggles from "What's wrong with me?" to "My brain works differently, and what can I do to support it?" This compassionate stance is a powerful first step in dismantling the shame that has been a constant companion. A woman's emotional volatility and difficulties with self-regulation, for example, can be reframed not as a sign of being "dramatic" but as a neurobiological reality that can be managed with the right tools.

Healing from the social cost of ADHD also requires a proactive approach to communication and connection. A woman can start by gently educating her loved ones about her ADHD, helping them understand that her behaviors are not a reflection of a lack of care but a result of a different brain wiring. By sharing resources and explaining the "why" behind her struggles, she can foster empathy and reduce the blame and misunderstanding that so often arise from these situations.

A woman's partner, for example, can be educated about how RSD works so that they can offer gentle reassurance and validate her feelings, even if they don't fully understand them.

Finally, a woman must actively seek out and find communities that are validating and affirming. Isolation amplifies distress, and a lack of a strong social network can be particularly damaging for women with ADHD.

A woman can connect with others who share her experience through online forums, support groups, or coaching groups that provide encouragement, understanding, acceptance, and support. This practice of finding her community is an essential step towards healing from a lifetime of masking and building a foundation of genuine self-acceptance and belonging.

When a woman with ADHD finds a community where she can feel seen and accepted for who she is, she can begin to heal from a lifetime of hurts and learn to embrace her authentic self.

The journey of healing from the social cost of ADHD is not a linear one, and there will be days when the inner critic gets loud and the shame resurfaces. The true strength lies not in achieving perfection, but in a woman's ability to consistently return to her toolkit of self-compassion, re-engage with her strategies, and approach each challenge with curiosity and kindness. You now have the blueprint to navigate a challenging social landscape with greater inner stability, resilience, and strength, giving you a powerful foundation for building a life of authentic connection and genuine self-acceptance.

CHAPTER 5

REDEFINING BALANCE: INTEGRATING LIFE AREAS WITH ADHD

For a woman with ADHD, a truly balanced life is not about achieving neurotypical perfection; it is about honoring her unique needs and building a life that accommodates her brain's natural rhythms. This involves a conscious integration of the different areas of her life, ensuring that she is not pouring all her energy into one area while neglecting others. It is critical to recognize that her ADHD symptoms, such as the love of novelty and the capacity for hyperfocus, can be powerful assets when managed intentionally.

A balanced life means recognizing that a woman needs to refuel on weekends, and that her needs for self-care are not a luxury but a fundamental necessity for her well-being. It means being compassionate with herself when a strategy fails and understanding that the journey is one of continuous learning and adaptation. The final chapter provides a holistic approach to living, where a woman can integrate her personal needs, her relationships, and her professional aspirations into a harmonious system that is uniquely her own.

The Myth of Perfect Balance and the Neurobiological Reality

The concept of a "balanced life" is often portrayed as a serene, perfectly orchestrated state where every area, work, family, health, and personal life, receives an equal amount of attention at all times. For a woman with ADHD, whose brain is not designed for this kind of rigid, sustained equilibrium, chasing this ideal can be a fast track to exhaustion and shame.

The "do it all" expectation that women should excel in both the public and private spheres often leaves them feeling overwhelmed and undervalued, a struggle that is profoundly exacerbated by ADHD symptoms. Research shows women report higher levels of stress than men, largely due to the "work-life conflict" that arises when they are expected to meet the demands of both family and work life simultaneously.

A woman's brain, with its executive function deficits in planning, prioritization, and time management, is simply not equipped to flawlessly juggle every demand in a way that feels seamless to a neurotypical individual. Her natural energy cycles are often unpredictable, with periods of intense focus and surges of energy followed by sudden crashes of exhaustion, a pattern that makes consistent, linear progress difficult.

Attempting to force a rigid, neurotypical definition of balance onto a neurodiverse brain is not only ineffective but also a source of significant mental fatigue, a constant, conscious effort to manage internalized symptoms that drains a woman's energy reserves and makes her more susceptible to burnout.

Harnessing Your ADHD Superpowers: Hyperfocus and Novelty

A truly balanced life for a woman with ADHD is not about eradicating her symptoms but about learning to see them as a source of unique strengths and adaptive capabilities when managed with intention. Her neurodiversity comes with inherent strengths that can be harnessed for extraordinary output.

- **The Power of Hyperfocus:** Hyperfocus, often viewed as a double-edged sword, is a state of intense and prolonged concentration on a specific task or activity. While it can lead to the neglect of other responsibilities, it can also be a powerful tool for productivity and creativity when channeled intentionally. A woman's ability to get so engaged in a project that she is unaware of her surroundings can be an asset in fields that require deep concentration, such as writing, research, or programming. The key is to direct this superpower toward high-leverage, meaningful tasks, using external reminders and alarms to break out of a hyperfocused state and prevent a work-life imbalance.
- **The Advantage of Novelty-Seeking:** The ADHD brain's natural inclination toward novelty is a neurobiological reality tied to its dopamine reward system. While this can lead to impulsivity and a trail of unfinished projects, it can also be the engine of innovation and creativity. Many ADHD brains excel at seeing connections others miss and approaching problems from unexpected angles. This strength can be leveraged by pursuing creative or entrepreneurial endeavors that provide a constant flow of new ideas and stimulating challenges. A balanced life means a woman can honor her need for novelty by engaging in hobbies or projects that provide this kind of stimulation without letting them derail her long-term goals or responsibilities.

The Framework for an Integrated Life

An integrated life is one where your various needs, professional, personal, emotional, and social, are not seen as separate domains to be balanced but as interconnected parts of a holistic system. This is an intentional way of living that acknowledges that what you do in one area of your life directly impacts all the others.

- **Schedule and Boundaries:** A woman can build a life that accommodates her brain's natural rhythms by creating a flexible but structured schedule that prioritizes her unique needs. This means scheduling in "deep work" during her peak energy hours, but also intentionally scheduling in "low-energy" tasks during her more distractible or fatigued periods. Critically, she must also set firm boundaries to protect her energy reserves. Learning to say "no" to commitments that do not serve her and actively avoiding "energy vampires"—people, tasks, or social media activities that drain her—is a fundamental part of self-care and emotional well-being.

- **Proactive Self-Care as a Necessity:** For a woman with ADHD, self-care is not a luxury but a fundamental necessity for sustainable productivity and emotional well-being. Burnout is a state of chronic exhaustion driven by the daily demands of managing ADHD symptoms, and women are particularly susceptible due to the added pressure to conform to neurotypical standards. A woman can build resilience against burnout by prioritizing good sleep hygiene, as quality sleep is critical for attention and working memory. She can use regular physical exercise as a powerful antidote to mental fatigue, as it helps regulate dopamine levels and improves mood. Nourishing her body with a balanced diet rich in protein, healthy fats, and complex carbohydrates is also crucial for maintaining stable energy levels, which in turn supports sustained focus and emotional regulation. By consistently engaging in these practices, she is building a physiological buffer against the mental and emotional fatigue that often accompanies ADHD.
- **Continuous Learning and Adaptation:** The journey of a balanced life is not a linear one. There will be days when strategies fail, deadlines are missed, and the inner chaos feels overwhelming. The key to sustainable progress is not rigid adherence to a perfect system, but a compassionate, iterative process of review and adaptation. A woman can learn to reframe setbacks as a source of valuable data, asking herself: "What happened here? What was the friction point? What made this system hard to maintain today?" By approaching these moments with curiosity and kindness, she can learn from them and make small, strategic adjustments to her systems, making them more resilient and effective over time. This continuous cycle of learning, adapting, and refining is the true foundation of a well-organized and peaceful life.

This final chapter has provided a woman with a holistic approach to living, where she can integrate her personal needs, her relationships, and her professional aspirations into a harmonious system that is uniquely her own.

The mastery of these practical skills, from leveraging her strengths to building systems of support, is the ultimate validation of a truly balanced and integrated life with ADHD. By embracing her neurodiversity and recognizing that her optimal life is one she designs for herself, she can move from feeling powerless against her symptoms to a place of profound self-acceptance and empowerment. This intentional approach to living is the final and most important step in her journey.

Conclusion: Your Integrated Success

A roadmap for navigating the complex challenges of money and relationships has been provided in this book, demonstrating that a woman can move from a place of overwhelm to a place of integrated success. By confronting financial challenges head-on with systems that work for her ADHD brain, strengthening her communication with loved ones, and actively building a community that validates her experience, a woman can build a truly resilient and fulfilling life. The mastery of these practical skills is the ultimate validation of a truly balanced and integrated life with ADHD.

The Foundation of Practical Systems: Working with Your Brain

For women with ADHD, the struggles with finances and relationships are not a reflection of their intelligence or character; they are a direct result of core ADHD symptoms that profoundly impact daily functioning. Executive function deficits, particularly in areas like planning, organization, impulse control, and emotional regulation, make managing these two vital areas of life feel like an impossible task. The result is a persistent feeling of being overwhelmed and a consistent struggle to navigate adulthood in a way that feels seamless to a neurotypical individual.

The financial toll of these struggles is a measurable phenomenon known as the "financial ADHD tax," a lifelong cost that can significantly impact a woman's long-term financial health. Research from a 2020 study found that between the ages of 25 and 30, adults with ADHD show considerably slower growth in income and savings and often remain financially dependent on their families. By age 30, a projected retirement gap for a person with ADHD could be as much as 40% less net worth in the best-case scenario, potentially ballooning to 64% less when accounting for inconsistent saving patterns, a hallmark of the condition. A primary driver of this is impulsivity, a neurobiological difficulty in delaying gratification that leads to spontaneous purchases and a lack of savings.

Another significant factor is time blindness, which is a difficulty in accurately perceiving the passage of time that leads to late payments, accumulating fines, and a feeling that deadlines appear out of nowhere. The work in this book has provided a woman with the tools to confront these challenges head-on with systems that work for her ADHD brain, such as using automation and visual budgeting apps to bypass deficits in planning and organization.

A woman's relationships are also a mirror for her underlying ADHD symptoms. Communication, in particular, can be a major source of friction, as her mind may wander during conversations or she may impulsively interrupt, leading a partner to feel unheard and unprioritized. A particularly difficult dynamic can emerge when a neurotypical partner unintentionally takes on the role of a taskmaster to manage shared household responsibilities, leaving the ADHD partner feeling like a scolded child.

To overcome these hurdles, a woman has been equipped with intentional communication strategies like using "I" statements to express her feelings without blame and leveraging visual aids like a whiteboard chore chart to externalize shared responsibilities. By building these external systems and intentional communication practices, a woman moves from a place of reactive chaos to one of proactive, collaborative partnership.

The Emotional Core of Integrated Success

The consequences of these financial and relational struggles are not just external; they create a pervasive and amplifying emotional burden. A lifetime of feeling misunderstood, coupled with a pattern of failures rooted in ADHD symptoms, can lead to a deep-seated belief that a woman is inadequate or "not good enough."

A woman with undiagnosed ADHD reported feeling that she was "actually a bad person... I was not an adequate human being." The constant pressure to meet impossible societal standards and the perpetual cycle of feeling overwhelmed and behind can erode a woman's self-esteem and feed a pervasive sense of shame.

A painful and debilitating manifestation of this emotional dysregulation is Rejection Sensitive Dysphoria (RSD), an extreme emotional responsiveness to perceived rejection or criticism that is highly common in women with ADHD. This profound hypersensitivity is fueled by a lifetime of internalizing struggles and the fear that her "perceived failures" will be discovered. A woman's emotional volatility and misinterpretations may be seen as a "melodramatic overreaction" by others, which further invalidates her pain and reinforces her sense of being unworthy.

The constant effort to "mask" her symptoms to conform to neurotypical standards is a major source of this emotional burden, and it can lead to chronic loneliness and a debilitating sense of not being able to be her authentic self. A woman may feel like an impostor, constantly fearing that her true self will be discovered and she will be rejected, a painful experience that reinforces the low self-esteem and shame that are so prevalent in women with ADHD.

The mastery of these practical skills, from managing finances with strategic systems to communicating with greater clarity, is a powerful antidote to this profound emotional burden. The mastery of these practical skills is the ultimate validation of a truly balanced and integrated life with ADHD.

The Empowerment of Community and Self-Acceptance

Healing from a lifetime of shame and self-blame requires a fundamental shift in a woman's relationship with her neurodiversity. It is a journey of moving from a place of self-loathing to a place of self-compassion and genuine self-acceptance. A woman can begin to cultivate a more compassionate and accepting relationship with her neurodiversity by actively challenging the negative narrative she has internalized.

She can reframe her struggles from "What's wrong with me?" to "My brain works differently, and what can I do to support it?" This compassionate stance is a powerful first step in dismantling the shame that has been a constant companion.

Healing from the social cost of ADHD also requires a proactive approach to communication and connection. A woman can start by gently educating her loved ones about her ADHD, helping them understand that her behaviors are not a reflection of a lack of care but a result of a different brain wiring. By sharing resources and explaining the "why" behind her struggles, she can foster empathy and reduce the blame and misunderstanding that so often arise from these situations.

Furthermore, a woman must actively seek out and find communities that are validating and affirming, as isolation amplifies distress and a lack of a strong social network can be particularly damaging for women with ADHD.

A study on girls with ADHD found that those with hyperactive/impulsive symptoms were "socially rejected" by peers, while those with the quieter, inattentive subtype were "socially neglected," or simply left out of social groups altogether. These patterns, which are deeply painful for women who have a greater need for social acceptance than men, persist into adulthood, reinforcing feelings of loneliness and a sense of never "fitting in".

A robust social support network can serve as a vital buffer against stress and emotional turmoil, a coping mechanism that women are more likely to rely on than men. This practice of finding her community is an essential step towards healing from a lifetime of masking and building a foundation of genuine self-acceptance and belonging.

Integrating the Five Pillars: The Holistic Whole

The journey through this guide has been about building a life that is not just manageable but truly integrated and fulfilling. A woman is now empowered to leverage her strengths, mitigate her challenges, and create a harmonious system that is uniquely her own. A truly integrated success is not about achieving neurotypical perfection; it is about honoring your unique needs and building a life that accommodates your brain's natural rhythms.

A seamless, integrated life is a product of all five books working in synergy. The organizational systems you have built in Book 1 provide a stable and predictable base for the complex skills of focus and emotional mastery. A woman who has a system for taming her digital world is better equipped to manage the digital distractions that derail her focus (Book 2).

A woman who has reduced her daily stressors through functional organization has more mental and emotional bandwidth to manage the intense feelings and emotional dysregulation that are so prevalent in ADHD (Book 4), and she is less likely to feel overwhelmed by minor inconveniences that can trigger a disproportionate emotional storm.

The mastery of these practical skills, from managing finances with strategic systems to communicating with greater clarity, is the ultimate validation of a truly balanced and integrated life with ADHD.

This book provides a roadmap for navigating the complex challenges of money and relationships, demonstrating that a woman can move from a place of overwhelm to a place of integrated success. By confronting financial challenges with systems that work for her ADHD brain, strengthening her communication with loved ones, and actively building a community that validates her experience, a woman can build a truly resilient and fulfilling life. The mastery of these practical skills is the ultimate validation of a truly balanced and integrated life with ADHD.

Reflection Questions

- This part discusses the "ADHD tax" on finances and relationships. What is one practical system you can put in place to reduce the financial "tax" (e.g., using a single-purpose account, automating bill payments)?
- The book encourages gentle education about ADHD with loved ones. What is one thing about your ADHD brain that you can share with a partner or close friend to foster empathy and reduce misunderstanding?
- How can finding a validating and affirming community help you heal from the social toll of ADHD?

OVERALL CONCLUSION:

THE EMPOWERED WOMAN WITH ADHD

The journey through this five-book series has been an in-depth exploration of the multifaceted experience of ADHD in women. It has been a process of peeling back the layers of misconception and shame to reveal a path to empowerment and self-mastery. This guide has established that ADHD is not a deficit to be cured, but a unique operating system to be understood and strategically managed.

The analysis has provided a woman with a powerful toolkit for:

- **Self-Awareness:** A deep understanding of her brain's unique wiring, its rhythms, and its challenges, which is the foundation of all effective self-management.
- **Practical Strategies:** Concrete, evidence-based tools across all vital areas of life, designed to work with her ADHD brain, not against it.
- **Emotional Resilience:** The capacity to navigate intense feelings and cultivate an inner dialogue that supports her well-being.
- **System Building:** The ability to create external structures that compensate for internal challenges, freeing up mental energy for what truly matters.
- **Self-Compassion:** The crucial understanding that progress, not perfection, is the goal, and that kindness toward herself is the most powerful catalyst for sustainable change.

A woman is no longer merely coping with ADHD; she is actively crafting a life that is aligned with her unique strengths and values. The power lies in her newfound ability to recognize when she's struggling, refer back to her toolkit, re-engage with the strategies that work for her, and continuously review, adapt, and iterate her approach. She is now an Empowered Woman with ADHD, and she possesses the knowledge, skills, and mindset to navigate her world with greater clarity, purpose, and peace. She can embrace her neurodiversity, celebrate her unique gifts, and continue to build the extraordinary life she is capable of living.

PART 2: ADHD WORKBOOK FOR WOMEN 5-IN-1

How to Declutter, Beat Overwhelm, Sharpen Executive Function, Sync Hormones, Tame Emotions, and Strengthen Relationships

REVIEW ON

ADHD Workbook For Women 5-In-1: How To Declutter, Beat Overwhelm, Sharpen Executive Function, Sync Hormones, Tame Emotions, and Strengthen Relationships

By: Carolina Estevez, Psy.D., Licensed Psychologist

The *ADHD Workbook for Women 5-in-1: How to Declutter, Beat Overwhelm, Sharpen Executive Function, Sync Hormones, Tame Emotions, and Strengthen Relationships* is a well-researched, compassionate, and practical guide that addresses the unique neurological, emotional, and hormonal factors affecting women with Attention-Deficit/ Hyperactivity Disorder (ADHD). As a psychologist, I found this workbook to be an empowering blend of science, therapeutic strategies, and hands-on tools for daily life. The author bridges neuroscience, psychology, and behavioral interventions with accessible language and relatable case examples that capture the lived experience of women managing ADHD amid modern demands.

The chapters on *decluttering your space* and *beating overwhelm* stand out as especially impactful. Rather than promoting rigid organizational systems that often fail for neurodivergent minds, the workbook emphasizes "micro-steps"—breaking down large tasks into tiny, achievable actions that prevent paralysis and perfectionism. Practical techniques such as "doubling" (doing two small related tasks together) and the use of visual timers help transform initiation difficulty into momentum. The chapter also introduces ADHD-friendly storage systems that reduce visual clutter and decision fatigue, reinforcing that environment strongly influences emotional regulation. The focus on *reset routines* and the acceptance that clutter will reappear normalizes the ADHD experience and supports progress over perfection.

The section on *beating overwhelm* further explores how ADHD-related time blindness undermines productivity. The workbook introduces *time blocking* and the *Pomodoro technique* as accessible methods for restoring a sense of temporal structure. It also integrates evidence-based tools to strengthen working memory, such as externalizing reminders, planning routines, and reducing digital overload to minimize cognitive fatigue. These strategies align well with cognitive-behavioral therapy principles used in clinical practice.

The chapter on *sharpening executive function* offers a comprehensive toolkit for managing deadlines, sustaining focus, and improving task follow-through. It emphasizes realistic goal- setting, environmental design, and the use of external supports—such as checklists and accountability systems—to compensate for executive weaknesses.

Perhaps the most groundbreaking section is *syncing hormones to optimize treatment.* Few ADHD resources address the hormonal fluctuations that shape cognition, energy, and emotion in women. The book guides readers to track symptoms across the menstrual cycle, identify "high- risk" hormonal phases, and collaborate with healthcare providers on stimulant dose adjustments. The author also covers perimenopause and menopause, highlighting how sleep, nutrition, and lifestyle stabilization can buffer mood and cognitive disruptions.

Finally, the chapter on *taming emotions and strengthening relationships* integrates dialectical and cognitive-behavioral techniques such as sensory grounding, opposite action, and self- validation to manage shame, rejection sensitivity, and impulsivity. Relationship-focused exercises using mirroring, "I" statements, and emotional transparency empower women to communicate more effectively and foster connection.

Overall, this workbook is a comprehensive and affirming guide that blends neuroscience, self- compassion, and real-world behavioral tools. It is a valuable therapeutic companion for clinicians and a transformative resource for women seeking to understand and work with their ADHD rather than against it.

INTRODUCTION
WELCOME TO YOUR EMPOWERED BRAIN

The journey of an adult woman with Attention-Deficit / Hyperactivity Disorder (ADHD) is often an invisible battle, fought in silence against a world and a mind that seem perpetually misaligned. For too long, the narrative of ADHD has been dominated by an outdated, male-centric view, leading to profound misunderstanding and delayed diagnosis for countless women. This workbook is a direct response to that historical oversight, offering a comprehensive, evidence-based roadmap designed specifically to meet the unique neurobiological and psychological needs of the female ADHD brain.

Historically, ADHD research and diagnostic criteria have centered on the externalized, hyperactive symptoms more common in boys: physical restlessness, disruptive impulsivity, and constant movement. This narrow lens has failed to capture the nuanced and often internalized presentation typical of women, whose struggles frequently manifest as profound inattention, chronic disorganization, intense emotional dysregulation, and a pervasive, invisible sense of internal restlessness. This diagnostic disparity is stark: studies show the mean age of diagnosis for women can be years later than for men, leaving them to spend years, or even decades, struggling in secret before receiving the proper framework for their challenges.

The delay in diagnosis forces women into a debilitating cycle of self-blame and shame. Without a neurobiological explanation for their difficulties, they internalize their struggles, believing their chronic disorganization, poor time management, and emotional volatility are personal failings rather than symptoms of a condition. This conflict is amplified by powerful societal expectations for women to be the organized, emotionally stable, and nurturing caretakers of their homes and families. The relentless pressure to conform directly clashes with core ADHD symptoms, compelling many to engage in **masking**: the exhausting effort to develop sophisticated compensatory behaviors to appear "neurotypical" and competent to the outside world. This constant, invisible performance is an immense cognitive burden that fuels anxiety, depression, and a shattered sense of self-worth.

This workbook transforms this struggle from a personal failure into a strategic challenge. It is built on the understanding that your challenges are not a deficit of character, but a consequence of a distinct neurological operating system that demands a tailored approach. The strategies and tools presented in these five books are designed to address the six core pillars of the female ADHD experience: how to **Declutter**, **Beat Overwhelm**, **Sharpen Executive Function**, **Sync Hormones**, **Tame Emotions**, and **Strengthen Relationships**. By addressing these interwoven challenges holistically, we move beyond mere coping to achieving genuine self-mastery and integrated success.

The Neurobiological Reality: Why Your Brain Works Differently

To effectively manage ADHD, we must first understand its neurobiological roots. ADHD is fundamentally characterized by challenges in **executive functions (EFs)**, a family of mental processes essential for regulating behavior, planning, reasoning, and maintaining focus. These core deficits are not a reflection of intelligence; rather, they are rooted in variations in brain structure and, critically, **neurotransmitter activity**, particularly concerning **dopamine** and **norepinephrine**.

Dopamine, the brain's key chemical for motivation, reward, and attention, is thought to be dysregulated in the ADHD brain. This often leads to lower effective levels in the brain's synapses. This reduction makes tasks that are not inherently stimulating or immediately rewarding feel incredibly difficult to initiate and sustain. This explains why boring or repetitive tasks are met with immense resistance or paralysis, a state often confused with laziness but which is, in fact, a neurological hurdle.

This difference in brain wiring gives rise to several critical challenges that deplete mental energy and lead to the ubiquitous feeling of being perpetually "frenzied, frazzled, and overwhelmed" :

The Burden of High Cognitive Load

A key factor in the struggle is **cognitive load**, which refers to the total amount of mental effort consumed by working memory. For a neurotypical person, the brain efficiently filters out irrelevant stimuli and prioritizes information. For the ADHD brain, this filtering mechanism is often less efficient, causing it to take in and process a disproportionate amount of incoming information, both internal and external. A stray object on a desk, a pending notification, or a fleeting intrusive thought can all compete for attention with the same intensity as the main task at hand.

Research indicates that high cognitive load can have a disproportionately negative impact on performance for people with ADHD. This means that a cluttered physical or digital space isn't just an inconvenience; it is a direct contributor to reduced cognitive function, as each piece of clutter represents a subtle, but persistent, demand on a brain already struggling to filter and prioritize. This immense, continuous mental effort is the measurable **ADHD Tax** on your energy, draining your executive function reserves and leading to chronic fatigue and burnout.

The Task Activation Deficit and Time Blindness

Two of the most frustrating executive function deficits are the difficulty in starting tasks and the struggle with time perception:

1. **Task Activation Deficit (ADHD Paralysis):** You may know exactly what needs to be done, but the gap between intention and action feels immense, like an uncrossable chasm. This paralysis is a neurological hurdle rooted in the brain's reward and motivation system. The sheer scope of a large, daunting project is perceived as too complex, triggering a cognitive shutdown rather than initiation. The solution, explored in **Book 1**, is not willpower, but creating external scaffolding by breaking tasks into their smallest component parts to reduce the activation energy required.
2. **Time Blindness:** This is the inability to accurately perceive or estimate the flow of time. Time blindness makes setting realistic schedules, remembering deadlines, and transitioning between activities exceptionally challenging. Because the future often feels less "real" than the present, the ADHD brain struggles to prioritize based on future deadlines, leading to chronic lateness and poor planning. **Book 3** focuses entirely on making abstract time concrete and visible to counteract this core deficit.

The Female Experience: Masking, Shame, and Hormonal Fluctuations

The neurobiological realities of ADHD are compounded for women by two critical factors: the pressure to conform and the dramatic influence of ovarian hormones.

The Emotional Cost of Masking and Internalization

A significant component of the female ADHD experience is the internalization of symptoms, leading to a profound sense of shame and inadequacy. While men are more likely to externalize frustration, women often turn the struggle inward, interpreting their functional difficulties, like a messy home or an impulsive outburst, as moral failings. This internalized struggle is the source of the persistent inner critic that erodes self-worth and contributes to high rates of co-occurring mental health challenges like anxiety and depression.

This internal pressure often manifests as **emotional dysregulation**, a core, significant, and often misunderstood aspect of ADHD. Emotional dysregulation is the difficulty in controlling and appropriately expressing emotions, leading to feelings that are **all-or-nothing**, where a small trigger can flip feelings from calm to an overwhelming "red" reaction without warning. This is rooted in a disconnect between the brain's emotional accelerator (the amygdala, which can be overactive) and the emotional brakes (the frontal cortex, which can be underactive), making it difficult to modulate the intensity and duration of feelings.

Rejection Sensitive Dysphoria (RSD): A Heightened Pain

A particularly debilitating manifestation of emotional dysregulation is **Rejection Sensitive Dysphoria (RSD)**, a term describing the extreme emotional pain and anxiety triggered by the perception of criticism or rejection. For women who have endured a lifetime of "chronic negative feedback" and shame, a perceived snub can unleash an immediate, overwhelming emotional pain that feels physically agonizing. This hypersensitivity often drives women to people-pleasing or perfectionism as a defense mechanism, a strategy that is ultimately exhausting and unsustainable. **Book 5** provides the tools to manage this extreme reactivity, offering strategies to create a crucial pause between emotional stimulus and intentional response.

The Critical Interplay of Hormones and Cognition

Perhaps the most overlooked factor in the female ADHD journey is the profound, dynamic influence of hormones. ADHD is not a static condition; its symptom severity changes across a woman's lifespan in concert with her hormonal cycle, a link that is often dismissed by practitioners who have not been trained on this gender-specific reality.

1. **The Neurochemical Link:** Research shows that **estrogen**, a primary female sex hormone, plays a crucial role in regulating neurotransmitters like dopamine. Because dopamine is already dysregulated in the ADHD brain, fluctuations in estrogen can significantly impact symptom severity. When estrogen levels are lower or unstable, the existing dopaminergic pathway dysregulation may intensify, leading to worsening core ADHD challenges.

2. **The Menstrual Cycle Impact:** This connection explains why many women anecdotally report that their attention, organization, and emotional volatility worsen during the low-estrogen, high-progesterone **luteal phase**—the period leading up to menstruation. During this phase, studies suggest that inattention and executive function deficits can become more pronounced. This shift can even make standard ADHD medication feel less effective.
3. **The Midlife Challenge ("ADHD Squared"):** For women entering perimenopause and menopause, the decline in both estrogen and progesterone can "unmask" a previously subtle ADHD presentation or significantly worsen diagnosed symptoms. Some experts refer to this as an "**ADHD squared**" effect—the compounding of low estrogen and low dopamine, leading to severe brain fog, increased anxiety, and unmanageable difficulties with memory and focus.

Book 4 provides the essential roadmap for tracking this hormonal roadmap, empowering you to advocate for a personalized, integrated treatment plan that addresses your unique neurobiological needs.

Blueprint for Empowerment: The 5-in-1 Book Solution

This workbook is a structured journey designed to move you from a state of chronic overwhelm and self-blame to one of strategic self-mastery. We will tackle the core challenges of living with ADHD in women by providing an evidence-based toolkit across five interconnected books, each building upon the foundational skills of the last.

Book 1: Declutter Your Space and Defeat Task Paralysis for the ADHD Woman

The first step toward beating overwhelm is establishing external order to reduce internal chaos. This book addresses organization not as a matter of moral superiority, but as a form of self-care designed to reduce cognitive load.

The primary barrier to an organized life is not laziness, but the neurological hurdle of **task paralysis** and the cognitive cost of

disorganization. When a task is perceived as too complex, the brain shuts down. This book provides the foundational blueprint for creating "functional organization," focusing on simple, repeatable systems that work with the ADHD brain's unique wiring:

- **Conquer Paralysis:** Systematically breaking down overwhelming tasks into **micro-steps** (e.g., separating "cleaning the entire living room" into steps like "collect dishes from the living room and place them in the kitchen sink").
- **Design Your Sanctuary:** Combating the "out of sight, out of mind" phenomenon by utilizing **visible storage** (e.g., containers without lids) and designating a predictable "home" for every item to eliminate decision fatigue.
- **Sustain Momentum:** Leveraging **Body Doubling**—performing a task in the presence of another person (in-person or virtually)—to initiate and sustain focus, which acts as an external executive function.

Book 2: Beat Overwhelm for the ADHD Woman

After establishing external order, **Book 2** provides the core strategies for managing your inner landscape, your focus, attention, and mental energy, to beat the pervasive feeling of being overwhelmed and frazzled. This involves moving past the myth of multitasking and embracing intentional, single-task focus.

This book trains your brain to regulate attention and utilize its energy efficiently:

- **Visualize Time:** Directly attacking **time blindness** by making abstract time concrete and visible through structured scheduling.
- **Schedule Success:** Shifting from ineffective, vague to-do lists to **Time Blocking**, which forces you to allocate specific, finite time durations for tasks, thereby reducing the cognitive guesswork involved in initiation and planning.
- **Customize Your Focus:** Implementing the **Pomodoro Technique** (short, focused work intervals followed by mandated breaks) to boost concentration, prevent burnout and hyperfocus, and provide the necessary novelty for the ADHD brain to remain engaged.

Book 3: Sharpen Executive Function in Women with ADHD

Building upon the foundations of organizational structure and intentional time management, **Book 3** focuses on advanced techniques to sustain focus and build the internal resilience necessary for long-term productivity. This work is fundamentally about protecting your mental energy and optimizing your cognitive resources.

The key strategies involve creating both an internal and external "attention zone":

- **Future-Proof Your Brain:** Strengthening crucial executive function skills, including inhibitory control and working memory, through structured activities and consistent routines.
- **Protect Your Energy:** Recognizing that sustained focus is a product of managing your energy, not just your time, by prioritizing sleep hygiene, nutrition (e.g., Omega-3s), and physical activity to regulate dopamine and mitigate the effects of chronic **mental fatigue**.
- **Embrace Single-Tasking:** Debunking the myth of multitasking, which is simply inefficient **task-switching** that drains the ADHD brain. You will learn to prioritize **deep work** by batching similar tasks and creating "pre-flight checklists" to smoothly transition into sustained focus.

Book 4: Sync Hormones and Optimize Treatment for the ADHD Woman

This is the gender-specific core of the workbook, providing the scientific context and practical tools to navigate the dynamic relationship between hormones and ADHD symptoms. Recognizing this link is crucial for achieving stable mental and emotional health.

This book empowers you to become a self-advocate for tailored medical care:

- **Map Your Cycle:** Learning to track your menstrual cycle and emotional / cognitive symptoms to pinpoint when the low-estrogen phases (such as the luteal phase) are likely to intensify symptoms like inattention, anxiety, and emotional volatility.

- **Advocate for Adjustment:** Gaining the knowledge to discuss **cycle dosing** of stimulant medication with your doctor, as research suggests the efficacy of treatment can fluctuate with hormonal status.
- **Manage the Transition:** Understanding the "ADHD squared" effect during **perimenopause and menopause**, where declining estrogen compounds ADHD symptoms, and exploring integrated treatment options like Hormone Replacement Therapy (HRT) combined with stimulants to support memory and focus.

Book 5: Tame Emotions and Strengthen Relationships in Women with ADHD

The emotional rollercoaster of ADHD, coupled with its profound impact on communication, requires a robust toolkit for self-regulation and interpersonal effectiveness. This book equips you with therapeutic skills to build emotional resilience and foster meaningful connection.

Drawing heavily on evidence-based approaches like Dialectical Behavior Therapy (DBT), this book teaches you how to manage intense emotional surges and communicate effectively:

- **Ground Yourself and Change the Script:** Implementing **Distress Tolerance** skills like sensory grounding (TIPP skills) to interrupt acute emotional distress and applying **Opposite Action** (doing the opposite of the emotional urge) to change the emotional trajectory.
- **Challenge the Critic:** Utilizing **Cognitive Behavioral Therapy (CBT)** tools to identify and challenge unhelpful thought patterns (cognitive distortions), such as catastrophizing or mind reading, which fuel shame and RSD.
- **Strengthen Relationships:** Mastering **Interpersonal Effectiveness** skills to reduce relational friction, including **Active Listening** (mirroring and validation) and using **"I" Statements** to express needs without blaming, thereby moving from a "parent-child" dynamic to a collaborative partnership.

Your Roadmap to Self-Mastery and Integrated Success

The journey you are about to begin is one of empowerment. It is built on the unwavering belief that your struggles are not a reflection of a personal deficit but a signal that your unique brain requires a strategic, tailored approach. This workbook provides the necessary framework to move you from a lifetime of self-blame, masking, and chaos to a life defined by intentional action and self-acceptance.

The path to integrated success is not about achieving neurotypical perfection; it is about honoring your unique needs, building a life that accommodates your brain's natural rhythms, and celebrating progress over flawlessness. The skills you cultivate here, from external organization and focused attention to hormonal awareness and emotional resilience, will work in synergy, creating a stable foundation that allows your considerable strengths and creativity to flourish.

You are no longer merely coping with ADHD; you are actively crafting a life that is aligned with your values. By embracing this holistic roadmap, you gain the knowledge, the skills, and the compassionate mindset to build the extraordinary life you are capable of living. The time for shame is over. The moment for self-mastery is now.

BOOK ONE

DECLUTTER YOUR SPACE AND BEAT OVERWHELM FOR THE ADHD WOMAN

INTRODUCTION

THE COGNITIVE COST OF DISORGANIZATION

For the adult woman with Attention-Deficit / Hyperactivity Disorder (ADHD), organization is not merely a matter of tidiness or a reflection of personal effort; it is a profound, daily struggle that consumes mental energy and fuels a persistent, debilitating sense of overwhelm. The chronic difficulty in maintaining order, whether in physical spaces like a home or digital environments like an inbox, is a direct, measurable symptom of the disorder, stemming from inherent challenges with **executive functions (EFs)**, such as planning, sustained attention, and working memory.

This constant friction between the desire for order and the neurobiological reality of disorganization carries a devastating cognitive and emotional cost that permeates every facet of a woman's life. Valuable time is perpetually lost in frantic searches for misplaced items, crucial opportunities are missed due to forgotten deadlines or buried paperwork, and the physical and mental clutter creates a pervasive **hum of anxiety** that depletes mental reserves. This struggle is often amplified by powerful societal expectations for women to be the organized, emotionally stable caretakers of their homes, leading to a deep, debilitating sense of shame and feelings of inadequacy.

This book approaches organization not as a rigid, perfectionistic ideal, but as a form of neurobiological **self-care**. The goal is to establish **"functional organization,"** a system designed intentionally to reduce cognitive load, minimize daily friction, and work **for** the unique wiring of the ADHD brain, rather than forcing the brain to operate against its natural impulses. By creating external structure, we can compensate for internal inconsistencies and free up the mental bandwidth necessary to master the more complex challenges of focus, emotions, and relationships.

The Neurobiological Reality: Why Your Brain Struggles with Order

The internal engine of the ADHD brain operates on a different, often more demanding, set of rules than its neurotypical counterpart, making traditional organizational advice ineffective or even counterproductive. The challenges you face are not a failure of character; they are a consequence of specific differences in how your brain processes and prioritizes information.

1. Executive Function Deficits: The Organizational Brain

Core executive functions, a family of mental processes essential for regulating behavior, planning, and maintaining focus, are significantly challenged in the ADHD population. These deficits are the root cause of chronic disorganization:

- **Working Memory as a Sieve:** Working memory, often described as the brain's temporary mental scratchpad, can feel unreliable for a woman with ADHD, making it nearly impossible to hold a multi-step organizational plan in mind or to reliably recall where an item was placed moments ago. This profound challenge is the clinical basis for the ubiquitous **"out of sight, out of mind"** phenomenon. If an item is put away in an opaque container or a cluttered drawer, it ceases to exist for the ADHD brain, necessitating systems that are deliberately visual to act as consistent, reliable external cues.
- **Reduced Prefrontal Cortex Activity:** Research indicates that the parts of the brain responsible for executive functions,

particularly the **prefrontal cortex** (the brain's "command center" for planning, working memory, and impulse control), tend to be less developed or less active in people with ADHD. This reduced activity makes it challenging to remember task goals, instructions, or rules, contributing to what is often described as "brain fog", a temporary sluggishness and slowdown of thinking abilities that compounds the difficulty of organizing complex environments.

2. The High Cognitive Cost of Clutter

A crucial factor in understanding why disorganization feels so debilitating is the concept of **cognitive load**, which refers to the total amount of mental effort consumed by working memory.

The neurotypical brain is designed to efficiently filter out irrelevant stimuli and prioritize information. For the ADHD brain, this filtering mechanism is often less efficient, causing it to take in and process a disproportionate amount of incoming information, both internal and external. A single stray object on a desk, an unread email notification, or an incomplete task all compete for attention with the same intensity as the main task at hand.

- **Visual Noise as Mental Drain:** This constant processing of non-essential stimuli creates a state of chronic, high cognitive load. A cluttered physical or digital space isn't just an inconvenience; it is a direct contributor to reduced cognitive function, as each piece of clutter represents a subtle, but persistent, demand on a brain already struggling to filter and prioritize. The constant effort required to fight against this neurobiological reality is a significant "ADHD Tax" on your mental energy, leading to the chronic fatigue and burnout that underpins the feeling of being perpetually "frenzied, frazzled, and overwhelmed."

3. Task Activation Deficit: The Root of Paralysis

The path to organizing is often obstructed by a profound neurological hurdle known as **task paralysis** or the "can't get started" syndrome. This paralyzing procrastination is not a moral failing or a deficit of willpower; it is a direct result of how the brain's motivation system operates.

- **Overwhelm Triggers Shutdown:** Task paralysis occurs when a project is perceived as too complex, involves too many steps, or when the task is repetitive and understimulating. The sheer scope of organizing a messy room or cleaning a cluttered inbox can trigger a feeling of overwhelm that makes task initiation nearly impossible. The brain's executive functions struggle to find a clear entry point, triggering an immediate shutdown response instead of action.
- **Dopamine and Novelty:** This deficit is tied to the dysregulation of **dopamine**, the brain's key chemical for motivation and reward. The ADHD brain craves novelty and immediate stimulation. Mundane, multi-step tasks like organizing or filing do not provide the necessary immediate reward, making them intensely difficult to initiate and sustain, which necessitates external structures to provide momentum.

The Emotional and Relational Toll of External Chaos

The organizational struggles driven by these neurobiological factors take a severe emotional and relational toll, particularly for women who face intense societal pressure to maintain a perfect home and life.

1. Shame, Self-Blame, and the Inner Critic

The emotional cost of chronic disorganization is profound and personal. Living with constant, visible messiness and the energy drain required to manage its consequences leads to low self-esteem, self-blame, and pervasive feelings of inadequacy.

- **Internalizing Failure:** Without a neurobiological explanation for their struggles, many women internalize their functional difficulties, believing their chaotic environment is evidence of a personal flaw or moral failure. This leads to a powerful **inner critic** that reinforces a narrative of shame: "I should be able to keep this house clean," or "I must be lazy if I can't even pay the bills on time." This pattern is exacerbated by the fact that women are more likely to internalize their struggles than men, contributing to high rates of co-occurring anxiety and depression.

- **The Shame of the Home:** Societal expectations for women to be the organized, nurturing caretaker often clash violently with ADHD symptoms. When a woman struggles to maintain an organized home, this failure feels like a violation of traditional feminine norms, leading to immense social anxiety and shame, often manifesting as avoidance, such as refusing to have people over due to the mess.

2. Relationship Friction and the "Mental Load"

The organizational struggles of ADHD are a frequent and profound source of friction in close relationships, often mediated by deficits in executive functions and emotional regulation.

- **The Parent-Child Dynamic:** When an organized, neurotypical partner is forced to constantly remind the ADHD partner about household tasks, a difficult and unhealthy **"parent-child" dynamic** can emerge. The ADHD partner feels scolded and shamed for their inability to initiate tasks, while the non-ADHD partner feels exhausted and unheard, leading to significant resentment and a breakdown in core partnership values.
- **Impaired Communication:** The same EF deficits that cause disorganization also affect communication. Poor working memory and impulsivity can lead to difficulty with active listening, frequent interruptions, and challenges in following through on relationship commitments, further eroding trust and intimacy.

The Strategic Shift: Building External Scaffolding

This book is dedicated to providing the cognitive scaffolding required to stabilize your external environment, reducing the debilitating effects of chaos and overwhelm. The solution is to strategically design systems that bypass the weaknesses of the ADHD brain by leveraging external structure and accountability.

The functional approach presented here relies on three core principles that will be developed in the following chapters:

1. **Externalizing the Brain:** You cannot rely on inconsistent internal memory. Instead, you must intentionally use physical and digital systems (planners, visual cues) to reliably hold information, deadlines, and the designated locations for every item, thereby offloading your working memory. This practice transforms organization from an exercise in mental effort to a reliable system of external recall.
2. **Minimizing Activation Energy:** To defeat task paralysis, every overwhelming project must be broken down into its smallest, most actionable micro-steps. This strategic reduction in complexity lowers the activation energy required to begin, transforming daunting goals into achievable, low-friction entry points that leverage the brain's need for novelty and immediate reward.
3. **Harnessing External Structure:** Overcoming the initiation deficit requires proactive, external anchors. Strategies like **Body Doubling**, performing a task in the presence of another person (in-person or virtually), provide gentle encouragement and non-judgmental accountability, acting as a temporary external executive function that anchors attention and sustains momentum. Furthermore, establishing visible, designated "homes" for every item (e.g., containers without lids, clearly labeled areas) creates a system of predictability that reduces decision fatigue and reinforces good habits.

The work of creating functional organization is the crucial first step toward building a truly resilient and fulfilling life. By mastering these foundational systems, you move past self-blame and equip yourself with the mental bandwidth necessary to succeed in the areas of focus, emotional regulation, and deep connection explored in the rest of this workbook.

CHAPTER 1

CONQUER PARALYSIS: BREAK DOWN OVERWHELMING TASKS INTO MICRO-STEPS

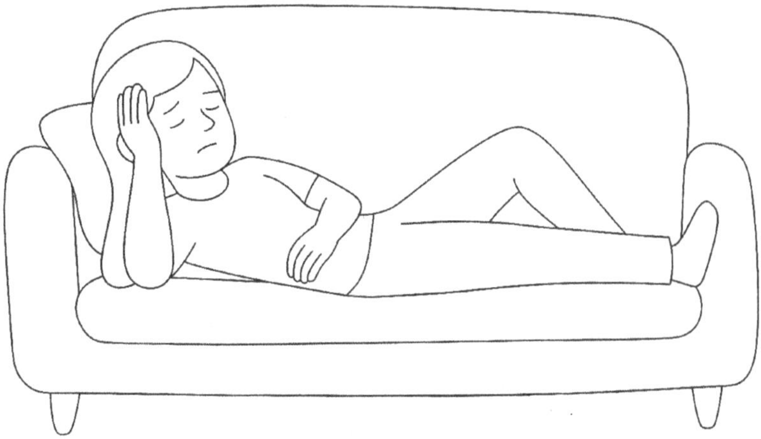

The overwhelming, chronic feeling of being "frenzied, frazzled, and overwhelmed" that many women with ADHD report is often rooted in one profound neurological hurdle: **task paralysis**. This state, often mislabeled as laziness or avoidance, is the invisible wall between intention and action, preventing you from starting or continuing projects that are crucial for creating order and stability in your life.

For the ADHD brain, organizing or initiating a demanding task is rarely about willpower. It is a neurological challenge rooted in the brain's unique wiring and its reward system. The sheer, undifferentiated scope of a large project, such as "Clean the entire house" or "Organize the finances", can trigger a cognitive shutdown, leaving you stuck in a state of avoidance and procrastination.

This chapter provides the strategic blueprint to dismantle this paralysis, transforming amorphous, daunting goals into a series of low-friction, achievable **micro-steps**. This approach fundamentally bypasses the initiation deficit, leveraging the power of momentum to move you from analysis and avoidance to consistent action.

The Neurobiology of the Paralysis Trap

To conquer task paralysis, you must first understand why your brain defaults to a frozen state when faced with a large project. This is not a character flaw, but a measurable neurobiological response tied to **Executive Function (EF) deficits** and the brain's internal reward system.

1. **Overload and Filtering Failure:** The ADHD brain struggles with filtering out irrelevant information and distractions. When faced with a cluttered room, every item, color, shape, and pending decision, *Where does this go? Do I need this? What if I toss it?*, competes for attention. The resulting sensory and visual overload exceeds the brain's capacity to process and prioritize, leading directly to a cognitive shutdown or mental paralysis.
2. **The Activation Deficit:** Task initiation, the ability to simply start a task, requires a burst of "activation energy" fueled by the neurotransmitter **dopamine**. When a project is new, complex, involves multiple steps, or is boring and repetitive, the brain struggles to produce enough dopamine to find the task stimulating or rewarding. This is why the gap between knowing *what* to do and actually *doing* it feels immense, forcing the person into procrastination and avoidance.

The solution to both overload and the activation deficit is the systematic reduction of complexity. By breaking down the daunting task, you dramatically lower the cognitive load and create clear, immediate entry points that are psychologically approachable.

Strategy: Deconstruct the Dragon into Micro-Steps

The most effective strategy to defeat paralysis is to relentlessly break down the overwhelming task into its smallest, most elemental component parts. A successful step is one that requires minimal thought, minimal movement, and generates an immediate, satisfying sense of completion.

The goal is to create steps that are so small they feel almost ridiculous to avoid. This process is structured in three phases:

Phase 1: The Brain Dump and Inventory

Before you can organize a task, you must first externalize all the thoughts, steps, and worries associated with it. This removes the mental clutter that consumes working memory and contributes to overload.

- **List Everything:** For a daunting project (e.g., "Organize the spare room"), write down every single step, thought, item, and worry related to it. Include abstract steps like "Figure out where to put the donation box" or "Call the donation center."
- **Identify Friction Points:** Review your list and circle every item that feels complex, vague, or emotionally charged. These are your "friction points" that are most likely to trigger paralysis.

Phase 2: Identify the "Next Action" (The Smallest Viable Step)

Once the friction points are identified, the objective is to simplify them into a **Next Action**, the specific, physical action that requires the least amount of energy to execute.

Overwhelming Task (Vague)	Dismantled Micro-Steps (Actionable)	Why it Works
Organize the entire living room	**Task #1: Collect dishes** from the living room and place them in the kitchen sink.	Specific and immediate. Bypasses the need to sort or find a "home."
Clean out the desk drawers	**Task #2: Empty all trash** from the desk area into a wastebasket.	Low-friction action. Provides instant visible progress.
Sort through paperwork pile	**Task #3: Find the utility bill** that needs to be paid and place it on the landing strip.	Focuses only on *one type* of item, not the entire pile.

Get started on laundry	**Task #4: Put all dirty clothes** from the bedroom floor into the hamper.	Simple physical movement. Doesn't require sorting or starting the washing machine yet.
Clear the kitchen counter	**Task #5: Wipe down one square foot** of counter space with a cleaning spray.	Time-bound and small enough to feel non-threatening.

Phase 3: Create Immediate Accountability (Toss, Donate, Keep)

When organizing items physically, the sorting process itself can induce paralysis, as the brain struggles to decide the fate of each object. A structured, predetermined set of categories eliminates decision fatigue during the active organizing phase.

1. **Designate Three Categories:** Label three distinct boxes or areas immediately: **Toss** (for true garbage), **Donate** (for items to be given away), and **Keep** (for items to be put back in a designated home).
2. **Schedule the Follow-Up:** Organizing only creates temporary clutter if the disposal steps are not completed. When a **Donate** box is full, immediately schedule the action into your calendar: "Drop off donation box at Goodwill at 2 PM Saturday". By making an appointment for that action, you maintain momentum and prevent the discarded items from becoming new, permanent clutter.
3. **The "Junk Drawer" Allowance:** To maintain a sustainable system, embrace functional organization over perfection. Designate at least one "junk drawer" in every room for temporary storage of items that do not yet have a determined home. Attempting to achieve impossible perfection often leads to immediate abandonment of the system; embracing this small allowance allows the overall system to remain sustainable.

The Dopamine Hit: Leveraging Momentum to Defeat Avoidance

The success of the micro-step strategy is rooted in the neurobiology of motivation. The ADHD brain is constantly seeking immediate feedback and reward.

By committing to, and completing, a simple micro-step, you achieve a rapid, tangible "win." This completion provides a small, satisfying burst of **dopamine** that reinforces productive behavior and makes the next step feel slightly easier to initiate. The feeling of accomplishment, even from putting a single dish in the sink, builds **momentum**, which is the most powerful antidote to task paralysis. Momentum means you rely less on inconsistent willpower and more on the positive feedback loop of immediate reward.

The mastery of this process, externalizing the cognitive load, deconstructing overwhelming tasks into their smallest actions, and utilizing the reward of momentum, is the essential first step toward reclaiming control over your environment and defeating the chronic feeling of overwhelm that defines unmanaged ADHD.

Chapter 1 Workbook: Conquer Paralysis: Break Down Overwhelming Tasks into Micro-Steps

Objective: To bypass **Task Paralysis** by reducing the **activation energy** of a single overwhelming project using the Micro-Step Strategy.

Activity 1.1: The Micro-Step Converter

1. **The Overwhelming Task:** Identify one organizing project you have been avoiding due to feeling overwhelmed (e.g., "Clean the entire closet," or "Organize the digital files").

   Task: ____

   ____

2. **Dismantle to Micro-Steps:** Break the task down into three physical actions that require **less than 2 minutes each** and **no decision-making** (minimal friction).

Action-Oriented Micro-Step	Why It Works (Low Friction)
Step 1: (Example: Find and place a trash bag next to the task zone.)	
Step 2: (Example: Clear the top three items from the surface and toss them in the bag.)	
Step 3: (Example: Set a 5-minute timer and press START.)	

Reflection 1.2: Activation Energy Audit

1. On a scale of 1 (Calm) to 10 (Paralyzed), rate your internal resistance **before** completing Step 1.

   Rating: ____

   ____

   ____

   ____

   ____

2. How did completing **Steps 1 and 2** (the physical actions) change your resistance level? (Focus on the immediate feeling of momentum).

   Change: ____

   ____

   ____

   ____

   ____

CHAPTER 2

DESIGN YOUR SANCTUARY: IMPLEMENT VISIBLE, ADHD-FRIENDLY STORAGE SYSTEMS

The immense, daily burden of overwhelm for a woman with ADHD is often amplified by the chaos of her environment. If Chapter 1 provided the blueprint for defeating the paralyzing inertia of clutter, this chapter offers the construction manual for building an external sanctuary, a physical and digital space intentionally designed to act as a **supportive ally** to the neurodiverse brain.

Traditional organizational advice often fails the ADHD population because it relies on two mental processes that are inherently compromised: robust **working memory** and seamless **executive planning**. When advice dictates that you "tuck everything away neatly," it sets you up for failure, as the moment an item is hidden, the ADHD brain registers it as permanently lost due to the "out of sight, out of mind" phenomenon.

This chapter champions **functional organization**: a strategic system built on principles of visual recall, predictable placement, and minimized decision-making. The goal is not a pristine home, but a reliably intuitive one that significantly reduces the daily friction and cognitive load that fuel internal anxiety and overwhelm. By externalizing your memory and creating visual cues, you transform your environment from a source of stress into a powerful co-regulator of your attention and emotional stability.

The Neurobiology of Visibility: Why Traditional Organization Fails

To build an effective system, we must first deeply understand the neurobiological deficits that make traditional, opaque organization, such as deep drawers, closed cabinets, or complex filing, counterproductive for the ADHD brain.

1. The Working Memory Deficit and Object Permanence

The most significant barrier to a tidy, functional home is the **working memory deficit** associated with ADHD. Working memory is the "mental scratchpad" that allows the brain to hold and manipulate information for a short period of time, such as remembering a complex instruction or where you placed your keys moments ago. For a woman with ADHD, this memory can feel inconsistent or unreliable.

This leads directly to the **"out of sight, out of mind"** experience: if an item is not in your immediate visual field, your brain essentially ceases to register its existence, location, or importance. While a neurotypical brain can easily retrieve the memory of an item's hidden location, the ADHD brain often struggles to initiate this retrieval process, particularly if the item is not needed immediately.

The implication is profound: forcing objects into opaque, hidden storage systems requires the ADHD brain to constantly expend energy fighting against its natural wiring. Every time you need an item, you must engage in a taxing cognitive search process, a task that consumes valuable mental bandwidth and contributes significantly to mental fatigue and burnout. The effective solution, therefore, is not to force the brain to remember, but to design the environment to *remember for the brain* through visual reinforcement.

2. The Cognitive Cost of Visual Noise and Clutter

While it may seem counterintuitive to advocate for more visible storage, the goal is not to create a chaotic mess but to manage **visual noise** strategically. Clutter is a direct contributor to high **cognitive load**, the amount of mental effort consumed by working memory, which is already a severe challenge for the ADHD brain.

A cluttered desk, a messy kitchen counter, or a chaotic digital desktop is not just an inconvenience; it represents a constellation of unfinished tasks, pending decisions, and unfiled items. Each of these competes for the attention of a brain that already struggles with an impaired **filtering mechanism**. The brain, unable to efficiently screen out irrelevant stimuli, processes every piece of visual input, a stray coffee cup, a pile of papers, a stack of books, as a subtle demand on its resources.

This constant, low-level mental effort is exhausting and generates a perpetual, low-grade hum of anxiety that significantly exacerbates ADHD symptoms. Studies have shown that cluttered environments can increase stress and anxiety, potentially raising stress hormones like cortisol, which can further impair executive functions like inhibitory control and emotional regulation. By strategically using clear, designated storage, we simplify the visual field. We replace the ambiguity of a messy surface with the predictable clarity of categorized storage, reducing the brain's processing burden and conserving executive function for more demanding tasks.

Section 1: The Design Strategy: Creating External Recall

The core principle of the ADHD-friendly sanctuary is to ensure that essential items remain visible and easily accessible. This strategy, known as **external recall**, compensates for compromised working memory by utilizing environmental design as an external reminder system.

1. Prioritize Visible Storage: Clear Containers and No Lids

To directly combat the "out of sight, out of mind" phenomenon, all organizational systems must favor transparency and accessibility.

- **Go Clear:** Use clear plastic or mesh containers and storage drawers wherever possible. Clear storage allows the eye to immediately register the contents, providing a constant visual cue of what is inside and eliminating the need for your working memory to recall the item's location. This is a simple yet powerful design shift that ensures items remain "in mind" even when stored.
- **Abolish the Lid:** For frequently used items or items prone to being lost (e.g., keys, mail, hats, snacks), use baskets, bins, or containers **without lids**. The friction of removing a lid, however small, can be enough to derail the moment of putting an item away, causing it to land on a nearby surface instead. Eliminating this tiny point of friction promotes the swift and easy return of the item to its designated "home," reinforcing the desired organizational habit. The basket serves as a **catch-all zone** that contains the mess without hiding the contents entirely.
- **Embrace the Tray:** Use small trays, dishes, or decorative plates on surfaces like nightstands, coffee tables, or desks. These function as miniature, contained landing zones for items that must remain visible (e.g., remote controls, reading glasses, medications). The tray visually signals that the items belong there while preventing them from spreading and creating generalized visual clutter.

2. Labeling for Specificity and Clarity

While clear storage is essential, it is often not enough. For items stored in opaque containers, or even clear containers with many similar items, clear, bold labeling is crucial. This serves two primary functions:

- **Externalizing Categorization:** The ADHD brain struggles with fluid categorization and can easily forget the specific contents or purpose of a bin once it is sealed or moved. A label, particularly one that is color-coded or uses pictures (for visual thinkers), serves as a constant, non-negotiable external reminder of the container's contents and purpose. The label prevents the mental effort of guessing or having to search through multiple drawers, thus saving precious executive function resources.

- **Promoting Consistency:** Labels reinforce the designated "home" of an item, making the act of putting things away automatic and low-friction. The label instantly communicates where an item should be returned, reducing the likelihood of it being placed on a random surface due to momentary decision fatigue. Labels should be simple and action-oriented (e.g., "Meds - AM / PM," "Office Receipts," "Car Keys / Wallet").

3. Vertical Organization vs. Piles

The ADHD brain is highly susceptible to the cognitive stress induced by piles. Piles are visually overwhelming, mentally ambiguous (is this a to-do pile or a finished pile?), and physically difficult to maintain. The solution is to move organization from a horizontal plane (piles) to a vertical one (display and file).

- **Vertical Filing:** For papers, rather than letting them accumulate in flat stacks that create visual noise, use vertical file folders, magazine holders, or wall-mounted clipboards. Displaying papers vertically keeps important documents visually accessible without creating a sense of chaotic mess. A paper on a clipboard is a visual cue for a "to-do," whereas a pile on a desk is a visual cue for "overwhelm."
- **Wall-Mounted Systems:** Utilize vertical wall space for external memory systems. Pegboards, hook racks, or command centers can keep frequently lost items (keys, headphones, backpacks) off flat surfaces and in a predictable, designated location. This leverages the principle that the ADHD brain benefits from the visual prominence of objects in its line of sight.

Section 2: Eliminating Decision Fatigue: The Power of a Designated "Home"

Once the environment is visually optimized, the next strategic step is eliminating the constant micro-decisions that plague the ADHD brain. **Decision fatigue** occurs when the sheer volume of choices, even mundane ones like *where should this pen go?*, drains mental energy, making the brain prone to poor judgment and eventual shutdown. The solution is the principle of the designated "home."

1. Give Every Item a "Home"

The foundational rule of functional organization is to commit to a specific, easily accessible "home" for every single item you own.

- **The Intentional Spot:** When organizing, you must proactively decide *where* each item belongs, and that location must be intuitive and easy to access. Putting the item away must be the simplest and lowest-friction choice available. If putting the item away is harder than leaving it out, the system will fail.
- **Anchor Points for Critical Items:** For items that are constantly lost, such as keys, wallets, phones, glasses, or medication, the **Landing Strip** is a crucial compensatory strategy. A landing strip is a small, designated zone (e.g., a dish, a tray, or a specific hook) near the entrance of your home where these items *must* be placed immediately upon entry. This intentional habit eliminates the frantic, time-consuming searches that typically accompany poor working memory and provides a vital feeling of predictability and control.

2. The Strategic Allowance: Embracing the "Junk Drawer"

The pursuit of absolute perfection is a common cause of system abandonment for the ADHD brain. Attempting to achieve impossible tidiness often leads to system failure and renewed overwhelm. To maintain sustainability, the organizational strategy must include an intentional allowance for functional imperfection.

- **The Role of the Catch-All:** The **Junk Drawer** is not a failure of organization; it is a strategically designated, contained zone of functional clutter. Designate at least one easy-to-access "junk drawer" or "miscellaneous basket" in high-traffic rooms (e.g., kitchen, office) for temporary storage of items that do not yet have a determined home, or items that are truly miscellaneous (e.g., loose batteries, rubber bands, spare change).
- **Preventing the Spillover:** The junk drawer acts as a controlled pressure release valve. It prevents small, ambiguous items from spreading onto countertops and tables, where they would otherwise create general visual clutter and increase cognitive load. It recognizes the reality that not every item can be perfectly categorized immediately, allowing the overall system

to remain sustainable by channeling the chaos into a single, predictable location.

Section 3: The Sanctuary Mindset: Emotional and Cognitive Benefits

The work of designing an ADHD-friendly sanctuary yields measurable, profound benefits that go far beyond a cleaner look. These changes actively regulate the nervous system and protect valuable mental resources.

1. Reducing Anxiety and Shame

Clutter is frequently a direct source of anxiety and shame for women with ADHD. The chronic feeling that one "should" be more organized but cannot achieve it creates a relentless cycle of self-criticism and inadequacy.

- **Dismantling the Inner Critic:** Functional organization acts as a powerful antidote to the harsh inner critic. When a woman can reliably find her essential items and her space is visually calm, the evidence of her "failure" is reduced. This shift helps dismantle the toxic narrative that she is "lazy" or "incompetent," replacing it with the reality that her brain simply requires a unique, supportive system.
- **Fostering Self-Compassion:** By intentionally designing a space that accommodates her neurobiology, a woman is engaging in a powerful act of **self-compassion**: treating herself with the understanding and support she would offer a close friend facing the same challenge. This reduces the emotional isolation and self-blame that are so prevalent in the female ADHD experience.

2. Conserving Executive Function and Mental Energy

Every element of the designed sanctuary, the clear bins, the labels, the landing strips, is a tool for **conserving executive function (EF) reserves**. EF is a finite resource, and when it is depleted by fighting clutter or constantly searching for items, a woman has less capacity for high-leverage tasks like deep work, emotional regulation, and planning.

- **Frictionless Living:** The goal is to move from a state of **high friction** (where every action requires significant mental effort) to **frictionless living** (where putting things away is the easiest choice). Eliminating decision fatigue and relying on visual recall allows the woman's working memory and planning centers to operate on a simpler, more efficient level.

- **Creating Predictability:** Predictability reduces the need for the ADHD brain to constantly engage in effortful monitoring and filtering. When items are in their designated homes, the environment becomes a source of stability, not surprise. This stability frees up immense cognitive bandwidth, reducing the overall cognitive load and the persistent mental fatigue that defines chronic overwhelm.

Conclusion: Your External Brain

The organizational struggle is a profound, lifelong challenge rooted in neurobiological differences. The work of designing your sanctuary is not about achieving perfection; it is about establishing a foundational system of functional organization that consistently supports your brain's unique wiring.

The mastery of this external scaffolding, from prioritizing visible storage to strategically utilizing the junk drawer, transforms your environment from a demanding adversary into a supportive "external brain." This system of visual recall and reduced decision-making is the prerequisite for the deeper work of focus, emotional mastery, and relational stability. By reducing the visual noise and cognitive burden of your space, you free up the mental energy necessary to transition from simply surviving to proactively thriving.

Chapter 2 Workbook: Design Your Sanctuary: Implement Visible, ADHD-Friendly Storage Systems

Objective: To compensate for poor **working memory** by creating a supportive, visually accessible environment that defeats the **"out of sight, out of mind"** phenomenon.

Activity 2.1: The Visible Recall Conversion

1. **Opaque Overload Zone:** Identify one area using hidden, opaque, or lidded storage where items consistently get lost (e.g., "Bathroom cabinet," or "Toolbox").
2. **Plan the Conversion:** Detail how you will convert this area to a visual system.

Item Type	Current Storage (Hidden)	ADHD-Friendly Conversion (Visible)
(Example: Vitamins)	Tucked away in a lidded bottle in a dark cabinet.	Moved to a **clear container** without a lid on a countertop.
(Example: Mail / Paper)	Piled on the kitchen counter.	Stored **vertically** in a clear wall-mounted file folder.
(Your Item):		

Action Check 2.2: Labeling for Clarity

Commit to creating bold, simple labels for three items in your identified zone. Labels should be functional, not decorative.

Label 1: ____

Label 2: ____

Label 3: ____

CHAPTER 3

ESTABLISH PREDICTABILITY: GIVE EVERY ITEM A DESIGNATED "HOME"

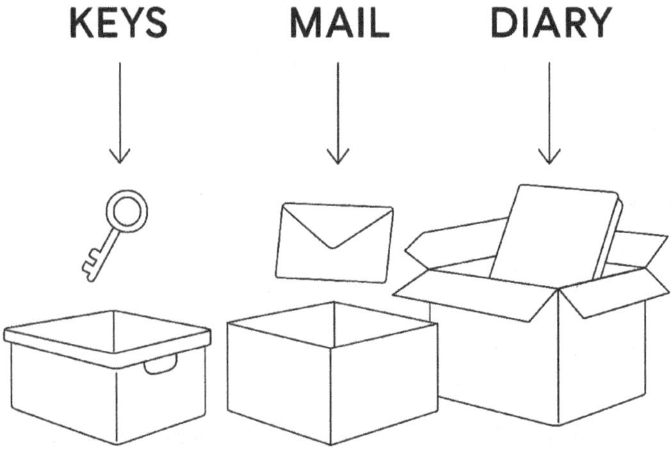

Following the vital work of confronting paralysis and designing a visually accessible environment, the next critical step in achieving functional organization is establishing unshakeable **predictability**. This chapter addresses the profound daily drain caused by **decision fatigue** and the constant expenditure of mental energy required to recall or find misplaced items. The solution is elegantly simple: to commit to a specific, easily accessible, and intuitive "**home**" for every item you own.

For the woman with Attention-Deficit / Hyperactivity Disorder (ADHD), the absence of a designated home for an object, whether it's her keys, a critical piece of mail, or a pair of reading glasses, forces her brain to make a series of exhausting, minute decisions every single time she interacts with it. *Where should this go? Where did I just set it down? Which pile is the right pile?* This relentless barrage of micro-decisions is not merely an inconvenience; it actively depletes the finite resources of her executive functions, contributing significantly to chronic overwhelm, anxiety, and the pervasive feeling of being perpetually "frenzied, frazzled, and overwhelmed."

This chapter moves past simple tidiness and into a strategy of neurobiological self-management. By creating a predictable and intuitive external system, you eliminate the daily cognitive friction of choice, reduce the reliance on compromised internal working memory, and conserve your precious executive function reserves for tasks that truly require focused, complex thought.

The Neurobiological Cost of Decision Ambiguity

The struggle to keep things organized and in their place is deeply rooted in the neurobiology of the ADHD brain. Understanding *why* ambiguity drains your energy is the key to building systems that are resilient to the challenges of inattention and memory deficits.

1. Decision Fatigue: The Silent Drain on Executive Function

Decision fatigue is a state of mental exhaustion caused by having to make a high volume of choices over a sustained period. This phenomenon is particularly devastating for the ADHD brain, whose executive function (EF) skills, the "mental toolkit for success", are already prone to inconsistency and rapid depletion.

Every time you encounter an item without a clear destination, your prefrontal cortex (the brain's command center for planning and logic) has to engage in a micro-analysis: *Analyze item; Recall potential locations; Evaluate importance; Select location; Initiate movement.* This process, repeated dozens of times daily for mundane items, burns through the limited cognitive bandwidth required for higher-leverage activities like complex problem-solving, emotional regulation, or sustained focus on work.

When EF reserves are depleted by constant micro-decisions, the brain defaults to its least energy-intensive choices, which inevitably leads to:

- **Impulsivity:** Less mental energy is available to inhibit the urge to leave the item where it is or to make poor decisions later in the day (e.g., impulsive spending or emotional outbursts).
- **Avoidance / Paralysis:** The prospect of confronting a pile of ambiguous items, each demanding a decision, becomes too cognitively taxing, triggering an overwhelm response that leads to complete task paralysis.

The commitment to giving every item a designated "home" is therefore an act of preservation. It proactively eliminates ambiguity, replacing taxing analysis with automatic, low-friction placement, thus conserving executive function for when it is truly needed.

2. Compensating for Compromised Working Memory

A significant barrier to maintaining order is the well-documented **working memory deficit** associated with ADHD. Working memory, the mental "scratchpad," is essential for holding temporary information, such as the location where you just placed an item. For a woman with ADHD, this memory can feel like a sieve, making the rapid recall of a non-designated spot nearly impossible.

This is the neurobiological root of the "out of sight, out of mind" phenomenon: the item effectively ceases to exist when it is no longer in the immediate visual field, because the memory system fails to reliably store or retrieve its location.

A designated "home" acts as a reliable **external memory cue** that bypasses this internal deficit. When you train yourself to place Item X at Spot Y, the association becomes muscle memory, or an automatic process that relies on habit rather than conscious effort and recall. The external structure compensates for the internal inconsistency, creating a reliable, low-effort pathway for maintenance.

The Foundational Principle: The Rule of Intentional Placement

Functional organization for the ADHD brain must be built on the principle of minimal friction. An item's designated "home" must be the easiest, most intuitive, and least energy-intensive choice for placement. If the effort required to put an item away is greater than the effort required to leave it out, the system will fail.

1. Assigning the Home: Proximity and Logic

The act of assigning a home must be intentional and logical, taking into account the item's use and the brain's preference for immediate gratification.

- **The Proximity Principle:** An item's home should be located immediately adjacent to where it is most frequently **used**. For instance, charging cables should live directly next to the charging station, not in a box across the room. Scissors and tape should live in the most common wrapping or craft area, not in a generic utility drawer in the kitchen. This reduces the physical and mental steps required for put-away, making the organized choice the path of least resistance.
- **The "First Touch" Rule:** Commit to determining a home for every new item the moment it enters your home. If a new receipt or piece of mail lands on the counter, address it immediately by moving it to its designated home (e.g., the "To-File" bin or the "Bill Pay" folder). Allowing ambiguous items to linger creates visual clutter that contaminates the predictable system and invites paralysis.

2. The Critical "Landing Strip"

The most significant drain on time and energy for many women with ADHD comes from losing critical, frequently used items: keys, phone, wallet, or daily medication. To combat this, the **Landing Strip** is a non-negotiable strategic system designed to eliminate the decision process for these high-value, high-loss items.

- **The Designated Zone:** The Landing Strip is a small, designated, and visually prominent zone immediately near your primary entry / exit point (e.g., a specific bowl, a tray, or a dedicated hook rack).
- **The Automatic Habit:** The habit must be rigid: Every critical item *must* be placed on the Landing Strip immediately upon re-entering the home, before jackets are removed or bags are put down. This ritual transforms placement from a conscious decision into a low-effort, automatic sequence that leverages muscle memory. By eliminating the question "Where are my keys?" from your daily life, you dramatically reduce pre-departure stress, saving both time and mental energy.

The Necessity of Functional Imperfection: The Designated "Junk Drawer"

Perfection is the enemy of sustainability for the ADHD brain. Attempting to achieve a flawless organizational system that accounts for every tiny, miscellaneous item often leads to immediate abandonment and a renewed sense of failure. The strategy must include an intentional allowance for functional imperfection.

The **Junk Drawer** is not a sign of failure; it is a strategically designated, contained zone of functional clutter that acts as a controlled pressure release valve.

1. The Purpose of the Pressure Release Valve

The junk drawer serves a crucial neurobiological purpose: it provides a predetermined, low-friction "home" for items that trigger decision fatigue due to their ambiguity or size.

- **Ambiguity Reduction:** It accommodates items that do not yet have a determined "home" (e.g., a spare Allen wrench, an unidentifiable small battery, a piece of wire) or items that are truly miscellaneous (rubber bands, spare change). Without this release valve, these small items would spread onto countertops and surfaces, creating generalized visual clutter that rapidly contaminates the entire space and increases overall cognitive load.
- **Preventing Paralysis:** When encountering an item whose home is not immediately obvious, the brain might freeze, triggering task paralysis. The junk drawer eliminates this pause by offering a swift, non-judgmental destination: *If I don't know where it goes, it goes in the drawer.* This simple, clear rule prevents the spread of chaos and conserves decision-making energy for high-leverage tasks.

2. Strategic Placement and Maintenance

The junk drawer must be managed strategically to remain functional and not become an overwhelming time capsule.

- **Controlled Containment:** Designate at least one easy-to-access junk drawer or miscellaneous basket in high-traffic rooms (e.g., kitchen, office). The key is that the clutter is contained, visually separated from the organized surfaces that serve as your core memory cues.

- **Periodic Review (Low-Stakes):** Schedule a very low-stakes, non-judgmental review of the junk drawer once every six months or so. Because the contents are already contained, the task of reviewing them is less overwhelming than facing general clutter. This ensures the drawer remains a functional holding zone rather than a black hole of permanent chaos.

Sustaining Predictability: Reinforcing the "Home"

Establishing the "home" is only half the battle; the long-term success of the system depends on transforming these intentional placements into automatic, low-effort **habits**. The ADHD brain often struggles with habit formation due to the dysregulated dopamine system, which seeks immediate reward and struggles with repetitive, mundane follow-through.

1. Leverage Habit Stacking for Automaticity

Habit stacking is an evidence-based technique that links a new, desired habit (putting an item in its home) to an existing, established habit. This technique leverages the automaticity of the existing routine to anchor the new, difficult behavior, reducing the reliance on inconsistent willpower.

- **Anchor the New Habit:** Structure the placement rule around an existing, reliable cue.
  - *Instead of:* "Remember to put your glasses in the case."
  - *Try:* "After I put my dinner plate in the sink **(Existing Habit)**, I immediately place my reading glasses in the designated tray on the counter **(New Habit)**."
- **Anchor the Daily Transition:** Use established transition points, which are often challenging for the ADHD brain, as predictable cues.
  - "After I turn off my computer for the night **(Existing Habit)**, I take my wallet and phone out of my bag and place them directly on the Landing Strip **(New Habit)**."

2. Implement the 15-Minute Daily "Reset" Ritual

Organization is not a static destination; it is a dynamic process of continuous maintenance. A key vulnerability of the ADHD brain is allowing small messes to escalate into paralyzing chaos. The solution is the **15-Minute Daily "Reset" Ritual**.

- **Prevent the Snowball Effect:** Dedicate a consistent, short period, approximately 15 minutes daily, to a focused "reset" of your core living or working areas. This is not a deep clean; it is merely an intentional effort to put things back in their designated homes, throw items out, and quickly file necessary documents.
- **Leverage Timers and Novelty:** To maintain engagement and overcome the boredom of repetition, use a timer or integrate elements of **Body Doubling** (working in the presence of a supportive partner or friend) during this 15-minute period. The short duration, enforced by a timer, makes the task feel finite and less overwhelming, leveraging the principle of the micro-step to sustain momentum.

The Emotional and Cognitive Liberation of Predictability

The commitment to establishing predictability through the "designated home" is a profound act of self-care with measurable psychological benefits that extend far beyond a tidy room.

1. Reducing Anxiety and Boosting Self-Efficacy

Chronic disorganization is a relentless source of anxiety for women with ADHD, fueling the pervasive belief that they are fundamentally incapable of self-management.

- **The Antidote to Shame:** Predictability directly counteracts the cycle of shame and self-blame that stems from lost items and chronic lateness. When a woman knows, without question, where her critical items are located, she reduces the internal stress and the subsequent external friction that often leads to outbursts or breakdowns.
- **Building Self-Efficacy:** Every successful instance of putting an item in its designated home, the keys on the hook, the mail in the basket, the remote on the tray, provides a small, satisfying

"win." This consistent, positive reinforcement builds **self-efficacy**, the belief in one's own ability to succeed, which is a powerful psychological resource that bolsters overall emotional resilience.

2. Reclaiming Cognitive Bandwidth

The most important result of this work is the liberation of cognitive bandwidth. By moving the organizational burden from the brain's inconsistent internal memory to reliable external systems, a woman frees up the immense mental energy that was once consumed by searching, worrying, and deciding.

This conserved executive function can now be redirected toward high-leverage pursuits: achieving deep work, mastering emotional regulation, engaging in intentional communication, and simply enjoying moments of focused peace. The unpredictable internal chaos begins to subside, replaced by the calm, supportive rhythm of a truly predictable, intentionally designed external environment. The result is a life that is no longer dominated by low-level anxiety and micro-decisions, but by purposeful, integrated action.

Chapter 3 Workbook: Establish Predictability: Give Every Item a Designated "Home"

Objective: To eliminate daily **decision fatigue** by assigning a specific, non-negotiable **"home"** to essential items, reducing reliance on inconsistent internal memory.

Activity 3.1: The Landing Strip Commitment

1. **High-Loss Stressors:** List the top three items you **always** search for before leaving the house.

   Items: ____

   ____

   ____

2. **Designate the Permanent Home:** Define the exact, exclusive location for these items near your main entrance (The Landing Strip).

   Location: ____

   ____

3. **Create the Habit Stack:** Anchor the new habit of using the Landing Strip to an existing, automatic habit you do when you enter the door (e.g., taking off your coat).
   - *Existing Habit:* "The moment I ______________________,"
   - *New Habit Stack:* "I immediately place my keys / wallet on the Landing Strip."

Reflection 3.2: The Anti-Friction Allowance

1. Name one type of ambiguous item (e.g., loose change, spare twist ties, old coupons) that often pollutes your clear spaces.

   Item: ____

   ____

2. To reduce decision fatigue, you commit to routing this item directly to a **Junk Drawer** or **Miscellaneous Basket**. How does this commitment reduce the friction on your organized surfaces?

   Benefit: ____

   ____

CHAPTER 4

SUSTAIN MOMENTUM: USE BODY DOUBLING AND TIMERS TO START TASKS

In the journey to defeat chronic disorganization, the most difficult challenge often remains **task initiation**: the ability to simply start a demanding or tedious project. While the previous chapters laid the critical foundation by breaking down overwhelming projects into manageable micro-steps and establishing predictable homes for items, a crucial neurological barrier persists: the **task activation deficit**. For the ADHD brain, the gap between *knowing* what to do and actually *doing* it can feel immense, like an uncrossable chasm, rooted in a fundamental challenge with motivation and executive control.

This chapter provides the strategic solution to this barrier, focusing on two evidence-based techniques that create **external scaffolding** to bridge the gap between intention and action: **Body Doubling** and the disciplined use of **Timers.** These tools work by strategically bypassing the internal deficits in focus and motivation, leveraging external structure and accountability to transform a state of paralyzing inertia into one of sustained momentum. The goal is to stop fighting your internal resistance with willpower, and start designing an environment that *forces* the first step, making the organized choice the path of least resistance.

The Neurobiology of the Activation Barrier

To effectively defeat the "can't get started" syndrome, we must recognize that this resistance is not a moral failure, but a neurobiological reality. Task paralysis and the difficulty in initiation are symptoms of the ADHD brain's unique wiring, particularly concerning **dopamine dysregulation** and **cognitive overload.**

1. The Dopamine-Driven Deficit

Dopamine, the brain's primary neurotransmitter for motivation, reward, and activation, is thought to be dysregulated in the ADHD brain. This neurochemical difference makes tasks that are not immediately stimulating or inherently rewarding feel exceptionally difficult to initiate and sustain. Mundane, multi-step activities inherent in organization, such as filing paperwork or cleaning a neglected corner, do not provide the necessary immediate reward, failing to trigger the dopamine release required for activation. This deficit explains why a woman may find herself procrastinating and avoiding tasks by doing other, more stimulating activities, or simply "zoning out" instead of engaging with the task she knows must be done.

2. Cognitive Overload and Filtering Failure

The ADHD brain struggles with efficiently filtering out irrelevant information and distractions, leading to a constant state of high **cognitive load.** When faced with an organizing project, the brain is instantly overwhelmed by the sheer volume of competing stimuli—the mess, the potential steps, the emotional weight of the task—which quickly exceeds its capacity to process and prioritize. This overload triggers a cognitive shutdown, or mental paralysis, as the brain seeks to protect itself from excessive stimulation.

The two strategies presented here, Body Doubling and Timers, work by providing powerful, external cues that bypass the need for internal dopamine generation or excessive cognitive filtering, creating a non-negotiable anchor for attention and initiation.

Section 1: Body Doubling: Creating External Executive Function

Body Doubling refers to the practice of performing a task in the presence of another person to enhance motivation, focus, and efficiency. This technique, which emerged from the self-help literature of the ADHD community, is a highly effective, low-risk strategy that utilizes a social framework to compensate for internal executive function deficits.

The Mechanism: Anchoring Attention and Accountability

While controlled research on Body Doubling is limited, anecdotal evidence strongly suggests its profound utility for individuals with ADHD who struggle with consistency and initiation. The mechanism is theorized to work by creating a form of **external executive functioning** that anchors the individual to the present moment, thereby reducing distraction and enhancing motivation.

1. **Anchoring Attention:** The presence of a body double, even a silent one working on a completely separate task, acts as a consistent, non-judgmental anchor for the ADHD brain. Because the brain struggles to filter out external stimuli, the quiet, focused presence of another person becomes a central point of focus that helps the individual stay oriented to the task at hand, reducing the risk of being pulled away by internal or external distractions.
2. **Social Accountability:** The mere act of committing to work in the presence of another person, whether in-person or virtually, provides a subtle yet powerful source of accountability that bypasses the internal motivation deficit. This sense of being observed, not critically, but supportively, can supply the necessary activation energy to overcome procrastination and keep the individual engaged when the task becomes boring or difficult. The pressure is externalized and positive, making the "cost" of not starting higher than the cost of initiation.

3. **Encouragement and Momentum:** The body double can also function as a source of gentle encouragement or help with challenging steps, particularly when the ADHD individual hits a common roadblock, such as emotional overwhelm or task confusion. This external encouragement helps the person maintain momentum, which, in turn, generates the internal dopamine reward necessary to continue working.

Implementing the Body Double Strategy

To maximize the effectiveness of Body Doubling, it must be implemented strategically, ensuring the environment supports focus rather than providing a new distraction:

- **Establish the Rules:** The most successful Body Doubling requires clear ground rules. The double's role is *not* to micromanage, perform the task for you, or criticize your pace. Their primary job is simply **to be visibly present** and engaged in their *own* work. This non-judgmental presence is crucial for women with ADHD who may already struggle with immense shame and a harsh inner critic.
- **Prioritize Visibility:** Whether the session is in-person or virtual, the body double must remain visible. If working virtually, use a video call with cameras on so you can see your double working. This visual cue acts as the constant, external anchor for your attention.
- **Set a Time Limit:** The Body Doubling session should have a clear, finite duration. Because individuals with ADHD struggle with accurately estimating the time needed for a task (**time blindness**), using a timer during the session is essential to prevent overwhelm and maintain focus. Short, manageable work intervals ensure that you only have to stay focused for a limited time, making the commitment feel less intimidating.

Section 2: Harnessing Time: Timers as External Cues

The strategic use of a timer is the second crucial component of creating external scaffolding. For the ADHD brain, which struggles profoundly with the flow and estimation of time, a timer transforms abstract time into a visible, concrete, and manageable resource.

The Challenge of Time Blindness

Time blindness, the inability to accurately feel or gauge the passage of time, is a core executive function deficit that severely impacts productivity and increases feelings of overwhelm. This challenge makes it exceptionally difficult to estimate how long a task will take, or to remember deadlines without constant, conscious effort.

- **Overwhelm by Infinity:** When a task is assigned, the ADHD brain may perceive the work as an infinite, unquantifiable time sink, which triggers anxiety and paralyzes initiation.
- **The Estimation Deficit:** Individuals with ADHD consistently underestimate how long tasks will take, leading to chronic rushing, missed deadlines, and increased stress.

The Solution: Making Time Concrete

Timers directly address time blindness by creating a **visual representation of time** that bypasses the abstract, internal sense of duration. This clear structure helps bring the task into focus, eliminating the cognitive guesswork of *what to do next* and *for how long*.

The Pomodoro Technique: Structured Focus and Reward

The **Pomodoro Technique** is a highly effective timer-based system that structures work into short, focused intervals (traditionally 25 minutes) followed by mandated short breaks (5 minutes). This technique is uniquely suited for the ADHD brain due to several key neurobiological advantages:

1. **Breaks Down Overwhelming Tasks:** By requiring the user to break a large, daunting task into smaller, clearer, 25-minute chunks, the Pomodoro Technique makes the project feel manageable and achievable, directly combating the task paralysis triggered by complexity.
2. **Boosts Concentration and Reduces Fatigue:** The knowledge that the focused effort is limited to a short burst, the duration of the timer, helps keep attention sharp and prevents the deep mental fatigue often caused by continuous, unstructured effort.
3. **Prevents Hyperfocus and Burnout:** For the woman who struggles with *uncontrolled* hyperfocus, where she becomes so engrossed she neglects other responsibilities, the mandated

break acts as a crucial, external circuit-breaker. The scheduled 5-minute pause provides a regular, guilt-free opportunity for the brain to seek novelty or reset, preventing burnout without derailing the entire work session.

4. **Leverages the Reward System:** Each completed interval provides a tangible sense of accomplishment, yielding a small burst of dopamine that reinforces productive behavior and builds momentum for the next interval.

Customizing the Timer for Personal Needs

While the standard 25 / 5-minute interval is a good starting point, the most powerful feature of the Pomodoro Technique for ADHD is its **customizability**. A woman must tailor the duration to match her personal attention span and energy cycle:

- If 25 minutes feels too long, start with a 15-minute interval.
- If you are deep in a flow state, extend the work block to 45 minutes, but keep the mandatory break scheduled to prevent hyperfocus from becoming avoidance or burnout.

The consistent use of structured intervals provides a reliable way to make time concrete, turning the work period into a manageable sprint rather than an overwhelming marathon.

Section 3: Leveraging Accountability and Momentum

The combination of Body Doubling and Timers does more than just start a task; it creates a structured environment for sustained momentum and proactive problem-solving, dramatically reducing the invisible energy cost of unmanaged ADHD.

Transforming Tasks into Actionable Appointments

One of the greatest struggles for the ADHD brain is translating a vague task on a to-do list (e.g., "Organize files") into a specific, executable commitment. The organizational process must treat tasks as non-negotiable, scheduled events.

- **Schedule Your Organization:** Every organizational step, whether it is a micro-step defined in Chapter 1 or a 25-minute Pomodoro interval, must be scheduled into your planner or calendar as an **actionable appointment**. For example, instead of writing "Laundry" on your list, schedule: "1:00 PM - 1:25 PM: Body Double Laundry: Sort, Load, and Start Wash Cycle." This shift provides a clear temporal cue that is crucial for a brain that struggles with internal time management.

- **Build in Buffer Time:** A key strategy to reduce stress and maintain flow is to intentionally schedule **more time than you initially estimate** for tasks, including buffers for transitions between activities. Acknowledging the estimation deficit and adding an extra 25-50% time to your scheduled appointment prevents the rush and stress that compound executive function deficits.

Defeating the "ADHD Tax" on Mental Energy

The chronic feeling of being perpetually "frenzied, frazzled, and overwhelmed" that many women with ADHD report is the emotional and mental cost of navigating daily life with compromised executive functions—often referred to as the **"ADHD Tax."** This cost includes the mental exhaustion of constantly compensating, self-correcting, and fighting internal disorganization.

By externalizing task initiation through Body Doubling and time management through Timers, you are actively mitigating this tax:

- **Reduces Cognitive Load:** These external structures reduce the mental effort required to start, stay on track, and manage transitions, thereby conserving precious cognitive bandwidth.
- **Mitigates Overwhelm:** The clear structure and defined limits combat the feelings of overwhelm that trigger paralysis, allowing the woman to operate from a place of calm control rather than panicked reaction.
- **Consistent Practice:** The use of short, scheduled intervals (like the 15 minutes recommended for daily de-cluttering) makes maintenance a consistent, low-friction routine rather than a stressful, all-or-nothing chore.

Conclusion: The Strategic Path to Action

Task initiation is the moment where the strategic work of organization meets the neurobiological reality of the ADHD brain. For the woman who has internalized her struggles as personal failings, the inability to start tasks fuels deep shame and feelings of inadequacy.

The combination of **Body Doubling** and **Timers** provides a powerful, compassionate, and evidence-based solution. You are no longer fighting internal motivation with inconsistent willpower. Instead, you are building an external system that provides the necessary social accountability to anchor your focus, and the clear structure to manage time, transforming overwhelming inertia into predictable, sustained momentum.

Mastering these tools creates a sense of confidence and control, moving you past the paralyzing gap between intention and action. This stability in task initiation is the final foundational skill in Book 1, providing the necessary platform of physical and temporal order upon which the more complex skills of focus, emotional regulation, and deep connection in the following books will be built.

Chapter 4 Workbook: Sustain Momentum: Use Body Doubling and Timers to Start Tasks

Objective: To bypass the internal motivation deficit by leveraging **external accountability** (**Body Doubling**) and **fixed time limits** (Timers) to sustain focus.

Activity 4.1: The External Scaffolding Trial

1. **The Boring Task:** Select one boring or repetitive organizing task that is difficult to start (e.g., "Filing old receipts," or "Cleaning the baseboards").

   Task: ____

   ____

   ____

   ____

2. **Set the Pomodoro Sprint:** Schedule a short, fixed work block using a timer to counteract **time blindness**.

Time Block	Activity	External Support Used
25 Minutes	Uninterrupted work on the Target Task.	**Body Double** Name:________________ ________________________ ________________________
5 Minutes	**Mandatory Break** (Stand up, stretch, get water—no social media).	Timer

Action Check 4.2: Accountability Script

1. If you get distracted or hit a wall during the 25-minute sprint, you need a non-judgmental cue. Write one sentence your Body Double can use to gently redirect you.
    - *Body Double Script:* (Example: "You've got 15 minutes left, let's go for one more micro-step.")

CHAPTER 5

STOP THE SNOWBALL: IMPLEMENT DAILY 15-MINUTE "RESET" ROUTINES

The work of achieving functional organization is not a one-time cleaning event; it is an ongoing process of strategic maintenance and habit formation. The most insidious challenge for a woman with Attention-Deficit / Hyperactivity Disorder (ADHD) is the **"Snowball Effect"**: the inevitable reality that a small, manageable mess, a few dishes in the sink, a handful of papers on the counter, an unread stack of emails, can rapidly escalate into an overwhelming, paralyzing avalanche of chaos.

This chapter addresses the final, crucial step in organization: building consistent, low-friction habits to maintain order. The solution lies in the disciplined implementation of the **Daily 15-Minute "Reset" Routine**, a non-negotiable, short burst of focused effort designed to interrupt the snowball effect before it can trigger the emotional and cognitive paralysis that leads to complete system breakdown.

For the ADHD brain, which struggles profoundly with **task initiation** and **consistency**, maintenance often feels impossible, a source of profound shame and failure. This is often because the approach is flawed: it attempts to impose rigid, perfectionistic standards that are neurobiologically unsustainable. This chapter rejects the "all-or-nothing" cycle and champions a compassionate, strategic model of **functional imperfection**, where consistency and self-forgiveness are prioritized over flawless tidiness. By consistently applying short, time-bound efforts, you transform organization from a stressful, all-consuming chore into a manageable, routine practice that systematically conserves your mental energy.

Section 1: The Neurobiological Imperative for Daily Maintenance

The struggle with consistent habit formation and maintenance for the ADHD brain is rooted in its unique neurobiology, particularly concerning its **reward system** and its vulnerability to **cognitive overload**. Understanding these mechanisms is key to building a resilient maintenance plan.

1. Dopamine, Novelty, and the Habit Deficit

Habits are typically formed and maintained through a psychological loop of **cue, routine, and reward**. For a neurotypical brain, the long-term rewards of organization, reduced stress, easier mornings, overall control, are often enough to sustain the mundane, repetitive effort of maintenance.

However, for a woman with ADHD, the **dopamine dysregulation** in her brain means that the rewards associated with routine, mundane activities are often too delayed or too small to motivate consistent follow-through. Her brain craves **novelty** and **immediate stimulation** (a fresh idea, a new project, a stimulating hobby) which provide a rapid, satisfying burst of dopamine. Mundane maintenance tasks, such as clearing the desk or filing paperwork, are repetitive, boring, and fail to generate the necessary neurochemical reward, causing the brain to struggle with activation and quickly lose interest.

This neurochemical reality explains why organizational systems fail: they demand consistent effort for a delayed, low-intensity reward. The solution is to leverage **external structure** (like a timer and a fixed routine) to force initiation, and then utilize **internal momentum** (the feeling of accomplishment from a quick win) to act as an immediate reward that reinforces the habit, bypassing the long-term dopamine deficit.

2. The Cognitive Cost of Clutter and the Snowball Effect

The core organizational principle established in previous chapters is that **clutter equals cognitive load**. The ADHD brain struggles with efficiently filtering out irrelevant stimuli. Every object without a home, every unfiled paper, and every dirty dish on the counter demands a fraction of mental attention, increasing the overall **cognitive load** on already limited **executive function (EF) reserves**.

The "Snowball Effect" occurs when small, initial points of clutter, which, individually, require minimal effort to address, begin to accumulate. This visual and mental mess quickly overwhelms the brain's filtering capacity, leading to a critical threshold where the cognitive load becomes unbearable.

At this threshold, the brain defaults to **task paralysis** and **avoidance**. The project of cleaning is perceived as too complex and daunting, triggering a neurological shutdown rather than initiation. Therefore, the strategic purpose of the Daily 15-Minute Reset is to **interrupt the accrual of cognitive debt** every single day, ensuring the clutter never crosses the threshold into paralyzing overwhelm.

3. Defeating the "All-or-Nothing" Perfectionism Trap

A significant emotional barrier to maintenance for women with ADHD is **perfectionism**, which is often a compensatory strategy developed to mask symptoms and avoid the deep pain of criticism or shame. If a woman believes a chore must be executed flawlessly or that the entire home must be perfectly organized, the task quickly becomes too large and intimidating to start.

- **The Shame Cycle:** The failure to meet this unrealistic, perfectionistic standard fuels shame and the inner critic: "*I missed one day of cleaning, so the whole system is ruined, and I'm a failure anyway.*" This shame then leads to the abandonment of the entire system, reinforcing the cycle of chaos, self-blame, and renewed overwhelm.

- **The Daily Reset as a Compromise:** The Daily 15-Minute Reset is designed to be intentionally imperfect. Its goal is **functionality**, not perfection. It focuses only on high-leverage areas (like the sink or the bedside table) and deliberately leaves larger, less critical messes for another time. This small, consistent win builds resilience and teaches the brain that partial effort is valuable effort, breaking the debilitating "all-or-nothing" mindset.

Section 2: Implementing the Daily 15-Minute Reset

The Daily Reset must be implemented as a non-negotiable **ritual** that is built on strict limits of time and scope. This structure compensates for the ADHD brain's difficulty with time estimation and initiation.

1. The Critical Role of the Timer

The timer is the single most important tool in this routine, transforming abstract time into a concrete, visible, and manageable resource.

- **Combating Overwhelm:** By limiting the task to 15 minutes, the timer prevents the project from feeling infinite or overwhelming, lowering the activation energy required to start. The brain knows the effort is finite and temporary.
- **Preventing Hyperfocus and Burnout:** For the woman who struggles with *uncontrolled hyperfocus* (getting lost in one area for hours), the timer acts as a crucial, external circuit-breaker. When the alarm sounds, the task **stops**, even if it's unfinished. This prevents the maintenance routine from consuming the entire evening and causing burnout.
- **Creating Urgency:** The presence of the timer creates a necessary sense of urgency, often referred to as "external deadlines," which provides the burst of activation energy that the ADHD brain struggles to generate internally.

2. Defining the "High-Leverage" Reset Zones

The 15 minutes must be directed toward the highest-impact areas, the **Landing Zones** that quickly accumulate clutter and cause the most stress.

- **The Kitchen Sink / Counter:** The kitchen counter and sink are often the fastest "chaos breeding grounds" in the home. The reset must prioritize clearing all dishes, wiping the counter, and putting away misplaced mail or groceries. A clean counter significantly reduces visual noise and cognitive load at the start and end of the day.
- **The Digital Desktop / Inbox:** The digital space must be included. Dedicate a few minutes to closing unnecessary browser tabs, moving files off the desktop into a single "To Sort" folder, and applying the **"Two-Minute Rule"** to the email inbox (delete, do immediately, or defer). This reduces the invisible mental clutter that fragments attention.
- **The Bedside Table / Landing Strip:** These are crucial high-loss zones. The reset ensures that keys, wallets, phones, and any essential medications are placed immediately on their designated "Landing Strip" home, preventing the frantic, time-consuming search that increases morning stress.

3. Scheduling the Reset as a Non-Negotiable Appointment

The routine must not be treated as an optional task on a vague list; it must be scheduled as a fixed, non-negotiable **actionable appointment** in your planner or calendar.

- **Fixed Time Slots:** Schedule the reset during a natural transition point, such as "immediately after dinner" or "the last 15 minutes before work ends." This utilizes **Habit Stacking** by anchoring the new routine to an established, automatic habit (eating dinner, finishing the workday) that already has momentum.
- **Visual Reminder:** Write the reset in your planner or on a whiteboard as "15-Min System Reset - Kitchen / Desk." This provides a clear, actionable visual cue that requires minimal decision-making.

Section 3: Strategies for Building and Sustaining the Maintenance Habit

Sustaining a habit requires leveraging the ADHD brain's need for reward and external cues. The following strategies ensure the Daily Reset becomes an automated, low-effort part of your life.

1. Leveraging the Momentum of Micro-Wins

The success of the Daily Reset lies in its ability to create frequent, rapid **micro-wins** that provide immediate, tangible feedback and a necessary dopamine hit.

- **Immediate Reward Loop:** When you complete a micro-step—clearing the sink, putting three items back in their designated home—the visible progress and the mental satisfaction act as an immediate reward that reinforces the productive behavior. This reliance on **momentum** makes the continuation of the task easier than the initial start.
- **The Visual Cue of the Timer:** The sound of the timer going off after 15 minutes is itself a reward, signaling that the difficult task is over and the focused effort was successfully completed. This concrete ending reinforces the brain's ability to engage with finite tasks.

2. Utilizing External Scaffolding: Body Doubling

When initiation is difficult, the organizational system must utilize external anchors. The practice of **Body Doubling**, typically used for large projects, can also be highly effective for anchoring the Daily Reset.

- **Accountability in Routine:** Working in the presence of another person (a supportive partner, friend, or virtual accountability buddy) provides a subtle, non-judgmental form of accountability that bypasses the internal motivation deficit. The body double's presence acts as a consistent anchor for the ADHD brain, making it easier to start the 15-minute routine and preventing distraction.
- **Simple Implementation:** The body double need only be present and engaged in their * own* quiet task (reading, paying bills, working). Their role is not to help clean, but simply to

provide a stable, non-distracting presence that helps the individual stay oriented to the 15-minute task at hand.

3. Embracing the "Junk Drawer" for Functional Imperfection

To ensure the maintenance habit remains sustainable, the system must tolerate functional imperfection.

- **The Pressure Release Valve:** The **Junk Drawer** (or designated "Miscellaneous Basket") is the essential companion to the Daily Reset. It provides a controlled, low-friction "home" for ambiguous items that do not yet have a determined destination. When the clock is ticking during the 15-minute reset, instead of pausing to decide where a stray item goes (triggering decision fatigue and slowing momentum), the rule is simple: *Put it in the junk drawer.*
- **Controlled Containment:** This strategy channels the natural chaos and ambiguity of daily life into a contained, visually separate zone, preventing the spread of clutter onto organized surfaces where it would increase cognitive load and trigger overwhelm. It is a deliberate choice to accept imperfection in one small area to maintain functionality in the entire system.

Section 4: Long-Term Resilience and Self-Compassion

Sustained organization is inherently tied to emotional resilience. A consistent maintenance routine reduces the shame associated with chaos and builds long-term self-efficacy.

1. The Weekly Review: Maintaining the Integrity of the System

While the Daily Reset tackles surface clutter, the deeper organizational integrity must be maintained through a periodic, low-stakes review.

- **Processing the Holding Zones:** Schedule a low-pressure **Weekly Review** session (e.g., 30 minutes on Sunday afternoon). This session focuses specifically on processing the **holding zones** created by the Daily Reset—the "To Sort" file, the Digital Downloads folder, and the Junk Drawer.

- **Low-Stakes Decluttering:** Because the items are already contained, the task of reviewing them is less overwhelming than facing generalized chaos. This periodic review prevents the holding zones from becoming permanent black holes and ensures the overall organizational structure remains functional and sustainable.

2. Reframing Failure with Self-Compassion

The greatest threat to long-term maintenance is not the mess itself, but the shame that arises when the routine is inevitably missed. A woman must consciously replace the automatic self-criticism with strategic self-compassion.

- **Mistakes as Data:** When the 15-minute reset is missed—whether due to fatigue, hyperfocus, or distraction—the moment must be reframed from a personal failure into a source of **valuable data**. Instead of: *"I'm lazy and ruined the system,"* ask: *"What was the friction point today? Was I too tired? Did I miss the alarm? Should I move the reset time slot?"*
- **Self-Kindness and Recovery:** This compassionate inquiry preserves the emotional energy that self-blame would have consumed. It allows the woman to return to the system without the crushing weight of guilt, making recovery easier and quicker. The goal is to start the next 15-minute reset immediately, without waiting for the "perfect" moment to restart the routine.

3. The Emotional Payoff: Sustained Calm and Control

The reward for building this resilient maintenance system is far greater than a tidy home. The most profound benefit is the sustained reduction in **chronic anxiety** and the daily feeling of being perpetually overwhelmed.

- **Reduced Anxiety:** A predictable, functional environment reduces the brain's need to constantly monitor for potential disaster (the lost keys, the forgotten bill, the overwhelming mess). This reduction in internal monitoring frees up immense mental bandwidth.

- **Sustained Self-Efficacy:** Every successful 15-minute reset provides consistent, positive reinforcement, building **self-efficacy**—the belief in one's own ability to succeed. This sustained feeling of competence is the antidote to the shame and inadequacy that characterize unmanaged ADHD, transforming a life of frantic reaction into one of intentional control.

Conclusion: Your Foundational Systems

This book has provided a comprehensive blueprint for constructing a resilient, ADHD-friendly organizational system. The core of this work has been about externalizing the burdens of your brain, creating physical and temporal structures that compensate for internal challenges with planning, working memory, and task initiation.

By committing to the **Daily 15-Minute Reset Routine**, you systematically interrupt the emotional and cognitive paralysis caused by the Snowball Effect. This final foundational skill ensures that the stability and order you have built are not just temporary states but sustainable features of your life.

This hard-won stability is the prerequisite for the more complex work that follows. A brain that is no longer consumed by the low-level noise of disorganization and the frantic search for lost items is a brain that has gained the mental bandwidth necessary for **sharpened focus** (Book 2), **emotional mastery** (Book 4), and **deepening relationships** (Book 5). You have moved beyond mere coping to building a reliable, supportive structure for a truly empowered life.

Chapter 5 Workbook: Stop the Snowball: Implement Daily 15-Minute "Reset" Routines

Objective: To systematically interrupt the **Snowball Effect** by making low-friction maintenance a consistent, manageable **ritual**, not a stressful chore.

Activity 5.1: The Daily Reset Blueprint

1. **Identify High-Impact Zones:** List the three areas that accumulate clutter fastest and cause the most anxiety.

   Zone 1: ____

Zone 2: ____

Zone 3: ____

2. **Define the Reset Routine:** Create a fixed, three-step checklist that takes **no more than 5 minutes per action** and targets only high-leverage maintenance.

Reset Action	Task (Specific, e.g., "Load all dishes from the sink")
Action 1:	
Action 2:	
Action 3:	

3. **Anchor the Routine:** Commit to performing this 15-minute routine at a fixed, anchored time each day.

Anchored Time: "Immediately after ________________________

____

____

____

____

____

____

____

(e.g., I shut down my computer for the day), I start my 15-Minute Timer."

Reflection 5.2: The Recovery Plan

1. **The All-or-Nothing Trap:** When you inevitably miss the 15-Minute Reset, the feeling of "I've ruined the system" can strike. Write a **Compassionate Recovery Plan** that rejects this shame and gets you back on track immediately.
    - *Recovery Statement:* (Example: "It's okay. Setbacks are data. I will not try to catch up, but I will do a **5-minute micro-reset right now** to stop the snowball.")

CHAPTER 6

REFLECT AND INTEGRATE: YOUR DECLUTTERING JOURNEY SO FAR

You have completed the foundational phase of your journey. The five preceding chapters were dedicated to constructing a stable, supportive external environment, a prerequisite for managing the more complex internal challenges of the ADHD brain. This chapter marks a moment of intentional pause, a crucial opportunity to **reflect and integrate** the organizational systems you have built, recognizing the profound transformation that has occurred in your emotional and cognitive landscape.

This work was not about achieving neurotypical perfection, but about embracing **functional imperfection**: creating external structures that work *for* your brain's unique wiring, rather than forcing your brain to operate against its natural impulses. By systematically implementing the tools of breaking down tasks, creating designated "homes," leveraging visual storage, utilizing external accountability, and performing daily resets, you have moved beyond the paralyzing cycle of chaos and shame. You have learned that your struggle was never a character flaw, but a neurobiological reality that required a strategic, tailored solution.

The integration of these skills, from defeating the initiation deficit to neutralizing the snowball effect, yields measurable, powerful results in three interconnected domains: the cognitive, the emotional, and the relational. This reflection is designed to solidify those gains, ensuring that the habits you have built are not temporary fixes, but sustainable, resilient features of your self-management toolkit.

Section 1: The Transformation of the Cognitive Landscape

The most immediate and profound impact of functional organization is the reduction of **cognitive load** and the recovery of previously consumed mental energy. Unmanaged ADHD creates a state of chronic, high cognitive demand, where the brain is perpetually exhausted from fighting against the chaos of its environment and its own internal inconsistencies. The systems built in this book directly counteract this drain.

1. Mitigating the ADHD Tax and Overwhelm

The pervasive feeling of being "frenzied, frazzled, and overwhelmed" is the emotional manifestation of continuous cognitive exhaustion. This chronic feeling of being perpetually behind is often referred to as the **"ADHD Tax"**, the measurable cumulative cost, financial, emotional, and mental, of navigating a world designed for neurotypical brains.

This tax is rooted in the constant effort required to mentally process and filter irrelevant stimuli. Every piece of visual clutter, every ambiguous pile, and every item without a designated "home" acts as an "open loop" in the brain, demanding a fraction of your working memory and attention.

By applying the principles of Book 1, you have fundamentally altered this equation:

- **Reduced Visual Noise:** Utilizing clear storage, bold labels, and ruthlessly clearing high-traffic surfaces minimizes the visual inputs that trigger overload, freeing up the brain's impaired filtering mechanism to focus on priority information.

- **Eliminated Decision Fatigue:** Giving every item a designated, predictable "home" and creating low-friction "Landing Strips" eliminates the dozens of micro-decisions (e.g., *Where does this pen go? Where did I put my keys?*) that were previously required every day. This conservation of executive function (EF) reserves significantly reduces overall cognitive load.
- **Defeated Paralysis:** The technique of breaking down overwhelming tasks into **micro-steps** and utilizing the structure of the **Daily 15-Minute Reset** systematically addresses the **task activation deficit**. This ensures that the brain is not triggered into paralysis by the perception of an infinite, daunting task, but is instead motivated by the low-friction initiation and the immediate dopamine reward of a small, achievable "win."

The result is a reclaimed sense of intellectual clarity. The mental energy that was once consumed by frantic searching, anxiety over deadlines, and fighting clutter is now available for higher-leverage activities like sustained focus, emotional regulation, and deep work. You have created an "external brain" that reliably holds the organizational load for you, allowing your internal mental energy to be conserved.

2. The Shift from Willpower to System

A major insight of this organizational journey is the understanding that consistent follow-through is not a matter of **willpower**, but of **system design**. For years, the struggle felt like a moral failing, a lack of motivation or discipline. Now, you recognize it as a neurobiological challenge that required strategic compensation.

The systems you built, the shared planner as an actionable document, the Body Doubling appointment as external accountability, and the timer as a concrete representation of time, act as external scaffolding, reliably performing the planning and initiation functions that are inconsistent in the ADHD brain. This move from inconsistent internal effort to reliable external structure is the key to long-term sustainability and reduced stress.

Section 2: The Emotional Liberation: Healing the Shame Cycle

The work of decluttering is inherently emotional work. For women with ADHD, chronic disorganization is one of the most significant sources of shame, self-blame, and inadequacy, largely due to intense societal pressure to be the organized caretaker. The systems built in Book 1 serve as a powerful antidote to this emotional burden.

1. Countering Shame and the Inner Critic

The emotional cost of chronic disorganization is profound, leading many women to endure years of feeling that they are "not an adequate human being" because their external chaos conflicts with neurotypical and gendered expectations. Without a framework for their struggles, they internalize their difficulties as personal flaws, fueling an aggressive inner critic that compounds anxiety and depression.

Functional organization directly counteracts this shame by creating irrefutable **evidence of competence** and by establishing a compassionate allowance for imperfection:

- **Evidence of Self-Efficacy:** Every time you successfully find your keys on the **Landing Strip** or successfully complete the **15-Minute Reset**, you generate a small, tangible win. This consistent, positive reinforcement builds **self-efficacy**, the belief in your own ability to manage tasks, which is the direct antidote to the feelings of helplessness and inadequacy that define shame.
- **Compassionate Design:** Embracing **functional imperfection**, such as the intentionally organized chaos of the designated **"Junk Drawer"**, actively rejects the toxic, "all-or-nothing" perfectionism that leads to system failure and renewed shame. By acknowledging that chaos is a neurobiological reality and channeling it into a contained zone, you practice self-kindness, reducing the emotional friction caused by self-judgment.

2. Reducing Relational Friction

Organizational challenges are a major source of friction in close relationships, often leading to an unhealthy **"parent-child" dynamic** where the non-ADHD partner becomes the taskmaster or reminder. This dynamic erodes intimacy and increases feelings of shame and resentment on both sides.

The establishment of clear, external systems serves as a mechanism for **de-personalizing** the struggle and promoting collaboration:

- **Externalizing Responsibilities:** By using shared calendars, chore charts, and systems that clearly externalize the organization of tasks, the burden of "remembering" is shifted from the neurotypical partner's mind to a neutral system. This reduces the need for constant verbal reminders, which mitigates the resentment and criticism that fuels the parent-child dynamic.
- **Fostering Partnership:** This move allows the relationship to shift from arguing over perceived failures (e.g., "Why didn't you put the keys away?") to problem-solving the system (e.g., "The key bowl must be moved closer to the door to reduce friction"). The focus shifts from blame to a collaborative effort toward a shared goal, which is essential for repairing disconnections and strengthening the core partnership.

Section 3: Sustaining the System: The Three Laws of Maintenance

The ultimate measure of organizational success is not how clean your home is today, but how easily you can recover when chaos inevitably creeps back in. The organizational systems you have mastered adhere to three core laws of long-term maintenance for the ADHD brain.

Law 1: The Law of External Scaffolding

The systems must always rely on external structures and human connection rather than inconsistent internal motivation. You cannot simply *wish* for motivation; you must **design** it into your environment.

- **Timers and Finite Effort:** The use of timers (e.g., Pomodoro, 15-Minute Reset) transforms amorphous, infinite tasks into finite, manageable sprints, which is a powerful antidote to both the estimation deficit and the activation deficit.
- **The Power of Presence (Body Doubling):** When inertia hits, Body Doubling leverages the power of social anchoring, providing external accountability that bypasses the internal motivation deficit and helps sustain focus.

Law 2: The Law of Low-Friction Design

The system must be designed to make the organized choice the path of least resistance. Friction points, small barriers like removing a lid, deciding where an item goes, or searching for a tool, are the primary cause of system breakdown for the ADHD brain.

- **Designated Homes:** Every item must have a predictable, accessible home, eliminating daily decision fatigue.
- **Visible Access:** Utilizing clear bins and open containers compensates for compromised working memory, ensuring that items remain "in mind" even when stored.
- **The Containment Valve:** The intentional use of the **Junk Drawer** channels ambiguous items into a controlled zone, preventing them from spreading onto high-leverage surfaces and maintaining the functional integrity of the overall space.

Law 3: The Law of Iteration (Review and Adaptation)

The system must be viewed as an ongoing, living process, not a rigid, fixed state. Failure is inevitable; recovery is strategic.

- **Consistent Reset:** The Daily 15-Minute Reset ensures that clutter is addressed before it reaches the paralyzing threshold of the "Snowball Effect," turning maintenance into a manageable ritual, not a major project.
- **Compassionate Review:** When the system fails (e.g., you miss a week of resets), the response is not self-criticism, but curious inquiry: *What was the friction point? Was the "home" too far away?* This stance treats setbacks as valuable **data collection** rather than moral judgment, allowing you to make strategic adjustments that lead to greater resilience over time.

Section 4: The Bridge to Internal Mastery

The foundational work of Book 1 is now complete, and it serves as the essential launchpad for the rest of your journey toward self-mastery. You have successfully externalized the chaos, creating a stable platform from which to address the complex internal challenges that follow.

1. From External Structure to Internal Focus

The cognitive bandwidth you conserved by systematizing your environment must now be actively redirected toward **sharpened focus** and **executive function training** (Book 2).

- **Reduced Distraction:** A clutter-free, predictable workspace directly minimizes sensory overload and visual distraction, which is crucial for a brain that struggles with filtering. The quiet of an organized desk is the necessary prerequisite for achieving deep, sustained concentration.
- **Redirected EF:** The EF resources freed up from searching for lost items and battling decision fatigue can now be used to engage in the cognitively demanding work of **time blocking**, **single-tasking**, and strengthening working memory—the core focus of the next book. You are moving from managing your *things* to managing your *attention*.

2. The Foundation for Emotional and Relational Stability

Organizational stability is the prerequisite for emotional and relational health. When a woman's daily life is a constant battle against chaos, her stress levels are chronically elevated, which severely impairs her capacity for self-regulation and emotional tolerance.

- **Stress Reduction:** The reduction in daily friction (e.g., no longer frantically searching for keys or worrying about the mess) lowers the overall physiological arousal in the nervous system, creating a more stable emotional baseline.
- **Bandwidth for Connection:** When you are less consumed by shame, anxiety, and task overwhelm, you have greater mental and emotional bandwidth available to engage in the sensitive, intentional work of **emotional regulation** (Book 4) and **active listening** within your relationships (Book 5).

The journey continues by shifting the focus inward. You are now equipped with the physical and temporal control needed to begin the challenging, but rewarding, work of mastering your attention, regulating your emotions, and building the resilience required for lasting success.

Chapter 6 Workbook: Reflect and Integrate: Your Decluttering Journey So Far

Objective: To solidify the cognitive and emotional gains, transforming the external systems into internal self-acceptance and strategic action.

Activity 6.1: The System vs. Shame Scorecard

Instructions: Rate the severity of your anxiety and shame related to two core organizational challenges, comparing your perspective **before** this book (relying on willpower) to **now** (relying on systems). (Scale: 1 = Low Shame / Anxiety, 5 = High Shame / Anxiety)

Challenge	Shame / Anxiety **Before** Systems	Shame / Anxiety **Now**	Reflection: The Tool That Helped
Finding Lost Keys / Wallet			(Example: Landing Strip)
Starting a Major Household Chore			(Example: Micro-Steps)

Reflection 6.2: Reclaiming Your Narrative

1. Identify one specific self-critical thought you had before this book (e.g., "I'm lazy because I can't keep a clean house").

   Old Thought: ____

   ____

   ____

   ____

2. Rephrase this thought using the compassionate language and neurobiological understanding you gained (e.g., "My brain is wired for novelty and needs external cues to initiate boring tasks. I am strategic, not lazy.").

   New, Empowered Narrative: ______________________________

   ____

   ____

   ____

3. **Bridge to Focus (Book 2):** In one sentence, state what you will do with the mental energy you conserved by eliminating clutter and searching.

   Action Plan: ____

   ____

   ____

   ____

CHAPTER 7

PRACTICE AND APPLY: YOUR DECLUTTERING ACTION TOOLKIT

You have completed the foundational work of understanding *why* disorganization plagues the ADHD brain. You now recognize that your struggles are not moral failures, but neurobiological realities rooted in challenges with **executive function (EF)**, **task activation**, and **working memory**. The previous chapters provided the neuroscientific framework and the theoretical principles for building functional organization: breaking down overwhelming tasks, creating visually supportive systems, establishing predictability, leveraging external accountability, and sustaining momentum with daily maintenance routines.

This chapter is the **Action Toolkit**, the essential bridge that moves you from theory and reflection to embodied, practical skill development. The goal is to take the abstract concepts of Chapters 1 through 5 and transform them into concrete, low-friction systems that are integrated into your daily rhythm. By systematically applying these tools, you are actively creating the external scaffolding required to consistently defeat overwhelm and sustain mental clarity.

The power of this practice lies not in achieving rigid perfection, but in achieving **consistent, intentional imperfection**. Every small action you take using these tools reinforces a positive feedback loop, provides a necessary **dopamine hit** (the reward your brain craves), and builds the self-efficacy that is the antidote to shame and paralysis.

Toolkit 1: The Task Activation Blueprint

Objective: Defeat Task Paralysis and Minimize Activation Energy

The largest barrier to organization is often the **task activation deficit**, the inability to simply start a complex or boring task. The sheer scope of an undifferentiated project triggers **cognitive overload** and an immediate **shutdown response** (paralysis). This toolkit utilizes the **Micro-Step Strategy** to systematically reduce the cognitive load, creating an entry point so small and low-friction that initiation becomes the path of least resistance.

Scientific Anchor: Dopamine and the Small Win

Task initiation requires a burst of "activation energy" that is often lacking in the ADHD brain due to dopamine dysregulation. Breaking a large project into minuscule, actionable steps creates more opportunities for **rapid feedback** and **immediate reward**. Each completed micro-step generates a small, satisfying "win," which provides the necessary dopamine reinforcement to fuel the subsequent step, creating **momentum** that bypasses reliance on inconsistent willpower.

Action Toolkit: The Brain Dump to Micro-Step Converter

This exercise requires you to externalize your mental clutter, identify a paralyzing project, and systematically dismantle it into low-friction actions.

Step 1: Externalize the Chaos (The Brain Dump)

- **Target:** Identify one major organizing project that you have been avoiding for weeks or months (e.g., The Garage, The Files, The Digital Inbox).

- **Action:** Take 10 minutes to write down *every single thought, step, worry, and task* associated with that project. Do not worry about order or logic; just empty the mental clutter onto the page. Include vague items (e.g., "Figure out what to do with the old tax papers," "Find the key to the cabinet," "Wipe the shelves").

Step 2: Isolate the Paralysis Point (The Friction Audit)

- **Action:** Review your list from Step 1. Circle the three tasks or worries that feel the most vague, most complicated, or most emotionally charged. These are your paralysis points.
- **Example Friction Point:** "Clean out the old filing cabinet."

Step 3: Convert to Micro-Steps (The Next Action Principle)

- **Action:** For your single most paralyzing friction point, break it down until the first two steps are undeniably simple, so small they require **no decision-making** and **no more than 2 minutes** of effort. The goal is to create steps that are entirely physical and immediate.

Paralyzing Friction Point	Low-Friction Micro-Steps (The Next Action)	Why It Bypasses Paralysis
Clean out the old filing cabinet	**Step 1:** Get one trash bag and place it next to the cabinet.	Requires zero mental decision-making; only physical movement.
	Step 2: Open the top drawer and pull out the first three folders.	A tiny, finite commitment (only three folders).
	Step 3: Immediately drop the three folders into the pre-placed trash bag. (Assume they are garbage for now).	Creates immediate, visible reduction in clutter.

Organize the laundry pile	**Step 1:** Grab the hamper and place it next to the pile.	Low initiation energy.
	Step 2: Pick up all socks and put them *in* the hamper. Do nothing else.	Focuses on one specific, easy-to-identify item.
	Step 3: Place the hamper outside the laundry room door.	Transfers the next required action to an external location.

Commitment: By converting the overwhelming goal into these low-friction micro-steps, you are supplying the necessary **activation energy** required for the ADHD brain to engage. Commit to completing only **Step 1** and **Step 2** right now, then immediately proceed to **Toolkit 3** to anchor the action with a timer.

Toolkit 2: The Environmental Memory Protocol

Objective: Establish Predictability and Externalize Working Memory

The "out of sight, out of mind" phenomenon is a direct consequence of a compromised **working memory** and the ADHD brain's struggle to retrieve memories of hidden objects. This toolkit designs the environment to reliably *remember for you*, reducing the daily friction caused by searching and decision ambiguity.

Scientific Anchor: Reducing Decision Fatigue

Giving every item a designated, predictable "home" eliminates constant **decision fatigue**, the daily mental exhaustion from deciding where an item belongs. This conserves the highly limited executive function resources that were previously wasted on searching and debating placement, reserving them for high-leverage tasks like planning and emotional regulation.

Action Toolkit A: The Landing Strip Audit

The Landing Strip is a crucial system for high-loss, high-stress items.

Step 1: Identify High-Loss Stressors

- **Action:** List the top three items you **always** spend time searching for before leaving the house. (Common examples: Keys, Wallet, Phone, Daily Medication, Work ID).

Step 2: Designate the Permanent Home (The Landing Strip)

- **Action:** Physically establish one small, contained, dedicated zone for these items near your main exit point (e.g., a specific decorative bowl, a small wall-mounted hook rack, or a dedicated spot on a shelf near the door).
- **Rule:** This zone must be **clear of all other clutter** to ensure the crucial items remain visually prominent and easily accessible.

Step 3: Implement the Habit Stacking Cue

- **Action:** Anchor the habit of using the Landing Strip to an existing, non-negotiable habit.
- **Example Habit Stack:** "The moment I unlock the door and drop my keys **(Existing Habit)**, I immediately place my wallet and keys in the blue bowl on the console table **(New Habit)**." This low-friction link makes the desired organizational action automatic.

Action Toolkit B: The Visual Recall Conversion

This exercise challenges the traditional, unhelpful approach of hidden storage by converting one space into a supportive, visual system.

Step 1: Identify an Opaque Overload Zone

- **Target:** Select one small, cluttered area that currently uses opaque storage and causes friction (e.g., the medicine cabinet, the utility closet shelf, a junk drawer, or a kitchen cabinet where spices are stored).

Step 2: Convert to Visible Containment

- **Action:** Replace opaque storage with **clear containers, open baskets, or trays** for the items (e.g., clear spice containers, a clear first-aid box).
- **Rule:** For frequently used items, ensure the containers are **without lids** to reduce the friction of opening / closing, making put-away easier and quicker.

Step 3: Label and Define

- **Action:** Use large, bold labels on the containers to define the contents. The labels must be simple and specific. (Example: Instead of "Stuff," use "Batteries - AA / AAA" or "Receipts - To File.")
- **Neuro-Benefit:** This intentional labeling externalizes the categorization process, eliminating the cognitive guesswork of retrieving the item and reinforcing the designated "home".

Toolkit 3: The Momentum Accelerator

Objective: Leverage External Accountability to Sustain Focus

Even with tasks broken down (Toolkit 1) and a clear environment (Toolkit 2), sustaining effort on boring, repetitive, or complex tasks remains challenging due to the internal motivation deficit. This toolkit provides the crucial external structures necessary to maintain attention and momentum.

Scientific Anchor: External Executive Functioning

The presence of a non-judgmental partner, or **Body Double**, acts as a source of **external executive functioning** that anchors the attention of the ADHD brain to the present moment, thereby reducing distraction and enhancing motivation. Similarly, timers compensate for **time blindness** by making abstract time concrete and visible, preventing the work from feeling infinite or overwhelming.

Action Toolkit A: The Body Double Protocol

This exercise sets the framework for a successful, non-judgmental Body Doubling session, whether in-person or virtual.

Step 1: Define the Task and Duration

- **Action:** Choose a single, defined task from **Toolkit 1** (e.g., "Sort paperwork from the red basket") and commit to a fixed duration.
- **Goal:** The goal is to work alongside a supportive partner or friend who is focused on their own work.

Step 2: Establish the Non-Negotiable Contract

- **Action:** Share this contract with your Body Double and commit to it:

My Role (The Worker)	Your Role (The Body Double)
I commit to working on the task for **30 minutes** without checking my phone.	You commit to being visibly present and working on *your own* task.
My check-in question is: "What is the very next tiny step?"	You agree to provide **zero criticism**, only gentle, factual support.
If I get up to wander, you gently say, "Timer is still running."	You agree **not to do the task for me** or judge my pace.

Step 3: Anchor with Visibility

- **Action:** If working virtually, ensure cameras are on. If in-person, sit in the same room. The visible presence of the Body Double acts as the continuous, external anchor for your attention.

Action Toolkit B: The Pomodoro Planning Grid

Use this grid to plan an organizing task, converting the abstract effort into timed, manageable sprints.

Step 1: Select and Estimate

- **Action:** Take a medium-sized organizing task (e.g., organizing a drawer) and estimate its duration in Pomodoro intervals (25 minutes of work).

Step 2: Schedule with Buffers

- **Action:** Create a time-blocked schedule for this task. **Crucially,** add 5-minute breaks after each Pomodoro and **add 25% extra time** to your total estimate to compensate for **time blindness**.

Time Block	Activity	Neuro-Benefit
3:00 – 3:25 PM	Pomodoro 1: Sort items in the right-side drawer (Work / Focus)	Finitude reduces overwhelm and task initiation deficit.
3:25 – 3:30 PM	**Break:** Stand, stretch, get water (Reward / Reset)	Prevents mental fatigue and hyperfocus.
3:30 – 3:55 PM	Pomodoro 2: Label containers and discard garbage (Work / Focus)	Creates momentum through a visible, tangible "win."
3:55 – 4:00 PM	**Break:** Listen to one song, quick mind-reset	Accommodates brain's need for novelty.
4:00 – 4:15 PM	Final 15-Min Push: Put items back in labeled containers (Completion)	Ensures the task is finished while energy is still high.

Commitment: By scheduling tasks this way, you are treating your organizing efforts as non-negotiable **appointments**, which the ADHD brain handles much better than abstract to-do list items.

Toolkit 4: The Sustainability Audit

Objective: Ensure Long-Term Maintenance and Prevent the Snowball Effect

The biggest threat to organization is the rapid accumulation of small items, the **Snowball Effect**, which quickly triggers overwhelming chaos. This toolkit creates a low-stakes, highly effective maintenance ritual.

Scientific Anchor: The 15-Minute Rule

The **Daily 15-Minute Reset** works by utilizing the principle of **low-friction maintenance**. Since organization fails when it demands excessive mental energy or time, limiting the routine to 15 minutes ensures the effort is finite and low-stakes. This consistent interruption prevents small clutter points from reaching the overwhelming threshold that triggers paralysis and contributes to chronic cognitive load.

Action Toolkit: Customizing Your Daily Reset Checklist

Step 1: Identify Your Three High-Impact Zones

- **Action:** List the three areas in your home that accumulate clutter the fastest and cause the most anxiety (e.g., The Kitchen Counter, The Digital Inbox, The Living Room Coffee Table).

Step 2: Create the Customized 15-Minute Checklist

- **Action:** Design a three-step checklist that takes no more than 15 minutes to complete, focusing only on the highest-leverage actions. This is your non-negotiable daily commitment.

Reset Zone	Action (Maximum 5 Minutes Each)	Completion Cue
Kitchen / Sink	Load all dishes from the sink and counter into the dishwasher.	Counter is cleared.
Landing Strip	Ensure keys, wallet, and phone are placed *on* the designated strip.	All high-loss items are secured.
Digital Space	Close all unnecessary browser tabs (leaving only 3 open) and file 5 emails (Delete, Do, Defer) into the "To Sort" folder.	Desktop / Inbox is visually calm.

Step 3: Integrate and Allow for Imperfection

- **Action:** Commit to performing this 15-minute sequence at the **same time** each day (e.g., right before starting the coffee maker, or immediately after turning off the TV).

- **Rule of the Junk Drawer:** If an item's "home" is not immediately obvious, place it in the designated **Junk Drawer / Basket** rather than stopping to make a decision. This maintains the momentum of the reset ritual and prevents decision fatigue from derailing the 15 minutes.

Conclusion: Your Commitment to Sustainable Action

The chaos of unmanaged ADHD is not a burden you must carry alone; it is a complex system that requires complex, compassionate, and strategic solutions. By working through this Action Toolkit, you have created a powerful suite of external structures that compensate for internal inconsistencies in focus, memory, and motivation.

Your commitment moving forward is to **consistency over perfection**. There will be days when the timer is ignored, and days when the Landing Strip is missed. The key is not to succumb to shame, but to engage the principle of **self-compassion** and return to your customized checklist immediately, treating the setback as valuable **data** for refining your system. The ultimate reward for this work is the liberation of your mental energy, creating the cognitive bandwidth necessary to engage fully with the deeper work of sharpening focus and emotional mastery that awaits you in the next books. Commit to using one tool from this kit every day for the next week.

CONCLUSION

SUMMARY: YOUR FOUNDATIONAL SYSTEMS

You have completed the foundational work of Book 1, moving through the essential stages of confronting chaos, establishing predictability, and anchoring sustainable habits. This work was dedicated to addressing the most significant external barrier to a fulfilling life with Attention-Deficit/ Hyperactivity Disorder (ADHD): **chronic disorganization** and the resulting **overwhelm** that characterizes the female experience of the condition.

The core principle of this entire process has been to recognize that your struggle was never a character flaw or a reflection of incompetence. Instead, it was a neurobiological reality stemming from predictable deficits in **executive function (EF)**—namely, working memory, task initiation, and filtering capacity. By completing this foundational phase, you have successfully moved away from the debilitating cycle of self-blame and avoidance, and you have constructed a resilient, external scaffolding that is designed to perform the organizational tasks your inconsistent internal memory cannot reliably manage.

This chapter synthesizes the five key organizational pillars into a cohesive, integrated system, demonstrating the profound **neurobiological payoff** of this hard work. This stability in your external life is the necessary prerequisite—the "clean desk"—that frees up the mental bandwidth required to master the more complex internal challenges of focus, emotions, and relational stability that await you in the subsequent books.

Section 1: The Integrated System: Five Pillars of External Scaffolding

The systems you have built over the course of this book work in synergy, with each chapter addressing a specific neurobiological deficit to systematically reduce the overall **cognitive load** and **task activation energy** that once led to paralysis.

1. Pillar of Initiation: Defeating Paralysis (Chapter 1)

The most immediate hurdle to organization is the **task activation deficit**—the inability to initiate tasks, which is often mistaken for laziness but is rooted in dopamine dysregulation and cognitive shutdown.

- **The Problem:** The overwhelming scale of a messy room or daunting project triggers an immediate **paralysis response** as the brain's filtering mechanisms struggle to find a single, manageable starting point.
- **The Solution:** The methodical breakdown of overwhelming tasks into **micro-steps** and the identification of the **"Next Action"** (an action so simple it requires minimal effort and no decision-making) provides the necessary **activation energy**.
- **Neurobiological Payoff:** This process creates rapid, tangible "wins," each providing a small but necessary burst of **dopamine** that reinforces productive behavior and builds **momentum**, thus bypassing the reliance on inconsistent internal motivation.

2. Pillar of Memory: Designing for Visibility (Chapter 2)

Once you begin a project, maintaining order requires that items remain "in mind" and accessible, a process challenged by the working memory deficit.

- **The Problem:** The **"out of sight, out of mind"** phenomenon, a direct consequence of compromised working memory, leads to chronic loss, constant searching, and the feeling that items cease to exist the moment they are put away in hidden storage.
- **The Solution:** The implementation of **visible storage**—prioritizing clear containers, open baskets without lids, and transparent labeling—transforms the environment into a functional **external memory system.**
- **Neurobiological Payoff:** This strategy ensures that items remain visually prominent, reducing the mental effort required for retrieval and actively compensating for the internal memory deficit. By eliminating the ambiguity of hidden spaces, you reduce the **cognitive cost of visual noise** in your immediate environment.

3. Pillar of Clarity: Establishing Predictability (Chapter 3)

The daily interaction with objects without a designated place consumes significant mental bandwidth. Predictability is the key to automating placement.

- **The Problem:** The absence of a defined destination for every item forces the brain to engage in constant, taxing micro-decisions (e.g., *Where does this pen go?*), leading to systemic **decision fatigue** that drains executive function reserves.
- **The Solution:** The commitment to a specific, low-friction **designated "home"** for every item, coupled with the establishment of the **"Landing Strip"** for high-loss items (keys, wallet, phone), eliminates ambiguity. The **"Junk Drawer"** strategically manages inevitable chaos by providing a contained release valve for items without a determined home, preventing their spread onto high-leverage surfaces.
- **Neurobiological Payoff:** This creates reliable **automaticity**. Placement becomes a simple habit rather than a conscious decision, conserving precious executive function for higher-leverage tasks like planning and sustained focus.

4. **Pillar of Accountability: Sustaining Momentum (Chapter 4)**

Internal motivation is notoriously inconsistent. Maintaining momentum requires strategic, external support to anchor attention.

- **The Problem:** The difficulty in maintaining sustained attention, coupled with **time blindness** (the inability to accurately gauge the passage of time), makes follow-through challenging and often results in abandonment of tasks before completion.
- **The Solution:** Leveraging **Body Doubling**—working in the presence of a supportive partner or peer—provides the **external accountability** needed to anchor attention and bypass the internal activation deficit. Simultaneously, using **Timers** (such as the Pomodoro Technique) transforms abstract time into **concrete, finite blocks**, preventing the work from feeling overwhelming.
- **Neurobiological Payoff:** The Body Double acts as an **external executive function**, and the timer ensures that effort is finite and rewarded quickly (dopamine hit from completion), which fuels sustained engagement and prevents the deep mental fatigue caused by unstructured work.

5. **Pillar of Resilience: Stopping the Snowball (Chapter 5)**

Even the best systems fail if small messes are allowed to escalate into paralyzing chaos. Long-term success relies on low-friction maintenance.

- **The Problem:** The **"Snowball Effect"**, where minor clutter rapidly accumulates, quickly crosses a threshold that triggers **paralysis** and a full system shutdown, often exacerbated by the **"all-or-nothing"** perfectionism trap.
- **The Solution:** The implementation of the **Daily 15-Minute "Reset" Routine**, focused only on the highest-leverage areas (e.g., kitchen counter, Landing Strip), ensures that the accumulation of clutter is interrupted before it becomes cognitively paralyzing.
- **Neurobiological Payoff:** This ritual prioritizes **consistency over perfection**, training the brain that **partial effort is valuable effort**. By performing frequent, short bursts of maintenance, you prevent the chronic accrual of **cognitive debt**, sustaining a lower, more manageable level of background anxiety.

Section 2: The Neurobiological Payoff: Reclaiming Your Mental Bandwidth

The integration of these five pillars yields a profound transformation that goes far beyond a tidy home. The organizational systems built in Book 1 are the foundational mechanism for achieving internal stability, reducing the **shame** that has accompanied unmanaged ADHD, and conserving the vital resources necessary for focused work.

1. The Critical Reduction of Cognitive Load

The most significant payoff of functional organization is the dramatic reduction in the brain's chronic **cognitive load**. Unmanaged, this load is the sum of mental effort consumed by:

- Searching for lost items (working memory drain).
- Filtering competing visual stimuli (filtering deficit).
- Making unnecessary micro-decisions (decision fatigue).
- Worrying about deadlines and forgetting tasks (time blindness anxiety).

By externalizing these burdens, you free up immense cognitive bandwidth. This liberation of mental energy is directly tied to an increased capacity for other executive functions. When the brain is no longer consumed by low-level chaos, its resources can be redirected toward the sustained, complex effort required for **deep work** and **emotional regulation**.

2. The Antidote to Shame and the Inner Critic

For a woman with ADHD, chronic disorganization is one of the most significant sources of shame, fueled by the societal pressure to maintain an organized home and family. The systems in Book 1 provide tangible, undeniable **evidence of competence** that actively counters the narrative of the inner critic.

- **Building Self-Efficacy:** Every successful use of the Landing Strip or completion of the Daily Reset provides a small, positive neurochemical reinforcement, building **self-efficacy**—the belief in one's ability to succeed—which is the direct psychological antidote to the shame and feelings of inadequacy that characterize unmanaged ADHD.

- **Practicing Self-Compassion:** The intentional design of a system that accommodates neurobiological challenges (e.g., clear containers, low-friction entry points) is a profound act of **self-compassion**. By rejecting the toxic ideal of perfectionism and embracing functional imperfection, you are treating yourself with the kindness and understanding you would offer a struggling friend, reducing the emotional friction caused by self-judgment.

3. Stabilizing the Nervous System and Relationships

Organizational friction is a direct cause of chronic stress and relational tension. Stability in the environment leads to predictability in relationships.

- **Reduced Anxiety:** A predictable environment reduces the brain's need to be constantly on high alert, monitoring for potential disasters (the lost keys, the forgotten chore). This stability calms the nervous system, reducing the **physiological arousal** that exacerbates emotional dysregulation and anxiety.
- **De-personalizing Conflict:** By externalizing shared household tasks onto a neutral system (e.g., a chore chart or a shared calendar), the couple can move from arguing over perceived failures ("You never put that away!") to collaboratively solving a system problem ("The home for this item is not clear enough, let's fix it"). This shifts the dynamic from an unhealthy "taskmaster / scolded child" relationship to a partnership, fostering greater empathy and trust.

Section 3: The Bridge to Internal Mastery (Book 2)

The work of Book 1 is a crucial first step, but it is not the destination. Its primary purpose is to clear the runway so that you have the mental resources, the structural platform, and the physical space necessary for the demanding work of **internal mastery**. The stability you have created provides the essential bridge to the focus strategies in Book 2.

- **The Foundation for Focus:** A brain that is constantly distracted by visual noise and the low-level anxiety of disorganization is a brain incapable of deep, sustained concentration. The clear desk, the organized digital space, and the reduced background anxiety achieved in Book 1 are the necessary prerequisites for achieving the state of **deep work** addressed in the next phase.

- **The Conserved Executive Function:** The EF resources you conserved by eliminating decision fatigue and task paralysis must now be actively redirected. Book 2, **Beat Overwhelm and Sharpen Executive Function for the ADHD Woman**, will teach you how to use this reclaimed mental bandwidth to engage in the cognitively demanding work of **Time Blocking**, strengthening your **working memory**, and mastering **single-tasking** to achieve intentional attention.
- **The System for Emotional Growth:** The emotional stability gained from a less chaotic external environment provides the bandwidth necessary for the intensive internal work of **emotional regulation** (Book 4) and **relational effectiveness** (Book 5). You have built the vessel; now you will learn how to steer it.

Commit to maintaining the foundational systems you have built. Consistency is the goal; self-compassion is the method. This mastery of your external world has transformed your relationship with overwhelm, paving the way for the profound transformation of your focus and emotional landscape.

BOOK TWO

BEAT OVERWHELM FOR THE ADHD WOMAN

INTRODUCTION

THE PARADOX OF FOCUS AND THE MASTERING OF TIME

The foundational work of organization (Book 1) created a sanctuary in your external world by clearing visual clutter, defeating task paralysis, and establishing predictable systems. This stability reduced the debilitating pressure of external chaos. Now, the journey shifts profoundly inward. This book is dedicated to mastering the internal landscape of the ADHD brain: regulating attention, conquering the elusive nature of time, and strengthening the core processes of **Executive Function (EF)** that are essential for long-term productivity and self-efficacy.

For many women with Attention-Deficit / Hyperactivity Disorder (ADHD), the concept of "focus" is a profound paradox, a double-edged sword that can feel both like a superpower and a cruel burden. On one hand, a woman's attention can be so fragmented that she experiences a "thousand-yard stare," daydreaming, or "zoning out" during conversations or meetings, which leads to forgotten details and a pervasive sense of being perpetually in a fog. This fragmented attention makes it difficult to remember instructions, organize a schedule, or stay on task, all vital components of daily functioning. On the other hand, when a task is intensely stimulating, novel, or engaging, the ADHD brain can lock into a state of intense, almost obsessive **hyperfocus**. While this state can lead to incredible bursts of productivity and creative output, it is often uncontrolled: a woman may lose track of time, forget to eat, and fail to attend to critical responsibilities, creating significant friction in her life.

The fundamental challenge is not a lack of ability to pay attention, but rather a profound **difficulty in regulating it**. The issue lies in the brain's struggle to control its "on / off" switch, preventing it from consistently directing its mental spotlight where it needs to be and sustaining it for mundane, but necessary, tasks. This inherent **dysregulation of attention** is a primary driver of the chronic overwhelm that defines the female ADHD experience, leading to a profound sense of mental fatigue, inadequacy, and being perpetually "frenzied, frazzled, and overwhelmed."

This book provides the strategic, evidence-based roadmap to move beyond this paradox. It is built upon the understanding that achieving control over your attention is the key to defeating overwhelm and unlocking your full potential.

The Neurobiological Reality: Executive Function and the Time Barrier

To master focus and time, we must first confront their neurological roots. The difficulties with planning, productivity, and sustained attention are not signs of poor intelligence or character; they are direct consequences of how the ADHD brain is wired, specifically in the areas governing executive functions and motivation.

1. Executive Function (EF) Deficits: The Command Center

Executive functions (EFs) are the high-level mental processes that allow us to regulate behavior, think before acting, meet new challenges with flexibility, and stay focused and concentrate. These functions, which include planning, goal setting, working memory, inhibitory control, and time management, are so essential to well-being that they have been described as the **"mental toolkit for success,"** often proving more predictive of academic and career success than either socioeconomic status or IQ.

For the significant percentage of adults with ADHD who experience EF deficits, the brain's **prefrontal cortex**, the "command center" for these skills, is often less developed or less active than in neurotypical individuals. This deficit leads to measurable difficulties in nearly every aspect of organization and productivity, from struggling to hold multi-step instructions in mind (poor working memory) to the inability to start a task (task activation deficit). This constant struggle creates a feeling of profound functional inadequacy, contributing directly to the shame and anxiety so common in women with ADHD.

2. The Dopamine-Driven Dysregulation

The ADHD brain's relationship with attention is distinct and deeply rooted in its **dopamine system**. Dopamine, the key neurotransmitter for motivation, reward, and activation, is thought to be dysregulated in the ADHD brain, often resulting in lower effective levels in the synapses.

This deficit creates a powerful, persistent craving for **novelty and immediate stimulation**. When a task is under-stimulating (boring, repetitive, or requiring sustained, effortful attention), the brain struggles to produce enough dopamine to find it interesting, leading to distraction, mind-wandering, and task avoidance. The opposite is true for hyperfocus. The strategies in this book are designed to strategically introduce external structure, like fixed time limits, novelty simulation, and immediate feedback, to supply the necessary cues and reward required to sustain attention on necessary tasks, thereby bypassing the internal dopamine deficit.

3. Time Blindness: The Invisible Barrier to Planning

Perhaps the most disruptive deficit for productivity and life management is **time blindness**, the inability to accurately perceive or estimate the flow of time. Time does not feel like a consistent, measurable resource; instead, the ADHD brain lives predominantly in the "now," making the future feel abstract and less urgent.

This difficulty in feeling the passage of time creates several critical challenges:

- **Estimation Deficit:** Individuals with ADHD consistently underestimate how long tasks will take, leading to chronic rushing, missed deadlines, and the inevitable stress that results from constant lateness.
- **Prioritization Failure:** Because the future is abstract, the urgency of a deadline that is a week away feels equal to the urgency of a deadline that is three months away. The brain struggles to prioritize based on true time sensitivity.
- **Overwhelm by Infinity:** When faced with a task, the time needed to complete it feels amorphous and infinite, which instantly triggers an overload response and **paralysis**.

The comprehensive solution explored in this book is to stop relying on inconsistent internal time perception and instead use **concrete, visual tools** and **intentional scheduling** to make time palpable, measurable, and manageable. This involves mastering techniques like **Time Blocking** to enforce duration and utilizing **Timers** to make abstract time visible.

The Emotional and Cognitive Toll of a Fragmented Mind

The daily struggle with attention dysregulation and EF deficits takes a significant toll on a woman's emotional and cognitive well-being, leading directly to the pervasive sense of overwhelm that this book seeks to defeat.

1. High Cognitive Load and Mental Fatigue

The ADHD brain often struggles with an impaired **filtering mechanism**, meaning it registers all incoming stimuli, a flickering light, a phone notification, a fleeting thought, with almost equal importance. This results in a constant, effortful struggle to filter distractions, creating a state of chronically high **cognitive load**: the mental effort consumed by working memory. Research indicates that this high cognitive load disproportionately impacts performance for people with ADHD.

This continuous mental fight leads to profound **mental fatigue**, a temporary sluggishness and slowdown of thinking abilities that results in poor focus, forgetfulness, and exhaustion. This chronic effort to manage an overstimulated mind is the **"ADHD Tax"** on energy reserves, leading to burnout and a diminished capacity for sustained effort. The strategic management of attention and task structure is designed to dramatically lower this baseline cognitive load, reserving mental energy for the actual work of focus.

2. Shame, Masking, and the Loss of Self-Worth

The persistent difficulties with focus, time management, and follow-through often lead a woman with ADHD to internalize her struggles and blame herself, interpreting her symptoms as moral or character failings. This internalized struggle is amplified by the intense societal pressure on women to be organized, calm, and effortlessly competent.

This conflict drives **masking**, the exhausting practice of developing sophisticated compensatory behaviors (e.g., meticulously over-preparing, building in extreme time buffers) to hide the internal chaos and appear "neurotypical" to the outside world. For instance, a woman might pretend to take notes in a meeting to mask the fact that she has a "thousand-yard stare" or is "zoning out." This continuous performance is an invisible burden that leads to a lifetime of internalized shame, anxiety, and a shattered sense of self-worth. By providing a clear, neurobiologically-grounded roadmap for focus and EF mastery, this book empowers a woman to replace the narrative of shame with a foundation of strategic self-efficacy.

The Strategic Roadmap for Sustained Focus

The path to defeating overwhelm involves strategically creating external and internal structures that compensate for EF deficits. This book guides you through a process of learning to work *with* your brain's unique wiring, not against it, through evidence-based practices drawn from Cognitive Behavioral Therapy (CBT) and specialized ADHD coaching.

1. Making Time Concrete and Visible: The primary barrier of **time blindness** must be solved with external tools. You will learn to use visual, concrete scheduling systems, such as **Time Blocking**, to enforce duration and assign a fixed time slot to every activity, task, and transition. This contrasts sharply with vague to-do lists, which the brain can easily skip because they lack context and duration. Time Blocking forces planning and prioritization, directly mitigating the time estimation deficit by scheduling intentional time buffers.

2. Creating Focused Sprints: Initiation and sustained attention must be anchored by structure. You will master the **Pomodoro Technique**, breaking work into short, focused sprints followed by mandatory breaks, customizing the duration to match your personal attention span. This structured interval provides the necessary **finitude** to reduce the overwhelm that triggers paralysis, while the scheduled breaks prevent burnout and interrupt the cycle of uncontrolled hyperfocus, serving as a critical external circuit-breaker for attention. The visible timer makes time palpable and reinforces productive effort.

3. Strengthening Internal Resilience: Sustained EF mastery requires building the internal mental muscles responsible for planning and recall. This involves utilizing structured, consistent planning routines and cognitive exercises designed to improve **working memory** and **inhibitory control** (thinking before acting). By establishing fixed, actionable daily and weekly planning rituals, you externalize task goals and instructions, supporting the prefrontal cortex. Furthermore, intentional practices, such as **single-tasking**, are employed to minimize the draining **context switching cost** that is so taxing on the ADHD brain.

4. Protecting Your Cognitive Sanctuary: True focus is maintained by ruthlessly eliminating external and internal noise that depletes your finite mental energy. You will learn to recognize and proactively minimize the sources of **digital noise** and unnecessary **stimuli** that fragment your attention and increase cognitive load. This includes strategies like **Notification Annihilation** across all devices and reducing the number of open browser tabs, which are all "open loops" consuming precious working memory. Sustaining focus is a product of protecting your energy through prioritizing fundamental well-being factors, such as optimizing sleep hygiene and incorporating intentional physical activity, to regulate dopamine and mitigate the effects of chronic **mental fatigue**.

The culmination of this strategic work is a profound sense of self-efficacy and control. You are replacing the frantic, reactive cycle of overwhelm with a calm, strategic rhythm of intentional action. The stability achieved in Book 1 (external structure) provides the critical platform, and the EF mastery achieved here (internal structure) provides the necessary skill set to move toward integrated success and prepare you for the complex work of emotional regulation and relational depth that lies ahead.

CHAPTER 1

VISUALIZE TIME: BANISH TIME BLINDNESS WITH CONCRETE SCHEDULING TOOLS

The foundational stability created by organizing your external environment (Book 1) now clears the path for the deepest internal challenge of Attention-Deficit / Hyperactivity Disorder (ADHD): the mastery of attention and time. For the woman with ADHD, the most insidious barrier to productivity and the primary driver of chronic stress is a core executive function deficit known as **Time Blindness**.

Time blindness is the neurological inability to accurately perceive, estimate, or feel the passage of time. Time does not feel like a consistent, measurable resource; instead, the ADHD brain operates predominantly in the "now," making the future feel abstract, distant, and therefore, less urgent. The consequence of this temporal vacuum is devastating: chronic lateness, perpetual underestimation of task durations, missed deadlines, poor long-term planning, and a debilitating feeling that deadlines emerge suddenly, as if out of nowhere. This struggle is not a character flaw or a failure to prioritize; it is a measurable neurocognitive reality that requires strategic, external compensation.

This chapter provides the critical first step in mastering Executive Function (EF): a shift in time management from abstract internal perception to **concrete, visible, and tangible tools**. By learning to externalize time and make it visually palatable, you systematically counteract the symptoms of time blindness, turning time from a source of anxiety and chaos into a predictable ally that you can manage and trust. The goal is to move from a reactive state, constantly rushing and playing catch-up, to a proactive, calm rhythm of intentional scheduling and focus.

Section 1: The Neurobiological Reality of Time Blindness

To effectively banish time blindness, we must first understand its neurobiological origins. The difficulty with time perception is a direct symptom of EF deficits rooted in the brain's "command center" for planning and self-regulation.

1. The Prefrontal Cortex and Time Perception

Executive functions, the suite of high-level mental processes that govern self-control, planning, and goal-directed behavior, are primarily controlled by the **prefrontal cortex**. Research indicates that in individuals with ADHD, this region is often less developed or less active, leading to compromised functioning in time-related skills.

- **Impaired Working Memory:** Time management requires **working memory**, the ability to hold and manipulate transient information, such as remembering how long a similar task took last time, or keeping multiple steps of a schedule in mind. A deficit here means the ADHD brain cannot reliably retrieve past temporal data, leading to a consistent struggle with accurate duration estimation.

- **Deficit in Inhibitory Control:** Time management also relies on **inhibitory control**—the ability to resist immediate gratification and prioritize long-term, abstract rewards (like future career success or financial security) over immediate, short-term rewards (like scrolling social media). Because the future feels abstract to the time-blind brain, the motivation to delay gratification for a distant reward is significantly weakened, contributing to chronic procrastination and poor future planning.

2. The Dopamine-Driven Urgency Gap

The struggle with time blindness is profoundly influenced by the ADHD brain's **dopamine dysregulation**. Dopamine, the neurotransmitter for motivation and reward, is released in anticipation of a reward, driving goal-directed action.

For the ADHD brain, the dysregulated dopamine system means that the sense of **urgency** required to initiate a task is not generated internally unless the reward is immediate or the consequence of avoidance is imminent (i.e., a looming deadline). Because the future is abstract:

- **Low Perceived Reward:** Tasks scheduled a week from now carry little to no emotional or chemical reward, making them impossible to initiate.
- **The Procrastination Loop:** Action is delayed until the deadline transforms the task into an immediate, high-stakes crisis, which finally triggers the intense dopamine / adrenaline response required for activation—a state often mistaken for working best under pressure, but which is neurobiologically driven crisis management.

The result is that the time-blind woman exists in a perpetual state of stress and shame, constantly rushing to meet self-imposed or external deadlines. The solution must provide external, visible cues that consistently generate the necessary sense of urgency and reward *before* the crisis hits.

Section 2: The Strategy Shift: Making Time Concrete and Visible

The core therapeutic strategy for time blindness is to stop relying on inconsistent internal perception and to replace it with a dependable **external visualization system**. Time must be made tangible—something the eye can see, the hand can touch, and the brain can anchor to.

1. Timers as External Cues

Timers are the most direct way to transform abstract time into a concrete, visible, and manageable resource. The ticking, counting-down clock bypasses the internal struggle with time estimation and provides a non-negotiable anchor for attention.

- **Finitude vs. Infinity:** The greatest source of overwhelm in time blindness is the feeling that a task requires an amorphous, infinite amount of time, which instantly triggers **paralysis**. A timer imposes **finitude**, a clear, visible end point (e.g., "This task requires only 25 minutes"), which significantly lowers the activation energy required to start. The commitment becomes manageable and approachable.
- **External Pacing:** For the brain that struggles with staying on task, the timer acts as a constant external reminder and pacer, reducing mind-wandering and sustaining concentration. It is a necessary external executive function that monitors the passage of time for you.
- **Visual Analog Clocks:** For deeper work on time blindness, visual analog clocks (like the Time Timer), which physically show the passage of time disappearing, can be profoundly helpful. These tools translate the duration into a visible, diminishing space, which is far easier for the time-blind brain to grasp than abstract numbers on a digital display.

2. Time Blocking: The Ultimate Visualization Tool

While traditional to-do lists serve a necessary purpose by simply externalizing tasks, they are fundamentally inadequate for the time-blind brain because they lack two crucial elements: **context and duration**.

Strategy	ADHD Challenge Addressed	Why It Often Fails the ADHD Brain
Traditional To-Do List	Working Memory Deficit (forgetting tasks)	Lacks time context, fails to enforce duration, and tasks feel equally urgent, leading to overwhelm and skipping.
Time Blocking	Time Blindness, Prioritization, Estimation	Forces the user to allocate a finite, visible block of time for *every* activity, making time concrete and scheduling transitions.

Time Blocking is the essential visualization strategy that directly addresses time blindness. It is a scheduling method that requires you to block out specific periods for activities, providing a clear, visible structure for the entire day.

- **Forces Estimation:** Time Blocking mandates that you pre-allocate a duration for every task (e.g., "Email Triage: 9:00 AM–9:45 AM"). This intentional allocation forces the engagement of the planning aspect of EF, mitigating the estimation deficit that plagues the ADHD brain.
- **Minimizes Guesswork:** When time is visually blocked, you eliminate the cognitive guesswork of "What should I do next?" The schedule becomes a clear, non-negotiable roadmap, which reduces feelings of overwhelm and supports better transitions between activities—a common sticking point for the neurodivergent brain.
- **Prioritizes by Finitude:** Instead of prioritizing by abstract importance, Time Blocking prioritizes by the finite reality of time. A task that is blocked from 10:00 AM to 11:00 AM has a clear boundary, which reduces the anxiety of the task feeling infinite.

Section 3: Structuring Your Time Blocks for ADHD Success

Implementing Time Blocking effectively requires customizing the system to accommodate the inherent neurobiological deficits of the ADHD brain, turning a rigid schedule into a flexible, supportive framework.

1. Compensating for the Estimation Deficit

People with ADHD consistently underestimate how long tasks will take—a phenomenon that fuels rushing, stress, and eventual system abandonment. The scheduling must proactively build in buffers to neutralize this deficit.

- **Schedule with Buffers:** The cardinal rule of ADHD time blocking is to **schedule more time than you think you need**. Intentionally add a time buffer of 25-50% to your initial estimate for every major task. If a report should take two hours, schedule 2.5 to 3 hours. This simple adjustment provides crucial breathing room, reducing the stress that comes from self-imposed, unrealistic temporal constraints.
- **Block Transitions:** Do not schedule tasks back-to-back. The process of shifting focus from one task to the next, known as **context switching**, is highly draining for the ADHD brain, which incurs a measurable cognitive cost each time it switches attention. Schedule specific, intentional transition periods (e.g., "5-Minute Break / Reset") between major blocks. This supports a smoother mental shift and maintains momentum.
- **Color-Coding:** Use a simple, consistent color-coding system to visually categorize blocks (e.g., blue for Work / Deep Focus, green for Health / Self-Care, yellow for Administrative / Errands). This visual cue allows the brain to quickly process and prioritize the schedule at a glance, minimizing the cognitive effort required to interpret the schedule.

2. Externalizing the Schedule (Visual and Digital Anchors)

The schedule must live in a location that is impossible to ignore, thereby acting as a constant **external working memory cue** that bypasses internal forgetfulness.

- **Visual Prominence:** Place your time-blocked schedule in a location of high visual traffic, a large wall calendar, a whiteboard in your office, or a prominent digital calendar view on your desktop. If the schedule is hidden away in a notebook or a deep folder, the time-blind brain will forget it exists.
- **Digital Reminders:** Leverage technology to provide automated, external cues. Use digital calendars (like Google Calendar) that provide multiple, automated reminders for transitions and task completion. Set alerts for a week before, a day before, and an hour before major deadlines to anchor the abstract future into the urgent present.

3. Structuring Work with Finitude (The Pomodoro Precursor)

While the full implementation of the Pomodoro Technique is covered in Chapter 3, the principle of **finite effort** must be integrated into your time blocks now. When scheduling a task, the time block must feel like a commitment to a manageable sprint, not an overwhelming marathon.

- **The Sprint Structure:** When you block out an hour for a project, mentally commit to that hour as a **focused sprint**. Break the hour down into smaller intervals (e.g., two 25-minute periods with a 10-minute break in between). This strategy reduces the urge to procrastinate because the commitment to start is short and finite, making the project psychologically approachable.
- **Clear Boundaries:** The most powerful rule of Time Blocking is to **respect the block**. When the scheduled time is up, the task stops, whether it is finished or not. This protects your boundaries and ensures that one hyperfocused task does not bleed into and derail the subsequent appointments, maintaining the integrity of the overall schedule.

Section 4: Time Blocking vs. To-Do Lists: A Neuroscientific Comparison

The reliance on traditional to-do lists, while common, fails to adequately support the EF deficits of time blindness and is a primary driver of overwhelm for women with ADHD. Understanding this distinction is key to embracing Time Blocking as the superior visualization tool.

The Failure of the To-Do List

Traditional to-do lists are simply a memory dump, a place to record tasks so they aren't forgotten. However, they fail the ADHD brain in critical ways:

- **Lack of Context:** They list tasks without assigning duration, effort, or location, making all tasks appear equally large and overwhelming. This ambiguity triggers **decision fatigue** and contributes to task paralysis.
- **Poor Prioritization:** A long, undifferentiated list of tasks (e.g., "Email boss," "Buy groceries," "Renew insurance," "Call friend") does not indicate which item is urgent or which requires the most time. The brain struggles to prioritize based on abstract importance, often defaulting to either the easiest / most stimulating task or, conversely, avoiding the list entirely.
- **Fueling Shame:** When a long list inevitably goes unfinished, it acts as a persistent source of shame and negative feedback, reinforcing the inner critic's narrative of failure and incompetence.

The Strength of Time Blocking

Time Blocking transforms the vague list into a functional map of reality, providing the structure and clear boundaries required for the ADHD brain to engage effectively.

- **Enforced Planning:** To create a time block, you *must* estimate duration and identify the steps involved, forcing the brain to engage the crucial **planning and organization** aspects of executive function.
- **Visual Urgency:** By turning the schedule into a visible, color-coded block, time is visually represented as a finite resource.

This external pressure creates a necessary sense of urgency that motivates initiation, bypassing the internal dopamine deficit required to start tasks that are not inherently stimulating.

- **Sustained Effort:** Time Blocking supports better transitions and reduces the cognitive load associated with making moment-to-moment decisions. This sustained, lower-friction effort is the key to maintaining momentum and avoiding the burnout caused by constant task-switching and chaotic urgency.

Conclusion: Reclaiming Your Time, Defeating Overwhelm

The journey of defeating overwhelm requires the mastery of time, the resource that is most often compromised by ADHD. Time blindness is a fundamental neurobiological challenge, but it is not an insurmountable one. By strategically externalizing your time perception, you systematically dismantle the planning, organization, and estimation deficits that have plagued your productivity.

The implementation of **visual timers** and the discipline of **Time Blocking** transform time from an abstract source of anxiety into a concrete, manageable, and predictable ally. You are moving past the frustrating cycle of self-blame and chronic lateness, replacing it with a strategic, intentional rhythm that honors your brain's unique need for structure and visible cues.

This new mastery of time is the crucial second pillar of your journey. By creating a reliable time map, you ensure that the mental energy you conserved through external organization (Book 1) is now actively redirected toward high-leverage, sustained focus. This is the foundation upon which true attention mastery, emotional resilience, and integrated success will be built.

Chapter 1 Workbook: Visualize Time: Banish Time Blindness with Concrete Scheduling Tools

Objective: To practice externalizing time and creating visual blocks that counteract the effects of **Time Blindness**.

Scientific Anchor: Time Blocking forces the ADHD brain to estimate task duration, which directly addresses the estimation deficit and provides a clear, non-negotiable external structure that reduces overwhelm.

Activity 1.1: The Estimation Deficit Audit

Instructions: Select three medium-sized, recurring tasks. **Before** you start the task, write down your estimate. **After** completing the task, record the actual time spent. This exercise trains your Executive Function's estimation skill by providing immediate, factual feedback.

1. **Task: Loading / Unloading Dishwasher & Wiping Counters**
   - *Initial Estimate:* ______________________ *minutes*
   - *Actual Time Spent:* ___________________ *minutes*
2. **Task: Processing Email Inbox (Triage 20 messages)**
   - *Initial Estimate:* ______________________ *minutes*
   - *Actual Time Spent:* ___________________ *minutes*
3. **Task: Preparing / Assembling Dinner**
   - *Initial Estimate:* ______________________ *minutes*
   - *Actual Time Spent:* ___________________ *minutes*

Activity 1.2: The Time Block Conversion Challenge

Instructions: Take your vague to-do list for tomorrow and convert it into a fully time-blocked schedule. Ensure every activity—including breaks, transitions, and personal care—has a fixed duration and time slot.

1. **Vague To-Do List Items:** List three general tasks for tomorrow (e.g., "Work on report," "Errands," "Laundry").

Vague Tasks: ____

____

____

____

____

____

____

____

____

____

____

____

____

____

____

____

____

2. **Time Block Schedule:** Convert these vague tasks into fixed, timed appointments. **Crucially, include buffers and transitions.**

Time Slot	Activity	Duration	Neuro-Adjustment (Buffer / Cue)
9:00 AM – 10:00 AM	**Deep Work: Report Draft (Pomodoro Sprint)**	60 mins	(Block time for only ONE task; close all other tabs.)
10:00 AM – 10:15 AM	**Transition Block: Walk to Mailbox & Water**	15 mins	(Scheduled break to support smooth transition.)

Time Slot	Activity	Duration	Neuro-Adjustment (Buffer / Cue)
10:15 AM – 11:30 AM	**Work: Email Triage / Admin**	75 mins	(This is the scheduled **only** time for email.)
Your Block 1:			
Your Block 2:			
Your Block 3:			

Reflection 1.3: Visualizing Urgency and Finitude

Instructions: Reflect on the emotional difference between viewing a long list and viewing a time-blocked schedule.

1. When you look at a traditional to-do list, what is the primary negative emotion that arises (e.g., anxiety, overwhelm, paralysis)? Why?

   Emotion: ____

   ____

   ____

   ____

   ____

2. When you look at your new Time Block Schedule, what positive sense or feeling is created? (Think: clarity, control, confidence, structure, or reduced anxiety).

   Positive Feeling: ____

   ____

   ____

   ____

   ____

   ____

   ____

3. How does the act of scheduling a task to end at a specific time (e.g., "Stop at 10:00 AM") make the task feel less daunting and reduce the risk of procrastination? (Hint: Think about **finitude** vs. infinity).

   Reduction in Daunt: ____________________________________

   ____

   ____

   ____

   ____

   ____

   ____

CHAPTER 2

SCHEDULE SUCCESS: SWITCH FROM ENDLESS TO-DO LISTS TO TIME BLOCKING

The journey to defeat the chronic, pervasive feeling of overwhelm for a woman with Attention-Deficit / Hyperactivity Disorder (ADHD) requires the establishment of rigorous, external structure. In Chapter 1, we learned that **Time Blindness**, the inability to accurately feel or estimate the passage of time, is a core neurobiological deficit that makes reliable planning nearly impossible. This chapter introduces the strategic solution: the abandonment of traditional, ineffective to-do lists in favor of **Time Blocking**, an evidence-based scheduling method that directly counteracts the planning and estimation deficits of the ADHD brain.

While to-do lists are intuitively appealing, they externalize tasks, preventing memory overload, they are profoundly inadequate for sustaining productivity and reducing anxiety for the time-blind individual. A simple list fails to provide the two elements most critical to the ADHD brain: **context** (when does this happen?) and **duration** (how long will this take?). Without these concrete boundaries, the brain perceives the list as an overwhelming, undifferentiated mass of obligations, leading inevitably to **overload, procrastination, and shame**.

This chapter provides the blueprint for mastering Time Blocking, transforming abstract aspirations into fixed, non-negotiable appointments. By forcing a specific time allocation for every task, break, and transition, you systematically embed external Executive Function (EF) into your schedule, turning your calendar from a mere record of events into a powerful, proactive map of your day. The goal is to replace the chaos of reactive time management with the calm, self-directed rhythm of intentional action.

Section 1: The Neurobiological Failure of the To-Do List

The struggle with the traditional to-do list is not a sign of laziness; it is a measurable cognitive failure rooted in the specific ways ADHD compromises executive functions required for effective planning.

1. The Estimation Deficit and Overwhelm

The core flaw of the traditional to-do list is that it provides no information about time or effort. For the ADHD brain, which struggles acutely with time estimation (**time blindness**), this lack of duration context is devastating. When faced with an undifferentiated list, such as "Work on report," "Call insurance," "Go grocery shopping", the brain registers every item as equally demanding and equally urgent.

This perceived uniformity of effort leads to **cognitive overload** and **paralysis**. The entire list feels amorphous and infinite, triggering the brain's natural shutdown response, a phenomenon often described as **task paralysis**. The psychological cost of facing a long list that inevitably goes unfinished is immense: it acts as a constant source of negative feedback, reinforcing the inner critic's narrative of failure and incompetence, thereby fueling shame and low self-worth.

2. Lack of Context and Priority Ambiguity

The to-do list is simply a **memory dump**, a place to record tasks so they aren't forgotten. However, it fails to engage the crucial EF skills of **planning and prioritization**.

- **Ambiguity:** Because the list lacks context (Where? When? For how long?), the brain must expend significant energy deciding what to do next. This contributes to **decision fatigue**, draining EF reserves before any actual work is done. The brain often defaults to either the easiest / most stimulating task (ignoring priorities) or avoiding the list entirely.
- **The Problem of Vague Tasks:** As research suggests, if a task on a list is too vague (e.g., "Exercise" or "Organize"), the brain tends to skip right over it because it doesn't provide a clear, actionable starting point. Time Blocking, conversely, forces the user to define the action: "Exercise: 30-minute power walk from 5:00 PM to 5:30 PM."

3. The Fuel for Shame

When a woman sees a long list of tasks that remains consistently incomplete, the list becomes a document of personal failure. This persistent external reminder of underperformance amplifies the shame that women with ADHD are already prone to internalizing, damaging self-efficacy and confidence. Time Blocking, by limiting the expectation to what is temporally possible, turns the schedule from a source of judgment into a realistic plan for action.

Section 2: The Neurobiological Power of Time Blocking

Time Blocking is a therapeutic strategy that transforms how the ADHD brain interacts with time and tasks, serving as a powerful **external executive** function tool. It directly addresses the core deficits of time blindness, planning, and prioritization through intentional structure and visualization.

1. Making Time Concrete and Visible

The primary strength of Time Blocking is its ability to take abstract time and render it concrete and visible.

- **Visual Representation:** When time is represented by a physical block of color or space on a calendar, it becomes tangible, something the eye can see and the brain can anchor to. This visualization helps counteract **time blindness**, allowing the brain to better grasp and respect duration, transforming time from an enemy into a predictable resource.

- **Enforced Finitude:** By assigning clear start and end times to every activity, Time Blocking imposes **finitude** on tasks, ensuring they do not feel amorphous or infinite. The brain knows the commitment is limited (e.g., 9:00 AM to 10:30 AM), which significantly reduces the anxiety that triggers **paralysis** and lowers the necessary **activation energy** to begin.

2. Forcing Planning and Estimation

Time Blocking forces the brain to engage the crucial executive functions of planning and estimation *before* the work begins, providing the necessary cognitive scaffolding.

- **Pre-Allocation of Effort:** To create a Time Block, you *must* estimate the task duration and define the steps involved. This intentional pre-allocation of time forces the brain to engage the planning aspect of EF, a skill that is often inconsistent in ADHD.
- **Minimizing Guesswork:** When the entire day is mapped out, the cognitive guesswork of "What should I do next?" is eliminated. The schedule becomes a clear, non-negotiable roadmap, which reduces feelings of overwhelm and conserves EF reserves that would otherwise be wasted on moment-to-moment decision-making, a process that leads to severe fatigue.
- **Better Transitions:** Time Blocking supports smoother transitions between activities, a common sticking point for the neurodivergent brain, which struggles with context switching. By scheduling specific start and end times, you create clear boundaries that help the brain disengage from one task and transition smoothly to the next, conserving mental energy.

3. Leveraging the Dopamine System

The ADHD brain is driven by the immediate reward of a dopamine release. Time Blocking provides structured opportunities for this necessary reinforcement:

- **Immediate Feedback:** When a Time Block is completed, the visible act of checking it off, removing it from the schedule, or moving the focus to the next block provides a tangible sense of accomplishment. This immediate positive feedback generates a small burst of dopamine, reinforcing the productive behavior and building the necessary **momentum** to tackle the next scheduled task.

- **Visual Urgency:** The sight of the scheduled time block marching toward its end creates a constructive sense of urgency. This external pressure provides the necessary **activation energy** that the brain struggles to generate internally for boring tasks.

Section 3: Strategic Implementation for the ADHD Brain

To ensure Time Blocking is sustainable and effective, the system must be customized to accommodate the inherent deficits of ADHD, turning a rigid schedule into a flexible, supportive framework.

1. Compensating for the Estimation Deficit (The Buffer Rule)

People with ADHD consistently **underestimate** how long tasks will take, a phenomenon that fuels rushing, anxiety, and eventual system abandonment. Time Blocking must proactively neutralize this deficit.

- **Schedule with Buffers:** The cardinal rule of ADHD time blocking is to **intentionally schedule more time than you think you need**. Add a time buffer of 25–50% to your initial estimate for every major block of work. If a report should take two hours, schedule 2.5 to 3 hours. This simple adjustment provides crucial breathing room, reducing the stress that comes from unrealistic temporal constraints and preventing the schedule from becoming a source of impossible pressure.
- **Block Transitions:** Do not schedule tasks back-to-back. Intentional transition periods (e.g., "15-Minute Break / Reset" or "Walk to next meeting location") must be blocked between major focus tasks. This supports the smooth mental shift required for the ADHD brain and mitigates the high **cognitive cost of context switching**, which occurs every time the brain changes its focus.

2. Enforcing Boundaries (The Respect Rule)

The most powerful rule of Time Blocking is to **respect the block**—both its beginning and its end.

- **Respect the Start:** When the time block begins, the task is the non-negotiable focus. All distractions (e.g., checking email, answering texts) must be suppressed, mirroring the approach used for Deep Work. This training strengthens **inhibitory control**, the ability to resist temptations, a core EF skill.
- **Respect the End:** When the scheduled time is up, the task **stops**, whether it is finished or not. This protects the integrity of the overall schedule, ensuring that one hyperfocused task does not bleed into and derail the subsequent appointments, which is a major source of chaos for the ADHD brain. If the task is unfinished, schedule a new, finite block for it immediately.

3. Integrating Deep Work and Single-Tasking

Time Blocking naturally integrates the principle of **single-tasking**, the necessary antidote to the inefficient and draining process of rapid task-switching.

- **Anchor One Task:** Within a defined time block (e.g., 9:00 AM–10:30 AM), only **one specific, defined task** should be anchored (e.g., "Draft Introduction to Report," not "Work on Report"). This focus minimizes the cognitive effort required to decide what to do and prevents the brain from engaging in rapid toggling, which drains mental energy.
- **Batch Similar Tasks:** To further reduce the draining cost of **context switching**, schedule similar activities together in the same block (e.g., dedicate one block for "Email Triage / Admin" and a separate block for "Creative Writing / Deep Work"). This allows the brain to stay in one cognitive mode for a longer period, conserving EF resources.

4. Externalizing the Schedule (Visual and Digital Anchors)

The schedule must live in a location that is impossible to ignore, thereby acting as a constant **external working memory cue** that bypasses internal forgetfulness.

- **Visual Prominence:** Your time-blocked schedule must be visually prominent, a large digital calendar view, a color-coded whiteboard, or a physical planner left open on your desk. If the schedule is hidden, the time-blind brain will forget it exists.

- **Color-Coding for Clarity:** Use a simple, consistent color-coding system to visually categorize blocks (e.g., blue for Work / Deep Focus, green for Health / Self-Care, yellow for Administrative / Errands). This visual cue allows the brain to quickly process and prioritize the schedule at a glance, minimizing the cognitive effort required to interpret the schedule.
- **Automated Reminders:** Leverage technology to provide automated, external cues. Use digital calendars that provide multiple, automated reminders for transitions, task completion, and upcoming deadlines. Set alerts for a week before, a day before, and an hour before major deadlines to anchor the abstract future into the urgent present.

Section 4: The Emotional and Economic Payoff: Defeating the ADHD Tax

Mastering Time Blocking is not merely about increasing productivity; it is a vital strategy for emotional stabilization and mitigating the profound economic costs associated with unmanaged ADHD.

1. Reducing Shame and Building Self-Efficacy

The consistent failure of the traditional to-do list fuels a cycle of shame and inadequacy in women with ADHD, reinforcing the narrative that they are incapable of consistent performance. Time Blocking directly interrupts this cycle:

- **Realistic Expectations:** Time Blocking forces the creation of a schedule that is temporally realistic. By building in buffers and limiting the number of tasks, it sets achievable expectations, reducing the likelihood of failure and self-criticism.
- **Evidence of Competence:** Each completed Time Block provides tangible evidence of competence and follow-through, building **self-efficacy**, the belief in one's own ability to succeed. This self-efficacy is a powerful psychological resource that bolsters overall emotional resilience.
- **Neutralizing Emotional Dysregulation:** The structure and predictability of Time Blocking help stabilize the nervous system, reducing the chaotic internal environment that triggers **emotional dysregulation**. When the day is predictable, the

brain is less likely to feel overwhelmed, which can prevent small triggers from escalating into a disproportionate emotional storm.

2. Mitigating the Financial and Economic ADHD Tax

Unmanaged ADHD symptoms carry a significant and measurable **"ADHD Tax,"** which includes the cumulative cost, financial, emotional, and mental, of operating in a world designed for neurotypical brains. Time Blocking is a direct weapon against the most costly elements of this tax:

- **Combating Productivity Loss:** The largest component of the societal excess cost of adult ADHD is indirect cost related to work loss and productivity. The total societal excess cost attributable to ADHD in US adults is estimated at **$122.8 billion annually**, with excess costs of unemployment and productivity loss comprising the largest proportion. Time Blocking enhances productivity by enforcing single-task focus and minimizing context switching, directly reducing the waste of time and effort.
- **Addressing the Core Financial Risk:** Time blindness, disorganization, and poor prioritization contribute to financial instability, including late fees and lower earnings. Time Blocking helps enforce vital, non-stimulating administrative tasks, such as "Pay Bills: 4:00 PM–4:30 PM, Friday", by giving them non-negotiable, visible appointments, mitigating the risk of financial penalties caused by forgetfulness and procrastination. Furthermore, improved planning and organization, which are trained through consistent Time Blocking, are linked to better long-term financial outcomes.

3. Reducing Relational Friction

Time Blocking reduces friction in relationships by externalizing planning and ensuring necessary household and relational tasks are addressed.

- **Managing Shared Responsibilities:** By scheduling specific blocks for shared responsibilities (e.g., "Laundry / Chores: 7:00 PM–8:00 PM"), the ADHD partner externalizes their commitment, reducing the neurotypical partner's need to act as a **taskmaster** or reminder.

- **Supporting Communication:** Time Blocking allows for the intentional scheduling of high-leverage relational habits, such as "Weekly Check-in / Roundtable" or "Active Listening Practice." As research suggests, scheduling brief weekly check-ins helps build a routine of open dialogue and lightens the load of daily stress.

Conclusion: The Strategic Path to Control

The journey of defeating overwhelm requires replacing the chaos of reactive living with the strategic structure of intentional scheduling. The traditional to-do list, while useful for memory, fails the ADHD brain because it lacks the context and duration required to overcome time blindness and the activation deficit.

The mastery of **Time Blocking** transforms your relationship with time. By rendering time concrete, enforcing estimation, and embedding buffers and transitions, you systematically build the external EF required for consistent follow-through. This structural stability reduces the pervasive anxiety of chaos, conserves precious mental energy, and mitigates the emotional and economic costs associated with unmanaged attention.

The mental bandwidth conserved by creating this reliable time map is the resource you need for the internal work that follows in this book. You are no longer merely coping; you are proactively commanding your focus and shaping your reality. This commitment to intentional structure is the key to unlocking your full potential and moving toward a life defined by self-efficacy and control.

Chapter 2 Workbook: Schedule Success: Switch from Endless To-Do Lists to Time Blocking

Objective: To practice converting vague to-do items into concrete, time-bound, actionable appointments that compensate for Time Blindness and the Estimation Deficit.

Scientific Anchor: Time Blocking forces the engagement of planning and estimation skills, which are core executive functions challenged by ADHD, while its visual nature counteracts time blindness by making time concrete.

Activity 2.1: The To-Do List Conversion Audit

Instructions: Identify three items from a recent or current vague to-do list that caused you stress or that you procrastinated on. Convert them into Time Block appointments, ensuring you include the necessary boundaries (start / end time) and specific action cues.

Vague To-Do Item (Problematic)	Time Block Appointment (Solution)	Neuro-Adjustment Added (Why it works)
(Example: "Organize files")	**2:00 PM – 2:45 PM: Process Invoices and File (45 min fixed block)**	Enforced duration reduces paralysis and stress.
(Your Item 1)		
(Your Item 2)		
(Your Item 3)		

Activity 2.2: The Buffer and Transition Rule

Instructions: Plan a critical 3-hour work block for tomorrow, intentionally building in two types of crucial buffers: **The Estimation Buffer** (extra time for the core task) and **The Transition Buffer** (a mandatory break between activities).

1. **Core Task:** (E.g., "Draft Client Proposal"). Your honest estimate for this task is 1.5 hours.
2. **Time Block Plan (3 Hours Total):**

Time Slot	Activity	Duration (Fixed)	Neuro-Strategy
9:00 AM – 10:45 AM	**Core Focus Work (Task)**	105 minutes	(1.5 hours + 30 min **Estimation Buffer**)
10:45 AM – 11:00 AM	**Mandatory Transition / Reset**	15 minutes	(Scheduled physical / mental break to mitigate context switching cost)
11:00 AM – 12:00 PM	**Secondary Task (Follow-up calls)**	60 minutes	

Reflection 2.3: Visualizing Control and Finitude

Instructions: Reflect on the emotional difference between the two scheduling methods.

1. When you look at a long, vague to-do list, the item "Draft Client Proposal" feels like it requires **infinite** time. How does seeing the task confined to a **105-minute block** on your calendar reduce the risk of you procrastinating? (Focus on the concept of **finitude**).

   Finitude Effect: ____

   ____

   ____

   ____

   ____

   ____

2. The goal of Time Blocking is to conserve EF. How does pre-scheduling the **Transition Block** (10:45–11:00 AM) reduce the daily cognitive load that would normally be wasted deciding when or how to stop the first task and start the next?

EF Conservation: ____

____

____

____

____

____

3. Name one specific way you plan to make your Time Block schedule **visually prominent** (e.g., using a large screen widget, a whiteboard, or color-coding) to counteract the effect of Time Blindness and externalize the schedule.

   Visualization Tool: ______________________________________

   ____

   ____

   ____

   ____

   ____

   ____

CHAPTER 3

CUSTOMIZE YOUR FOCUS: APPLY THE POMODORO TECHNIQUE TO YOUR ATTENTION SPAN

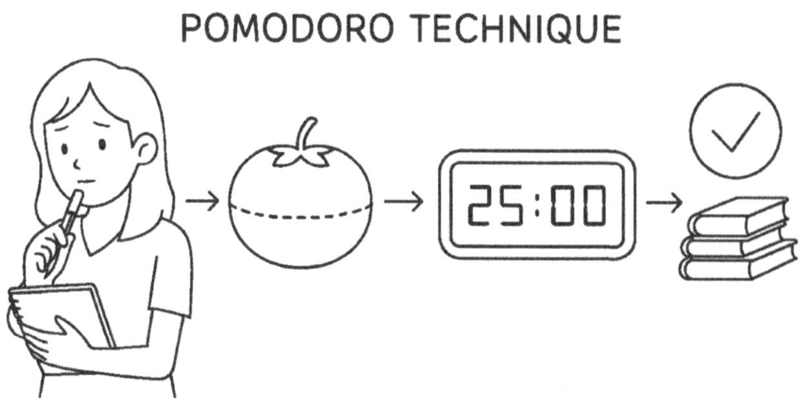

In Chapter 2, you mastered **Time Blocking**, transforming abstract time into a concrete schedule and enforcing the necessary boundaries of duration and transition. This structural discipline, however, still faces a formidable opponent: the difficulty of sustaining focus *within* those blocks, a struggle rooted in the dual paradox of ADHD attention, the unpredictable swing between acute **inattention** and disabling **hyperfocus**.

This chapter provides the tactical solution to this dilemma: the disciplined and customized application of the **Pomodoro Technique**. This evidence-based time management system utilizes short, fixed work sprints followed by mandatory, short breaks. For the ADHD brain, the Pomodoro Technique is more than a productivity hack; it is a neurological strategy that systematically addresses three core executive function deficits:

1. **Task Activation Deficit (Paralysis):** It makes the commitment to start feel short and manageable.
2. **Time Blindness:** It makes time visible, eliminating the feeling of infinite, overwhelming duration.
3. **Attention Dysregulation:** It provides a critical external "circuit-breaker" to prevent burnout from sustained, uncontrolled hyperfocus.

By customizing the duration of your focus sprints to match your current energy levels and attention span, you stop fighting your internal resistance and begin harnessing your inherent bursts of attention with intentional, reliable structure. This is the key to transforming chaotic energy into consistent, high-quality output.

Section 1: The Neurobiology of Finitude: Defeating Paralysis and Time Blindness

The first and most critical function of the Pomodoro Technique is to counteract the anxiety, paralysis, and overwhelm triggered by the perception of an infinite, daunting task. This intervention relies on the powerful psychological effect of **finitude**.

1. The Threat of Infinite Time

Time blindness, the inability to accurately perceive or estimate the flow of time, is a core neurobiological reality of the ADHD brain. When faced with a large, undifferentiated project, the brain perceives the commitment as amorphous, unquantifiable, and potentially unending.

- **Overwhelm Triggers Paralysis:** This perception of infinity instantly triggers **cognitive overload** and the **paralysis response**. The brain attempts to protect itself from the immense, unknown mental effort required, leading to procrastination and avoidance.
- **The Activation Deficit:** The task is too boring or too complex to generate the necessary internal burst of **dopamine** (activation energy) required to start. The commitment of working for an unknown, potentially long period feels too high.

The Pomodoro Technique directly attacks this anxiety by imposing **clear, fixed boundaries**. Committing to a task for only 25 minutes (or less) transforms the project from a paralyzing marathon into a manageable sprint. The visible, ticking timer serves as a constant, non-negotiable external cue, providing the brain with the precise structure it requires to initiate the effort. This dramatically lowers the activation energy, making the organized choice the easiest choice.

2. The Power of Visibility and Momentum

The use of a physical or digital timer as a countdown mechanism serves as a continuous external representation of time passing, which is vital for the time-blind brain.

- **Concrete Time:** The timer translates the abstract concept of duration into a visual or auditory cue, allowing the brain to anchor its attention to the external environment rather than relying on unreliable internal time perception. This makes the time spent feel tangible and measurable.
- **Momentum and Dopamine:** Each completion of a fixed work interval provides an immediate, tangible "win." This sense of success generates a small, but powerful burst of **dopamine** (the brain's reward chemical), reinforcing the productive behavior and building **momentum** for the next sprint. This positive feedback loop is crucial for overcoming the motivation deficit associated with the ADHD brain and is far more reliable than relying on abstract, distant rewards.

Section 2: The Mechanism: Pomodoro as External Regulator

The genius of the Pomodoro structure for ADHD is its symmetrical approach to the problem of attention dysregulation: it effectively manages both **inattention** (difficulty starting / staying on task) and **hyperfocus** (difficulty stopping / transitioning).

1. Managing Inattention and Distraction

The short, fixed work interval is specifically designed to work *with* the ADHD brain's tendency toward novelty-seeking and restlessness, rather than fighting against it.

- **Sustaining Engagement:** The limited duration of the work period (e.g., 25 minutes) is less intimidating than a long, unstructured block. The brain knows the commitment is short, which makes it easier to sustain concentration and reduces the mental fatigue often caused by continuous effort. The timer itself serves as a constant, gentle redirection mechanism, pulling the attention back to the task whenever it wanders.

- **Reducing "Mental Friction":** By committing to a single task within the fixed interval, you enforce the discipline of **single-tasking**, which is the necessary antidote to the inefficient and draining cost of constant **task-switching**. You are telling your brain, "You only need to focus on this one thing until the bell rings." This clear boundary reduces the cognitive load associated with filtering distractions and making constant choices about priority.

2. The Circuit Breaker: Preventing Hyperfocus and Burnout

While hyperfocus can generate impressive productivity, it is ultimately a form of attention dysregulation that can lead to burnout, missed appointments, and relationship friction (e.g., forgetting to eat, neglecting family needs, failing to transition to a critical deadline). The mandated break is the Pomodoro Technique's most critical feature for the hyperfocus-prone ADHD brain.

- **Enforced Disengagement:** The scheduled break acts as an **external circuit-breaker**. The timer going off forces the individual to stop working, even if they feel they are in a productive flow state. This external boundary protects the integrity of the overall schedule and prevents the hyperfocused task from bleeding into and derailing subsequent appointments, which is a major source of chaos for the ADHD brain.
- **Preventing Mental Fatigue:** The **mandatory 5-minute break** provides a regular, guilt-free opportunity for the brain to reset and seek the novelty and low-effort stimulation it craves (e.g., stretching, getting a drink of water, listening to one song, or stepping away from the desk). This strategically scheduled break prevents the deep mental fatigue and burnout often associated with prolonged, continuous concentration, ensuring that the next work interval starts with higher energy reserves.

Section 3: Customization: Tailoring the Sprint to Your Brain

The traditional 25-minute Pomodoro is merely a suggestion. For the ADHD brain, the technique is only effective and sustainable when the duration is **customized** to match the individual's unique attention span and energy cycle. Rigidly adhering to a standard that causes excessive struggle simply creates a new source of shame.

1. Matching Duration to Attention Span

Your focus intervals should be low-friction and achievable. The duration should be challenging enough to facilitate deep work, but short enough to avoid triggering anxiety or burnout.

- **Start Short and Build:** If 25 minutes feels daunting, start with a shorter interval, such as **15 minutes** of focused work followed by a **5-minute break**. Successfully completing three 15-minute sprints builds more confidence and momentum than struggling through one 25-minute block. Over time, you can gradually extend the work interval as your attentional muscle strengthens.
- **The "Energy Matching" Rule:** Match your work duration to your daily energy cycle. Schedule longer Pomodoro sprints (e.g., 45–50 minutes) during your peak mental energy hours (often the morning) and shorter, high-impact sprints (e.g., 10–15 minutes) during your afternoon energy slump or when transitioning between complex tasks.

2. Customizing the Break for Optimal Reset

The break is as important as the work interval, serving as a restorative reset for the brain. The break must be low-stakes and intentionally non-productive.

- **Movement Over Screens:** While the ADHD brain craves the stimulation of a screen (email, social media), engaging with these during the break risks fragmenting attention and increasing context-switching cost, making it harder to return to focus. Prioritize **physical movement** (e.g., stretching, walking, drinking water) during the break to discharge pent-up physical restlessness and stimulate the dopamine system in a healthy way.

- **Sensory Reset:** Use the break to engage in a simple **sensory reset**. For instance, step outside to feel the air, or engage in a quick **grounding technique** (e.g., the 5-4-3-2-1 method) to pull the attention away from internal chatter and into the present environment. This prepares the brain to re-engage with focus.

Section 4: Advanced Implementation and Momentum

Integrating the Pomodoro Technique with other EF strategies ensures that the method becomes a resilient tool for **Deep Work**, not just a timer for busywork.

1. The Pre-Flight Checklist Ritual

Before starting any Pomodoro sprint, the ADHD brain requires a consistent ritual to ensure the environment and mind are prepared for focus, minimizing the cognitive load of initiation.

- **Define the Single Task:** Review the Time Block schedule (Chapter 2) and confirm the **single, specific task** for the next interval (e.g., "Draft the conclusion paragraph," not "Work on report"). This specificity is a direct antidote to the paralysis caused by ambiguity.
- **Minimize Distraction:** As the timer is set, perform a quick **Notification Annihilation** ritual: silence all devices, close unnecessary browser tabs (each is an "open loop" consuming working memory), and clear the immediate desk area of everything not related to the task. This intentional preparation saves valuable executive function during the sprint.

2. Integrating External Accountability

When the internal motivation is low, the Pomodoro timer should be anchored with the external support of **Body Doubling** (Chapter 4, Book 1).

- **Accountability Anchor:** The physical presence or visible virtual presence of a Body Double provides the non-judgmental accountability necessary to ensure the Pomodoro sprint begins on time and continues uninterrupted until the timer rings. The double serves as an external pacer and a stable, non-distracting focal point, which is crucial for maintaining attention during the focused interval.

- **Shared Structure:** If working with a partner or peer, commit to synchronized Pomodoro cycles (e.g., everyone starts their 25-minute timer at the same moment). This shared structure leverages social commitment to enforce the schedule, making the transition back to work easier for all parties.

3. Leveraging Momentum for Larger Projects

The goal of the Pomodoro Technique is to transform large, daunting projects into chains of achievable sprints. This harnesses the power of **momentum** to sustain effort.

- **Chaining Micro-Steps:** Use the Pomodoro intervals to execute the **micro-steps** defined in Chapter 1. A 25-minute sprint should be used to complete two or three small, defined micro-steps, rather than tackling a vague, large chore. The satisfaction of checking off multiple micro-steps during the break provides a powerful burst of dopamine that reinforces the next sprint.
- **Tracking the Sprints:** Visually track the number of Pomodoro sprints completed each day or week (e.g., a simple tally mark on a whiteboard). This externalizes progress and provides a concrete, visible record of effort, which helps the ADHD brain appreciate progress and build confidence in its ability to sustain focus over time.

Section 5: The Emotional Payoff: Self-Compassion and Sustainable Focus

Mastering the Pomodoro Technique yields significant emotional benefits, creating a sustainable foundation that actively protects against shame and burnout, the primary emotional drivers of overwhelm.

1. Reducing Shame and the Inner Critic

The chronic failure to meet deadlines or sustain focus fuels a cycle of shame and self-blame in women with ADHD. The Pomodoro Technique provides tangible proof of competence, directly countering this inner critic.

- **Evidence of Competence:** Each successfully completed 25-minute sprint provides undeniable evidence of focus and follow-through, building **self-efficacy**, the belief in one's own ability to succeed. This steady accumulation of small wins gradually dismantles the pervasive feeling of inadequacy.

- **Guilt-Free Breaks:** The mandated 5-minute break is a built-in act of self-compassion. It legitimizes rest, ensuring that the woman does not feel guilty for pausing her effort. The break becomes an integral, non-negotiable part of the system, not a reward earned through punishing effort. This shifts the focus from rigid self-criticism to compassionate self-management.

2. Preventing Burnout and Protecting Energy Reserves

The cycle of burnout, uncontrolled hyperfocus followed by exhaustion, task avoidance, and crisis management, is a major source of chaos for the ADHD brain.

- **Energy Regulation:** By enforcing regular breaks, the Pomodoro Technique ensures that mental energy is managed proactively, preventing the total depletion of EF reserves that occurs during uncontrolled hyperfocus. This protects the brain from the chronic fatigue and mental sluggishness that define the "ADHD Tax" on energy.
- **Sustainable Effort:** The technique promotes **sustainable effort** rather than sporadic, intense bursts of productivity. By working in short, manageable chunks and recovering frequently, the woman creates a predictable, consistent rhythm that is resilient to the chaos of overwhelm.

Conclusion: Your Focused Edge

The journey through this chapter has provided the tactical mastery necessary to sustain focus within the structure established by Time Blocking. The customized application of the **Pomodoro Technique** systematically addresses the core attentional challenges of the ADHD brain, time blindness, task paralysis, and hyperfocus—by leveraging external cues and fixed boundaries.

You are no longer leaving focus to chance or fighting internal resistance with sheer willpower. Instead, you are using the timer as a reliable external regulator, transforming daunting commitments into manageable, rewarding sprints. This disciplined, yet compassionate, approach empowers you to command your mental spotlight, achieving higher-quality work with less mental fatigue. This cultivated focus is the definitive step toward defeating overwhelm and preparing your entire system for the essential work of strengthening your core Executive Function skills that follows.

Chapter 3 Workbook: Customize Your Focus: Apply the Pomodoro Technique to Your Attention Span

Objective: To customize the Pomodoro Technique to match your unique attention span and energy cycle, transforming work into manageable, timed sprints.

Scientific Anchor: Customizing the Pomodoro interval (e.g., starting shorter) reduces the anxiety that triggers task paralysis, while mandated breaks prevent hyperfocus and burnout, thereby maintaining executive function reserves.

Activity 3.1: Attention Span Customization Audit

Instructions: Identify your current optimal focus interval (Work) and the necessary duration of a true mental break (Rest). This moves beyond the standard 25 / 5 interval.

1. **Work Interval Assessment:** If a task is boring, what is the *shortest* amount of time you can commit to before feeling the urge to check your phone or move? (Select one: 10 min, 15 min, 25 min, 30 min).
    - *My Custom Work Interval (A):* ________ *minutes*
2. **Break Interval Assessment:** How long do you need to stand, stretch, and move your body before you can successfully re-engage? (Select one: 3 min, 5 min, 10 min).
    - *My Custom Break Interval (B):* ________ *minutes*
3. **My Customized Pomodoro Cycle: A (Work)** minutes / **B (Break)** minutes.

Activity 3.2: The Anti-Hyperfocus Break Protocol

Instructions: The break is mandatory and must be designed to interrupt the flow of hyperfocus and truly reset the brain. Design your three go-to **Break Actions** that are low-friction and actively avoid screens (to prevent context-switching cost).

Break Action	Duration (Fixed)	Neuro-Benefit (Why it works)
Action 1: Physical Movement	(E.g., 2 minutes)	(Example: Standing, 5 jumping jacks, or brisk walk to the window. Discharges physical restlessness)
Action 2: Sensory Reset	(E.g., 1 minute)	(Example: Splash cold water on face, hold ice cube, or use 5-4-3-2-1 grounding technique.)
Action 3: Hydration/ Dopamine Reward	(E.g., 2 minutes)	(Example: Get a specific drink of water / tea. Quick, safe reward that reinforces follow-through.)

Reflection 3.3: Anchoring Focus and Defeating Guilt

Instructions: Reflect on how the structure of this technique supports both your focus and your emotional well-being.

1. **Defeating Paralysis:** You are about to start a task you hate. How does seeing the timer set for your **Custom Work Interval (A)** instantly reduce the anxiety that would otherwise lead to procrastination? (Focus on **finitude**).

   Reduction in Anxiety: ____________________________________

   ____

   ____

   ____

   ____

   ____

   ____

   ____

   ____

2. **Stopping Hyperfocus:** When the timer rings and you are deep in hyperfocus, what is the single biggest challenge you face (e.g., guilt, feeling the loss of momentum, urgency)?

   Challenge: ____

   ____

   ____

   ____

   ____

   ____

   ____

   ____

   ____

3. **Self-Compassion and the Break:** How does knowing the break is **mandatory** (an integral part of the system, not a reward you must earn) reduce the feeling of **guilt** or self-criticism when you pause your work?

   Guilt Reduction: ____

   ____

   ____

   ____

   ____

   ____

   ____

   ____

   ____

CHAPTER 4

FUTURE-PROOF YOUR BRAIN: STRENGTHEN WORKING MEMORY WITH PLANNING ROUTINES

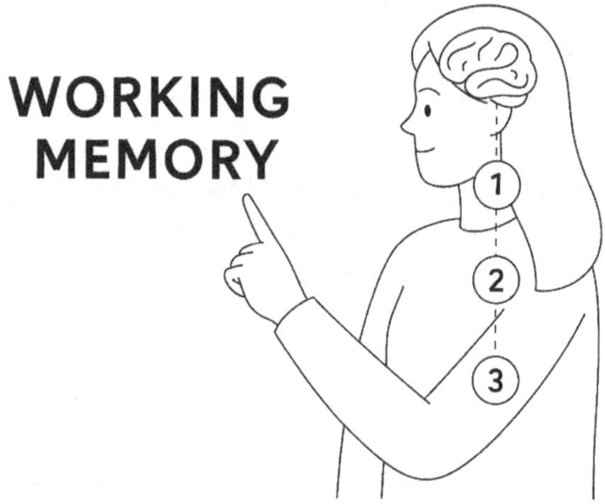

The work completed in the preceding chapters, establishing external organization (Book 1) and mastering time visualization through Time Blocking and Pomodoro sprints (Chapters 1–3), has provided the essential structural scaffolding for your life. You have successfully reduced the chaotic, reactive demands on your attention. Now, the journey shifts to the deepest level of Executive Function (EF) mastery: **internal strengthening and resilience**.

This chapter is dedicated to the core cognitive skills required for sustained adult function: **Working Memory (WM)** and **Inhibitory Control (IC)**. WM is your brain's "mental scratchpad", the ability to hold and manipulate information for short-term use, while IC is your brain's "brakes" , the capacity to resist temptation and think before speaking or acting. Both are crucial EF skills that are often inconsistent in the ADHD brain, leading to forgetfulness, poor follow-through, and impulsive decisions.

This chapter is about building a powerful, long-term cognitive strategy. While external tools compensate for deficits, consistent practice and the establishment of reliable, fixed planning routines are necessary to truly **future-proof your brain** against the stress, inconsistency, and shame that define unmanaged ADHD. By training these skills and reducing the internal friction associated with planning, you create a foundation for resilience that is less susceptible to the chaos of fatigue and distraction.

Section 1: The Neurobiology of Core Executive Function Deficits

To effectively strengthen WM and IC, we must first understand the specific neurobiological deficits that make these processes challenging for women with ADHD. Both WM and IC are highly dependent on the function of the **prefrontal cortex (PFC)**, the brain's command center for higher-level cognitive functions.

1. Working Memory: The Inconsistent "Mental Scratchpad"

Working memory (WM) is the system that allows you to temporarily hold multiple pieces of information in mind and manipulate them simultaneously, such as remembering a multi-step instruction while executing the first step, or keeping track of conversation points while formulating a response. For a woman with ADHD, WM can feel like a sieve.

- **Impact on Multi-Step Tasks:** This deficit makes it difficult to follow lengthy verbal instructions, remember the location of an item moments after placing it down, or retain the steps of a task management plan. When WM fails, follow-through suffers, tasks are often left unfinished, and the brain is quickly overwhelmed by the number of steps required for a goal.
- **The Planning Barrier:** WM is essential for effective **planning**. You must be able to hold the goal, the steps, and the available resources in mind simultaneously to map out a strategy. A compromised WM means this planning stage is taxing, leading to frustration, avoidance, and reliance on spontaneous, often inefficient, action rather than intentional, planned execution.

2. Inhibitory Control: The Weakening of the "Brakes"

Inhibitory control (IC) is the ability to resist an urge or temptation, curb impulsivity, and think before acting or speaking. It is the EF responsible for discipline, perseverance, and delayed gratification.

- **Impulsivity and Regulation:** When IC is inconsistent, it manifests as impulsive interruptions during conversations, difficulty resisting the urge to check a notification, or the inability to stay on task despite boredom or setbacks. For women with ADHD, this can contribute significantly to both **emotional dysregulation** (impulsive outbursts) and **relational friction** (interrupting a partner).
- **Dopamine's Role in Delay:** IC is heavily tied to the **dopamine dysregulation** in the ADHD brain. Because the brain struggles to generate internal motivation for tasks that lack novelty, the impulse to seek immediate stimulation (e.g., procrastination, checking social media) is often prioritized over the long-term, abstract reward of the task at hand. Strengthening IC means strengthening the "brakes" to resist this immediate gratification.

Section 2: Strengthening Inhibitory Control: Training the "Brakes"

Improving any executive function skill, including inhibitory control, requires consistent practice and challenge. The work is similar to physical exercise: the muscle must be challenged to grow. By intentionally engaging in activities that require you to override an automatic response, you strengthen the neural pathways responsible for IC.

1. Intentional Resistance Games

Behavioral therapies and EF training often utilize activities that require the individual to think before acting and to curb impulses, which are essential components of IC.

- **Structured Behavioral Games:** Engaging in structured activities that require suppression of a dominant response helps build IC. Simple games like "Simon Says" (where the command must be filtered before execution) are clinically noted to improve inhibitory control by training the brain to resist the automatic urge. These can be adapted for adults (e.g., intentionally performing the opposite of a simple command).

- **Delayed Gratification Practice:** Actively creating small, intentional opportunities for **delayed gratification** trains the brain to resist immediate reward. This could involve using a specific "Waiting Basket" for non-urgent notifications or committing to a **"Ten-Minute Rule"** before making a non-essential purchase or responding to a heated text message. This crucial pause allows the PFC to engage and override the amygdala's impulsive reaction, which is key to reducing both financial impulsivity and emotional volatility.

2. The Power of Single-Task Focus

The deliberate practice of **single-tasking** (Chapter 4, Book 2) is a form of intensive IC training.

- **Resisting Context Switching:** When committing to a Pomodoro sprint, every time the urge to check email, open a new browser tab, or look at your phone arises, you are engaging and strengthening your IC. The act of resisting the distraction and maintaining focus on the primary task forces the brain to suppress the impulse, building the attentional muscle required for long-term concentration.
- **Managing Internal Distraction:** IC also involves suppressing internal cognitive noise. During a focused block, the appearance of an intrusive thought or a fleeting idea is inevitable. Instead of immediately pursuing the thought, IC trains you to acknowledge the thought without judgment and gently redirect your focus back to the task at hand, reinforcing the discipline of internal self-control.

Section 3: Enhancing Working Memory: Supporting the "Mental Scratchpad"

WM training requires a dual approach: building a reliable external system that compensates for memory deficits and engaging in consistent cognitive challenge to improve retrieval and retention.

1. Externalizing Memory with Fixed Routines

The most effective strategy for managing WM deficits is to consistently offload all essential information onto a reliable **external system**, preventing the mental scratchpad from becoming overloaded. The Time Blocking structure (Chapter 2) and organizational systems

(Book 1) are already serving this function. This section focuses on the **routine** of using those tools.

- **Fixed Planning Rituals:** WM is strengthened when the need for it is reduced. Establishing a daily, non-negotiable planning ritual ensures all necessary instructions and objectives are externalized and placed in a visible, predictable location (e.g., your Time Block schedule). This ritual should involve:
    - **The Daily Prep:** At the start of the workday, visually review the day's schedule and mentally rehearse the first two transition points. This loads the instructions into short-term memory with minimal effort.
    - **The End-of-Day Review:** Before shutting down, capture all new tasks and ideas (the **Brain Dump**) and immediately process them into the planner for future scheduling. This prevents "open loops" from consuming WM overnight and causing sleep anxiety.
- **Creating Checklists and Templates:** To compensate for forgetting steps or instructions, create visual **checklists and templates** for repetitive tasks (e.g., "The Meeting Prep Checklist," "The Morning Routine Checklist"). These external scaffolds ensure consistency without requiring the brain to expend WM energy recalling multi-step sequences.

2. Cognitive Challenge and Practice

While systems are essential for daily function, consistent, targeted cognitive practice challenges the underlying WM capacity.

- **Cognitive Exercises:** Engaging in brain training exercises designed to stress working memory, such as dual N-back tasks, memory games, or structured puzzles that require multi-step recall, can strengthen the neural connections associated with WM function over time. This intentional practice challenges the EF muscle to adapt and improve its capacity for sustained information processing.
- **Verbalizing Steps:** When faced with a multi-step project, verbalize the steps aloud (or write them down immediately). This externalization reinforces the instruction and aids the process of encoding information into memory, improving the likelihood of retention and follow-through.

Section 4: Future-Proofing through Routine: The Fixed Planning Rituals

For the ADHD brain, the greatest enemy is inconsistency. The intentional, fixed planning rituals outlined below are the mechanism for translating the skills of WM and IC into resilient, long-term habits.

1. The Weekly Review (The Strategy Session)

The Weekly Review is a non-negotiable appointment (scheduled and time-blocked) designed to proactively engage the planning aspect of EF, ensuring the abstract future is made concrete and manageable.

- **Goal Setting and Prioritization:** Dedicate 60–90 minutes each week (e.g., Sunday afternoon) to review the past week's progress and the upcoming week's commitments. This process forces engagement with **goal setting** and **prioritization**, identifying the few high-leverage tasks that must be accomplished, rather than allowing a massive to-do list to create overwhelm.
- **Scheduling the "Boring" Tasks:** Use the review to specifically time-block tasks that lack intrinsic reward and are prone to avoidance (e.g., administrative tasks, bill paying, follow-up calls). By scheduling them into the Time Block as non-negotiable appointments, you bypass the reliance on future internal motivation, which is often inconsistent.
- **Resource Management:** This review is used to ensure you have the necessary materials and resources for the upcoming week, mitigating the risk of starting a task only to discover a key item is missing, a common frustration that triggers task abandonment.

2. The Daily Execution Prep (The Launch Sequence)

The Daily Execution Prep is the launch sequence that ensures the WM is loaded with the necessary instructions for the day, minimizing morning chaos and uncertainty.

- **The Nightly Offload:** The most critical step occurs the night before: reviewing the Time Block schedule for the next day, collecting all materials needed for the first task (e.g., reports, specific pens, water bottle), and performing the **Digital Reset** (clearing the desktop / closing tabs) to ensure a clean start. This prevents "open loops" from disrupting sleep and minimizes decision fatigue in the morning.

- **The Morning Activation:** Upon waking, immediately check the Time Block for the first appointment and the corresponding materials. This intentional, structured beginning activates the Task Positive Network (TPN) and ensures the WM is loaded with the immediate instructions, transitioning the brain smoothly from the Default Mode Network (DMN) (rest / mind-wandering) to focused effort.

Section 5: The Holistic Context: Sustaining Cognitive Growth

The PFC's capacity for WM and IC is highly vulnerable to impairment from internal psychological states. Sustaining cognitive growth requires actively minimizing the things that impair EF and enhancing the things that support it.

1. Reducing the Impact of Stress and Sadness

Research is clear: EF skills **blossom most when we lessen things that impair them (like stress or sadness) and enhance the things that support them (like joy or feelings of belonging).** This means the intentional emotional regulation and self-compassion work (to be addressed in Book 4) is a non-negotiable part of improving focus and WM.

- **Emotional Resilience is Cognitive Resilience:** Stress, anxiety, and feelings of shame consume immense EF resources, making focus and planning exponentially harder. By utilizing the external structures of Time Blocking and Pomodoro sprints, you reduce the systemic stress of daily chaos, thereby providing the necessary emotional buffer for your cognitive skills to flourish.
- **Mindfulness and Re-Entry:** Mindfulness practices (Chapter 3, Book 2) are crucial for strengthening attention regulation. They train the brain to gently observe internal chaos without judgment and return to the chosen focus, reinforcing the IC muscle required for sustained effort.

2. Physiological Support for the Prefrontal Cortex

The PFC requires optimal fuel for peak function. Sustaining cognitive growth requires prioritizing the physiological factors that directly support neurotransmitter regulation.

- **Sleep Hygiene:** Quality sleep is non-negotiable for WM and IC. Sleep deprivation can be as impairing as the core symptoms of ADHD themselves. Consistent, prioritized sleep hygiene is essential for restoring the PFC's capacity and mitigating the chronic mental fatigue that drains EF reserves.
- **Nutrition and Movement:** Consistent protein and complex carbohydrates maintain stable energy and blood sugar, preventing the crashes that exacerbate WM / IC deficits. Regular physical exercise is a powerful, evidence-based tool that promotes dopamine release, improving attention and inhibitory control, acting as a natural cognitive enhancement.

Conclusion: Your Future-Proofed Mind

The work of this chapter moves beyond mere compensation into true cognitive enhancement. By establishing fixed planning rituals, intentionally training your Inhibitory Control to resist distraction, and supporting your Working Memory through external offloading, you are actively increasing your long-term resilience.

You have transformed WM and IC from unreliable, internal deficits into skills supported by a robust, predictable system. This intentional, disciplined practice is the definitive step toward conquering the fragmented mind and replacing chronic overwhelm with the quiet confidence of self-mastery. The mental energy conserved by this internal structure is the final resource you need to ensure that the effort of focus is not only powerful but also sustainable, preparing you for the final stage of Executive Function mastery: ruthlessly protecting your cognitive space from digital and mental noise.

Chapter 4 Workbook: Future-Proof Your Brain: Strengthen Working Memory with Planning Routines

Objective: To practice strengthening **Working Memory (WM)** and **Inhibitory Control (IC)** using fixed planning routines and targeted exercises.

Scientific Anchor: Executive Function (EF) skills, including WM and IC, improve through continuous challenge and consistent practice. Fixed planning rituals externalize the cognitive burden, allowing the core skills to stabilize.

Activity 4.1: The Weekly Review: Future-Proofing Your Plan

Instructions: Schedule a 60-minute appointment this week for a **Weekly Review.** This process proactively engages WM and planning EFs.

1. **Identify Three High-Leverage Tasks:** What are the three **most important, non-urgent** tasks for the upcoming week? (These are the items most likely to be forgotten or avoided).

   Task 1: ____

   Task 2: ____

   Task 3: ____

2. **Externalize Resources:** For your first task, list every resource, material, and contact you need. (This offloads instructions from WM).

   Resources Needed: ______________________________________

   ____

   ____

   ____

   ____

3. **Time Block Commitment:** Commit these three tasks to your Time Block schedule for the upcoming week (Chapter 2), ensuring you add a **25% Estimation Buffer** to each block.

   Task 1 Block: (Time / Duration): ___________________________

   ____

   ____

Activity 4.2: Training Inhibitory Control (IC)

Instructions: Practice intentionally resisting an urge for 10 minutes, strengthening your brain's "brakes" (IC).

1. **Identify Your #1 Impulse:** What is the most common, low-stakes impulse that derails your focus? (E.g., Checking your phone, opening a social media tab, getting a snack, interrupting a conversation).

   Impulse: ____

   ____

   ____

2. **The 10-Minute IC Sprint:** Set a timer for 10 minutes. During this time, commit to working on an existing task while actively, mindfully **resisting** the identified Impulse whenever it arises. Each resistance is a "rep" for your IC muscle.

   IC Practice: ____

   Start time: ____

   End time: ____

Reflection 4.3: Analyzing Executive Function Gain

Instructions: Reflect on how your consistent routine supports your focus and conserves EF energy.

1. **WM Conservation:** How does performing the **Nightly Offload** (capturing tasks for the next day) reduce your brain's tendency to ruminate or worry before sleep? (Focus on how the external system manages the "open loops").

   Sleep / WM Benefit: ____

   ____

   ____

   ____

   ____

2. **EF and Emotional Load:** The PFC's ability to plan and focus is impaired by stress and sadness. How does the structure of a predictable Time Block schedule, which reduces rushing and late penalties, act as a psychological buffer that supports your EF?

Emotional / EF Support: ________________________________

____

____

____

____

3. **The Strength of Routine:** What is one checklist or template (e.g., "The Meeting Prep Checklist," "The Morning Routine") you can create this week to offload a multi-step instruction from your Working Memory?

   Checklist to Create: ____________________________________

   ____

   ____

   ____

   ____

   ____

CHAPTER 5

PROTECT YOUR ENERGY: REDUCE COGNITIVE LOAD BY ELIMINATING DIGITAL NOISE

The mastery of focus, achieved through Time Blocking, customized Pomodoro sprints, and the strengthening of Working Memory (WM) and Inhibitory Control (IC), is not solely about increasing output; it is fundamentally about the intelligent management and **protection of your finite mental energy**. The entire effort of setting up structural scaffolding (Book 1) and time discipline (Chapters 1–4) can be instantly negated by one insidious, pervasive threat: **Digital Noise** and the neurological drain caused by **Context Switching**.

For the woman with Attention-Deficit / Hyperactivity Disorder (ADHD), the modern world, a hyper-stimulating landscape of flashing notifications, open browser tabs, and constantly refreshing inboxes, is perfectly designed to dismantle sustained concentration. Each digital "ping" is a siren call for the novelty-seeking, dopamine-driven brain, forcing a taxing shift in attention that rapidly depletes the finite resources of the Executive Functions (EFs).

This chapter provides the final, essential stage of focus mastery: the strategy of **Cognitive Load Annihilation**. It details how to ruthlessly eliminate the digital and environmental friction that fragments attention, thereby protecting the mental energy necessary for consistent follow-through and preventing the descent into profound **mental fatigue** and burnout. By minimizing context switching and eliminating digital noise, you systematically reduce the chronic effort required to fight distraction, allowing your newly strengthened EF skills to operate at their most efficient, sustainable level. This is the difference between sporadic productivity and enduring, integrated self-mastery.

Section 1: The Neurobiology of Noise: Why Digital Distraction is Draining

The core challenge in sustaining focus for the ADHD brain is its impaired ability to filter out irrelevant stimuli, leading to a state of perpetually high mental effort, the **Cognitive Load (CL)**.

1. Cognitive Load and the Filtering Deficit

Cognitive load refers to the total amount of mental effort consumed by your working memory during a task. For a neurotypical individual, the brain effortlessly filters out background stimuli, prioritizing the central task. However, for a woman with ADHD, the brain's filtering mechanism is often less efficient, registering all incoming information, internal thoughts, external noise, and digital cues, with nearly equal significance.

- **Disproportionate Impact:** This inefficient filtering means that a stray notification or a distracting sound does not simply divert attention; it forces the brain to expend immense, measurable energy processing and suppressing that irrelevant stimulus. Research indicates that as CL increases, individuals with ADHD experience reduced performance and increased reaction time variability compared to their neurotypical peers.
- **The "Open Loop" Drain:** Every unread email, every ignored text message, and every open browser tab represents an "open loop", an unresolved task or piece of information that the brain is subconsciously tracking. These open loops consume valuable

WM resources, placing a constant, low-level demand on EF reserves and contributing significantly to the feeling of being perpetually "frenzied, frazzled, and overwhelmed." The goal of energy protection is to systematically close these loops and reduce the background noise that consumes CL.

2. The Cost of Context Switching: Debunking the Multitasking Myth

The pervasive myth that one can efficiently multitask is the single greatest drain on the ADHD brain's energy. Multitasking is scientifically inaccurate; what it describes is rapid **Context Switching**, the act of quickly shifting attention between two or more cognitively demanding tasks (e.g., drafting a report while responding to instant messages).

- **The Task Switch Penalty:** Each time the brain switches tasks, it incurs a measurable **cognitive penalty**. This penalty involves the mental effort required to disengage from the first task, reorient attention, and load the new set of information and rules into the compromised Working Memory. This process is highly inefficient, leading to increased errors, slower overall completion time, and significant mental exhaustion.
- **Dopamine's Role in the Switch:** The ADHD brain is highly susceptible to this switching because the act of checking a new notification provides an immediate, low-effort burst of dopamine (novelty / reward), while resisting it requires the challenging, high-effort function of Inhibitory Control (IC). The brain favors the path of least resistance, leading to constant toggling that fragments focus and rapidly depletes the finite EF reserves. By minimizing context switching, we protect the brain's energy from this continuous, self-imposed tax.

Section 2: The Strategy of Annihilation: Eliminating Digital Friction

Protecting your focus begins with a ruthless, strategic annihilation of the digital cues that are actively pulling your attention and demanding context switches. This must be a systematic, environment-wide commitment.

1. Notification Annihilation: Silence as Self-Care

Notifications are the primary culprit in fragmentation, turning devices from tools into demanding masters. The strategy must be absolute and uncompromising: turn off all non-essential pings.

- **The Rule of Essential Only:** Go through every app on your phone, tablet, and computer and turn off all alerts for social media, news applications, and non-critical email accounts. Only notifications that signal an **immediate, non-deferrable emergency** (e.g., calendar reminder for a critical meeting, high-priority work alert) should remain active.
- **Creating the Digital "Do Not Disturb" Zone:** Commit to using your device's "Do Not Disturb" or "Focus Mode" feature during all scheduled **Time Blocks** (Chapter 2) and **Pomodoro Sprints** (Chapter 3). This creates a clear, non-negotiable external boundary that physically and digitally protects your concentration and reduces the temptation to check a new ping.
- **The Cost of the Vibrate:** Even a silent vibration or a flashing light should be managed, as these subtle cues still register in the background, consuming a fraction of CL and tempting a context switch. Placing your phone out of immediate sight (e.g., in a drawer or face-down across the room) during deep work intervals is crucial for reinforcing IC.

2. Browser Management: Closing Open Loops

The modern desktop, with its multitude of open browser tabs, is a perfect visual representation of the ADHD brain's tendency toward accumulation and cognitive overwhelm. Each open tab is a subtle demand on Working Memory (WM) and a potential distraction for IC.

- **The Three-Tab Rule:** Implement a strict rule: you may only have **three browser tabs open** at any given time, one for the current task, one for immediate reference, and one for your planner / timer. This physically limits the number of cognitive "open loops" your brain is tracking.
- **The "Later" Parking Lot:** When a thought or distraction related to a new, non-essential website arises during a focus sprint, use a dedicated external system (e.g., a "Brain Dump" note, a digital bookmark folder) as a "parking lot" for the idea. Write down the thought immediately and return to the main task. This offloads the thought from WM without allowing the brain to reward the distraction impulse.

- **Digital Triage:** Perform a **Digital Reset** (Chapter 5, Book 1) at the end of every work session or day. This includes closing all unnecessary tabs and moving all temporary files from the desktop into a single, designated "To File" folder. A clean, quiet desktop is the necessary environmental cue for a successful launch into the next day's focused effort.

3. Email and Communication Batching

Managing the constant influx of digital communication as it arrives is a guaranteed path to continuous context switching and mental exhaustion. The brain must be trained to engage with communication on its own terms, not the sender's.

- **Scheduled Triage:** Dedicate specific, **Time Blocked** intervals (e.g., 9:00 AM–9:30 AM and 3:00 PM–3:30 PM) solely for checking and processing emails and messages. Turn off the email client entirely outside of these designated blocks. This intentional "email batching" minimizes context switching and allows the brain to remain in a "Deep Work" mode for longer, conserving EF resources.
- **The "Two-Minute Rule":** When engaging with communication during a scheduled triage block, implement the classic "Two-Minute Rule": if an email or message can be dealt with in two minutes or less (delete, respond briefly, or schedule a Time Block appointment), do it immediately. Otherwise, defer it by moving it to a **"To Do"** folder or scheduling an appointment for the necessary work. This low-friction triage system prevents the inbox from becoming an ambiguous, overwhelming to-do list that triggers paralysis.

Section 3: Sustaining Energy: Proactive Burnout Prevention

The persistent struggle with filtering, context switching, and sustained effort makes women with ADHD significantly more susceptible to **Mental Fatigue and Burnout** than their neurotypical peers. This chronic exhaustion is the culmination of the **ADHD Tax** on energy. Sustaining focus requires proactive strategies that protect the brain's overall physiological and cognitive reserves.

1. Managing Mental Fatigue as a Core Symptom

Mental fatigue is not merely feeling tired; it is a temporary physiological sluggishness and slowdown of thinking abilities caused by the chronic, high cognitive demands placed on the ADHD brain. This state directly impairs Working Memory and Inhibitory Control, making focus and emotional regulation exponentially harder.

- **Scheduled Recovery:** Schedule mandatory, non-negotiable **rest and recovery blocks** into your weekly Time Block schedule (Chapter 2). These are not blocks for chores or errands; they are for genuine passive rest, such as reading for pleasure, intentional relaxation, or quiet time without digital stimuli. This scheduled recovery is essential for restoring the prefrontal cortex's capacity.
- **The Power of Movement:** Regular physical movement is a powerful, evidence-based tool for combating mental fatigue, promoting dopamine release, and enhancing focus. Utilize the **Pomodoro Break** (Chapter 3) to enforce short bursts of movement (e.g., stretching, brisk walk to the water cooler). This proactive physical reset is crucial for discharging pent-up restlessness and stimulating the neurochemistry required for renewed attention.

2. Physiological Foundations for Cognitive Health

Sustaining focus requires protecting the physiological systems that directly support EF and neurotransmitter regulation.

- **Sleep Hygiene as EF Protection:** Quality sleep is non-negotiable for EF and WM function. Sleep deprivation can be as impairing as the core symptoms of ADHD themselves. Consistent, prioritized sleep hygiene is essential for restoring the prefrontal cortex's capacity and mitigating the chronic mental fatigue that drains EF reserves. The **Nightly Offload** routine (Chapter 4) should be performed to externalize worries and clear the mental space required for restorative sleep.
- **Fueling the PFC:** The brain relies on stable fuel for peak performance. Consistent consumption of lean protein and complex carbohydrates prevents the blood sugar crashes that exacerbate WM and IC deficits. Intentional hydration is also

crucial for maintaining optimal brain function and mental clarity. By stabilizing your physiological environment, you provide the necessary, steady foundation for sustained attention.

Section 4: The Emotional and Economic Payoff of Annihilation

The commitment to ruthless distraction elimination yields profound benefits that extend beyond a few extra hours of productivity, directly addressing the shame and economic costs associated with unmanaged attention.

1. Economic Gains: Mitigating the Cost of Work Loss

Unmanaged attention and context switching are direct causes of reduced productivity and work loss—the largest components of the overall societal **ADHD Tax**.

- **Quantified Cost:** The excess costs associated with ADHD in US adults are estimated at **$122.8 billion annually**, with costs of unemployment ($66.8 billion) and productivity loss ($28.8 billion) comprising the largest proportion.
- **Protecting Income:** By enforcing single-task focus and minimizing context switching through Cognitive Load Annihilation, you are directly increasing your efficiency and quality of work. This strategic focus is an active measure against productivity loss, providing a measurable economic gain by supporting career stability and performance.

2. Emotional Liberation: Defeating Shame and Overwhelm

The constant failure to maintain focus and follow through, often caused by digital distraction, is a significant driver of shame and the pervasive feeling of being overwhelmed for women with ADHD.

- **Building Self-Efficacy:** Successfully completing a focused Pomodoro sprint (Chapter 3) without being derailed by notifications provides tangible evidence of **competence and control**. This consistent success builds **self-efficacy**, the belief in your ability to manage your focus, which is the direct antidote to the shame and inadequacy that characterize unmanaged attention.

- **Sustained Calm:** By eliminating the sources of fragmented attention, you reduce the chronic internal turmoil and anxiety that arises from fighting digital noise. This creates a state of sustained calm, allowing you to operate from a place of intentional control rather than frantic, reactive chaos.

Conclusion: Your Focused Sanctuary

The work of **Protecting Your Energy** is the final, non-negotiable step in mastering focus. By ruthlessly applying the strategy of Cognitive Load Annihilation, you move beyond merely coping with distraction and actively design an environment that compels focus.

You have transformed your relationship with your attention: it is no longer a fragile, easily fragmented resource, but a powerful, sustained tool, supported by the external structure of Time Blocking and protected by the boundaries of digital silence. This systematic effort conserves the mental energy needed for sustained self-mastery.

This cultivated internal stability, the quiet confidence of a mind no longer fragmented by noise, is the essential prerequisite for the next stage of your journey. You are now equipped to manage your attention, making you resilient against the profound **hormonal fluctuations** that can destabilize focus and emotions. The mastery of your mental energy is the critical bridge to managing your body's rhythm and achieving true integrated success.

Chapter 5 Workbook: Protect Your Energy: Reduce Cognitive Load by Eliminating Digital Noise

Objective: To identify and eliminate key sources of digital noise and unnecessary context switching, thereby protecting finite Executive Function resources.

Scientific Anchor: Digital notifications and open browser tabs create "open loops" that consume Working Memory and increase Cognitive Load, disproportionately impacting performance for individuals with ADHD. Strategic elimination of these distractions conserves EF energy.

Activity 5.1: The Digital Noise Annihilation Audit

Instructions: Audit your primary work device (phone or computer) and immediately turn off notifications for non-essential apps. Use the three categories below to guide your decision.

1. **Phone Notification Audit (Be Ruthless):**
    - *Apps You Silence Immediately (Non-Essential):* (Example: Social Media, News, Games, Most Shopping Alerts)
    - *Apps You Keep ON (Critical):* (Example: Calendar Alerts, Emergency Calls Only)
2. **Browser / Desktop Audit:** How many browser tabs do you currently have open? Commit to closing all but the three most essential tabs and turning off all pop-up notifications for non-essential websites.

    Current Open Tabs:; ____

    Cognitive Benefit of Closing Tabs: (How does this feel, or what mental benefit do you anticipate?)

Activity 5.2: Measuring the Cost of Context Switching

Instructions: Select a focused work block (e.g., a Pomodoro sprint) and intentionally track how often you switch tasks or succumb to digital temptation.

1. **Task:** (Select a specific, single task, e.g., "Draft the summary paragraph.")
2. **Duration:** Set a timer for 25 minutes.
3. **Context Switch Tally:** Every time you switch away from your designated task (e.g., check phone, open a new browser tab, start a different chore), place a tally mark below.

    Tally: ____

    ____

    ____

    ____

    ____

    ____

    ____

    ____

    ____

    ____

    ____

4. **Analysis:** Each tally mark represents a cognitive penalty, a drain on EF. If you had zero context switches, what would be the most important task you could accomplish with that conserved energy?

   Conserved Energy Use: ________________________________

   ____

   ____

   ____

   ____

   ____

   ____

Reflection 5.3: Energy Gain and Resilience

Instructions: Reflect on how eliminating digital noise creates a foundation for sustained energy and emotional resilience.

1. **EF Conservation:** How does intentionally closing all notifications and tabs *before* starting work reduce the mental energy (Cognitive Load) required for your brain to engage the task, compared to trying to filter them out *while* you work?

   Mental Energy Reduction: ____________________________

   ____

   ____

   ____

   ____

2. **Burnout Prevention:** The constant fight against distraction leads to mental fatigue. How does the discipline of **Batching Email** (only checking at fixed times) help prevent the chronic sense of being "frenzied" and "frazzled" throughout the day? (Think about the neurological shift from **reactive** to **proactive**).

   Proactive Calm: ________________________________

   ____

   ____

   ____

   ____

3. **Bridge to Hormones:** Stress, anxiety, and mental fatigue severely impair Executive Functions, and hormonal shifts exacerbate these symptoms. How does the reduction of digital noise and cognitive load provide a stable, protected mental baseline that prepares you to better manage the **hormonal fluctuations** that can destabilize focus and mood?

   Hormonal Resilience: ____________________________________

   ____

   ____

   ____

   ____

   ____

   ____

CHAPTER 6

REFLECT AND INTEGRATE: YOUR FOCUS JOURNEY SO FAR

You have reached a pivotal moment in your journey toward integrated self-mastery. The work of Book 2 has been dedicated to the deepest, most taxing internal struggle of the ADHD brain: the mastery of **attention dysregulation** and the pervasive chaos of **Time Blindness**. You have moved beyond simply coping with distraction to actively commanding your focus, transforming your mind from a source of perpetual fragmentation into a powerful, reliable tool.

This chapter is a moment of necessary pause, a time to **reflect and integrate** the profound cognitive and emotional gains achieved through the disciplined practice of the strategies you have mastered: **Time Blocking**, **Pomodoro sprints**, and **Cognitive Load Annihilation**. The aim is to solidify the foundational shift from a life defined by **reactive chaos** and **overwhelm** to a state of **proactive, intentional action.**

The core insight of this book is that consistent focus is not a matter of willpower; it is a measurable, neurobiological function directly tied to **energy management** and **strategic structure**. You have learned that the struggle was never laziness, but a challenge of **Executive Function (EF)** that required an evidence-based toolkit to compensate for deficits in time perception, task initiation, and filtering capacity. By systematically reducing the external noise and structuring your time to work *with* your brain's need for novelty and finitude, you have reclaimed precious mental bandwidth, creating the stability required to manage the complex emotional and physiological challenges addressed in the books that follow.

Section 1: The Cognitive Transformation: Conquering Time and Load

The most powerful outcome of mastering the EF strategies in this book is the mitigation of two core, debilitating deficits: the inability to perceive time accurately and the chronic drain of high cognitive load. This transformation of the cognitive landscape is the tangible benefit of replacing inconsistent internal effort with predictable external structure.

1. The Banishment of Time Blindness and the Estimation Deficit

The feeling of being perpetually behind, rushing deadlines, and being surprised by the sudden emergence of appointments is the emotional reality of **Time Blindness**, the inability to feel or accurately estimate the passage of time. This neurobiological deficit makes effective long-term planning virtually impossible, leading to the financial and relational penalties of chronic lateness and poor prioritization. The strategies in this book directly counteract this deficit by making time concrete and visible, thereby reducing the anxiety and overwhelm that triggers **task paralysis**.

- **Time Blocking as an External Clock:** By enforcing the practice of **Time Blocking** (Chapter 2), you replaced the abstract, amorphous nature of time with a tangible, visual map of your day. This technique directly addresses the **estimation deficit** by forcing you to pre-allocate duration for every task, break, and transition. The visible schedule minimizes the cognitive guesswork of "What to do next?", conserving EF resources that were previously wasted on moment-to-moment decisions and providing the necessary external context that the time-blind brain lacks. This methodical approach ensures that even tasks that lack intrinsic interest are assigned a fixed, non-negotiable temporal slot, circumventing the dopamine deficit that fuels procrastination.

- **The Power of Finitude and Momentum:** The customized application of the **Pomodoro Technique** (Chapter 3) strategically attacks the paralysis triggered by the perception of an infinite, daunting task. By committing to short, fixed sprints, you impose **finitude** on the task, lowering the psychological barrier to initiation. The visible timer provides a constant, external cue, anchoring attention and generating the necessary **momentum** through the immediate reward of completing a structured sprint. This systematic approach transforms work from an overwhelming marathon into a chain of manageable, dopamine-rewarding sprints, allowing you to sustain attention over periods that were previously impossible to command.

2. Cognitive Load Annihilation and EF Conservation

The chronic state of overwhelm in the ADHD experience is rooted in the high **Cognitive Load (CL)**, the relentless mental effort consumed by an overstimulated mind that struggles to filter stimuli. The mastery of **Cognitive Load Annihilation** (Chapter 5) is the most direct defense against this drain.

- **Defeating Context Switching:** By enforcing **single-tasking** and **email / notification batching** (Chapter 5), you systematically eliminated the draining cost of **Context Switching**—the rapid shifting of attention between different cognitive demands. This practice is crucial because each switch, particularly for the ADHD brain with its inefficient filtering, incurs a measurable cognitive penalty, rapidly depleting EF resources (like Working Memory and Inhibitory Control) and leading to significant mental exhaustion. By reducing digital noise and minimizing "open loops" (e.g., closing unnecessary browser tabs), you conserved the mental energy that was once consumed by fighting internal and external distractions.

- **Strengthening Internal Resilience:** The consistent practice of **Inhibitory Control (IC)** and **Working Memory (WM)** training within fixed planning routines (Chapter 4) created a powerful internal structure. IC was strengthened by intentionally resisting the urge to check notifications during Pomodoro sprints, and WM was supported by externalizing all task instructions onto fixed checklists and planners. This dual approach, externalizing the burden while strengthening the internal "brakes", builds a long-term cognitive resilience that is less susceptible to collapse under stress. Furthermore, this deliberate training of IC (thinking before acting) is the very muscle needed for emotional regulation (resisting impulsive emotional reactions), a key component for future mastery (Book 4).

Section 2: The Emotional and Economic Payoff: Mitigating the ADHD Tax

The structured focus achieved in this book yields profound benefits beyond mere mental clarity; it actively reduces the quantifiable **"ADHD Tax"**, the cumulative financial, emotional, and mental cost of navigating life with unmanaged executive function deficits. This mitigation leads directly to increased self-efficacy and emotional stability.

1. Mitigating the Economic Cost of Work Loss and Financial Strain

Unmanaged attention dysregulation is a direct cause of work loss and reduced productivity, the largest components of the societal economic burden associated with ADHD. The commitment to Time Blocking and sustained focus is a fundamental economic defense strategy.

- **Addressing Productivity Loss:** The total societal excess cost attributable to ADHD in US adults is estimated at **$122.8 billion annually**, with excess costs of unemployment ($66.8 billion) and productivity loss ($28.8 billion) comprising the largest proportion. Time Blocking and Pomodoro sprints directly counteract this economic drain by enforcing single-task focus and consistent follow-through, increasing efficiency and quality of work. This stability is a proactive measure against the financial toll that includes lower savings and earnings that affect adults with a history of ADHD.

- **Reducing Penalties:** The banishment of time blindness ensures that crucial administrative tasks (like bill payment, follow-up calls, or administrative work) are scheduled as non-negotiable appointments (Time Blocks), mitigating the risk of financial penalties, late fees, and lost opportunities that stem from inattention and poor prioritization. The systematic scheduling enforces the kind of reliable behavior that protects credit and financial standing, areas often compromised by ADHD impulsivity and poor memory.

2. Defeating Shame and Building Self-Efficacy

The chronic failure to maintain focus and follow through, a frequent result of digital distraction and time blindness, is a significant driver of shame and the pervasive feeling of overwhelm for women with ADHD.

- **The Antidote to the Inner Critic:** The mastery of Time Blocking replaces the long, overwhelming to-do list (a document of perceived failure) with a realistic, manageable schedule, thereby setting **achievable expectations** and reducing the likelihood of failure and self-criticism. The fact that you are setting a realistic schedule, complete with buffers and recovery time, is an act of **self-compassion** that actively disarms the "all-or-nothing" perfectionism trap.
- **Evidence of Competence:** Each successfully completed Time Block or Pomodoro sprint provides tangible, undeniable evidence of competence and follow-through. This consistent success builds **self-efficacy**, the belief in one's ability to manage their focus and time, which is the direct psychological antidote to the inadequacy that characterizes unmanaged attention. The power lies in realizing that success is due to a deliberate, effective strategy, not inconsistent willpower.

3. Protecting the Emotional Baseline and Relationships

The continuous fight against distraction and chaos creates a state of chronically elevated stress and anxiety, which directly triggers or exacerbates **emotional dysregulation**, the sudden, intense emotional surges common in ADHD.

- **Stress Reduction:** The structural predictability of a Time Blocked schedule, coupled with the digital silence of the focus sprints, stabilizes the nervous system by reducing the chaotic inputs that trigger anxiety. This conserved emotional bandwidth creates a more stable baseline, reducing the likelihood of minor triggers escalating into disproportionate emotional storms (the "green-to-red" phenomenon).
- **Reducing Relational Friction:** By clearly blocking time for necessary tasks and reducing chronic lateness (Time Blindness), the focus skills directly reduce friction in relationships. Consistent follow-through, supported by the scheduled Time Blocks, lessens the neurotypical partner's need to act as a **taskmaster** or reminder, mitigating the resentment and the unhealthy "parent-child" dynamic that often develops in neurodiverse couples.

Section 3: The Bridge to Resilience: Preparing for Hormonal and Emotional Challenges

The structural stability of focus achieved in Book 2 is not an end goal; it is the essential **prerequisite** for engaging with the complex internal work of the upcoming books. The Executive Functions you have strengthened are necessary to build resilience against the profound physical and emotional volatility that characterizes the female ADHD experience.

1. EF Stability as a Buffer Against Hormonal Chaos (Book 3)

The brain's Executive Function skills, particularly Working Memory and attention, are known to be highly sensitive to hormonal fluctuations. Research suggests that the decline in **estrogen** during the low-estrogen phases of the menstrual cycle (e.g., the luteal phase) can exacerbate core ADHD symptoms like inattention and disorganization.

- **The Problem of Hormonal Fluctuation:** Preliminary pilot data suggests that within-person declines in estrogen, particularly in the context of rising levels of progesterone just post-ovulation, are associated with meaningful increases in ADHD symptoms (e.g., inattention and hyperactive-impulsive features). These fluctuations, which are unique to the female lifespan (puberty, menstrual cycle, perimenopause), act as a "double whammy" on an already dysregulated system.

- **Neutralizing the Effect:** By maintaining a robust, external EF system (Time Blocking, predictable Pomodoro routines), you create a functional buffer against these inevitable internal shifts. When hormonal changes inevitably cause an internal drop in dopamine-linked focus, the external system (the schedule, the timer, the task boundaries) remains intact, preventing the system from collapsing into chaos. This stability ensures that the impact of the hormonal fluctuation is absorbed by the structure, rather than leading to a complete functional failure.
- **Data Collection for Advocacy:** The disciplined use of the scheduled Pomodoro sprints and Time Blocks provides objective **data** on performance consistency (e.g., how many sprints were completed, how accurate were the time estimates). This data becomes the essential tool for tracking the impact of hormonal cycles on your productivity, enabling you to advocate for personalized treatment approaches (like "cycle dosing") with your healthcare professional, a practice that is necessary given the established **gender health gap** in ADHD research.

2. Focus as the Foundation for Emotional Mastery (Book 4)

Emotional dysregulation is the most impairing symptom for many women with ADHD, and its effective management relies heavily on the EF skills you have practiced.

- **Activating the "Brakes":** The practice of **Inhibitory Control (IC)**, resisting the urge to check a notification or interrupt a conversation (Chapter 4), is the very same EF muscle required for **emotional regulation**, resisting the urge to react impulsively during an intense emotional surge. You are training the brain's "brakes" (the PFC) to successfully override the emotional accelerator (the amygdala).
- **Mindfulness and Attention:** The capacity for sustained attention, honed through the Pomodoro Technique, is the prerequisite for effective **Mindfulness** (a cornerstone of DBT). Mindfulness is the ability to gently anchor attention to the

present moment without judgment. This EF skill creates the critical **"pause"** between feeling an intense emotion and reacting to it, allowing the cognitive strategies of CBT (challenging the thought) to engage before the emotional storm takes over. By stabilizing focus, you build the internal toolkit necessary to navigate the complexities of intense feelings and Rejection Sensitive Dysphoria (RSD), which is often exacerbated by emotional volatility.

Section 4: The Laws of Sustained Attention

To ensure the focus gained is resilient, we must integrate the key principles of Book 2 into a set of non-negotiable laws that govern your attention. These laws solidify the shift from chaos to command.

Law 1: Time is Visible, Finite, and Blocked

- **Principle:** Never leave time or task duration vague. Every activity must be scheduled as a fixed appointment with a clear start and end time (Time Blocking).
- **Rule:** Always apply an **Estimation Buffer** (25–50% extra time) and schedule mandatory **Transition Blocks** between activities to compensate for the estimation deficit and the cognitive cost of context switching.

Law 2: Attention is Anchored by Finitude and Structure

- **Principle:** Sustain focus by structuring effort into small, manageable sprints that reduce the psychological cost of commitment.
- **Rule:** Use the **Customized Pomodoro Cycle** to match work periods to your current attention span, and always enforce the **mandatory break** to prevent burnout and interrupt hyperfocus.

Law 3: Energy is Conserved by Annihilation, Not Effort

- **Principle:** The best way to create focus is to ruthlessly eliminate the sources of distraction and cognitive load that consume Working Memory.
- **Rule:** Enforce **Cognitive Load Annihilation** by minimizing context switching (single-tasking), strictly implementing **Notification Annihilation** across all devices, and maintaining a clean **Digital Desktop** to protect your limited EF reserves.

Conclusion: Your Empowered Attention

The journey through Book 2 marks the completion of the structural foundation required for integrated self-mastery. You have systematically defeated Time Blindness, conquered the paradox of focus, and reclaimed valuable mental bandwidth from the chaos of digital noise and fragmented attention.

The stability achieved here is your most valuable asset. The mental energy that was once consumed by fighting your own brain is now a conserved resource, a stable platform upon which you can build emotional resilience and navigate the complex, dynamic landscape of your hormonal health.

You are no longer a passive victim of your neurobiology, but an active, strategic commander of your attention. This powerful new sense of competence and control is the definitive antidote to the shame and overwhelm that has characterized your struggle, equipping you for the profound work of self-mastery that lies ahead.

Chapter 6 Workbook: Reflect and Integrate: Your Focus Journey So Far

Objective: To synthesize the cognitive and emotional gains achieved in Book 2, solidifying the shift from reliance on willpower to resilient system design.

Scientific Anchor: Reflective practice reduces the impact of stress and sadness on Executive Functions, allowing the functional systems built to flourish. Acknowledging neurobiological reality counters the shame cycle.

Activity 6.1: The Time Blindness & Load Reduction Scorecard

Instructions: Rate the severity of your challenges **before** Book 2 and **now**, focusing on the impact of the new time and focus strategies. (Scale: 1 = Minimal Challenge, 5 = Severe Challenge)

Challenge Area	Before Book 2 (Initial)	After Book 2 (Current)	Reflection: The Tool That Helped Most
Chronic Lateness/ Time Estimation			(Example: Estimation Buffer / Time Block)
Task Paralysis / Starting Boring Work			(Example: Pomodoro Finitude)
Distraction from Digital Notifications			(Example: Notification Annihilation)
Mental Fatigue / Brain Fog			(Example: Scheduled Recovery / IC Practice)

Reflection 6.2: Shifting from Shame to Strategy

Instructions: Use this space to integrate the core concept that struggles with focus are neurological, not moral, and assess your progress in building self-efficacy.

1. **The Overwhelm to Control Shift:** Identify one specific moment this week where you felt an urge to procrastinate or switch tasks. How did remembering a specific tool (**IC Practice** or the **Customized Pomodoro**) create a crucial pause that allowed you to choose a strategic action?

   The Intervention: ____

   ____

   ____

   ____

   ____

2. **The Shame Antidote:** Identify one self-critical thought you had about your focus (e.g., "I'm lazy for losing focus after 30 minutes"). Rephrase this thought using the compassionate, neurobiological reality you learned (e.g., "My brain is wired for novelty and needs a mandated break after 30 minutes to reset. I am managing my energy strategically.")

   New, Empowered Narrative: ______________________________

   ____

   ____

   ____

   ____

   ____

3. **Building Self-Efficacy:** What is the most important piece of **evidence of competence** you created this week (e.g., sticking to a Time Block, ignoring a notification, completing three Pomodoros)? How does this tangible "win" counteract a previous feeling of inadequacy?

   Evidence of Competence: ______________________________

   ____

   ____

   ____

   ____

Activity 6.3: Bridge to Hormonal Resilience (Book 3 Prep)

Instructions: The capacity for focus (EF) is highly vulnerable to hormonal fluctuations, stress, and anxiety. Use this activity to analyze your current EF stability.

1. **Vulnerability Audit:** Thinking about the week before your menstrual cycle (the low-estrogen phase) or a period of high stress, what three EF skills are most likely to fail first? (e.g., Working Memory, Inhibitory Control, Time Estimation).

   Vulnerable Skill 1: ______________________________

   Vulnerable Skill 2: ______________________________

   Vulnerable Skill 3: ______________________________

2. **External Buffer Plan:** For the three vulnerable skills you identified, name the specific **external system** from Book 2 that you will use to compensate for that weakness when your focus dips due to hormonal shifts or stress.

   External Buffer 1 (System): ________________________________

   External Buffer 2 (System): ________________________________

   External Buffer 3 (System): ________________________________

CHAPTER 7

PRACTICE AND APPLY: YOUR EXECUTIVE FUNCTION ACTION TOOLKIT

You have mastered the core neurobiological strategies for managing attention, time blindness, and chronic overwhelm. This chapter provides the final **Action Toolkit** for Book 2, designed to transform these concepts into consistent, low-friction habits that build lasting Executive Function (EF) resilience. The consistent use of these tools ensures that the mental bandwidth you reclaimed from fighting external chaos is now actively utilized for intentional, sustained focus.

Toolkit 1: Time Blocking and Buffer Application

Objective: To systematically defeat **Time Blindness** by creating fixed, time-bound appointments that include estimation and transition buffers.

Scientific Anchor: Time Blocking forces the engagement of planning and estimation skills, which are core executive functions challenged by ADHD, while mandatory buffers reduce the stress caused by the Estimation Deficit.

Activity 7.1: The Bounded Work Block

1. **Select a Task:** Choose one specific, demanding task for tomorrow (e.g., "Draft the summary," not "Work on report").
2. **Estimate:** Write your honest, quick estimate for how long it will take: minutes.
3. **Schedule the Block:** Create a fixed Time Block, adding a **25% Estimation Buffer** to your original time (e.g., if you estimated 60 min, block 75 min).

Time Slot	Activity	Fixed Duration (Includes Buffer)
(Example: 9:00 AM)	**Focus Sprint: Your Task**	---- minutes
(Time after Task)	**Mandatory Transition Block**	**15** minutes

Commitment: Commit to respecting the **Transition Block.** When your work time is up, physically move away from your desk for the 15 minutes to clear your mind and prevent the cognitive cost of context switching.

Toolkit 2: Inhibitory Control (IC) Training

Objective: To actively strengthen your brain's "brakes" (Inhibitory Control) by resisting a common, low-stakes digital distraction during a short work sprint.

Scientific Anchor: Resisting immediate gratification strengthens the neural pathways responsible for self-control (IC), which is essential for sustained focus and emotional regulation.

Activity 7.2: The Digital Resistance Sprint

1. **Identify Your #1 Impulse:** Name the primary, non-essential impulse that derails your focus (e.g., Checking text messages, opening the news app, grabbing a snack).

   Impulse: ____

   ____

   ____

2. **The Sprint:** Set a timer for **10 minutes**. Work on your most boring task. Every time the urge to act on your Impulse arises, perform a **micro-pause**: acknowledge the urge without judgment, take one deep breath, and gently redirect your focus back to the task.

3. **Tally:** Record how many times you successfully resisted the impulse in 10 minutes.

   Successful Resistances: _______________________________

   ____

   ____

   ____

   ____

   ____

   (Each resistance is a "rep" for your IC muscle.)

Toolkit 3: Cognitive Load Annihilation

Objective: To reduce **Cognitive Load** and free up Working Memory by systematically eliminating digital "open loops."

Scientific Anchor: Unresolved tasks (open tabs, unchecked notifications) consume Working Memory. Closing these "open loops" conserves mental energy and prevents fragmentation of attention.

Activity 7.3: The Digital Reset

1. **Browser Cleanup:** How many browser tabs do you have open right now?

   Current Tab Count: ___________________________________

Action: Immediately close all but the **three most essential tabs.**

2. **Notification Audit:** Check your phone's notification settings for three non-essential apps (e.g., social media, shopping, non-critical news).

   Action: Immediately set these three apps to **silent** or **turn off all alerts**. This is **Notification Annihilation**, silence as self-care.

3. **Email Batching Commitment:** Commit to checking your email only during two fixed, Time Blocked windows tomorrow.

   Email Block 1 (Start / End Time): ___________________________

   Email Block 2 (Start / End Time): ___________________________

Reflection 7.4: Focus System Assessment

1. **Pomodoro Efficacy:** The core benefit of the Pomodoro Technique is **finitude**. How does knowing a work session is limited to 25 minutes reduce the feeling of **overwhelm** that often leads to procrastination?

   Finitude Effect: ____

   ____

   ____

   ____

2. **Relational Benefit:** How does consistently using **Time Blocking** to schedule fixed time for non-work tasks (e.g., "6:00 PM–7:30 PM: Dinner / Family Time") reduce the internal guilt or external pressure that often arises when the ADHD brain is hyperfocused on work?

   Guilt Reduction: ____

   ____

   ____

   ____

CONCLUSION

SUMMARY: YOUR EMPOWERED ATTENTION

You have reached a definitive inflection point in your journey toward self-mastery. The work of Book 2 has been a disciplined, sustained assault on the internal chaos that defines unmanaged Attention-Deficit / Hyperactivity Disorder (ADHD): the systemic fragmentation of attention, the tyranny of **Time Blindness**, and the profound exhaustion of **Cognitive Load (CL)**. You have successfully moved beyond the reactive struggle, where your focus was a victim of distraction, to a state of **proactive, intentional command**.

The core insight solidified here is that consistent focus is not a mysterious gift of willpower; it is the measurable result of disciplined **Executive Function (EF) management** and the strategic application of **external scaffolding**. By systematically reducing the external noise and structuring your time to work *with* your brain's need for novelty and finitude, you have reclaimed precious mental bandwidth. This stability is the necessary foundation for managing the complex emotional and physiological challenges addressed in the books that follow. You have not just managed your focus; you have successfully future-proofed your capacity for consistent follow-through, providing the ultimate antidote to the pervasive feeling of being "frenzied, frazzled, and overwhelmed."

Section 1: The Victory Over Time and Load (Cognitive Synthesis)

The most powerful outcome of mastering the EF strategies in this book is the mitigation of two core, debilitating deficits: the inability to perceive time accurately and the chronic drain of high cognitive load. This transformation of the cognitive landscape is the tangible benefit of replacing inconsistent internal effort with predictable external structure.

1. The Banishment of Time Blindness: Finitude and Planning

Time blindness, the inability to accurately perceive or estimate time, is the primary driver of chronic lateness, poor prioritization, and the anxiety that triggers task paralysis. The strategies in this book directly counteract this neurobiological deficit by making time concrete and measurable.

- **Time Blocking as an External Clock:** The discipline of **Time Blocking** (Chapter 2) replaced the amorphous chaos of the to-do list with a tangible, visual map of your day. By forcing the allocation of fixed duration for every task and transition, you directly addressed the **estimation deficit** (the tendency to underestimate time), ensuring that your schedule is temporally realistic and includes the necessary **Estimation Buffers** (25–50% extra time). This enforced planning minimized the cognitive guesswork of "What to do next?", conserving EF resources.
- **The Power of Pomodoro Finitude:** The customized application of the **Pomodoro Technique** (Chapter 3) strategically attacks the paralysis triggered by the perception of an infinite, daunting task. By committing to short, fixed sprints (e.g., 25 minutes), you impose **finitude** on the task, lowering the psychological barrier to initiation. The timer serves as a constant, non-negotiable external cue, anchoring attention and generating the necessary **momentum** through the immediate reward of completing a structured sprint, systematically bypassing the internal dopamine deficit.

- **Strengthening Working Memory:** The practice of utilizing **fixed planning rituals** and external scaffolds (Chapter 4), such as reviewing your plan nightly, actively offloaded instruction-following and multi-step tasks from your unreliable **Working Memory (WM)**. This systematic offloading ensured that your WM was not overloaded, which is crucial for preventing the "brain fog" and forgetfulness that accompany high cognitive load.

2. Cognitive Load Annihilation: Conserving Energy from Digital Noise

The chronic state of overwhelm is rooted in the high **Cognitive Load (CL)** caused by an overstimulated mind that struggles to filter stimuli and manage multiple **"open loops."** The mastery of **Cognitive Load Annihilation** (Chapter 5) is the most direct defense against this drain.

- **Defeating Context Switching:** By enforcing **single-tasking** and **email / notification batching**, you systematically eliminated the draining cost of **Context Switching**, the rapid shifting of attention between different cognitive demands. Each switch incurs a measurable cognitive penalty, rapidly depleting EF resources and leading to severe mental fatigue.
- **Digital Sanctuary:** The strict implementation of **Notification Annihilation** and the maintenance of a clean **Digital Desktop** (closing open tabs) systematically closed digital "open loops," conserving the mental energy that was once consumed by fighting internal and external digital distractions. This intentional environment management protected your **Inhibitory Control (IC)**, your brain's "brakes", from the constant temptation of novelty, ensuring those resources are conserved for higher-leverage tasks, such as sustained focus and emotional regulation.

Section 2: The Emotional and Economic Payoff: Mitigating the ADHD Tax

The structured focus achieved in this book yields profound benefits beyond mere mental clarity, actively reducing the quantifiable **"ADHD Tax"**, the cumulative financial, emotional, and mental cost of navigating life with unmanaged EF deficits.

1. Mitigating the Economic Cost of Work Loss

Unmanaged attention dysregulation is a direct cause of work loss, reduced productivity, and financial instability, the largest components of the societal economic burden associated with ADHD.

- **Quantified Cost Reduction:** The total societal excess cost attributable to ADHD in US adults is estimated at **$122.8 billion annually** ($14,092 per adult), with excess costs of unemployment and productivity loss comprising the largest proportion. Time Blocking and Pomodoro sprints directly counteract this drain by enforcing single-task focus and consistent follow-through, actively increasing efficiency and the quality of work. This stability serves as a crucial defense against the financial consequences, such as lower earnings and savings, that affect adults with a history of childhood ADHD, even in adulthood.
- **Reducing Penalties:** The banishment of time blindness ensures that crucial administrative tasks (like bill payment or scheduling) are scheduled as non-negotiable appointments, mitigating the risk of financial penalties, late fees, and lost opportunities that stem from inattention and poor prioritization.

2. Defeating Shame and Building Self-Efficacy

The chronic failure to maintain focus and follow through, a frequent result of digital distraction and time blindness, is a significant driver of shame and the pervasive feeling of overwhelm for women with ADHD.

- **The Antidote to the Inner Critic:** The mastery of Time Blocking replaces the long, overwhelming to-do list (a document of perceived failure) with a realistic, manageable schedule, thereby setting **achievable expectations** and reducing the likelihood of failure and self-criticism. The fact that your schedule is realistic, complete with buffers and recovery time, is an inherent act of **self-compassion** that disarms the "all-or-nothing" perfectionism trap.
- **Evidence of Competence:** Each successfully completed Time Block or Pomodoro sprint provides tangible, undeniable evidence of competence and follow-through. This consistent

success builds **self-efficacy**, the belief in one's ability to manage their focus and time, which is the direct psychological antidote to the inadequacy that characterizes unmanaged attention.

Section 3: The Bridge to Resilience: Preparing for Hormonal and Emotional Challenges

The structural stability of focus achieved in Book 2 is the essential **prerequisite** for engaging with the complex internal work of the upcoming books. The Executive Functions you have strengthened are necessary to build resilience against the profound physical and emotional volatility that characterizes the female ADHD experience.

1. EF Stability as a Buffer Against Hormonal Chaos

The brain's Executive Function skills, particularly Working Memory and attention, are known to be highly sensitive to hormonal fluctuations. This link is critical, as estrogen directly influences the dopamine system that governs focus.

- **The Vulnerability:** Research suggests that the decline in **estrogen** during the low-estrogen phases of the menstrual cycle (e.g., the luteal phase and perimenstrual periods) can exacerbate core ADHD symptoms, including inattention and poor organization, due to the corresponding dip in dopamine support. Furthermore, progesterone's influence can increase anxiety and emotional reactivity. These fluctuations impose a "double whammy" on an already vulnerable system.
- **Neutralizing the Effect:** By maintaining a robust, external EF system (Time Blocking, predictable routines), you create a functional buffer against these inevitable internal shifts. When hormonal changes inevitably cause an internal drop in focus, the external system (the clear schedule, the mandatory breaks, the strict task boundaries) remains intact, preventing the entire system from collapsing into chaos. This stability ensures that the impact of the hormonal fluctuation is absorbed by the structure, rather than leading to a complete functional failure.

- **Data Collection for Advocacy:** The disciplined use of the scheduled Pomodoro sprints and Time Blocks provides objective **data** on performance consistency. This data becomes the essential tool for tracking the impact of hormonal cycles on your productivity, enabling you to advocate for personalized treatment approaches (like "cycle dosing") with your healthcare professional, a necessary step given the established **gender health gap** in ADHD research.

2. Focus as the Foundation for Emotional Mastery

Emotional dysregulation, the most impairing symptom for many women with ADHD, is profoundly linked to the EF skills you have practiced. Effective emotional management relies on the ability to pause and redirect attention, skills honed in Book 2.

- **Activating the "Brakes":** The practice of **Inhibitory Control (IC)**, resisting the urge to check a notification or interrupt a conversation (Chapter 4), is the very same EF muscle required for **emotional regulation**, resisting the urge to react impulsively during an intense emotional surge. You are training the brain's "brakes" (the PFC) to successfully override the emotional accelerator (the amygdala).
- **Mindfulness and the "Pause":** The capacity for sustained attention, honed through the Pomodoro Technique, is the prerequisite for effective **Mindfulness** (a cornerstone of DBT). Mindfulness is the ability to gently anchor attention to the present moment without judgment. This EF skill creates the critical **"pause"** between feeling an intense emotion and reacting to it, allowing the cognitive strategies of CBT (challenging the thought) to engage before the emotional storm takes over. By stabilizing focus, you build the internal toolkit necessary to navigate the complexities of intense feelings and **Rejection Sensitive Dysphoria (RSD)**.

Section 4: The Laws of Sustained Attention

To ensure the focus gained is resilient, we must integrate the key principles of Book 2 into a set of non-negotiable laws that govern your attention. These laws solidify the shift from chaos to command, allowing you to sustain focus indefinitely.

Law 1: Time is Visible, Finite, and Blocked

- **Principle:** Never leave time or task duration vague. Every activity must be scheduled as a fixed appointment with a clear start and end time (Time Blocking).
- **Rule:** Always apply an **Estimation Buffer** (25–50% extra time) and schedule mandatory **Transition Blocks** between activities to compensate for the estimation deficit and the cognitive cost of context switching.

Law 2: Attention is Anchored by Finitude and Structure

- **Principle:** Sustain focus by structuring effort into small, manageable sprints that reduce the psychological cost of commitment.
- **Rule:** Utilize the **Customized Pomodoro Cycle** to match work periods to your current attention span, and always enforce the **mandatory break** to prevent burnout and interrupt hyperfocus.

Law 3: Energy is Conserved by Annihilation, Not Effort

- **Principle:** The best way to create focus is to ruthlessly eliminate the sources of distraction and cognitive load that consume Working Memory.
- **Rule:** Enforce **Cognitive Load Annihilation** by minimizing context switching (single-tasking), strictly implementing **Notification Annihilation** across all devices, and maintaining a clean **Digital Desktop** to protect your limited EF reserves.

The journey through Book 2 marks the completion of the structural foundation required for integrated self-mastery. You have systematically defeated Time Blindness, conquered the paradox of focus, and reclaimed valuable mental bandwidth from the chaos of digital noise and fragmented attention.

You are no longer a passive victim of your neurobiology, but an active, strategic commander of your attention. This powerful new sense of competence and control is the definitive antidote to the shame and overwhelm that has characterized your struggle, equipping you for the profound work of self-mastery that lies ahead.

BOOK THREE

SHARPEN EXECUTIVE FUNCTION IN WOMEN WITH ADHD

INTRODUCTION

The structural discipline initiated in the foundational work, clearing the external chaos of disorganization and creating predictable physical systems, has successfully established a crucial sanctuary in your life. This hard-won stability reduced the debilitating, reactive pressure on your attention and conserved mental energy that was previously consumed by fighting clutter. Now, this book marks the transition to the most demanding phase of self-mastery: the conquest of **Time Blindness** and the intensive, systematic sharpening of the core cognitive engine of the brain. This volume is dedicated to mastering the internal landscape of the ADHD brain, focusing relentlessly on regulating attention, prioritizing complexity, and sharpening **Executive Function (EF)** skills, the very "mental toolkit for success" required for long-term productivity and emotional self-regulation.

For many women with Attention-Deficit / Hyperactivity Disorder (ADHD), the concept of "focus" is a profound paradox, often presenting as a debilitating struggle rather than a steady capacity. This experience is defined by the dual extremes of attention dysregulation: the chaotic fragmentation of the mind and the intense, often uncontrolled absorption known as **hyperfocus**. On one hand, a woman's attention can be so fragmented that she experiences a "thousand-yard stare," mind-wandering, or "zoning out" during essential conversations or tasks, which leads to forgetfulness, missed details, and a pervasive, anxious sense of being perpetually in a fog. On the other hand, when a task is intensely stimulating, novel, or provides immediate reward, the ADHD brain can lock into the state of hyperfocus. While this state can lead to incredible bursts of creativity and productivity, where hours vanish without notice, it is often uncontrolled, leading a woman to neglect critical responsibilities, miss scheduled appointments, or disregard basic physiological needs, thereby creating significant friction and imbalance in her life.

The fundamental challenge is not a lack of ability to pay attention, but rather a profound **difficulty in regulating and directing it**. The issue lies in the brain's struggle to control its "on / off" switch, preventing it from consistently sustaining its mental spotlight on mundane, but necessary, tasks. This inherent **dysregulation of attention** is a primary, internal driver of the chronic overwhelm that defines the female ADHD experience, leading to a profound sense of mental fatigue, inadequacy, and the feeling of being perpetually "frenzied, frazzled, and overwhelmed."

This book provides the strategic, evidence-based roadmap to move beyond this paradox. It is built on the understanding that conquering overwhelm requires the systematic strengthening of EF skills, allowing you to proactively harness your attention, manage your time effectively, and achieve a state of intentional, sustained focus rather than reactive distraction. The goal is to replace the chaotic demands of an easily fragmented mind with the calm, self-directed structure of cognitive command.

The Neurobiological Reality: Executive Function and the Cognitive Tax

To achieve mastery over focus and productivity, we must first confront the neurological roots of these challenges. The difficulties with planning, sustained attention, prioritization, and impulse control are not signs of poor intelligence or laziness; they are direct consequences of neurobiological differences in how the ADHD brain processes information and regulates itself.

1. Executive Function (EF) Deficits: The Command Center

Executive functions (EFs) are the high-level mental processes that allow us to organize, plan, regulate behavior, meet new challenges with flexibility, and stay focused and concentrate. These functions, which include planning, goal setting, **working memory**, **inhibitory control**, and time management, are essential for success in adult life, proving highly predictive of academic and career outcomes. EFs have been described as the **"mental toolkit for success."**

For individuals with ADHD, these EF skills are prone to inconsistency and functional impairment. The brain's **prefrontal cortex (PFC)**, the "command center" for these skills, is often less developed or less active than in neurotypical individuals. This deficit leads to measurable difficulties in nearly every aspect of organization and productivity, from struggling to hold multi-step instructions in mind (poor working memory) to the difficulty initiating a boring task (task activation deficit). Research consistently highlights the essential nature of these executive skills to success, noting that problems with EFs are among the core ways ADHD affects a person. This constant struggle to execute intentions creates a feeling of profound functional inadequacy, contributing directly to the shame, self-blame, and anxiety so common in women with ADHD.

2. The Dopamine-Driven Dysregulation

The ADHD brain's relationship with attention is distinct and deeply rooted in its **dopamine system**. Dopamine, the key neurotransmitter for motivation, reward, and activation, is thought to be dysregulated in the ADHD brain, often resulting in lower effective signaling in the synapses.

This deficit creates a powerful, persistent craving for **novelty and immediate stimulation**. When a task is under-stimulating (boring, repetitive, or requiring sustained, effortful attention), the brain struggles to produce enough dopamine to find it interesting, leading to distraction, mind-wandering, and task avoidance. The strategies in this book are designed to strategically introduce external structure, like fixed time limits and immediate feedback, to supply the necessary cues and reward required to sustain attention on necessary tasks, thereby effectively bypassing the internal dopamine deficit.

3. Time Blindness: The Invisible Barrier to Planning

Perhaps the most disruptive deficit for productivity and life management is **Time Blindness**, the inability to accurately perceive or estimate the flow of time. Time does not feel like a consistent, measurable resource; instead, the ADHD brain lives predominantly in the "now," making the future feel abstract, distant, and less urgent.

This profound difficulty in feeling the passage of time creates several critical challenges:

- **Estimation Deficit:** You consistently underestimate how long tasks will take, leading to chronic rushing, missed deadlines, and the inevitable stress that results from constant lateness.
- **Overwhelm by Infinity:** When faced with a large task, the time needed to complete it feels amorphous and infinite, which instantly triggers an overload response and **paralysis**. This neurobiological shutdown against overwhelming mental effort is a frequent cause of procrastination.

The comprehensive solution explored in this book is to stop relying on inconsistent internal time perception and instead use **concrete, visual tools** and **intentional scheduling** to make time palpable, measurable, and manageable. This involves mastering techniques like **Time Blocking** to enforce duration and utilizing **Timers** to make abstract time visible.

The Emotional and Cognitive Toll of a Fragmented Mind

The daily struggle with attention dysregulation and EF deficits takes a significant toll on a woman's emotional and cognitive well-being, leading directly to the pervasive sense of overwhelm that this book is designed to defeat.

1. High Cognitive Load and Mental Fatigue

The ADHD brain often struggles with an impaired **filtering mechanism**, meaning it registers all incoming stimuli, a flickering light, a phone notification, a fleeting thought, with almost equal importance. This results in a constant, effortful struggle to filter distractions, creating a state of chronically high **Cognitive Load (CL)**, the mental effort consumed by working memory. Research consistently shows that high cognitive load disproportionately impairs performance for people with ADHD, reducing brain network efficiency.

This continuous mental fight leads to profound **mental fatigue**, a temporary sluggishness and slowdown of thinking abilities that results in poor focus, forgetfulness, and exhaustion. This chronic effort to manage an overstimulated mind is the **"ADHD Tax"** on energy reserves, a measurable cumulative cost that depletes mental capacity and leads to burnout and a diminished capacity for sustained effort. The entire strategy of focus mastery is designed to dramatically lower this baseline cognitive load, reserving mental energy for high-leverage tasks.

2. Shame, Masking, and the Loss of Self-Worth

The persistent difficulties with focus, time management, and follow-through often lead a woman with ADHD to internalize her struggles and blame herself, interpreting her symptoms as moral or character failings. This internalized struggle is amplified by the intense societal pressure on women to be organized, calm, and effortlessly competent.

This conflict drives **masking**, the exhausting practice of developing sophisticated compensatory behaviors to hide the internal chaos and appear "neurotypical" to the outside world. This continuous performance is an invisible burden that leads to a lifetime of internalized shame, anxiety, and a shattered sense of self-worth. Studies confirm that girls are more likely to mask their symptoms than boys, and this practice prevents authentic connection and reinforces feelings of inadequacy.

The Strategic Roadmap for Sustained Focus

The path to defeating overwhelm involves strategically creating external and internal structures that compensate for EF deficits. This book guides you through a process of learning to work *with* your brain's unique wiring, not against it, through evidence-based practices drawn from specialized ADHD coaching and therapeutic principles.

The upcoming chapters will provide you with a comprehensive toolkit to sharpen your cognitive command:

- **You will master the schedule:** You will move beyond vague deadlines by learning the **Reverse Timeline** method, transforming overwhelming projects into sequential, manageable **Milestones**. This strategic method systematically minimizes the **Task Activation Deficit** that triggers paralysis, anchoring the project to the immediate present.

- **You will prioritize effectively:** You will gain techniques to identify high-leverage tasks and allocate resources with intention, countering the brain's tendency to get bogged down in an undifferentiated mass of obligations and achieving clarity in decision-making.
- **You will harness attention:** You will utilize structured time management techniques, including the **Pomodoro Technique**, to break work into short, focused sprints. This provides the necessary **finitude** to reduce overwhelm and prevents burnout from uncontrolled hyperfocus, transforming chaotic energy into reliable output.
- **You will strengthen resilience:** You will build the internal mental muscles responsible for planning and recall by mastering fixed planning routines and engaging in cognitive exercises designed to improve **working memory** and **inhibitory control** (thinking before acting).
- **You will protect your sanctuary:** You will learn to recognize and ruthlessly eliminate the sources of **digital noise** and unnecessary **context switching** that fragment your attention and increase cognitive load (CL). This involves implementing strategies like **Notification Annihilation** to protect your precious mental energy reserves.

This book provides the strategic roadmap for replacing the chaotic demands of an easily fragmented mind with the calm, self-directed structure of cognitive command. This cultivated focus and sense of control are not only vital for career and productivity but are the foundation upon which emotional resilience and strong relationships are built, preparing you for true integrated success.

CHAPTER 1

MASTER YOUR SCHEDULE: TRANSFORM DEADLINES INTO MANAGEABLE MILESTONES

The greatest internal hurdle for women with Attention-Deficit / Hyperactivity Disorder (ADHD) is the mastery of time. The experience of **Time Blindness**, the inability to accurately perceive or estimate the flow of time, is the core neurobiological deficit that makes reliable planning impossible and fuels chronic stress. Deadlines always feel abstract until they become immediate crises, triggering the adrenaline-fueled cycle of last-minute overwhelm and shame.

This chapter provides the strategic toolkit to dismantle this chaos by transforming daunting deadlines into concrete, manageable **Milestones**. By proactively converting vague future requirements into visible, tangible steps anchored to the present, you systematically counteract the symptoms of time blindness, turning time from a source of anxiety into a predictable, functional ally. The shift is from relying on inconsistent internal urgency to utilizing strategic, external structure.

Section 1: The Neurobiology of the Crisis Cycle

The chronic cycle of procrastination, crisis, and last-minute rushing is not a character flaw; it is a neurobiological consequence of how the ADHD brain processes time and motivation, directly impacting Executive Function (EF) skills like planning and initiation.

1. Time Blindness and the Estimation Deficit

The inability to accurately gauge the passage of time creates the **Estimation Deficit**, the tendency to consistently and severely underestimate how long tasks will take. When faced with a multi-day project, the time-blind brain may incorrectly allocate only a fraction of the necessary hours, leading to predictable failure and frustration.

- **Abstract Future, Urgent Present:** Because the future feels abstract to the ADHD brain, tasks scheduled far away carry little **dopamine reward** or internal sense of urgency, making them impossible to initiate. Action is delayed until the deadline becomes an imminent threat, which finally generates the intense adrenaline / dopamine response required for task activation (the crisis cycle).
- **Overwhelm and Paralysis:** The perception of a large, complex deadline (e.g., "Finish the entire report") feels amorphous and infinite, which instantly triggers **cognitive overload** and the **paralysis response**. The complexity overwhelms the brain's filtering mechanisms, leading to a neurobiological shutdown against overwhelming mental effort.

The solution is to eliminate the concept of one giant deadline and replace it with a series of small, low-friction, rewarding Milestones that anchor the project to the immediate present.

2. The Power of Finitude and Visibility

To counteract the feeling of infinite, overwhelming duration, time management must impose **finitude**, a clear, visible end point, on tasks.

- **Milestones as Finitude:** Breaking a long project into **Milestones** (e.g., "Milestone 1: Outline complete by Tuesday morning") transforms the commitment from a marathon into a manageable sprint. This dramatically lowers the **activation energy** required to start, making the initial step psychologically approachable.

- **Visible Anchors:** Visual tools, such as calendars, planners, and timers, are essential for anchoring the project to the present. The visual display of a project's timeline bypasses reliance on inconsistent internal memory, acting as a reliable **external Executive Function** cue. This intentional structuring helps the brain manage the complexity often associated with EF challenges like planning, goal setting, and time management.

Section 2: The Strategic Milestone Framework

This framework provides a systematic approach to converting any large deadline into a series of predictable, manageable, and rewarding actions, leveraging the planning and organizational executive skills that are compromised by ADHD.

1. Deconstruct the Deadline (The Reverse Timeline)

Instead of planning forward from the start date, the ADHD brain benefits from planning backward from the final deadline. This process forces the abstract deadline into the immediate present, generating necessary urgency.

- **Define the Finish Line:** Start with the **Final Deadline** (e.g., Report Due: Friday, 5 PM).
- **Identify Critical Milestones:** Work backward, listing 3–5 non-negotiable **Milestones** (Mini-Deadlines) that must be completed to meet the final goal. These should be 20–30% of the overall project.
    - *Example Milestone 1:* Final Draft to Editor: Wednesday, 10 AM.
    - *Example Milestone 2:* Data Analysis / Outline Complete: Monday, 3 PM.
- **Establish Actionable Steps:** For the very first Milestone (Milestone 2, due Monday), break it down into the smallest possible **Actionable Steps** (micro-steps). This micro-commitment reduces the cognitive load and is essential for task initiation, ensuring the first step is low-friction (e.g., "Task #1: Collect dishes from the living room and place them in the kitchen sink" is easier than "Clean the entire living room").

2. Time Block and Buffer Application

Every Actionable Step and Milestone must be immediately scheduled into your calendar as a non-negotiable appointment using **Time Blocking** (introduced in Book 2). This ensures the task has the necessary **context and duration** that the traditional to-do list lacks, a significant failure point of vague to-do lists for the ADHD brain.

- **Forced Estimation and Buffers:** For each time block, intentionally schedule **more time than you think you need** (the Estimation Buffer) to compensate for the Estimation Deficit. This prevents the stress of constant rushing, a common trigger for emotional dysregulation, and provides crucial breathing room, reducing the likelihood of failure and self-criticism.
- **Block Transitions:** Schedule **Transition Blocks** (e.g., 15 minutes) between Milestones and major work periods. This is crucial as it supports better transitions between activities, which is often a sticking point for ADHD brains, mitigating the draining **context switching cost**.

3. Anchor with Visual Cues and Alerts

The schedule must live in a location that is visually prominent and supported by automated cues to overcome internal forgetfulness and the abstract nature of future time.

- **Visual Prominence:** Use a calendar or planner that is visible on your wall or desktop. Use **Color-Coding** and clear labels to categorize the project and its Milestones to minimize the cognitive effort required to interpret the schedule.
- **Automated Urgency:** Set multiple, automated digital reminders for Milestones: one **two days before** (to check progress) and one **one hour before** the scheduled Time Block (to generate activation energy). This anchors the abstract future into the urgent present, supplying the necessary external cue to act, bypassing the internal motivation deficit.

Section 3: The Emotional and Cognitive Payoff

Transforming deadlines into manageable Milestones is profoundly effective because it addresses the emotional and cognitive barriers that fuel overwhelm, leading to increased self-efficacy and resilience.

1. Reducing Paralysis and Overwhelm

By breaking down the project into defined Milestones, you reduce the perceived complexity that triggers **task paralysis**. This strategic reduction in complexity systematically lowers the cognitive load, allowing the brain to engage without immediate shutdown. This contrasts with traditional to-do lists, which often contribute to disappointment because the items are too large or vague to be actionable.

2. Building Self-Efficacy and Momentum

Each completed Milestone, a fixed, tangible win, generates an immediate **dopamine hit** that reinforces productive behavior and builds **momentum**. This steady accumulation of small, visible successes builds **self-efficacy** (the belief in one's ability to succeed), which is the direct psychological antidote to the shame and inadequacy that characterize unmanaged ADHD. This proof of competence replaces the reliance on inconsistent willpower with a strategic system you can trust, empowering clients to build lasting improvements in both personal and professional domains.

3. Mitigating the ADHD Tax on Time

The disciplined use of this Milestones framework directly combats the financial and time cost of the **ADHD Tax**, the cumulative cost, emotional, mental, and financial, of navigating life with the condition. By systematically prioritizing and meeting deadlines, you reduce the likelihood of late fees, lost opportunities, and the excess time spent compensating for mistakes, all measurable consequences of unmanaged time blindness and poor organization.

Chapter 1 Workbook: Master Your Schedule: Transform Deadlines into Manageable Milestones

Objective: To practice converting one complex deadline into a fixed, manageable series of Milestones and Actionable Steps.

Scientific Anchor: Breaking deadlines into Milestones reduces cognitive load and task paralysis by imposing finitude and structure on an otherwise overwhelming project, which is critical for the ADHD brain.

Activity 1.1: The Reverse Timeline Deconstruction

Instructions: Identify one complex project or deadline you are currently facing (work, school, or personal).

1. **The Final Deadline (Fixed Date):** ______________________________
2. **Milestone Mapping (Work Backward):** List 3 non-negotiable Milestones that must be achieved on fixed days *before* the Final Deadline.
   - **Milestone 1 (First Step)**
      - Date Due ________________________________
      - Action (What must be 100% complete?)

        ____

        ____

        ____
   - **Milestone 2 (Mid-Point Check)**
      - Date Due ________________________________
      - Action (What must be 100% complete?)

        ____

        ____

        ____
   - **Milestone 3 (Final Review / Prep)**
      - Date Due ________________________________
      - Action (What must be 100% complete?)

        ____

        ____

        ____
3. **Actionable Steps:** Take **Milestone 1** (your first step) and break it down into the smallest possible actions that take less than 15 minutes each (Micro-Steps).
   - **Step 1:** (Example: Open the correct folder / document)
      - Micro-Step ______________________________
      - Time Estimate (Actual Effort) ______________
      - Neuro-Strategy (Low Friction) ______________

- Step 2:
  - Micro-Step ______________________________
  - Time Estimate (Actual Effort) _______________
  - Neuro-Strategy (Low Friction) ______________
- Step 3:
  - Micro-Step ______________________________
  - Time Estimate (Actual Effort) _______________
  - Neuro-Strategy (Low Friction) ______________

Activity 1.2: Time Block and Buffer Commitment

Instructions: Take the Actionable Steps from Activity 1.1 and schedule them into your calendar for tomorrow, applying the necessary EF buffers.

1. **Time Block Commitment:** Select the time slot you will use tomorrow for this task.

Time Slot	Scheduled Activity	Duration (with 25% Buffer)
10:00 AM (example)	Focus Sprint: Actionable Steps 1 & 2	______ minutes

2. **Anchor Commitment:** What **external alert** will you set one hour before this Time Block to ensure you initiate the task?

   Alarm / Reminder Text: __________________________________

   ____

   ____

   ____

   ____

Reflection 1.3: The Shame / Paralysis Antidote

Instructions: Reflect on how this strategic framework impacts the emotional challenges of the ADHD brain.

1. **Paralysis to Momentum:** When you first thought of the Final Deadline, on a scale of 1 to 10 (10 = Total Paralysis), what was your resistance level? How did breaking it into Actionable Steps reduce that feeling?

   Initial Resistance: ____

   Reduction in Paralysis: ____________________________________

2. **Defeating the Inner Critic:** The inner critic often says, "You're going to miss that deadline, you always do." How does looking at your Time Blocked Milestones provide **tangible, visual evidence** to counter that thought?

   Visual Evidence: ____

   ____

   ____

   ____

   ____

   ____

   ____

CHAPTER 2

PRIORITIZE LIKE A PRO: TECHNIQUES TO IDENTIFY WHAT TRULY MATTERS

In Chapter 1, you mastered the critical first step in managing Executive Function (EF) deficits: transforming paralyzing deadlines into actionable Milestones, imposing structure on the chaos of **Time Blindness**. This intentional scheduling provided the necessary external scaffolding. Now, the challenge moves from mastering *when* tasks happen to mastering *which* tasks should happen at all.

For the woman with Attention-Deficit / Hyperactivity Disorder (ADHD), the inability to effectively prioritize is a core symptom of EF dysfunction that fuels chronic overwhelm. When faced with an undifferentiated mass of obligations, a long to-do list, competing demands from work and family, and an avalanche of new ideas, the brain registers every item as equally urgent and equally demanding. This ambiguity triggers **cognitive overload**, leading to ineffective prioritization where the brain often defaults to the path of least resistance: either tackling the most stimulating, low-leverage task, or avoiding the entire list altogether in a state of **paralysis**.

This chapter provides the strategic toolkit to conquer this ambiguity. By implementing clear mental frameworks, you will learn to systematically identify your high-leverage tasks, allocate your finite energy reserves with intention, and simplify the daunting process of decision-making. The goal is to replace the chaotic demands of an overstuffed schedule with a calm, self-directed focus on activities that truly drive your goals and reduce overall stress.

Section 1: The Neurobiological Roots of Prioritization Failure

Effective prioritization requires the sustained, simultaneous engagement of several complex Executive Function skills, all of which are inconsistent in the ADHD brain.

1. Cognitive Overload and the Filtering Deficit

Prioritization relies on the ability to filter out non-essential information and hold the importance of tasks in **Working Memory (WM)**. However, the ADHD brain struggles with an impaired filtering mechanism, meaning every task, notification, and demand consumes measurable mental energy, the **Cognitive Load (CL)**.

- **Ambiguity is Energy Drain:** When the brain is unable to quickly determine if a task is important (high reward) or urgent (high deadline), it expends valuable CL resources on continuous internal debate. This ambiguity, inherent in a long, undifferentiated list, is draining. Research shows that as CL increases, the ADHD brain's performance and efficiency decrease disproportionately compared to neurotypical peers.
- **The Paradox of Urgency:** Because the brain struggles to generate internal urgency for future rewards, it often falls into the trap of prioritizing "crisis-of-the-moment" tasks or small, trivial, high-dopamine tasks (e.g., answering easy emails) over complex, high-leverage work (e.g., report drafting). This pattern leaves the woman perpetually busy but ineffective, increasing the overall sense of stress and inadequacy.

2. Planning Deficits and the Fear of Choice

Prioritization is fundamentally an act of planning and choice, both of which trigger anxiety when EF skills are compromised.

- **Lack of Goal Coherence:** Effective prioritization requires holding long-term goals and their necessary sub-steps in WM. When planning skills are inconsistent, the connection between a small daily task and a large future goal is weak, making it difficult to allocate energy correctly. The ADHD brain loses sight of the long-term payoff, making the immediate, easy task more appealing.
- **Decision Paralysis:** Prioritization involves making difficult decisions about what to *not* do. For the ADHD brain, which already struggles with the decision process, the immense volume of choices presented by an unprioritized to-do list (e.g., 50 tasks) triggers **decision paralysis**, a state of mental shutdown caused by overload, leading to task avoidance and immobilization.

Section 2: Strategic Prioritization Frameworks

The solution to prioritization failure is to introduce external mental frameworks that bypass cognitive ambiguity, forcing the brain to analyze tasks based on clear, visual boundaries rather than subjective feeling or internal debate.

1. The Eisenhower Matrix: The Essential Filter

The Eisenhower Matrix (Urgent / Important Matrix) is a powerful, visually simple tool that forces the brain to categorize tasks based on two critical criteria, eliminating the ambiguity that triggers overload.

- **The Quadrants:** Tasks are categorized into four quadrants:

Quadrant	Priority	Action (EF Strategy)	ADHD Neuro-Benefit
Q1: Urgent & Important	Crisis	**DO NOW.** Firefighting, immediate deadlines.	Reserves energy for true emergencies; minimizes impulse to delay.
Q2: Not Urgent & Important	Goal	**SCHEDULE** (Time Block). Strategy, planning, health.	Forces attention onto long-term rewards, countering dopamine deficit.

Q3: Urgent & Not Important	Delegation / Minimize	**DELEGATE** or **REJECT**. Interruptions, others' priorities.	Protects boundaries and reduces time wasted on low-leverage demands.
Q4: Not Urgent & Not Important	Eliminate	**DELETE**. Distractions, time-wasters, digital noise.	Ruthlessly reduces Cognitive Load (CL) by closing "open loops."

- **Applying the Matrix:** When using a long to-do list, the woman must physically move each item into one of the four quadrants. This simple, forced categorization prevents the brain from treating all tasks as equally demanding, reducing CL and focusing effort on the high-leverage **Q2 (Goal) tasks**, the ones most critical for long-term EF mastery and success.

2. The Rule of Three: Limiting Cognitive Scope

The greatest antidote to decision paralysis is severely limiting the scope of choice. The "Rule of Three" limits the brain's focus to the absolute essentials, preventing the overwhelm associated with a massive to-do list.

- **Defining Daily Success:** At the start of the day (during your scheduled planning routine), review your entire list and select **only three high-leverage tasks** (ideally pulled from the Q2 / Goal quadrant) that, if completed, would make the day feel successful.
- **Benefits:** This technique bypasses the complexity of having 50 choices. The brain receives a clear, finite signal: "These three items are the only things that matter." This drastically reduces the ambient anxiety and frees up WM to concentrate solely on the primary goals, reserving remaining mental energy for unexpected interruptions or lower-priority maintenance tasks.

3. Energy Matching and Allocation

Traditional prioritization often ignores the brain's internal energy state, leading to scheduling failures. The ADHD brain's EF performance fluctuates throughout the day due to energy cycles and medication timing. **Energy Matching** aligns task difficulty with mental resource availability.

- **Identify Energy Peaks:** Schedule your most cognitively demanding tasks (Q2 work, planning, writing, problem-solving) for your **peak energy window** (e.g., morning, post-medication peak).
- **Allocate Low-Energy Tasks:** Reserve low-stakes, routine, or repetitive work (e.g., email batching, filing, chores, passive learning) for **trough periods** (e.g., late afternoon, pre-meal slump). Scheduling low-demand work during low-energy times prevents the collapse of EF performance and reduces the stress of trying to force focus when resources are depleted.

Section 3: Simplifying Decision-Making (The Cognitive Offload)

The goal of prioritization is not just to decide what to do, but to systematically reduce the need for constant, taxing decision-making throughout the day, ensuring EF reserves are conserved for truly important choices.

1. The Power of Routines and Checklists

Prioritization failure often happens when routine tasks (e.g., morning prep, bill paying) require spontaneous decision-making. Fixed routines eliminate this cognitive drain.

- **Routines as Automation:** Establishing fixed routines (e.g., the **Daily Reset** from Book 1) automates sequences of behavior, shifting control from the inconsistent PFC to reliable habit loops. This eliminates the need to expend mental energy deciding *when* or *how* to start a chore, saving EF for complex problem-solving.
- **Checklists for WM Offload:** For complex or multi-step routine processes (e.g., travel preparation, weekly grocery list, meeting setup), create permanent, external **Checklists**. These checklists offload instructions and sequences from your unreliable WM, ensuring consistency and accuracy without requiring mental effort, thereby reserving WM for immediate task execution.

2. The Decision Matrix for Financial and Digital Clarity

Prioritization frameworks can be applied to digital life and financial management—areas where ADHD-related impulsivity and inattention create significant chaos and economic cost.

- **Digital Triage:** When processing an email inbox or digital files, the decision should be instant, based on the Eisenhower Matrix: **Delete** (Q4 / Q3), **Do Now** (Q1, if < 2 min), or **Time Block** (Q2 / Q3, if complex). This structured triage eliminates the ambiguity that causes many with ADHD to leave emails open, creating an unmanaged "open loop" that drains CL.
- **Financial Pause:** Impulsive buying is a form of prioritization failure (prioritizing immediate dopamine reward over long-term financial health). Implementing a mandatory **"24-Hour Rule"** for non-essential purchases, forcing a delay between impulse and action, allows the PFC's Inhibitory Control to engage, changing the priority from immediate novelty to long-term value.

Section 4: The Holistic Impact on Overwhelm and Shame

Mastering prioritization frameworks is a crucial psychological intervention that directly addresses the shame and emotional volatility that define overwhelm for women with ADHD.

1. Reducing Shame and Building Self-Efficacy

The consistent failure to prioritize correctly leads to missed deadlines and the sense of constant rushing, reinforcing the inner critic's narrative of inadequacy.

- **Realistic Expectations:** The use of the **Rule of Three** and **Time Blocking** enforces a schedule that is temporally realistic. By consciously limiting daily expectations, you set achievable goals, reducing the likelihood of failure and self-criticism. This is a crucial practice of **self-compassion**, honoring your capacity rather than fighting against it.
- **Evidence of Competence:** Successfully completing the three daily prioritized tasks provides tangible evidence of competence and follow-through, directly countering shame and building **self-efficacy** (the belief in one's ability to execute a plan).

2. Protecting Emotional Resilience

Overwhelm is often the precursor to **emotional dysregulation** (the sudden shift from calm to intense emotion). Prioritization acts as a psychological buffer against this emotional trigger.

- **Stress Management:** When the schedule is prioritized, the brain experiences less background anxiety. Reducing the chaotic inputs that trigger stress conserves the emotional bandwidth required for resilience, preventing minor setbacks from escalating into disproportionate emotional storms.
- **Clear Boundaries:** Prioritization provides a rational framework for setting boundaries (Q3 / Delegate / Reject), allowing a woman to decline external demands that would overwhelm her schedule, thereby protecting her finite EF reserves and overall well-being. This assertive self-protection is vital for sustainable emotional health.

Conclusion: Prioritization as Cognitive Command

The mastery of prioritization frameworks is the definitive step in moving beyond the reactive chaos of overwhelm. By applying tools like the **Eisenhower Matrix** and the **Rule of Three**, you transform your to-do list from an ambiguous source of anxiety into a clear, actionable map of intentions.

You have now learned to not only control *when* you work (Milestones) but also *where* to direct your finite energy (Prioritization). This dual mastery, of time and task allocation, is the ultimate expression of Executive Function command. This structure conserves the mental energy needed for the sustained concentration, memory enhancement, and decision simplification techniques that will follow, setting the stage for true cognitive resilience.

Chapter 2 Workbook: Prioritize Like a Pro: Techniques to Identify What Truly Matters

Objective: To practice using external frameworks to systematically analyze and prioritize tasks, thereby reducing cognitive overload and decision paralysis.

Scientific Anchor: Categorizing tasks into matrices or limited scopes (e.g., Rule of Three) reduces the ambiguity that consumes Working Memory and triggers ADHD paralysis.

Activity 2.1: The Eisenhower Matrix Filter

Instructions: List 10 tasks currently weighing on your mind (work, home, personal). Use the Eisenhower Matrix below to categorize them based on **Urgency** (requires immediate attention) and **Importance** (moves you toward a major life goal).

1. **List of 10 Tasks:** (e.g., A. Pay electricity bill, B. Plan next vacation, C. Answer low-priority emails, D. Buy groceries, E. Outline new project, F. Call partner's doctor, G. Clean kitchen counter, H. Research new hobby, I. Organize old files, J. Call insurance company).
2. **Categorization:** Place each letter (A–J) into the most appropriate quadrant.

Quadrant	Tasks (A–J)	Action Commitment	Neuro-Benefit
Q1: **Urgent & Important**	(Crisis - Do Now)		Reserve for true emergencies.
Q2: **Not Urgent & Important**	(Goal - Time Block)		Forces focus onto long-term goals.

Q3: **Urgent & Not Important**	(Delegation/ Minimize)		Reduces time wasted on others' demands.
Q4: **Not Urgent & Not Important**	(Eliminate / Delete)		Reduces Cognitive Load (CL).

Activity 2.2: The Rule of Three Commitment

Instructions: Take the tasks you placed in the **Q2 (Not Urgent & Important)** and **Q1 (Urgent & Important)** quadrants and select **only three** high-leverage tasks to prioritize for tomorrow. This limits the cognitive scope to the essential.

1. **High-Leverage Task 1 (Must Do):** ------------------------------
2. **High-Leverage Task 2 (Should Do):** ----------------------------
3. **High-Leverage Task 3 (Could Do):**------------------------------

Time Block Commitment: Immediately schedule these three tasks into your Time Block calendar for tomorrow, ensuring they have fixed start / end times and buffers (Chapter 1).

Reflection 2.3: Analyzing Paralysis and Energy Allocation

Instructions: Reflect on how these frameworks impact the emotional and cognitive challenges of the ADHD brain.

1. **Defeating Decision Paralysis:** How does forcing every task into one of the four boxes (Activity 2.1) reduce the feeling of **paralysis** that often occurs when looking at a long, undifferentiated list?

Reduction in Ambiguity: ______________________________________

____

____

____

____

____

____

2. **Energy Matching:** Identify your **peak energy window** tomorrow (e.g., 9:00 AM–11:00 AM). Which of the three prioritized tasks will you intentionally schedule during this peak window to maximize your focus?

   Task and Time Slot: ____

   ____

   ____

   ____

   ____

   ____

   ____

3. **Shame and Self-Efficacy:** If you only complete the **three** high-leverage tasks tomorrow (and ignore the rest of the list), how does that outcome feel compared to the shame of completing 10 random, low-value tasks?

   Feeling of Efficacy: ____

   ____

   ____

   ____

   ____

   ____

   ____

CHAPTER 3

HARNESS YOUR ATTENTION: STRATEGIES TO BUILD LASTING FOCUS

You have successfully established external order by converting deadlines into manageable Milestones (Chapter 1) and proactively prioritizing tasks (Chapter 2), ensuring your efforts are directed toward high-leverage goals. Now, the challenge moves to the micro-level: sustaining **attention** during the actual work block, systematically defeating the neurobiological forces of distraction, impulsivity, and the dual paradox of inattention and **hyperfocus**.

For the woman with Attention-Deficit / Hyperactivity Disorder (ADHD), the difficulty lies not in a lack of intelligence, but in a profound inability to **regulate** attention. The brain struggles to control its "on / off" switch, making it difficult to maintain focus on mundane tasks and challenging to disengage from stimulating ones. This struggle is fueled by the ADHD brain's craving for novelty and immediate reward, often leading to rapid **task-switching**, a drain on Executive Function (EF) reserves that results in significant mental fatigue and chronic overwhelm.

This chapter provides the tactical toolkit to anchor your focus. You will learn to utilize structured time management techniques, such as the **Pomodoro Technique**, to impose **finitude** on tasks, leverage **external accountability** to bypass motivation deficits, and embrace **single-tasking** to transform fragmented effort into consistent, high-quality output. The goal is to move beyond wishing for focus to proactively commanding your attention with strategic, evidence-based structure.

Section 1: The Neurobiological Foundations of Attention Failure

To harness attention effectively, we must first understand the core neurobiological mechanisms that fragment it, particularly the role of motivation and the cost of task-switching.

1. The Dopamine Deficit and the Craving for Novelty

The ADHD brain's relationship with attention is deeply rooted in the dysregulation of **dopamine**, the neurotransmitter critical for motivation, reward, and sustained engagement.

- **Low Activation Energy:** When a task is under-stimulating (boring, repetitive, or complex), the brain struggles to produce enough dopamine to find it interesting, leading to a constant search for novelty, distraction, or mind-wandering. This deficit is the core reason why initiating and sustaining focus on necessary, non-stimulating tasks is so difficult.
- **Hyperfocus as Uncontrolled Flow:** Conversely, a task that is intensely stimulating or provides immediate, satisfying feedback can cause a dopamine surge, leading to the state of **hyperfocus**. While productive, this state is uncontrolled, consuming time and energy at the expense of other critical responsibilities.

The strategy must provide consistent, external cues and frequent, small rewards to compensate for the inconsistent internal dopamine system, making sustained, mundane effort neurologically palatable.

2. The Cognitive Cost of Task-Switching

The single greatest threat to sustained attention is the illusion of **multitasking**, which is actually rapid **task-switching**, a process highly inefficient and mentally exhausting for the ADHD brain.

- **Executive Function Drain:** Each time the brain switches tasks (e.g., from drafting a report to checking an email notification), it incurs a measurable **cognitive penalty**, the effort required to disengage from the first task, reload new rules and information into **Working Memory (WM)**, and reorient attention. This switching rapidly depletes the finite resources of the Prefrontal Cortex (PFC), leading to increased errors, slower pace, and severe **mental fatigue**.
- **The Impulse Trap:** The brain favors the path of least resistance, often preferring the low-effort dopamine hit of checking a notification (novelty) over the high-effort task of resisting it (Inhibitory Control). This leads to chronic toggling that fragments focus and prevents the attainment of *deep work*, the focused effort needed for high-quality output.

Section 2: The Pomodoro Technique: Anchoring Attention with Finitude

The **Pomodoro Technique**, breaking work into short, fixed work sprints followed by mandatory breaks, is the foundational tactical tool for anchoring attention in the ADHD brain. It works by imposing **finitude** and structure on work, neutralizing the anxiety that triggers procrastination and hyperfocus.

1. Finitude: Defeating Paralysis and Overwhelm

The core strength of Pomodoro is its ability to transform an overwhelming, amorphous project into a manageable sprint by providing a clear, fixed boundary for effort.

- **Lowering Activation Energy:** Committing to a task for only 25 minutes (or a customized shorter duration) dramatically reduces the commitment cost, which is essential for bypassing the **Task Activation Deficit**. The visible, ticking timer acts as a non-negotiable external cue, providing the brain with the precise structure it requires to initiate the effort.

- **Making Time Concrete:** For the time-blind brain, the timer translates the abstract concept of duration into a tangible, visual cue, anchoring attention to the external environment rather than relying on unreliable internal perception. This makes the time spent feel measurable and manageable, systematically reducing the mental stress caused by the Estimation Deficit (Chapter 1).

2. Breaks: The External Circuit-Breaker

The mandatory break is the most critical feature for sustaining attention in the ADHD brain.

- **Preventing Hyperfocus and Burnout:** The scheduled break acts as an **external circuit-breaker**, forcing the individual to stop working even if they are deep in hyperfocus. This protects the integrity of the overall Time Block schedule and prevents the task from consuming energy reserves and leading to exhaustion or missed appointments.
- **Restorative Reset:** The **mandatory 5-minute break** provides a regular, guilt-free opportunity for the brain to reset and seek the novelty and low-effort stimulation it craves (e.g., stretching, getting water). This strategically scheduled recovery prevents the deep mental fatigue associated with prolonged, continuous concentration, ensuring the next work interval starts with higher energy reserves.

3. Customization: Tailoring the Sprint to Your Brain

The Pomodoro Technique is only sustainable when the duration is **customized** to match the individual's unique attention span and energy cycle.

- **Matching Duration to Flow:** If a 25-minute sprint feels daunting, shorten it to **10 or 15 minutes** (e.g., 10 minutes of work, 5 minutes of rest). Successfully completing multiple shorter sprints builds more confidence and momentum than struggling through one long block.
- **Intentional Breaks:** Ensure your break is low-friction and actively restorative (e.g., physical movement, sensory reset, or grabbing a drink of water). Avoid engaging in distracting

activities like checking email or social media during the break, as this increases the draining cost of context switching.

Section 3: Leveraging External Accountability and Single-Tasking

The structured sprint must be supported by external accountability and the discipline of single-tasking to maximize efficiency and minimize the drain from fragmentation.

1. External Accountability: The Body Double Anchor

For tasks that are particularly difficult to initiate or sustain, **Body Doubling**, working alongside another person (in-person or virtually) who is focused on their own work, provides an essential source of external Executive Function.

- **Anchoring Attention:** The physical presence of a Body Double, even a silent one, acts as a consistent, non-judgmental anchor for the ADHD brain, pulling attention back to the task and reducing the risk of being pulled away by internal or external distractions.
- **Bypassing Motivation Deficits:** The mere act of committing to work in the presence of another person provides a subtle yet powerful source of **social accountability**, supplying the necessary external cue to overcome procrastination and initiate the work.

2. Embracing Single-Tasking: The Antidote to Chaos

The discipline of single-tasking is the necessary antidote to the inefficient and draining cost of constant task-switching.

- **Single Focus, Fixed Block:** Within a Time Block (Chapter 1) and a Pomodoro sprint, commit to focusing on **one specific, defined task** (e.g., "Draft the outline," not "Work on the project"). This clear boundary minimizes the cognitive effort required to decide what to do and prevents the brain from engaging in rapid toggling.
- **Batching Similar Tasks:** To further reduce context switching cost, schedule similar activities together in the same work session (e.g., dedicating a block for "Email / Admin" separate from "Deep Work"). This allows the brain to stay in one cognitive mode for longer, conserving precious EF resources.

Section 4: The Emotional and Cognitive Payoff

Mastering attention through structure yields immediate emotional and cognitive dividends, reinforcing the positive feedback loop necessary for long-term consistency.

1. Building Self-Efficacy and Momentum

Each successfully completed Pomodoro sprint provides tangible, immediate evidence of **competence and follow-through**. This steady accumulation of small wins generates a positive burst of dopamine, systematically dismantling the pervasive feeling of inadequacy and building **self-efficacy** (the belief in one's ability to succeed) that is the direct psychological antidote to shame.

2. Preventing Mental Fatigue and Burnout

The constant effort required to manage attention is the primary cause of chronic mental fatigue. By enforcing regular, restorative breaks and structured work intervals, you are proactively managing your energy, preventing the total depletion of EF reserves that leads to burnout. This controlled rhythm promotes **sustainable effort** rather than sporadic, intense bursts of productivity, creating a resilient foundation for the rest of your life.

Chapter 3 Workbook: Harness Your Attention: Strategies to Build Lasting Focus

Objective: To customize the Pomodoro Technique to match your unique attention span and utilize external accountability to anchor focus.

Scientific Anchor: Customizing the Pomodoro interval reduces the anxiety that triggers task paralysis, while mandated breaks prevent hyperfocus and burnout, thereby maintaining executive function reserves.

Activity 3.1: Attention Span Customization Audit

Instructions: Identify your current optimal focus interval (Work) and the necessary duration of a true mental break (Rest). This moves beyond the standard 25 / 5 interval.

1. **Work Interval Assessment:** If a task is boring, what is the *shortest* amount of time you can commit to before feeling the urge to check your phone or move? (Select one: 10 min, 15 min, 25 min, 30 min).
    - *My Custom Work Interval (A): _________ minutes*
2. **Break Interval Assessment:** How long do you need to stand, stretch, and reset your mind before you can successfully re-engage? (Select one: 3 min, 5 min, 10 min).
    - *My Custom Break Interval (B): _________ minutes*
3. **My Customized Pomodoro Cycle: A (Work)** minutes / **B (Break)** minutes.

Activity 3.2: The External Accountability Anchor

Instructions: Commit to using external accountability for one difficult task this week to leverage the momentum generated by social anchoring.

1. **Target Task (High Resistance):** Select one task that you consistently procrastinate on (e.g., administrative paperwork, detailed planning).

    Task: ____

    ____

    ____

2. **Accountability Anchor:** Commit to using either **Body Doubling** (working on a video call or in person with a friend) or **Public Accountability** (telling a trusted person a fixed time you will finish).

    Anchor Method: ______________________________________

    ____

    ____

    ____

3. **The Finitude Commitment:** Schedule the task using **3 cycles** of your Customized Pomodoro Cycle (from Activity 3.1).

    Total Time Block: __________________________ minutes

Reflection 3.3: Analyzing Focus and Shame

Instructions: Reflect on how the structure of this technique supports both your focus and your emotional well-being.

1. **Defeating Paralysis:** You are about to start a task you hate. How does seeing the timer set for your **Custom Work Interval (A)** instantly reduce the anxiety that would otherwise lead to procrastination? (Focus on **finitude**).

   Reduction in Anxiety: ______________________________________

   ____

   ____

2. **Stopping the Switch:** During your last Pomodoro sprint, what was the biggest distraction you successfully resisted (e.g., checking email, opening a new tab)? How did the simple act of resisting that temptation conserve mental energy?

   Distraction Resisted: ______________________________________

   ____

   ____

3. **Shame Reduction:** How does the frequent, tangible reward of completing a Pomodoro sprint counteract the feeling that you are "lazy" or "unproductive?"

   Self-Efficacy Gain: ______________________________________

   ____

   ____

CHAPTER 4

STRENGTHEN YOUR MEMORY: TOOLS TO BOOST WORKING MEMORY POWER

You have established structural command over your schedule (Chapter 1) and mastered intentional prioritization and focused work sprints (Chapters 2 and 3). These external strategies are highly effective compensations for the challenges of attention and initiation. Now, the journey shifts to the core internal cognitive skills required for sustained adult function: **Working Memory (WM)** and **Inhibitory Control (IC)**.

For the woman with Attention-Deficit / Hyperactivity Disorder (ADHD), **Working Memory (WM)**, the brain's "mental scratchpad", can feel like an inconsistent sieve. WM is the essential ability to hold and manipulate transient information for short-term use, such as remembering a multi-step instruction while executing the first step, or keeping track of conversation points while formulating a response. When WM is compromised, tasks are often left unfinished, instructions are forgotten, and the brain is quickly overwhelmed by the number of details required for a goal, leading to the pervasive anxiety of forgetfulness and the constant need to double-check information.

This chapter provides the strategic toolkit to actively strengthen your WM and, critically, to reduce the cognitive burden on this vital resource. We will explore how to build reliable **external memory systems** that compensate for internal inconsistency and integrate targeted cognitive practice to build long-term resilience, ensuring your EF reserves are conserved for high-leverage tasks.

Section 1: The Neurobiological Reality of Working Memory Deficits

The struggle with memory in ADHD is a measurable cognitive reality rooted in the function of the **prefrontal cortex (PFC)**, the brain's command center for Executive Functions (EFs).

1. WM and the Inconsistent "Mental Scratchpad"

WM deficits are a core characteristic of ADHD, often resulting in difficulties that are mistakenly attributed to carelessness or lack of effort.

- **Impact on Multi-Step Tasks:** A compromised WM makes it difficult to follow multi-step verbal instructions (e.g., in a recipe or meeting), retain the location of an item moments after placing it down, or hold the necessary data in mind to complete a complex calculation. This functional difficulty is a major contributor to poor follow-through and the feeling of being perpetually overwhelmed by detail.
- **The Planning Barrier:** WM is essential for effective **planning and prioritization** (Chapters 1 and 2). You must be able to hold the overall goal, the necessary resources, and the immediate steps in mind simultaneously to map out a strategic approach. When WM is taxed, this planning stage collapses, leading the brain to rely on spontaneous, often inefficient, action rather than intentional, planned execution.

2. Inhibitory Control (IC): The "Brakes" for Focus

Strengthening WM is intrinsically linked to strengthening **Inhibitory Control (IC)**, your brain's capacity to resist distraction and suppress impulsive responses. IC is vital for protecting WM from being hijacked by irrelevant stimuli.

- **Protecting WM from Noise:** The ADHD brain's filtering deficit means that internal thoughts and external stimuli constantly compete for WM resources. IC provides the "brakes" necessary to suppress these distractions, ensuring WM remains focused on the primary task. Without strong IC, WM is continuously overloaded, leading to fragmentation and mental fatigue.
- **Resisting Impulsivity:** IC governs discipline and perseverance, resisting the urge to procrastinate, check a notification, or interrupt a conversation. Strengthening IC means strengthening the capacity to override the brain's preference for immediate reward (a dopamine hit from novelty) and prioritize the sustained, focused effort that WM requires.

Section 2: Externalizing Memory: Building Reliable Systems

The most effective strategy for managing WM deficits is to consistently and aggressively offload all essential information onto a reliable **external system** that does not rely on inconsistent internal memory. This frees the WM from the taxing burden of constant recall.

1. The Power of Fixed, External Routines

WM is strengthened when the need for it is reduced. Fixed planning and execution routines ensure that all necessary instructions and objectives are externalized and placed in a visible, predictable location.

- **Checklists for WM Offload:** To compensate for forgetting steps or instructions, create visual **Checklists and Templates** for repetitive or multi-step tasks (e.g., "The Morning Routine Checklist," "Meeting Prep Checklist," or "Bill Payment Checklist"). These external scaffolds ensure consistency and accuracy without requiring the brain to expend energy recalling complex sequences, thereby reserving WM for immediate execution.
- **Visualizing Instructions:** For complex tasks, use physical visual cues. Instead of trying to hold the steps in your mind, physically lay out the tools and materials in sequential order. This environmental cue serves as a tangible reminder of the task sequence, offloading the memory burden onto the external world.

- **The Power of Writing:** The simple act of writing down instructions, commitments, or deadlines, even if you use a digital planner, reinforces encoding into memory. Commit to writing down any important information immediately, preventing it from being lost in the sieve of your WM.

2. The Nightly Offload and Morning Activation Ritual

WM is significantly impacted by anxiety and sleep quality. Establishing fixed rituals around transitions conserves WM and prevents "open loops" from consuming resources.

- **The Nightly Offload (Closing Open Loops):** The most critical step occurs the night before. Before bed, perform a **Brain Dump** (externalizing all new thoughts and worries) and process them into your Time Block schedule (Chapter 1). This intentional act of closing all "open loops" prevents them from consuming WM overnight and disrupting sleep, which is non-negotiable for EF restoration.
- **The Morning Activation:** Upon waking, immediately check your **Time Block schedule** and verbally rehearse the first two transition points of the day. This intentional, structured beginning activates the brain's **Task Positive Network (TPN)** and loads the immediate instructions into WM with minimal effort, ensuring a smooth transition into focused effort.

Section 3: Targeted Training: Strengthening the Memory Muscle

While systems compensate for deficits, consistent, targeted cognitive practice challenges the underlying WM capacity, similar to physical exercise.

1. Practice Inhibitory Control (IC) through Resistance

IC training is crucial because it protects WM. The goal is to strengthen the "brakes" so you can choose to suppress distraction and maintain focus.

- **Intentional Resistance:** During focused work sprints (Pomodoro, Chapter 3), use the urge to check a notification or open a new browser tab as a deliberate training opportunity. The act of resisting the distraction and maintaining focus on the primary task forces the brain to suppress the impulse, strengthening the IC muscle required for sustained effort.

- **The "Ten-Minute Rule":** For non-urgent impulses (e.g., an interesting but irrelevant thought, a desire to buy something), commit to a mandatory **"Ten-Minute Rule."** Write down the impulse immediately, and then force yourself to wait ten minutes before acting on it. This crucial pause allows the PFC to engage and override the amygdala's impulsive reaction, which is key to reducing both financial impulsivity and emotional volatility.

2. Cognitive Challenge and Dual-Task Practice

Consistent, low-stakes practice is essential for improving WM retrieval and retention over time.

- **Sequential Recall:** Practice activities that require you to hold multiple pieces of information in sequence (e.g., complex instructions, grocery lists, or phone numbers). Verbalizing the sequence out loud or writing it down immediately reinforces encoding.
- **Dual-Tasking (Controlled):** Engage in tasks that force you to hold focus on one item while simultaneously resisting the pull of a competing stimulus. For example, listen to an informative podcast while performing a simple, routine physical task (e.g., washing dishes). This controlled, low-stakes dual-tasking challenges WM to filter background information while maintaining a primary focus.

Section 4: The Holistic Context: Sustaining Cognitive Health

The PFC's capacity for WM and IC is highly vulnerable to impairment from internal psychological and physiological states. Sustaining cognitive growth requires actively minimizing the things that impair EF.

1. Sleep Hygiene and Physiological Support

Quality sleep and stable physical health are non-negotiable foundations for robust EF.

- **Sleep as Restoration:** Quality sleep is critical for WM and IC restoration. Sleep deprivation is as impairing as the core symptoms of ADHD themselves. Consistent, prioritized sleep hygiene is essential for restoring the PFC's capacity and mitigating the chronic mental fatigue that drains EF reserves.

- **Movement for Neurochemistry:** Regular physical exercise is a powerful, evidence-based tool that promotes dopamine release, improving attention and inhibitory control, acting as a natural cognitive enhancement. Use short bursts of movement during Pomodoro breaks (Chapter 3) to discharge restlessness and enhance focus.

2. Minimizing Stress and Sadness

Research is clear: EF skills **blossom most when we lessen things that impair them (like stress or sadness)** and enhance the things that support them.

- **Stress Reduction:** The structural predictability of Time Blocking and Milestone planning (Chapter 1) reduces the systemic stress of daily chaos, providing the necessary emotional buffer for your cognitive skills to flourish.
- **Self-Compassion:** Embracing self-compassion (to be addressed in Book 5) is essential. Self-criticism and shame consume immense EF resources. By replacing the inner critic with a supportive inner dialogue, you conserve mental energy, allowing your WM and IC to operate efficiently.

Conclusion: Your Resilient Internal Command

You have transformed Working Memory and Inhibitory Control from unreliable, internal deficits into skills supported by a robust, predictable system. By establishing fixed planning rituals, intentionally training your IC to resist distraction, and supporting your WM through external offloading, you are actively increasing your long-term resilience.

This intentional, disciplined practice is the definitive step toward conquering the fragmented mind and replacing chronic overwhelm with the quiet confidence of self-mastery. The mental energy conserved by this internal structure is the final resource you need to ensure that the effort of focus is not only powerful but also sustainable, preparing you for the final stage of Executive Function mastery: ruthlessly protecting your cognitive space from digital and mental noise.

Chapter 4 Workbook: Strengthen Your Memory: Tools to Boost Working Memory Power

Objective: To practice strengthening **Working Memory (WM)** and **Inhibitory Control (IC)** using fixed planning routines and targeted exercises.

Scientific Anchor: Executive Function (EF) skills, including WM and IC, improve through consistent challenge and practice. Fixed planning rituals externalize the cognitive burden, allowing the core skills to stabilize.

Activity 4.1: The WM Offload Checklist

Instructions: Identify one repetitive task you frequently forget steps for (e.g., getting ready for work, preparing a specific meal, sending a weekly report). Create an external WM Offload Checklist for it.

1. **Target Task:** ____
2. **External Checklist:** List 5 sequential non-negotiable steps for this task. Commit to referencing this physical or digital list every time you start the task.

Step	Action (Keep it simple)	WM Offload Benefit
1.		(Example: Reduces cognitive burden of recall)
2.		
3.		

Step	Action (Keep it simple)	WM Offload Benefit
4.		
5.		

Activity 4.2: Training Inhibitory Control (IC)

Instructions: Practice intentionally resisting an urge for 10 minutes, strengthening your brain's "brakes" (IC).

1. **Identify Your #1 Impulse:** What is the most common, low-stakes impulse that derails your focus? (E.g., Checking phone, opening new browser tab, getting a snack, interrupting).

   Impulse: ____

2. **The 10-Minute IC Sprint:** Set a timer for 10 minutes. Work on an existing task while actively, mindfully **resisting** the identified Impulse whenever it arises. Each successful resistance is a "rep" for your IC muscle.

   IC Practice: ____

   Start time: ____

   End time: ____

Reflection 4.3: Analyzing Executive Function Gain

Instructions: Reflect on how your consistent routine supports your focus and conserves EF energy.

1. **WM Conservation:** How does performing the **Nightly Offload** (writing down tomorrow's plan / worries) reduce your brain's tendency to ruminate or worry before sleep? (Focus on how the external system manages the "open loops").

2.

Sleep / WM Benefit: ______________________________________

____

____

____

____

____

____

3. **EF and Emotional Load:** The PFC's capacity to focus is impaired by stress and self-criticism. How does the structure of a predictable schedule, which reduces rushing and late penalties, act as a psychological buffer that supports your EF?

   Emotional / EF Support: _________________________________

   ____

   ____

   ____

   ____

   ____

4. **Future-Proofing:** Name one activity or task you will commit to resisting tomorrow (using your IC strength) that will save you at least 30 minutes of time.

   Time-Saving Resistance: _________________________________

   ____

   ____

   ____

   ____

   ____

CHAPTER 5

SIMPLIFY DECISIONS: REDUCE OVERWHELM WITH CLEAR MENTAL FRAMEWORKS

You have successfully established external command over your schedule (Chapter 1), mastered prioritization (Chapter 2), harnessed your attention (Chapter 3), and strengthened your memory (Chapter 4). This cumulative effort has created a structural and cognitive foundation that conserves vast amounts of mental energy. Now, this chapter targets one of the most critical, yet subtle, drains on Executive Function (EF) reserves: **Decision Fatigue**.

For the woman with Attention-Deficit / Hyperactivity Disorder (ADHD), the constant barrage of choices, from mundane (e.g., *Which laundry detergent to buy?*) to profound (e.g., *Which task to start next?*), rapidly depletes the finite resources of the prefrontal cortex (PFC). This neurological exhaustion leads directly to feelings of **overwhelm,**

anxiety, and, critically, **Task Paralysis**, as the brain shuts down to avoid the pain of continuous negotiation. Decision-making is inherently taxing, but for the ADHD brain, the effort is disproportionately high due to deficits in Working Memory (WM) and Inhibitory Control (IC).

This chapter provides the strategic toolkit to systematically **annihilate decision points** wherever possible. By implementing clear mental frameworks, routines, and external automation, you will eliminate the need for constant negotiation, ensuring your EF is conserved solely for high-leverage, important choices. The goal is to make the simplest, most effective choices automatic, reducing the daily friction that fuels chronic overwhelm.

Section 1: The Neurobiological Cost of Decision Fatigue

Decision fatigue is a state of mental exhaustion that arises from having to make a high volume of choices over a sustained period. For the ADHD brain, this exhaustion has immediate and measurable consequences on focus, mood, and productivity.

1. WM Overload and the Paralysis Trigger

Prioritization and choice require holding multiple options, goals, and consequences in **Working Memory** simultaneously. When a woman with ADHD faces a mountain of undifferentiated choices (e.g., a chaotic to-do list, a cluttered desk, a busy email inbox), her WM rapidly overloads.

- **Ambiguity is Painful:** Every ambiguous choice (e.g., *Where does this go? Do I need this?*) forces the brain to expend energy. This constant internal debate, a taxing form of **Cognitive Load (CL)**, drains the PFC.
- **The Shutdown Response:** When CL reaches a critical threshold, the brain defaults to avoidance. This is the physiological mechanism behind **Task Paralysis** and **Decision Paralysis**, the brain shuts down to avoid the pain of continuous negotiation, leading to procrastination and immobilization.

2. Impulsivity and the Breakdown of Inhibitory Control (IC)

Decision fatigue directly compromises **Inhibitory Control (IC)**, the ability to resist temptation and think before acting.

- **Weakened Brakes:** As EF resources are depleted, the brain's "brakes" weaken, making it harder to resist immediate gratification or make rational, long-term choices. This manifests as:
    - **Impulsive Buying:** Susceptibility to spontaneous purchases and going over credit limits (financial ADHD tax).
    - **Emotional Outbursts:** Reduced capacity to manage frustration, leading to impulsive words or emotional volatility (compromised IC for emotional regulation).
    - **Avoidance:** Impulsively choosing a low-effort, stimulating distraction (e.g., social media) over a high-effort, important task.

The strategies in this chapter are designed to automate or eliminate choices, thereby preserving IC for the moments when rational self-control is truly needed.

Section 2: Frameworks for Eliminating Decision Points

The solution is to introduce simple, external rules that force the brain to execute a choice without expending energy on deliberation. This shifts choice from an internal debate to an automatic system execution.

1. The Power of Default Settings and Automation

The most effective way to eliminate choice is to make the desired choice the **default setting** for your life. This bypasses the need for the PFC to engage entirely.

- **Financial Automation:** Automate all repetitive financial tasks, such as bill payments, savings transfers, and investment contributions, to occur immediately after payday. This eliminates the monthly decision (and risk of forgetting) associated with these high-stakes tasks, directly mitigating the financial **ADHD Tax** caused by poor working memory and time blindness.
- **The Digital Default:** Set your computer and phone environments to default to **Focus Mode** or "Do Not Disturb" (Chapter 5, Book 2) during peak working hours. This eliminates

the daily choice to turn off notifications, which would otherwise rely on inconsistent IC. Similarly, automate backups and file saving to eliminate the decision of *where* and *when* to save files.

2. The Binary Rule: The "Two-Minute Rule" and "One-Touch Rule"

For processing inputs like email, mail, or small organizational tasks, the decision must be reduced to a binary (two-choice) system that requires zero deliberation.

- **The Two-Minute Rule (for Digital / Admin):** If an incoming item (email, physical mail, small task on a list) can be dealt with in **two minutes or less**, do it immediately. Otherwise, it is deferred (Time Blocked or delegated). This rule instantly eliminates the ambiguity of deferral vs. action, reducing the item's burden on WM.
- **The One-Touch Rule (for Physical Items):** When you pick up a piece of physical clutter (e.g., mail, a dish, an article of clothing), you must act on it immediately—either put it in its **Designated Home** (Book 1), or put it in the **Trash / Junk Drawer** (the low-friction containment zone). It cannot be set down elsewhere. This simple rule prevents "piles" from forming, which are the visible manifestation of accumulated decision fatigue.

3. The Constraint Principle: Limiting Choice for Energy

The decision-making process is simplified when the number of available options is intentionally limited, the **Constraint Principle**.

- **The Capsule Wardrobe:** Reduce decision fatigue related to clothing by intentionally limiting your wardrobe to a cohesive "capsule" collection of items that mix and match easily. This eliminates the daily energy expenditure of choosing an outfit, reserving morning WM for high-leverage tasks.
- **Routine Meal Planning:** Establish a **Meal Rotation Schedule** or use a fixed set of recipes for weeknights. This eliminates the agonizing daily decision of "What's for dinner?", which is a classic source of executive fatigue for women managing family responsibilities.

Section 3: Leveraging Structure for Complex Choices

For unavoidable, complex choices (e.g., project strategies, financial investments), the goal is to use clear frameworks to externalize the pros and cons, minimizing internal cognitive negotiation.

1. The Externalized Pros and Cons List

The ADHD brain often struggles to hold and weigh multiple variables in WM simultaneously, leading to impulsive or delayed decisions. The solution is to externalize the variables.

- **The T-Chart Method:** For any non-urgent, high-stakes decision, create a simple, visible T-Chart that externalizes the variables. Title one column "Pros / Goals" (Q2, long-term payoff) and the other "Cons / Costs" (Q4, immediate friction). Visually comparing the lists reduces the reliance on inconsistent WM and allows the logical PFC to engage effectively.
- **The "Ten-Minute Rule" for Impulses:** For high-stakes, tempting impulses (e.g., impulsive spending or committing to a new project), enforce a mandatory **Ten-Minute Wait** (Chapter 4). Write down the impulse and the **Pros / Cons** immediately, then wait. This pause allows the PFC's **Inhibitory Control** to kick in, reducing the emotional urgency that drives poor decisions.

2. The Prioritization Filter (Review of Chapter 2)

Prioritization frameworks mastered in Chapter 2 must be used as the ultimate mental filter for simplifying demands.

- **The Eisenhower Matrix (Q2 Check):** When a new commitment arises (e.g., joining a committee, starting a new project), filter it immediately through the **Q2 (Important / Goal)** matrix. If it does not actively move you toward a major goal, the automatic decision is to **Delegate or Reject** (Q3 / Q4), eliminating the need for deliberation. This protects your time and energy from commitments that don't serve your purpose.

Section 4: The Emotional and Cognitive Liberation

The systematic annihilation of decision points yields a profound emotional and cognitive payoff, reinforcing self-efficacy and reducing the pervasive anxiety of overwhelm.

1. Conservation of Executive Function (EF)

The most direct benefit is the significant conservation of EF resources. By automating or eliminating dozens of micro-decisions daily, you free up mental bandwidth that was previously consumed by fighting ambiguity.

- **Fueling Focus:** This conserved EF is the resource you need to fuel sustained concentration (Pomodoro sprints) and engage in challenging cognitive practice (WM training). The mind is quieter, less cluttered, and more capable of engaging in **Deep Work** (high-leverage, non-fragmented focus).
- **Reduced Mental Fatigue:** Eliminating the chronic effort required for decision-making directly combats the **Mental Fatigue and Brain Fog** that characterize chronic overwhelm, creating a more stable internal environment that promotes clarity and motivation.

2. The Antidote to Shame and Paralysis

Decision fatigue fuels the negative emotional cycle of the ADHD experience, leading to shame over missed opportunities and an inability to act.

- **Building Trust:** Relying on robust, automatic systems builds **trust** in your ability to manage your life (self-efficacy). When high-stakes tasks (bills, savings) are executed reliably by automation, you no longer feel the shame associated with poor memory or inconsistent follow-through.
- **Self-Compassion:** The conscious use of the **Constraint Principle** (e.g., limiting wardrobe, fixed meal plans) is an act of self-compassion. You are acknowledging your neurobiological limits and designing a supportive system, replacing the impossible demand for perfection with a realistic, low-friction framework for success.

Conclusion: Your Automated Life

The journey through this chapter marks the final strategic step in maximizing your Executive Function. By systematically applying frameworks like the **Two-Minute Rule** and **Financial Automation**, you have eliminated the chaotic friction of endless micro-decisions.

You have transformed your daily experience from one defined by decision paralysis and exhaustion to one rooted in clarity and automaticity. This mastery of simplicity is the final, essential foundation for long-term self-mastery, ensuring that your conserved mental energy is now fully available for the crucial emotional regulation work (Book 4) and relational connection (Book 5) that builds a truly resilient and fulfilling life.

Chapter 5 Workbook: Simplify Decisions: Reduce Overwhelm with Clear Mental Frameworks

Objective: To practice using external frameworks to automate decisions and reduce the cognitive burden associated with choice and ambiguity.

Scientific Anchor: Reducing the volume of daily micro-decisions conserves Working Memory and Inhibitory Control, mitigating Decision Fatigue and Task Paralysis.

Activity 5.1: The Binary Rule Audit

Instructions: Identify one area where daily decision-making consistently creates friction (e.g., laundry, dish management, email). Apply a binary rule to eliminate ambiguity.

1. **Friction Area:** ____
2. **The Rule (Yes / No Action):** Create a clear, two-choice action plan for items encountered in this area.
    - *Example (Email):* If < 2 minutes, DO NOW. If > 2 minutes, **TIME BLOCK or DELETE.**
    - *Your Binary Rule:* If Item is picked up, it must be ______ OR _______ (e.g., Put in Home OR Put in Junk Drawer).

Activity 5.2: Decision Automation Commitment

Instructions: Commit to implementing three automated systems to bypass reliance on inconsistent Working Memory and follow-through.

1. **Financial Automation:** What is one high-stakes bill or savings transfer you will automate this week?

   Automated Action: ________________________________

   ____

2. **Routine Automation (Constraint Principle):** What is one area you will reduce choice in to eliminate morning energy drain? (e.g., Lunch Prep, Outfit Choice).

   Constraint: ____________________________________

   ____

   (e.g., "I will only choose from three work outfits on Monday morning.")

3. **Digital Automation (IC Protection):** What will you set your phone / computer to automatically do during your main Time Block hours to eliminate the choice of checking notifications?

   Default Setting: ________________________________

   ____

   (e.g., "Set to Do Not Disturb / Focus Mode automatically 9 AM-12 PM.")

Reflection 5.3: Analyzing Freedom from Choice

Instructions: Reflect on how eliminating small choices impacts your emotional and cognitive energy.

1. **Paralysis to Action:** How does the mere existence of the **Binary Rule** (Activity 5.1) reduce the anxiety that leads to task paralysis? (Focus on the elimination of internal debate).

   Reduction in Debate: ____________________________

   ____

   ____

   ____

   ____

2. **IC Conservation:** How will the automation of high-stakes financial tasks (Activity 5.2, #1) free up mental energy that was previously consumed by worry, fear of late fees, or guilt?

   Worry / Guilt Reduction: ________________________________

   ____

   ____

   ____

   ____

   ____

3. **The New Priority:** If you save 30 minutes of decision time each day, where will you intentionally re-invest that conserved Executive Function (e.g., starting a Pomodoro sprint, engaging in mindful relaxation)?

   Re-investment Plan: ________________________________

   ____

   ____

   ____

   ____

   ____

CHAPTER 6

REFLECT AND INTEGRATE: INSIGHTS AND GROWTH IN YOUR EXECUTIVE FUNCTION JOURNEY

You have reached a significant milestone in your journey toward self-mastery. The preceding chapters of this book have been a disciplined, sustained campaign against the core internal chaos of the ADHD brain: the systemic fragmentation of attention, the tyranny of **Time Blindness**, and the pervasive exhaustion of **Cognitive Load (CL)**. You have moved beyond the reactive struggle, where your focus was a victim of distraction and procrastination, to a state of **proactive, intentional command** over your mental resources.

This chapter marks a critical moment of pause, a dedicated space to **reflect and integrate** the profound cognitive and emotional gains achieved through the disciplined practice of the strategies you have mastered: **Milestone Planning**, **Prioritization Frameworks**, **Attention Anchoring**, and **Decision Simplification**. The aim is to solidify the foundational shift from a life defined by **reactive chaos** and **overwhelm** to a state of **proactive, intentional action**.

The core insight solidified here is that consistent focus is not a mysterious gift of willpower; it is the measurable result of disciplined **Executive Function (EF) management** and the strategic application of **external scaffolding**. You have learned that the struggle was never laziness, but a profound neurobiological challenge that required an evidence-based toolkit to compensate for deficits in time perception, task initiation, and filtering capacity. By systematically structuring your time, ruthlessly prioritizing your energy, and training your cognitive functions, you have established the resilient internal command necessary to manage the complex emotional and physiological challenges that lie ahead.

Section 1: The Cognitive Victory: Annihilating Time Blindness and Overload

The most powerful outcome of mastering the EF strategies in this book is the mitigation of two core, debilitating deficits: the inability to perceive time accurately and the chronic drain of high cognitive load. This transformation of the cognitive landscape is the tangible benefit of replacing inconsistent internal effort with predictable external structure.

1. The Banishment of Time Blindness: Finitude and Planning

Time blindness, the inability to accurately perceive or estimate the flow of time, is the primary driver of chronic lateness, poor prioritization, and the anxiety that triggers task paralysis. The Milestones framework directly counteracted this deficit by making time concrete and visible.

- **Milestones as an External Map:** You replaced the overwhelming abstract nature of deadlines with a series of sequential, manageable **Milestones** (Chapter 1). This technique directly addressed the **estimation deficit** (the tendency to underestimate time) by forcing you to apply the **Reverse Timeline** method and intentionally schedule **Estimation Buffers** (25–50% extra time), ensuring your schedule is temporally realistic. This structured approach minimized the cognitive guesswork of "What to do next?", conserving EF resources.

- **The Power of Finitude and Pomodoro:** The implementation of **Time Blocking** (Chapter 1) and the customized application of the **Pomodoro Technique** (Chapter 3) strategically attacks the paralysis triggered by the perception of an infinite, daunting task. By committing to short, fixed sprints, you impose **finitude** on the task, lowering the psychological barrier to initiation. The visible timer provides a constant, external cue, anchoring attention and generating the necessary **momentum** through the immediate reward of completing a structured sprint, systematically bypassing the internal dopamine deficit.

2. Cognitive Load Annihilation and WM Conservation

The chronic state of overwhelm in the ADHD experience is rooted in the high **Cognitive Load (CL)** caused by an overstimulated mind that struggles to filter stimuli and manage multiple "open loops." The mastery of **Decision Simplification** (Chapter 5) and **Prioritization** (Chapter 2) provided the defense against this drain.

- **Annihilating Decision Fatigue:** By implementing binary frameworks like the **Eisenhower Matrix** (Chapter 2) and **The Rule of Three**, you eliminated the chaotic friction of endless micro-decisions (e.g., *Which task should I start?*). The systematic annihilation of decision points, achieved through automation and the **One-Touch Rule** (Chapter 5), conserved EF resources that were previously consumed by continuous internal negotiation.
- **Strengthening Internal Resilience:** The consistent practice of **Inhibitory Control (IC)** training (Chapter 4)—intentionally resisting the urge to check a notification or interrupt a task—actively protected your limited **Working Memory (WM)** from being fragmented by distraction. Furthermore, utilizing **fixed planning rituals** and external checklists actively offloaded multi-step instructions from your unreliable WM, ensuring that your cognitive resources are available for high-leverage thinking, not constant recall.

Section 2: The Emotional and Psychological Liberation

The EF mastery achieved in this book yields profound emotional dividends, reinforcing the positive feedback loop necessary for long-term consistency and challenging a lifetime of internalized shame.

1. Defeating Shame and Building Self-Efficacy

The chronic failure to maintain focus and follow through—a frequent result of time blindness and fragmentation—is a significant driver of shame and the pervasive feeling of inadequacy for women with ADHD.

- **The Antidote to the Inner Critic:** The mastery of EF strategies replaces the long, overwhelming to-do list (a document of perceived failure) with a realistic, manageable schedule, thereby setting **achievable expectations** and reducing the likelihood of failure and self-criticism. The fact that your schedule includes **Estimation Buffers** is an inherent act of **self-compassion** that disarms the "all-or-nothing" perfectionism trap.
- **Evidence of Competence:** Each successfully completed Milestone or Pomodoro sprint provides tangible, undeniable evidence of competence and follow-through. This consistent success builds **self-efficacy** (the belief in one's ability to execute a plan), which is the direct psychological antidote to the inadequacy that characterizes unmanaged attention. The realization that success is due to a deliberate, effective strategy, a system, replaces the reliance on inconsistent willpower.

2. Mitigating the ADHD Tax and Chronic Fatigue

The chronic, high effort required to manage attention is the primary cause of severe **Mental Fatigue** and burnout. This continuous cognitive effort is the **"ADHD Tax"** on energy reserves, a measurable cumulative cost that depletes mental capacity.

- **Energy Conservation:** By eliminating unnecessary **Context Switching** (Chapter 3) and automating decisions (Chapter 5), you directly conserved the mental energy that was previously consumed by fighting internal friction. This conserved energy directly combats the chronic fatigue and brain fog that characterize overwhelm, leading to a more stable emotional and cognitive baseline.

- **Sustaining Effort:** The structured use of the **Pomodoro Technique**, with its mandated restorative breaks, ensures that mental energy is managed proactively. This disciplined rhythm promotes **sustainable effort** rather than sporadic, exhausting bursts of productivity, which is crucial for the long-term health of the prefrontal cortex.

3. The Economic and Relational Dividend

The EF mastery achieved here translates into measurable improvements in the outside world, directly mitigating the financial and relational costs of the condition.

- **Economic Stability:** The use of the Milestones framework and Decision Simplification (automation) directly combats the financial costs associated with unmanaged time blindness (late fees, financial instability) and impulsivity (impulsive buying). By systematically prioritizing and meeting deadlines, you reduce the time and money wasted on compensation and mistakes.
- **Relational Predictability:** The predictability established through structured scheduling reduces the friction caused by forgetfulness and lateness. Furthermore, the practice of **Inhibitory Control** (Chapter 4) provides the internal capacity needed to pause before responding impulsively in relationships, which is a foundational skill for constructive communication (Book 5).

Section 3: The Bridge to Future Mastery: Preparing for Emotional Regulation

The structural stability of focus achieved in this book is the essential **prerequisite** for engaging with the complex internal work of emotional mastery (Book 4). A brain that is constantly battling chaos and cognitive fatigue lacks the resources necessary to manage intense feelings.

1. EF as the Foundation for Emotional Control

Emotional dysregulation, the most impairing symptom for many women with ADHD, relies heavily on the EF skills you have practiced.

- **Activating the "Brakes":** The muscle of **Inhibitory Control (IC)**, honed through resistance practice (Chapter 4), is the very same EF required for **emotional regulation**, resisting the urge to react impulsively during an intense emotional surge. You are training the brain's "brakes" (the PFC) to successfully override the emotional accelerator (the amygdala).
- **Mindfulness and the "Pause":** The capacity for sustained, anchored attention (Pomodoro / Single-Tasking) is the prerequisite for effective **Mindfulness** (a cornerstone of DBT / CBT). This EF skill creates the critical **"pause"** between feeling an intense emotion and reacting to it, allowing the cognitive strategies (challenging thoughts, etc.) to engage before the emotional storm takes over. Without the focus you have cultivated, the "pause" is impossible.

2. The Command Shift

You have transformed from a reactive participant in your life to a strategic commander of your time and attention. Your new system is governed by the following laws of sustained EF:

- **Law of Finitude:** You conquer paralysis by breaking all large projects into small, finite, manageable Milestones and Pomodoro sprints.
- **Law of Conservation:** You conserve energy by ruthlessly eliminating distractions (CL Annihilation) and automating decisions, preserving WM and IC for high-leverage tasks.
- **Law of Proactive Structure:** You replaced vague intentions with predictable, scheduled action, ensuring that your motivation is anchored to the external calendar, not inconsistent internal dopamine.

This powerful new sense of competence and control is the definitive antidote to the shame and overwhelm that has characterized your struggle, equipping you for the profound work of self-mastery that lies ahead.

Chapter 6 Workbook: Reflect and Integrate: Insights and Growth in Your Executive Function Journey

Objective: To synthesize the cognitive and emotional gains achieved in Book 3, solidifying the shift from reliance on inconsistent willpower to resilient system design.

Scientific Anchor: Reflective practice reduces the impact of stress and sadness on Executive Functions, allowing the functional systems built to flourish. Acknowledging neurobiological reality counters the shame cycle.

Activity 6.1: The Executive Function Gain Scorecard

Instructions: Rate the severity of your challenges **before** Book 3 and **now**, focusing on the impact of the new time and focus strategies. (Scale: 1 = Minimal Challenge, 5 = Severe Challenge)

Challenge Area	Before Book 3 (Initial)	After Book 3 (Current)	Reflection: The Tool That Helped Most
Task Paralysis (Starting Projects)			(Example: Milestones/ Micro-Steps)
Chronic Underestimation of Time			(Example: Estimation Buffer / Time Block)
Distraction / Context Switching			(Example: Single-Tasking / CL Annihilation)
Daily Decision Overwhelm			(Example: Rule of Three / Automation)

Reflection 6.2: Shifting from Shame to Strategy

Instructions: Use this space to integrate the core concept that struggles with EF are neurological, not moral, and assess your progress in building self-efficacy.

1. **The Overwhelm to Control Shift:** Identify one specific moment this week where you felt the pressure of **Decision Fatigue**. How did using a specific tool (e.g., **The Binary Rule** or **The Constraint Principle**) create an immediate sense of relief and simplification?

   The Intervention: ____

   ____

   ____

   ____

   ____

2. **The Shame Antidote:** Identify one self-critical thought you had about your productivity (e.g., "I'm lazy for procrastinating on that report"). Rephrase this thought using the compassionate, neurobiological reality you learned (e.g., "The task lacked clear Milestones, triggering a Task Activation Deficit. My brain needs finitude to start.")

   New, Empowered Narrative: ________________________________

   ____

   ____

   ____

   ____

3. **Evidence of Self-Efficacy:** What is the most important piece of **evidence of competence** you created this week (e.g., sticking to a Time Block, completing a full Pomodoro without switching, meeting a Milestone)?

   Evidence of Competence: __________________________________

   ____

   ____

   ____

   ____

Activity 6.3: Bridge to Emotional Mastery (Book 4 Prep)

Instructions: The capacity for emotional regulation (Book 4) relies on the EF skills (IC / Attention) you have strengthened.

1. **IC and the Emotional Surge:** When you feel an intense emotion (e.g., frustration, anger) that threatens to trigger an impulsive reaction, you need a **"Circuit-Breaker"** (IC in action). What single tool from Book 3 (e.g., The 10-Minute IC Rule, a physical Pomodoro break) will you commit to using as your first line of defense to create a **pause**?

   Circuit-Breaker Commitment: ____________________________

   ____

   ____

   ____

   ____

   ____

2. **CL and Stress:** How does the reduction in daily background noise (CL Annihilation / Digital Silence) provide more **emotional bandwidth** to handle a sudden conflict or intense feeling without immediately escalating to overwhelm?

   Emotional Bandwidth Gained: ____________________________

   ____

   ____

   ____

   ____

   ____

CHAPTER 7

PRACTICE AND APPLY: YOUR EXECUTIVE FUNCTION ACTION TOOLKIT

You have completed the intensive work of Book 3, systematically defeating the core internal challenges of the ADHD brain, **Time Blindness**, **Prioritization Failure**, and **Memory Inconsistency**. This final chapter provides the essential **Action Toolkit**, designed to transform the neurobiological strategies mastered in the preceding six chapters into resilient, low-friction habits that automate Executive Function (EF).

The goal of this Practice and Apply chapter is to move beyond theory and solidify the crucial shift from a life governed by inconsistent **willpower** to one governed by reliable **systems**. For the woman with ADHD, sustained success is achieved not by trying harder, but by strategically creating external structures that compensate for neurological deficits in Working Memory (WM) and Inhibitory Control (IC).

This toolkit consolidates the highest-leverage strategies into a single, cohesive daily ritual, ensuring that the mental bandwidth you reclaimed from fighting chaos is now actively utilized for intentional, high-quality focus. Consistency in applying these tools is the key to building long-term EF resilience.

Section 1: The Neurobiological Mandate: Automating Executive Function

The chronic feeling of overwhelm experienced by women with ADHD is rooted in the constant effort required to manage fundamental Executive Functions that are inconsistent. This chapter's strategies aim to automate these functions:

1. **Automating Planning (Time Blindness):** We must externalize time management, using visual cues and fixed schedules (Time Blocking) to anchor the present and make the future predictable, neutralizing the **Estimation Deficit**.
2. **Automating Prioritization (Cognitive Load):** We must impose frameworks (Eisenhower, Rule of Three) to eliminate ambiguity and conserve **CL** (Cognitive Load) and **WM**, ensuring energy is directed only toward high-leverage tasks.
3. **Automating Initiation (Task Paralysis):** We must use structures that impose **finitude** (Pomodoro, Milestones) to lower the **Activation Energy** required to start difficult tasks, leveraging momentum and dopamine reward for follow-through.

The exercises below are designed as your daily EF launch sequence, systematically checking these three boxes every morning.

Toolkit 1: The Time and Task Command Center

Objective: To master the initial planning and scheduling phase by converting abstract deadlines into actionable, time-bound Milestones, directly counteracting **Time Blindness** and **Estimation Deficits** (Chapters 1 & 2).

Scientific Anchor: Time Blocking and Milestones impose **finitude** on tasks, which lowers the cognitive resistance associated with paralyzing, open-ended work. Scheduling buffers compensates for the tendency to underestimate duration, reducing daily stress.

Activity 7.1: The Daily Planning Ritual (Morning / Nightly Prep)

Instructions: Commit 15 minutes each day to this structured planning routine, which externalizes your entire day's agenda.

1. **The Reverse Timeline Check (Chapter 1):** Review your **Weekly Milestones** and identify the single most critical, actionable step required today to move that project forward. This focuses your morning intention on a high-leverage task.

   Today's Primary Milestone Action: ________________________

   ____

2. **The Eisenhower / Rule of Three Filter (Chapter 2):** Review your digital inbox / list and select **only three** high-leverage tasks (one Q1 / Urgent, two Q2 / Goal) that define a successful day. All others are deferred, delegated, or deleted (Q3 / Q4). This protects against **Cognitive Overload.**

   High-Leverage Task 1 (Must Do / Q1 or Q2): ______________

   High-Leverage Task 2 (Goal / Q2): ________________________

   High-Leverage Task 3 (Goal / Q2): ________________________

3. **Time Block with Buffer Application:** Schedule your three tasks into your calendar using fixed time slots, applying the **Estimation Buffer** (add 25% more time than you think you need) and the **Transition Block** (10-15 minutes of scheduled rest) between sessions.

   Task 1 Time Block (Start / End): __________________________

   Task 1 Buffer / Transition: _______________________________

Reflective Commitment: If I only complete these three tasks today, my day will be (Successful / Productive / Calm).

Toolkit 2: Focus and Resistance Anchors

Objective: To proactively manage attention dysregulation by anchoring focus to structure (Pomodoro) and training **Inhibitory Control (IC)** against distraction (Chapter 3 & 4).

Scientific Anchor: The Pomodoro Technique provides the necessary **finitude** and frequent reward that the dopamine-dysregulated brain needs to sustain effort. IC training directly strengthens the prefrontal cortex's ability to resist the impulse to switch tasks or seek novelty.

Activity 7.2: The Focused Sprint and IC Training

Instructions: For your first scheduled **Time Block** of the day, commit to a focused sprint supported by external structures.

1. **Set the Stage for Single-Tasking:** Before you start the timer, perform a **Cognitive Load Annihilation** ritual:
   - Close all browser tabs except the one needed for Task 1.
   - Silence ALL notifications on all devices (Notification Annihilation).
   - Clear your immediate desk area of physical clutter (Visual Noise Reduction).
2. **The Custom Pomodoro Sprint:** Set a timer for your optimal work interval (e.g., 25 minutes).
   - *Work Interval:_______________________ minutes.*
   - *Mandatory Break: ____________________minutes.*
3. **IC Resistance Practice:** During the work sprint, actively practice **Inhibitory Control**. Every time the urge to check your phone or switch tasks arises, take one deep breath and place a tally mark below (A "rep" for your IC muscle).

   IC Resistance Tally:____

   ____

   ____

   (The goal is not zero, but to track and acknowledge the effort).
4. **The Restorative Break:** When the timer rings, honor the break immediately. Use a **Sensory Reset** technique to calm the nervous system (e.g., 5 deep breaths, walk to get water, light stretch). Avoid consuming digital media during this time to prevent **Context Switching Cost**.

Toolkit 3: Cognitive Offload and Automation

Objective: To simplify daily existence by automating decisions and reducing the mental effort required for constant recall, conserving Working Memory (WM) (Chapters 4 & 5).

Scientific Anchor: Automating routine tasks and implementing binary rules eliminates ambiguity that consumes WM and triggers Decision Fatigue, preserving EF for high-leverage thinking.

Activity 7.3: The Automation and Offload Ritual

Instructions: Focus on eliminating unnecessary mental friction by implementing external systems for memory and decision-making.

1. **The Binary Decision Rule (Chapter 5):** Apply the **Two-Minute Rule** to your email triage. For every email / small task:
    - If it takes < 2 minutes: **DO NOW.**
    - If it takes > 2 minutes: **TIME BLOCK or DELETE.**
    - *Commitment:* I will not leave any email in my inbox to "decide later."
2. **The WM Offload Checklist (Chapter 4):** Identify one repetitive, multi-step task you constantly forget or rush (e.g., leaving the house, shutting down the kitchen). Create a **permanent, visible checklist** to externalize the steps from your unreliable WM.

    Target Task Checklist: ______________________________________

    ____

    ____

    (Commit to reviewing it tonight).
3. **The Decision Simplification Commitment (Chapter 5):** Identify one area where you will apply the **Constraint Principle** this week (e.g., meals, clothing, exercise).

    Constraint: I will only wear ________________________________

    ____

    ____

    (pre-selected outfits this week to conserve morning decision energy.)
4. **The Nightly Offload (Closing Open Loops):** Before turning off your lights, perform this two-step ritual to clear your mind and conserve WM overnight:
    - **Step A:** Process any new tasks / worries from the day into your **Time Block Schedule** for future scheduling (Milestone planning).

- **Step B:** Place your **Landing Strip Items** (keys, wallet, phone) in their designated home.

Section 2: Integration and Long-Term Resilience (Reflective Summary)

The consistent, simultaneous application of these five toolkits, Milestones, Prioritization, Pomodoro, Memory Strengthening, and Simplification, creates a synergistic system that is far more resilient than any single strategy applied in isolation. This integrated approach addresses the chronic, cumulative nature of ADHD challenges.

1. The Synergistic EF Gain

The power of this toolkit lies in how each strategy supports the next, leading to a profound conservation of EF:

- **Milestones** (finitude) enable **Prioritization** (clarity of scope).
- **Prioritization** (focus on Q2 / Goals) enables **IC** (Inhibitory Control) because you know exactly what to resist.
- **IC** (resistance) protects **WM** (Working Memory) from CL drain.
- **WM** conservation and **Decision Simplification** reduce the overall **Mental Fatigue**, ensuring energy is available for the next day's activation.

This continuous positive feedback loop replaces the old cycle of chaos, paralysis, and shame with a new cycle of clarity, momentum, and self-efficacy.

2. The Emotional Fuel for the Next Journey

The Executive Function skills you have conserved and strengthened are the essential **psychological fuel** required for the profound emotional mastery work that lies ahead in Book 4 (Tame Intense Emotions).

- **Attention as a Prerequisite for Mindfulness:** The capacity for sustained, anchored attention, honed through **Pomodoro** and **IC practice**, is the critical prerequisite for effective **Mindfulness** (the cornerstone of DBT / CBT). Without the ability to maintain focus, the crucial mindful "pause" between feeling an intense emotion and acting impulsively is impossible.
- **IC as the Emotional Brake:** The muscle of **Inhibitory Control** (resisting the urge to check a notification) is the very same EF muscle required for **emotional regulation**—resisting the urge to

react impulsively or explode during conflict. Your IC practice in this book is, fundamentally, training your emotional "brakes."

- **Reduced Anxiety:** The structural predictability of Time Blocking and the knowledge that high-stakes tasks are automated (Toolkit 3) stabilize the nervous system, reducing the chaotic internal anxiety that often triggers emotional dysregulation.

By completing the work of Book 3, you have moved beyond merely coping with the symptoms of ADHD to strategically commanding your cognitive function. You are now equipped with the robust internal and external resilience needed to embark on the crucial journey of emotional mastery and true self-acceptance.

CONCLUSION:

SUMMARY: YOUR EMPOWERED ATTENTION

You have completed the intensive, strategic work of Book 3, systematically defeating the core internal challenges of the ADHD brain: **Time Blindness**, **Prioritization Failure**, and **Memory Inconsistency**. This accomplishment represents a profound transformation, shifting your state from chaotic reactivity to one of intentional, sustained command over your mental resources.

The core realization solidified here is that consistent focus and productivity are not born from relentless willpower, but from the disciplined, strategic application of **Executive Function (EF) management** and robust **external scaffolding**. You have learned that your struggle was never laziness; it was a neurobiological reality that required an evidence-based toolkit to compensate for deficits in time perception, task initiation, and filtering capacity.

By systematically reducing the internal noise and structuring your time to work *with* your brain's needs, you have reclaimed precious mental bandwidth. This cognitive stability is the most valuable asset you possess, providing the foundation necessary to manage the complex emotional and physiological challenges that lie ahead. You have not just managed your focus; you have successfully future-proofed your capacity for consistent follow-through, providing the ultimate antidote to the pervasive feeling of being perpetually "frenzied, frazzled, and overwhelmed."

Section 1: The Cognitive Victory: Annihilating Time Blindness and Overload

The most powerful outcome of mastering the EF strategies in this book is the mitigation of two core, debilitating deficits: the inability to perceive time accurately and the chronic drain of high cognitive load. This transformation of the cognitive landscape is the tangible benefit of replacing inconsistent internal effort with predictable external structure.

1. The Banishment of Time Blindness: Finitude and Planning

Time blindness—the inability to accurately perceive or estimate the flow of time—is the primary driver of chronic lateness, poor prioritization, and the anxiety that triggers task paralysis. The Milestone framework directly counteracted this deficit by making time concrete and measurable.

- **Milestones and Time Blocking as an External Clock:** You replaced the overwhelming abstract nature of deadlines with a series of sequential, manageable **Milestones** (Chapter 1), forcing the abstract future into the urgent present. This technique directly addressed the **estimation deficit** (the tendency to underestimate time) by forcing you to apply the **Reverse Timeline** method and intentionally schedule **Estimation Buffers** (25–50% extra time), ensuring your schedule is temporally realistic. The visible, structured schedule minimized the cognitive guesswork of "What to do next?", conserving EF resources.
- **The Power of Pomodoro Finitude:** The customized application of the **Pomodoro Technique** (Chapter 3) strategically attacks the paralysis triggered by the perception of an infinite, daunting task. By committing to short, fixed sprints, you impose **finitude** on the task, lowering the psychological barrier to initiation. The visible timer provides a constant, external cue, anchoring attention and generating the necessary **momentum** through the immediate reward (dopamine hit) of completing a structured sprint, systematically bypassing the internal motivation deficit.
- **Working Memory Conservation:** The consistent implementation of **fixed planning routines** (Chapter 4) and the use of external checklists actively offloaded multi-step instructions from your unreliable **Working Memory (WM)**. This systematic offloading ensured that your cognitive resources are available for high-leverage thinking, not constant recall, thereby mitigating "brain fog" and forgetfulness.

2. Cognitive Load Annihilation: Prioritization and Simplification

The chronic state of overwhelm is rooted in the high **Cognitive Load (CL)** caused by an overstimulated mind that struggles to filter stimuli and manage multiple "open loops." The mastery of **Decision Simplification** (Chapter 5) and **Prioritization** (Chapter 2) is the most direct defense against this drain.

- **Annihilating Decision Fatigue:** By implementing binary frameworks like the **Eisenhower Matrix** (Chapter 2) and **The Rule of Three**, you eliminated the chaotic friction of endless micro-decisions (e.g., *Which task should I start?*). The systematic annihilation of decision points, achieved through automation and the **One-Touch Rule** (Chapter 5), conserved EF resources that were previously consumed by continuous internal negotiation.
- **Defeating Context Switching:** By enforcing **single-tasking** and **Cognitive Load Annihilation** (Chapter 5), you systematically eliminated the draining cost of **Context Switching**—the rapid shifting of attention between different cognitive demands—which incurs a measurable cognitive penalty that rapidly depletes EF reserves and leads to mental exhaustion. The strict implementation of **Notification Annihilation** protected your **Inhibitory Control (IC)**—your brain's "brakes"—from the constant temptation of novelty.

Section 2: The Emotional and Economic Payoff: Building Resilience

The structured focus achieved in this book yields profound emotional dividends, reinforcing the positive feedback loop necessary for long-term consistency and challenging a lifetime of internalized shame.

1. Defeating Shame and Building Self-Efficacy

The chronic failure to maintain focus and follow through—a frequent result of time blindness and fragmentation—is a significant driver of shame and the pervasive feeling of inadequacy for women with ADHD.

- **The Antidote to the Inner Critic:** The mastery of EF strategies replaces the long, overwhelming to-do list (a document of perceived failure) with a realistic, manageable schedule, thereby setting **achievable expectations** and reducing the likelihood of failure and self-criticism. The consistent success in meeting **Milestones** provides tangible, undeniable evidence of competence and follow-through, systematically chipping away at the internalized shame and building **self-efficacy** (the belief in one's ability to execute a plan).

- **Emotional Conservation:** The structured use of the **Pomodoro Technique**, with its mandated restorative breaks, ensures that mental energy is managed proactively, preventing the total depletion of EF reserves that leads to burnout and emotional volatility.

2. Mitigating the ADHD Tax and Economic Strain

The EF mastery achieved here translates into measurable improvements in the outside world, directly mitigating the financial and time cost of the **ADHD Tax**.

- **Economic Stability:** The use of the Milestones framework and Decision Simplification (automation) directly combats the financial costs associated with unmanaged time blindness (late fees, financial instability) and impulsivity (impulsive buying). By systematically prioritizing and meeting deadlines, you reduce the time and money wasted on compensation and mistakes, actively safeguarding your financial well-being.
- **Relational Predictability:** The predictability established through structured scheduling reduces the friction caused by forgetfulness and lateness. Furthermore, the practice of **Inhibitory Control** (Chapter 4) provides the internal capacity needed to pause before responding impulsively in relationships, which is a foundational skill for constructive communication (Book 5).

Section 3: The Bridge to Future Mastery: Preparing for Emotional Regulation

The structural stability of focus achieved in this book is the essential **prerequisite** for engaging with the complex internal work of emotional mastery (Book 4). A brain that is constantly battling chaos and cognitive fatigue lacks the resources necessary to manage intense feelings.

1. EF as the Foundation for Emotional Control

Emotional dysregulation—the most impairing symptom for many women with ADHD—is profoundly linked to the EF skills you have practiced.

- **Activating the "Brakes":** The muscle of **Inhibitory Control (IC)**, honed through resistance practice (Chapter 4), is the very same EF required for **emotional regulation**—resisting the urge to react impulsively during an intense emotional surge. Your IC practice in this book is, fundamentally, training your emotional "brakes" (the PFC) to successfully engage before the emotional accelerator (the amygdala) takes over.
- **Mindfulness and the "Pause":** The capacity for sustained, anchored attention, honed through the **Pomodoro Technique** and **Single-Tasking**, is the critical prerequisite for effective **Mindfulness** (a cornerstone of DBT / CBT). This EF skill creates the critical **"pause"** between feeling an intense emotion and reacting to it, allowing the cognitive strategies (challenging thoughts, etc.) to engage before the emotional storm takes over.

2. The Laws of Sustained Executive Function

You have transformed from a reactive participant in your life to a strategic commander of your time and attention. Your new system is governed by the following laws of sustained EF, which you must commit to maintaining:

- **Law of Finitude:** You conquer paralysis by breaking all large projects into small, finite, manageable **Milestones** and **Pomodoro sprints**.
- **Law of Conservation:** You conserve energy by ruthlessly eliminating distractions (**CL Annihilation**) and automating decisions, preserving WM and IC for high-leverage tasks.
- **Law of Proactive Structure:** You replaced vague intentions with predictable, scheduled action (**Time Blocking**), ensuring that your motivation is anchored to the external calendar, not inconsistent internal dopamine.

The stability achieved here is your most valuable asset. The mental energy that was once consumed by fighting your own brain is now a conserved resource—a stable platform upon which you can build emotional resilience (Book 4) and navigate the complex dynamics of your relationships (Book 5). This powerful new sense of competence and control is the definitive antidote to the shame and overwhelm that has characterized your struggle, equipping you for the profound work of self-mastery that lies ahead.

BOOK FOUR

SYNC HORMONES AND OPTIMIZE TREATMENT FOR THE ADHD WOMAN

INTRODUCTION

The journey toward defeating chronic overwhelm for a woman with Attention-Deficit / Hyperactivity Disorder (ADHD) requires profound mastery over the structural demands of organization and the cognitive challenges of attention (as addressed in the foundational work of the previous books). However, for women, these struggles are not static; they are dynamically and intensely influenced by a factor often overlooked in mainstream ADHD literature: the powerful and intricate ebb and flow of **hormonal cycles** throughout her entire lifespan.

For many women, living with ADHD is akin to trying to stabilize a ship in a perpetually shifting tide. They report, anecdotally, yet consistently, that their core symptoms of inattention, poor time management, anxiety, and emotional dysregulation can intensify without warning during certain times of the month or at specific life stages, such as puberty, the menstrual cycle, or perimenopause. This crucial link has historically been minimized or dismissed by medical practitioners, leading to a profound sense of not being "believed" when a woman reports that her medication efficacy fluctuates or her focus completely collapses in the days leading up to her period.

This book is a direct intervention into this critical knowledge gap. It provides an evidence-based roadmap that validates the woman's lived experience with rigorous scientific research, empowering her to understand, track, and strategically manage the dynamic role of her hormones. The goal is to move beyond the traditional, male-normed view of ADHD treatment, which often assumes a static neurochemistry, and transition to a holistic, personalized approach that accounts for the powerful hormonal reality unique to the female brain. By syncing your management strategies with your natural hormonal rhythm, you move from reacting to chaos to creating predictable, sustainable stability.

Section 1: The Gender Health Gap and the Unseen Burden

The struggle to have the hormonal connection validated is a stark symptom of the wider **gender health gap** in ADHD research. Historically, research and diagnostic criteria were developed almost exclusively using male populations, leading to a limited understanding of the nuances of female symptom presentation and the profound influence of the female endocrine system.

- **Delayed Diagnosis and Shame:** The female presentation of ADHD, often characterized by internalized struggles, pervasive inattention, disorganization, and emotional volatility, is frequently overlooked or misdiagnosed entirely as anxiety or a mood disorder. This diagnostic disparity is severe: studies confirm that women tend to be diagnosed much later than men, with some finding the mean age of diagnosis for females to be up to 28.6 years, compared to 22.7 years for males. This delayed diagnosis leaves women without a framework to understand their struggles, fueling intense internalization, shame, and a belief that their functional difficulties are personal or moral failings.
- **The Neurochemical Reality of Worsening Symptoms:** When a woman reports that her symptoms worsen cyclically, it is not subjective fluctuation; it is a measurable consequence of her neurobiology being under additional, predictable hormonal pressure. The constant pressure to meet societal expectations for organization and emotional maturity further exacerbates this struggle, compelling many women to engage in **masking**,

the exhausting effort to hide their internal chaos. This book provides the language and objective data needed to overcome this invalidation and command a tailored, individualized treatment plan.

Section 2: The Core Neurochemical Link: Estrogen, Dopamine, and Attention

To understand the profound impact of hormones on ADHD, one must first grasp the intricate link between key sex hormones and the brain's neurochemical systems, particularly **dopamine**. This neurochemical connection provides the powerful, scientific explanation for why ADHD is not a static condition in women.

1. Dopamine: The Fuel for Focus and Motivation

At the core of the ADHD experience is a distinct neurochemical reality centered on the dysregulation of **dopamine**. Often called the brain's "motivation" or "reward" chemical, dopamine is crucial for regulating attention, initiation, and sustained focus. For individuals with ADHD, this dysregulation, often manifesting as lower effective dopamine signaling in the synapses, makes it exceptionally difficult to sustain engagement on tasks that are not inherently stimulating or rewarding. This is the neurobiological basis for procrastination, inattention, and the search for novelty.

2. Estrogen: The Supportive Ally

Estrogen, a primary female sex hormone, acts as a crucial supportive ally to this system. Research has consistently shown that estrogen plays a pivotal role in regulating dopamine synthesis and activity. Higher levels of estrogen are linked to increased dopamine levels and receptor sensitivity, which provides a **protective and enhancing effect** on the brain's attentional and emotional systems. This natural boost can make executive functions feel more robust and mood more stable.

Conversely, when estrogen levels drop or fluctuate erratically, this supportive effect diminishes. Lower estrogen levels are linked to lower dopamine levels, which can dramatically exacerbate core ADHD challenges like poor motivation, inattention, and executive dysfunction. This sudden change can feel like a complete collapse of organizational capability or focus, often leading to deep frustration and renewed self-blame.

3. Progesterone: The Complicating Regulator

Progesterone, the other major female sex hormone, further complicates this dynamic. Often referred to as the "calming hormone" due to its role in boosting the inhibitory neurotransmitter GABA, progesterone regulates mood, sleep, and emotional stability. However, its influence is complex: while it promotes calm, its rise, particularly in the context of declining estrogen during the late luteal phase, can increase the sensitivity of the brain's emotional center (the amygdala). This hormonal combination can lead to increased anxiety, irritability, poor emotional regulation, and heightened sensitivity to stress, contributing to the distinct symptoms of the premenstrual phase.

Section 3: The Dynamic Lifespan: Vulnerable Phases of Hormonal Fluctuation

ADHD symptoms are known to correlate with hormonal shifts, creating distinct periods of vulnerability across a woman's entire reproductive lifespan. This dynamic nature is why a static treatment plan often fails to provide stable support.

1. Puberty: The Initial "Double Whammy"

The onset of puberty is a pivotal time when many girls, previously managing their subtle symptoms, begin to struggle. As estrogen and progesterone levels surge and fluctuate, the balance of the brain's neurochemistry is disrupted. Experts refer to this phase as a **"double whammy,"** where the combination of transient hormonal effects and long-lasting organizational changes sets the stage for increased impairment in adulthood. This hormonal shift can exacerbate ADHD symptoms, including increased irritability and impulsivity, making the girl's presentation harder to manage and often leading to misdiagnosis as a mood or anxiety disorder, further widening the diagnostic gap.

2. The Menstrual Cycle: A Monthly Challenge

The natural, rhythmic fluctuations of the menstrual cycle create a constant, predictable source of internal volatility. Research and clinical monitoring strongly suggest that attention and executive function are significantly impaired during the low-estrogen phases of the cycle.

- **The High-Risk Luteal Phase:** Symptoms demonstrably worsen during the **luteal phase**, the period immediately following ovulation and preceding menstruation, which is characterized by declining estrogen and rising progesterone. This low-estrogen environment exacerbates the existing dopaminergic dysregulation, leading to more pronounced challenges in:
  - **Inattention and Focus:** Difficulty sustaining concentration and increased distractibility.
  - **Emotional Volatility:** Heightened anxiety, irritability, and stress.
  - **Executive Function:** Worsening of organization, planning, and task initiation deficits.
- **The PMDD Intersection:** This period of vulnerability is further intensified for the significant percentage of women with ADHD who also experience **Premenstrual Dysphoric Disorder (PMDD)**, a severe form of PMS characterized by debilitating emotional and physical symptoms. The combination of ADHD and PMDD creates a neurobiological perfect storm that makes emotional regulation nearly impossible during the premenstrual days.

3. Perimenopause and Menopause: The "ADHD Squared" Effect

The hormonal influence culminates in midlife, during the transition into **perimenopause and menopause**. As estrogen and progesterone levels undergo a significant, sustained decline, underlying ADHD symptoms that a woman may have compensated for throughout her life often become unmanageable.

- **Cognitive Collapse:** Experts refer to this as the **"ADHD squared"** effect, the compounding of already low dopamine with the sustained decline of estrogen. The symptoms of menopause, such as **"brain fog," memory lapses, poor organization, and difficulty with concentration**, often mirror and drastically intensify the symptoms of ADHD, leading to a confusing and frustrating experience that can feel like early-onset dementia.

- **Emotional Vulnerability:** The decline in progesterone during this phase further exacerbates anxiety, irritability, and emotional dysregulation by reducing its supportive, calming effect on the nervous system (GABA). This loss of neurochemical buffer makes the woman more susceptible to stress and emotional overwhelm, highlighting the intense need for individualized, integrated treatment.

Section 4: Implications for Optimized Treatment and Self-Advocacy

The knowledge of this hormonal connection is the key to moving from reactive coping to proactive, personalized treatment. You are now equipped to advocate for a plan that is dynamic, not static, addressing a long-standing **gender health gap** in medical care.

1. Cycle Dosing: Tailoring Medication Efficacy

One of the most critical implications of this research is the finding that the effectiveness of stimulant medication used to treat ADHD may be **menstrual cycle-dependent**. Because estrogen influences the dopamine system that these medications target, the natural decline in estrogen during the low-estrogen phases can lead to a diminished response to the stimulant, causing a temporary, frustrating return of symptoms.

- **The Guidance for Personalization:** Clinical observations and preliminary studies strongly suggest the potential benefit of **"cycle dosing"**, tailoring medication dosages to a woman's hormonal status, often involving a slight increase in dose during the premenstrual week when symptoms and medication challenges are most pronounced. This must be implemented only under the supervision of a specialized physician, but the evidence empowers the woman to initiate the conversation for a safe, optimal, and individualized treatment approach.
- **HRT Integration:** For women in perimenopause and menopause, combining **Hormone Replacement Therapy (HRT)** to increase estrogen with existing ADHD medication often yields the most effective improvement in memory, reasoning, and overall symptom control, demonstrating the critical interplay between neurochemistry and endocrinology.

2. The Power of Tracking: Moving from Anecdote to Data

The most powerful tool a woman possesses in this journey is objective data collection. For years, women were dismissed because their reports were subjective. Now, you can transform that anecdotal experience into undeniable evidence.

- **The Symptom Log:** By diligently tracking your menstrual cycle alongside your ADHD symptoms (inattention score, anxiety level, medication efficacy) for two to three months, you create a clear, measurable pattern. This data provides the concrete proof necessary to validate your experience and present an informed, strategic request to your healthcare provider for a dosage adjustment or personalized therapy plan.
- **The Bridge to Self-Compassion:** Tracking shifts the narrative from "I am failing to focus" to **"My body is currently experiencing a neurochemical shift due to lower estrogen levels, and this is a predictable, manageable challenge."** This perspective fosters **self-compassion**, recognizing that the struggle is a neurobiological reality, not a moral failure, and actively counters the shame that has long accompanied the female ADHD experience.

Section 5: The Holistic Path: Building Resilience Against Fluctuations

The structural stability achieved through organization and focus (Books 1 and 3) is the vital buffer that prevents hormonal fluctuations from leading to emotional or cognitive collapse. Sustaining hormonal harmony requires a proactive, holistic commitment to physiological self-care.

- **Proactive Scheduling:** Use the Time Blocking skills (Book 3) to strategically schedule high-leverage, cognitively demanding tasks (e.g., report writing, complex planning) during the high-estrogen phases and save routine, low-energy tasks (e.g., administrative work, organizing simple areas) for the challenging low-estrogen phases. This works with, rather than against, your fluctuating energy.

- **Physiological Buffering:** Prioritize factors that stabilize neurochemistry. Consistent, high-quality **sleep hygiene** is crucial, as sleep deprivation exacerbates both ADHD and hormonal symptoms. Regular **physical exercise** is a potent, natural tool for regulating dopamine levels, reducing restlessness, and improving mood, acting as a direct buffer against the emotional volatility of the luteal phase.
- **Stress Management:** High stress levels further disrupt hormonal balance and cognitive function. Maintaining a low baseline of stress through the elimination of chaos (Book 1) and the use of **mindfulness and grounding techniques** is crucial for protecting the Executive Functions that hormonal dips make vulnerable.

Conclusion: A Holistic Approach to Hormonal Harmony

The journey through this book provides a groundbreaking validation of the female ADHD experience. You have learned that your symptoms are not static; they are dynamic, measurable, and profoundly influenced by the ebb and flow of your hormonal cycles.

By understanding the neurochemical link between estrogen and dopamine, navigating the vulnerabilities of the menstrual cycle and menopause, and embracing the necessity of personalized treatment and proactive self-care, you move from feeling powerless against your symptoms to a place of informed, strategic action. This knowledge empowers you to command a truly holistic treatment plan, ensuring that your journey toward balance is not a rigid prescription but a dynamic, lifelong process that accounts for the complete reality of your unique neurobiology.

The harmony you cultivate here is the essential foundation for the intense internal work that follows: managing the unique emotional volatility and building the robust, stable connections that define integrated success.

CHAPTER 1

MAP YOUR CYCLE: TRACK SYMPTOMS TO PINPOINT HORMONAL HIGH-RISK DAYS

The journey to achieve sustainable calm and focus requires the integration of all facets of your neurobiology. As established in previous books, structural stability (Book 1) and cognitive command (Book 3) are essential, but for the female brain, these efforts are continuously modulated by the predictable, powerful rhythm of your **hormonal cycle**. For women with Attention-Deficit / Hyperactivity Disorder (ADHD), core symptoms, inattention, anxiety, and emotional volatility, are not static; they intensify dynamically with the ebb and flow of **Estrogen** and **Progesterone**.

This chapter provides the critical first step in taking command of this dynamic system: the transformation of subjective experience into objective, actionable data. By systematically tracking your menstrual cycle alongside your Executive Function (EF) deficits and emotional shifts, you move from feeling like a victim of unpredictable chaos to becoming a strategic commander of your own physiology. This data is the single most powerful tool for **self-advocacy**, enabling you to identify your personalized **Vulnerability Window**—the high-risk days when low estrogen levels demand a strategic adjustment to your work, self-care, and treatment protocols.

The goal is not to eliminate hormonal shifts, but to **anticipate** them. By recognizing the pattern, you neutralize the shame that accompanies the sudden, overwhelming dips in performance, allowing you to replace self-criticism with strategic self-compassion and proactive buffering.

Section 1: The Neurobiological Blueprint of the Monthly Shift

The need for cycle tracking is rooted in the measurable neurochemical reality of how ovarian hormones interact with the brain's attention system, which is already dysregulated in ADHD. This interaction provides the scientific basis for the worsening of symptoms.

1. The Low-Estrogen Trigger: Dopamine Diminishment

The effectiveness of the brain's attention and motivation system is highly dependent on **dopamine**. Since ADHD is fundamentally characterized by dopamine dysregulation, the supporting role of **Estrogen**, which increases dopamine synthesis and receptor sensitivity, is critical.

- **The Follicular Advantage:** During the late follicular phase (pre-ovulation), when estrogen levels are high and steadily rising, women often report experiencing a period of relative cognitive clarity and focus, and may find it easier to stay organized. This high-estrogen environment provides a **neurochemical buffer**, offering temporary support to the dopamine system, which can enhance motivation and Executive Functions.
- **The Luteal Collapse (The Vulnerability Window):** The challenge emerges during the **luteal phase** (post-ovulation and pre-menstruation), which is characterized by a significant drop in estrogen and a sharp rise in **Progesterone**. As estrogen diminishes, its supportive effect on the dopamine system collapses, exacerbating the underlying dopaminergic deficit of

ADHD. This predictable neurochemical dip leads to a pronounced worsening of core ADHD symptoms, including:

- **Exacerbated Inattention:** Difficulty sustaining focus and planning, and increased distractibility.
- **Emotional Volatility:** Heightened irritability, anxiety, and stress, often linked to the drop in the supportive, calming effects of progesterone on GABA.

This phenomenon is not anecdotal; studies suggest that within-person declines in estrogen are associated with **meaningful increases in ADHD symptoms** (specifically hyperactivity-impulsivity post-ovulation and inattention perimenstrually). Recognizing this pattern transforms a confusing, painful experience into a predictable neurobiological event that can be planned for.

2. The Link to Emotional Dysregulation and PMDD

The cyclic hormonal shifts intensify the most impairing aspects of female ADHD, particularly emotional dysregulation. For women with ADHD, this struggle is often compounded by a high incidence of **Premenstrual Dysphoric Disorder (PMDD)**, a severe form of PMS.

- **Emotional Amplification:** The low-estrogen, high-progesterone environment of the late luteal phase makes the brain's emotional center (the amygdala) more reactive while simultaneously reducing the inhibitory control of the prefrontal cortex. This combination leads to rapid, unpredictable mood shifts, where minor triggers can escalate into a disproportionate emotional storm, the "green-to-red" phenomenon often reported by those with emotional dysregulation.
- **Heightened Sensitivity:** This period of heightened emotional vulnerability also exacerbates sensitivity to perceived criticism or rejection, magnifying the debilitating pain of **Rejection Sensitive Dysphoria (RSD)**. During the vulnerability window, a woman may be more prone to catastrophizing and internalizing negative feedback, reinforcing the cycle of shame and self-blame.

Section 2: The Tracking Toolkit: From Anecdote to Objective Data

The most powerful form of self-advocacy and strategic management is moving from subjective reports of feeling "bad" to objective data that clearly identifies the correlation between your cycle day and symptom severity. Tracking is the process of building an **objective, measurable pattern** that your Executive Function can use to plan and that your doctor must respect.

1. Designing Your Symptom Log (The Four-Point Data Set)

Your log must track four key data points simultaneously to reveal the pattern:

Data Point	What to Track	Why It Matters
1. Cycle Day	Track Day 1 as the first day of your period (menses). This is the anchor for all subsequent hormonal phases.	Pinpoints the predictable decline in estrogen that triggers the dip.
2. Core ADHD Symptoms (Cognitive)	Rate Inattention, Task Initiation, and Working Memory (Forgetfulness) using a consistent scale (e.g., 1 to 5, where 5 is Severe).	Quantifies the functional impact on productivity and focus.
3. Emotional / Physical Symptoms	Rate Irritability / Anxiety, Fatigue / Brain Fog, and Sleep Quality (1 to 5).	Identifies the compounding effect of low Progesterone / low Estrogen on mood and energy.
4. Medication Efficacy	Rate how effective your stimulant medication feels each day (1 to 5, where 1 is Highly Effective, 5 is Ineffective).	Provides the necessary data for discussing **cycle dosing** options with your physician.

Consistency is the Goal: The tracking does not need to be complex; a simple journal or a dedicated app is sufficient. The key is to rate your symptoms **at the same time each day** (e.g., end of the workday) for a minimum of two to three full cycles. This consistency ensures the data is reliable and not influenced by transient events.

2. Pinpointing Your Vulnerability Window

After two cycles, review your data log to identify the predictable **Vulnerability Window**, the high-risk phase where scores for Inattention and Irritability consistently spike (e.g., Days 22–28, or the final week before menses).

- **Predictability is Power:** By pinpointing this window, you gain the ability to **anticipate** the dip. This pre-knowledge is an immense act of self-compassion, as it transforms the sudden onset of chaos into a predictable event. Instead of internalizing the sudden inability to focus as "I am falling apart," the thought becomes, "This is Cycle Day 24; my estrogen is low, and my system needs to buffer."
- **Strategic Planning Anchor:** This window now becomes the central anchor for your **Optimize Your Flow** plan (Chapter 2). During these days, you know you must enforce your external EF scaffolding (Time Blocking, micro-steps) more rigorously and reduce external demands to protect your finite energy reserves.

Section 3: Data as Self-Advocacy: Overcoming the Gender Health Gap

The intentional collection of objective data is the most crucial tool in navigating the often-skeptical medical environment and addressing the historical lack of research into female-specific ADHD symptoms, the **gender health gap**.

1. Challenging the Narrative of Dismissal

For years, women were dismissed because their reports were subjective. Clinicians often lack training in the dynamic relationship between hormones and neurochemistry, relying instead on a static model of ADHD.

- **From Anecdote to Evidence:** Your Symptom Log provides the concrete evidence needed to shift the conversation from general mood reporting to a specific correlation between hormonal status and functional impairment. You are presenting **measurable data** that demands a tailored response, effectively bypassing the historical tendency toward dismissal.
- **Targeted Request:** Instead of saying, "My medication doesn't work right before my period," the advocacy statement becomes: "My data shows that during Cycle Days 22–28, my average Inattention score increases by 4 points, and my stimulant efficacy drops by 50%. I would like to discuss evidence-based options for managing this predictable impairment, starting with cycle dosing."

2. The Intersection of ADHD and PMDD

For a significant number of women, the symptoms of the Vulnerability Window are so severe they align with **Premenstrual Dysphoric Disorder (PMDD).** Tracking is essential here because PMDD, like ADHD, is a condition rooted in neurochemical sensitivity, and its high co-occurrence with ADHD creates a perfect storm of emotional and cognitive distress.

- **Dual Diagnosis:** Tracking allows you to isolate the predictable, cyclical nature of severe mood swings, hopelessness, and intense irritability. This data is critical for seeking a PMDD diagnosis alongside your ADHD, which can open up specialized treatment options (often involving SSRIs or hormonal contraceptives) tailored to stabilize the emotional volatility of the luteal phase, thereby reducing the stress that exacerbates your core ADHD symptoms.

Section 4: The Emotional Payoff: Self-Compassion and Predictability

The most profound outcome of cycle tracking is the liberation from shame and the cultivation of radical self-compassion.

1. Neutralizing Shame with Knowledge

For the woman with ADHD, the sudden, unpredictable collapse of focus and control leads to immediate **shame** and internal judgment ("I'm a failure," "I'm lazy").

- **Anticipation is Self-Kindness:** By anticipating the symptom spike, you neutralize the shame. You replace the harsh self-judgment with **radical acceptance**, acknowledging the reality of the emotional / cognitive state without judgment. The thought is transformed from: *"Why can't I just focus today? I'm useless."* to *"Ah, my energy is low because my body is following a predictable hormonal rhythm. I need to pivot to a lower-effort task and engage my self-care buffer."*
- **Conserving Emotional Energy:** This compassionate response stops the cascade of self-criticism and stress, which would otherwise consume the limited emotional bandwidth required for resilience. You conserve vital emotional energy by refusing to fight against a temporary, neurobiological reality.

2. The Bridge to Long-Term Resilience

The data collected in this chapter is the essential link that connects all the pillars of this guide. It allows you to transform the external stability of time and focus management (Book 3) into a flexible, dynamic system that is resilient to internal volatility. You are using the language of science to honor the unique complexity of your brain and body, creating a foundation for true, integrated hormonal harmony.

Chapter 1 Workbook: Map Your Cycle: Track Symptoms to Pinpoint Hormonal High-Risk Days

Objective: To systematically collect objective data on how hormonal fluctuations impact ADHD symptoms and cognitive function, transforming subjective experience into actionable evidence.

Scientific Anchor: Tracking links perceived symptoms (e.g., anxiety, inattention) to measurable hormonal phases, providing the evidence needed to predict symptom spikes (especially in the low-estrogen luteal phase) and advocate for tailored support.

Activity 1.1: The Monthly Symptom / Cycle Tracker (Initial Audit)

Instructions: Commit to tracking for 30 consecutive days (Cycle Day 1 is the first day of your period). Use a scale of 1 (Minimal Impact) to 5 (Severe / Debilitating Impact) for consistency.

1. **Identify High-Risk Symptoms:** List the three ADHD symptoms that cause you the most distress during your known challenging times.

   Symptom 1 (Cognitive / Focus): ______________________________

   ____

   ____

   Symptom 2 (Emotional / Mood): ______________________________

   ____

   ____

   Symptom 3 (Functional / Task Initiation): ____________________

   ____

   ____

2. **Daily Tracking Log (Sample):** Record your data daily. After 30 days, identify your **Vulnerability Window** (the 3 to 7 days where the scores are consistently highest).

Cycle Day	Symptom 1 (Focus Score 1-5)	Symptom 2 (Irritability Score 1-5)	Medication Efficacy (1-5)	Notes (e.g., High Stress Day, Poor Sleep)
Day 1 (Period Start)				
Day 14 (Approx. Ovulation)				

Day 24 (Late Luteal)				
Day 28 (Premenstrual)				

Activity 1.2: Identifying Your Vulnerability Window

Instructions: Based on your completed 30-day log, review the data to pinpoint the predictable window where your EF and emotional resilience consistently dip.

1. **Peak Impairment Window:** Identify the range of days where your symptoms (scores of 4 or 5) consistently spike.

   My Vulnerability Window (Cycle Days):

   From Day ____

   To Day ____

2. **The Neurobiological Cause:** During this window, what functional change do you feel is the most detrimental (e.g., Working Memory collapses, or Task Activation is impossible)?

   Functional Collapse: _______________________________

   ____

   ____

   ____

   ____

Reflection 1.3: Data as Self-Advocacy

Instructions: Reflect on how this objective data shifts your emotional narrative and empowers your treatment plan, transforming anecdote into evidence.

1. **Shift from Shame:** Before tracking, when your symptoms worsened, what was your automatic internal thought (e.g., "I'm falling apart," "I can't handle this")?

   Old Thought: ____

   ____

   ____

   ____

2. **New Narrative:** How does having the **objective data** from your log allow you to replace that thought with a compassionate, non-judgmental, neurobiological explanation (e.g., "My estrogen is low; this dip is predictable")?

   New, Empowered Narrative: ____________________________

   ____

   ____

   ____

3. **Advocacy Preparation:** Create one specific, data-informed sentence you can now use to start a conversation with your healthcare provider about your symptoms during the Luteal Phase.

   Advocacy Sentence (e.g., "My tracking data shows a 40% drop in focus during Days X-Y, which aligns with low estrogen. What are our options for addressing this?"):

CHAPTER 2

OPTIMIZE YOUR FLOW: STRATEGICALLY SCHEDULE TASKS AROUND ENERGY PEAKS

In Chapter 1, you achieved the critical first step in managing hormonal chaos: systematic tracking of your cycle and the objective identification of your **Vulnerability Window**, the high-risk days characterized by low estrogen and a corresponding dip in neurochemical support. This data transforms your struggle from a confusing, subjective experience into a predictable, measurable pattern that demands strategic action.

This chapter moves from data collection to **strategic application**. The goal is to leverage the robust scheduling skills you mastered in Book 3 (**Time Blocking**, **Task Breakdown**) to intentionally **Optimize Your Flow** by aligning your cognitive demands with your hormonal energy peaks and troughs. This practice, often referred to as **Cycle Syncing**, is the definitive method for transforming unpredictable internal volatility into a manageable, structured rhythm. It is a necessary intervention for the

ADHD brain, whose executive functions (EFs) are already inconsistent and become exacerbated by hormonal shifts.

For the woman with Attention-Deficit / Hyperactivity Disorder (ADHD), the key to defeating chronic overwhelm is to stop fighting her fluctuating neurochemical energy and start working *with* her unique neurobiology. By proactively scheduling high-leverage, complex tasks during periods of natural cognitive enhancement (high-estrogen phases) and reserving low-stakes, routine tasks for periods of inevitable cognitive drain (low-estrogen phases), you systematically buffer the impact of hormonal shifts, conserve precious mental energy, and achieve a sustainable state of control.

Section 1: The Neurochemistry of Cognitive Peaks and Troughs

The foundation of flow optimization lies in recognizing the distinct cognitive profiles associated with the two main phases of the menstrual cycle, the **Follicular Phase** and the **Luteal Phase**. These differences are a direct result of the varying levels of **Estrogen** and **Progesterone** and their powerful influence on the brain's neurotransmitter systems.

1. Estrogen: The Fuel for Focus and Organization

Estrogen, the primary hormone of the first half of the cycle, is a powerful ally to the ADHD brain. Research consistently confirms that estrogen plays a pivotal role in regulating the synthesis and activity of **dopamine**, the key neurotransmitter for attention, motivation, and Executive Function. Given that ADHD is fundamentally characterized by dopamine dysregulation, the level of estrogen directly dictates the brain's baseline capacity for focus and organization.

- **High Estrogen (Follicular / Ovulatory Phase):** When estrogen levels are high and rising (during the late follicular phase, leading up to ovulation), women often report finding it **easier to focus, sustain attention, stay organized, and engage in high-level cognitive tasks**. This is the period of peak cognitive function, your natural productivity advantage, making it ideal for deep work, planning, and problem-solving.
- **Low Estrogen (Luteal / Perimenstrual Phase):** The symptoms spike during the **luteal phase** (post-ovulation and preceding menstruation), which is characterized by a significant drop in

estrogen. As estrogen diminishes, its supportive effect on the dopamine system collapses, exacerbating the underlying dopaminergic deficit of ADHD. This predictable neurochemical dip leads to a pronounced worsening of core ADHD symptoms, including **inattention, organization deficits, and executive dysfunction**.

2. Progesterone: The Complicating Factor in Emotional Regulation

Progesterone, which rises significantly during the **Luteal Phase**, further complicates the cognitive and emotional landscape. While often termed the "calming hormone" due to its role in boosting the inhibitory neurotransmitter GABA, its sustained presence in the context of declining estrogen leads to distinct challenges for the emotionally vulnerable ADHD brain:

- **Emotional Volatility:** The low-estrogen environment, coupled with the influence of progesterone, can increase the sensitivity of the brain's emotional center (the amygdala), leading to heightened irritability, anxiety, and low frustration tolerance.
- **Mental Sluggishness ("Brain Fog"):** The decline in both estrogen and progesterone in the late luteal / perimenstrual phase directly contributes to the feeling of **"brain fog,"** increased forgetfulness, mental fatigue, and sleep disturbances, which further impair focus and memory, core EF skills already challenged by ADHD.

The intentional goal of flow optimization is to use the structural integrity of your schedule (Time Blocking) to buffer these neurochemical dips, preventing the **Vulnerability Window** from triggering functional collapse and emotional overwhelm.

Section 2: The Cycle Syncing Framework: Aligning Task Demand

Cycle Syncing is the strategic process of aligning the **demand** of your scheduled tasks with the **supply** of your neurochemical energy. This framework utilizes the predictable energy shifts to schedule work that is easiest for your brain to manage in that specific phase, conserving your limited EF when support is low.

1. Phase 1: The Follicular / Ovulatory Phase (Peak Cognitive Function)

When: Typically from the end of the period until ovulation (approximately Days 6–14). Estrogen levels are rising or high.

Cognitive Profile: This is your **peak cognitive window**. Attention is generally more stable, motivation is higher (dopamine supported), and executive functions are most robust. You possess the greatest capacity for deep, sustained work and resistance to frustration.

Strategic Task Scheduling (High-Leverage Work):

- **Deep Work and Focused Sprints:** Schedule your most complex, cognitively demanding tasks, such as report writing, coding, complex planning, studying, and learning new skills. Utilize your longest **Pomodoro sprints** (e.g., 45–50 minutes) during this time, maximizing the mental acuity provided by high estrogen.
- **Goal Setting and Planning:** Dedicate time for strategic planning, setting major goals, tackling ambiguous projects (which require high EF), and initiating new creative work.
- **Communication and Socializing:** Schedule high-stakes meetings, difficult conversations, or challenging social engagements, as your emotional regulation, confidence, and verbal fluency are at their best.

2. Phase 2: The Luteal / Perimenstrual Phase (Strategic Conservation)

When: Typically from post-ovulation until the start of the period (approximately Days 15–28). Estrogen is dropping, and symptoms are worsening. This is your **Vulnerability Window** identified in Chapter 1.

Cognitive Profile: This is your low-energy phase. Focus, working memory, and emotional regulation dip. Irritability, anxiety, and task initiation deficits (paralysis) increase. The brain is conserving energy due to low estrogen support.

Strategic Task Scheduling (Low-Friction / Routine Work):

- **Routine and Maintenance:** Prioritize low-stakes, routine, and highly structured maintenance tasks that require minimal EF input. Examples include filing, performing the **Daily 15-Minute**

Reset (Book 1), simple administrative chores, running established errands, or answering low-priority emails.

- **Review and Editing:** Schedule tasks that require detailed, but non-creative, focus—such as proofreading, editing a report drafted in the Follicular Phase, or organizing established systems (e.g., sorting the Junk Drawer).
- **Self-Care and Recovery:** Schedule mandatory blocks for rest, relaxation, and proactive stress management. This is the time to aggressively enforce boundaries and decline commitments that will overextend your limited EF reserves.

Section 3: Tactical Adaptation of Executive Function Tools

The Time Blocking system you built in Book 3 must be flexible enough to adapt its parameters during the low-energy Luteal Phase. Successfully optimizing your flow requires modifying your approach to planning and focus based on your current neurochemical reality.

1. Adjusting Time Blocks and Buffers (Chapter 1, Book 3)

During the Luteal Phase, the **Estimation Deficit**, the tendency to underestimate task duration, is likely to be exacerbated by mental fatigue and compromised Working Memory. Your scheduled blocks must adjust proactively.

- **Increase the Estimation Buffer:** Double your usual time buffer. If you typically schedule 25% extra time for a task, increase it to **50% extra time** during the Vulnerability Window. Acknowledge that the process of loading information into your working memory will be slower, and transitions will be harder. This proactive adjustment reduces the stress of rushing, which would otherwise compound EF deficits.
- **Shorter, More Frequent Transition Blocks:** The high cognitive cost of **context switching** is intensified when focus is low. Schedule a **mandatory 10-minute break** between all major time blocks, rather than the standard 5-minute break. Use this time for physical movement (a brief walk) or sensory grounding to clear the mental slate before the next activity, conserving EF.

- **Color-Code for Energy:** When creating your time-blocked calendar, use a specific color (e.g., red or gray) to designate the high-risk Luteal Phase days, serving as a constant **external cue** to manage expectations for performance and prioritize self-compassion.

2. Modifying the Pomodoro Technique (Chapter 3, Book 3)

The customized Pomodoro cycle must contract during the low-energy phase to maintain its effectiveness and prevent burnout. The goal is to maximize the short bursts of attention available.

- **Contract the Work Sprint:** If your optimal work sprint is usually 45 minutes, contract it to **20 or 25 minutes** during the low-energy window. The commitment must feel short and finite to overcome the **task activation deficit** (paralysis) that flares up when motivation is low.
- **Lengthen the Break (Intentional Recovery):** Increase the break duration to 7 or 10 minutes. Use this mandated time for active recovery, movement, stretching, or engaging in a simple, non-productive reward. This intentional recovery period counteracts the high levels of **mental fatigue** that accompany the drop in estrogen, providing the novelty needed for the ADHD brain to re-engage.
- **Anchor with External Accountability:** During the low-motivation Luteal Phase, the need for **external scaffolding** is highest. Proactively schedule Body Doubling sessions (Book 1) for the tasks that you know will be difficult to initiate, as the presence of a non-judgmental peer provides the external executive function necessary to bridge the gap between intention and action.

Section 4: Holistic Buffering: Protecting Vulnerable Energy

Optimizing your flow is not just about moving tasks on a calendar; it is about building holistic resilience against the stress and emotional volatility that impair executive functions. When hormonal support is low, proactive self-care becomes the most critical EF strategy.

1. Prioritizing Sleep Hygiene and Physiological Support

Quality sleep and stable physical health are the non-negotiable foundations for robust EF and mood regulation. Sleep deprivation exacerbates both ADHD and hormonal symptoms.

- **The Circadian Anchor:** Enforce strict, consistent sleep hygiene, particularly during the Vulnerability Window, by maintaining a fixed bedtime and wake time. This regularity helps anchor the brain's circadian rhythm, which is vital for stabilizing the neurochemistry that governs attention and mood.
- **Movement for Neurochemistry:** Regular **physical exercise** is a potent, evidence-based tool for regulating dopamine levels, reducing restlessness, and improving mood, acting as a direct buffer against the emotional volatility of the luteal phase. Schedule a brisk walk or light exercise during this time, ensuring movement is prioritized over static work.
- **Nutritional Stability:** Maintain stable blood sugar levels through consistent consumption of lean protein and complex carbohydrates. Avoiding the sharp energy spikes and crashes from excessive sugar intake is essential, as these crashes exacerbate EF and mood deficits, particularly when estrogen levels are already low.

2. Enforcing Emotional Boundaries and Self-Compassion

Stress consumes immense EF resources. During the high-risk Luteal Phase, you must ruthlessly enforce boundaries to minimize stress and engage compassionate self-talk.

- **Enforce the Boundary Matrix:** Limit exposure to emotionally taxing situations and people (Q3 demands) that are harder to handle when emotional regulation is compromised by hormonal shifts. Use the prioritization frameworks from Book 3 to confidently decline external demands that would overwhelm your schedule.
- **Mindfulness and Stress Reduction:** Schedule brief, non-negotiable **mindfulness practices**, such as deep breathing or the 5-4-3-2-1 grounding exercise, to manage the increased anxiety and internal restlessness. The goal is to prevent the

physiological arousal of stress from further depleting your already limited EF reserves.

- **Radical Acceptance:** When a symptom spike occurs during the Vulnerability Window, the response is not criticism, but **self-compassion**, treating yourself with the same kindness and understanding you would offer a friend. This compassionate response stops the cascade of self-criticism and stress, which would otherwise consume the limited emotional bandwidth required for resilience. The narrative shifts from "I am failing" to "My body is following a predictable pattern."

Conclusion: Sustaining Predictability in a Dynamic System

The journey of optimizing your flow is the definitive step toward integrated self-mastery for the ADHD woman. By recognizing the profound, dynamic influence of your hormones on your executive functions, you stop fighting against your own neurobiology and start building a supportive, resilient framework.

You have learned to align the powerful, external structure of **Time Blocking** with the internal reality of your **hormonal cycle**. This strategic approach ensures that the mental energy you conserved through organization and focus mastery is deployed with maximum efficiency. You are moving from a frantic cycle of reactive overwhelm and symptom spikes to a calm, self-directed rhythm that honors your brain's unique need for both structure and self-compassion.

This mastery of cyclical stability is the essential platform for the high-stakes conversations that follow, advocating for medication adjustment (Chapter 3) and navigating the profound cognitive shifts of perimenopause (Chapter 4), and for engaging in the deep emotional work of the rest of the guide.

Chapter 2 Workbook: Optimize Your Flow: Strategically Schedule Tasks Around Energy Peaks

Objective: To practice aligning cognitive demands with the specific energy peaks and troughs of your Follicular (High Energy) and Luteal (Low Energy) phases.

Scientific Anchor: Strategically scheduling high-demand tasks during high-estrogen phases and low-demand tasks during low-estrogen phases conserves EF resources and reduces the shame of underperformance, providing a necessary buffer against hormonal shifts.

Activity 2.1: The Task Alignment Audit

Instructions: Identify the cognitive demands of your common tasks and assign them to the most supportive hormonal phase.

1. **Follicular / Ovulatory Phase (High Energy / Focus):** List three tasks requiring high **Working Memory, planning, or Inhibitory Control**.

   Task 1 (Example: Financial Planning / Budgeting):

   Task 2 (Complex Communication / Deep Work):

   Task 3 (Goal Setting / Strategy):

   ----

2. **Luteal / Vulnerability Phase (Low Energy / Routine):** List three tasks requiring minimal cognitive effort or tasks that are routine and established (low activation energy).

   Task 1 (Routine Maintenance): (Example: Filing receipts, simple chores.)

   Task 2 (Low-Cognitive Output / Review):

   Task 3 (Self-Care / Recovery):

Activity 2.2: Adapting Your Time Block Parameters

Instructions: Select a standard, recurring task (e.g., "Work on project X"). Show how you will change the **Time Block** and **Pomodoro** parameters during your identified **Vulnerability Window** (Luteal Phase) to compensate for low focus.

1. Standard Follicular Phase (High Focus):

Time Block / Interval	Duration	Neuro-Adjustment
Core Work Block	90 minutes	Standard commitment.
Pomodoro Cycle	45 min Work / 5 min Rest	Long, sustained effort.
Time Buffer	15% extra time	Standard Estimation Buffer.

2. Luteal / Vulnerability Phase (Low Focus):

Time Block / Interval	Duration	Neuro-Adjustment (The Buffer)
Core Work Block	90 minutes	Reduce work time to **60 minutes** or break into shorter blocks.
Pomodoro Cycle	Min Work ____ Min Rest _____	Contract work sprint (e.g., 20 / 10) to honor low focus and lengthen break for recovery.
Time Buffer	Extra time _____%	Increase buffer to 50% extra time for slow processing / fatigue.

Reflection 2.3: Shifting from Shame to Acceptance

Instructions: Reflect on how proactive planning impacts the emotional burden of performance.

1. **Defeating the Inner Critic:** When you fail to complete a complex task during the Luteal Phase, the inner critic often says, "You're useless, you should be able to do this." How does the simple act of looking at your calendar and seeing the block color-coded as "Low-Energy / High-Risk" provide a compassionate, factual response to that critic?

   Factual Response: ____

   ____

   ____

   ____

2. **Conserving Energy:** How does scheduling intentional, low-friction tasks (like maintenance) during the Luteal Phase contribute to your overall **Executive Function conservation**?

   EF Conservation: ____

   ____

   ____

   ____

3. **Future-Proofing:** What is one specific, non-work activity (e.g., physical movement, social buffer) that you will now **proactively schedule** during your next Vulnerability Window to act as a buffer against emotional volatility?

   Scheduled Buffer: ____

   ____

   ____

   ____

CHAPTER 3

ADVOCATE FOR ADJUSTMENT: DISCUSS CYCLE DOSING OF STIMULANTS WITH YOUR DOCTOR

You have successfully achieved the essential foundation of hormonal self-management: objective tracking of your cycle and the identification of your **Vulnerability Window**, the high-risk days when low estrogen causes a predictable collapse in focus, organization, and emotional resilience (Chapter 1). This data is not just for internal use; it is your single most powerful tool for **self-advocacy** in the medical setting.

This chapter addresses the critical next step: translating your personal data into an informed discussion with your healthcare provider about **optimizing your pharmacological treatment**. The traditional, male-normed approach to ADHD often assumes a static effective dose of medication, but a woman's neurochemistry is dynamic, fluctuating monthly with her hormones. The goal is to initiate a dialogue about **Cycle Dosing**, tailoring the dose of psychostimulants to align with your hormonal status, a strategy that addresses the documented **gender health gap** and aims to stabilize your cognitive function during your most challenging days.

This is a powerful act of informed self-care, moving you from passively accepting a fluctuating standard of care to proactively commanding a treatment plan that is personalized, dynamic, and neurobiologically accurate.

Section 1: The Neurochemical Reality of Medication Efficacy

The anecdotal experience of many women, that their ADHD medication seems to "stop working" in the days leading up to their period, is validated by the core neurochemistry of ADHD and the hormonal cycle. This phenomenon has a clear, scientific basis rooted in the interaction between estrogen and dopamine.

1. Estrogen's Role in Stimulant Response

Stimulant medications, such as amphetamines, work by increasing the availability and efficacy of **dopamine** and **norepinephrine** in the brain, thereby improving attention and executive function. However, the efficacy of this process is not independent of hormonal context.

- **Dopamine Dependence:** Estrogen acts as a supportive ally to the dopamine system, enhancing dopamine synthesis and receptor sensitivity.
- **Diminished Response:** Research, including clinical monitoring and preliminary studies, suggests that during the **late luteal phase** (the days preceding menstruation), the significant drop in estrogen levels diminishes this supportive effect. This hormonal drop can reduce the overall dopamine baseline, making the prescribed static dose of psychostimulant medication less effective at managing symptoms.
- **The Symptom Spike:** Consequently, during this low-estrogen phase, women often report a return or worsening of core ADHD symptoms, including pronounced **inattention, task paralysis, and emotional volatility**, even while taking their regular medication.

This neurochemical reality provides the foundation for demanding a dynamic, rather than static, approach to dosage.

2. The Unmet Need and the Gender Health Gap

The recognition of this cycle-dependent efficacy highlights a significant **gender health gap** in ADHD treatment. For decades, the fluctuations experienced by women were often dismissed as subjective or attributed to premenstrual moodiness, leaving a major unmet clinical need.

- **Lack of Research:** Only a very limited number of studies have formally investigated the effects of sex hormones on stimulants in women with ADHD, and even fewer have provided specific treatment recommendations tailored to the menstrual cycle.
- **Mismatched Treatment:** The current standard of care, a fixed, unchanging dose, is often mismatched to the dynamic neurobiological reality of the menstruating female brain, potentially leading to unnecessary suffering and self-blame during the high-risk Luteal Phase.

Section 2: The Strategy of Cycle Dosing

Cycle dosing refers to the clinical strategy of tailoring psychostimulant medication dosages to align with a woman's hormonal status. This approach aims to proactively counteract the anticipated neurochemical dip before symptoms intensify.

1. The Rationale for Dose Adjustment

The goal of increasing the dose during the vulnerability window is to compensate for the reduction in estrogen's supportive effect, thereby stabilizing the dopamine system and preventing the symptomatic collapse that typically occurs premenstrually.

- **Targeted Intervention:** Preliminary studies suggest that increasing the dosage of psychostimulant medication premenstrually may help combat the worsening of cognitive and emotional symptoms in vulnerable women with ADHD. This strategy offers a more refined, individualized approach to treatment, addressing a period where treatment outcome is often compromised.

- **Clinical Guidance:** While extensive research is still required, clinical monitoring and small studies provide guidance for the management of women with ADHD, suggesting that dosage adjustments in the late luteal phase may be beneficial for those who experience predictable, clinically significant symptom worsening.

2. The Necessity of Physician Oversight

Crucially, cycle dosing must be individually explored and implemented only under the close supervision of a physician or psychiatrist specialized in adult female ADHD. The process is highly individualized and depends on the specific medication, dosage, and a woman's unique symptom profile.

- **Implementation Strategy:** The typical approach involves identifying the specific **Vulnerability Window** (e.g., the 5–7 days before the period begins) and establishing a structured protocol for a minor, temporary increase in the prescribed stimulant dose during that window, followed by a return to the standard dose for the remainder of the cycle.
- **Focus on Symptoms:** The decision to adjust the dose should be based entirely on the **functional impairment** experienced during the low-estrogen phase (e.g., severe collapse in Working Memory, profound emotional dysregulation, or task paralysis), not merely on the calendar date.

Section 3: Empowering Self-Advocacy with Objective Data

To initiate a successful discussion about dose adjustment, you must provide your physician with objective data that transforms your anecdotal experience into measurable, quantifiable evidence of a cycle-symptom correlation. This is where the tracking completed in Chapter 1 becomes indispensable.

1. The Data Presentation: From Feeling to Factual Evidence

Instead of reporting vague feelings of being "more irritable" or "less focused," you should present your **Symptom Log** (Chapter 1) as factual evidence:

- **Quantify the Dip:** "My data shows that during Cycle Days 23–28 (the late luteal phase), my average score for **Inattention / Focus** increases from 2 to 5, and my self-rated **Medication Efficacy** drops by 40%. This decline consistently impairs my ability to perform scheduled work tasks during this window."
- **Target the Problem:** This shifts the conversation from addressing a mood issue to managing a documented neurochemical fluctuation that impairs executive function, aligning the discussion with the mechanisms of ADHD treatment.
- **Frame the Solution:** Propose the strategy as a proactive measure for stability: "Given this predictable pattern, I would like to explore evidence-based options for compensating for this dip, starting with a monitored, temporary dose increase during the last five days of my luteal phase."

2. Partnering with Specialized Professionals

Navigating hormonal treatment requires a multidisciplinary approach, often involving coordination between several professionals:

- **ADHD Specialist:** Seek a psychiatrist or medical doctor who has explicit experience treating **adult female ADHD** and is knowledgeable about the impact of hormonal fluctuations (the **ADHD health gap**).
- **Hormone Therapy Integration (Midlife):** For women in perimenopause or menopause (Chapter 4), coordinating treatment with a gynecologist or endocrinologist who is open to **Hormone Replacement Therapy (HRT)** is essential. HRT often works synergistically with stimulant medication to stabilize cognitive and emotional symptoms by increasing the baseline level of supportive estrogen.

Section 4: The Holistic Context: Conserving Energy and Defeating Shame

The strategy of cycle dosing is an essential part of a holistic plan, not the entire solution. Its true power is realized when it works in conjunction with the structural strategies you have already mastered.

1. EF Strategies as a Buffer Against Hormonal Chaos

Even with optimized medication, the low-estrogen phase still presents a challenge. The structural stability you created in Book 3 acts as the critical behavioral and cognitive buffer that prevents the internal dip from becoming an external crisis.

- **Time Blocking and Prioritization:** During the Vulnerability Window, you should rigidly enforce your **Time Block schedule** and **Prioritization Frameworks** (Q2 / Goal tasks only). The external structure compensates for the internal loss of Working Memory and Inhibitory Control, ensuring functional stability even when the brain is struggling internally.
- **Reducing Cognitive Load:** Aggressively reduce **Cognitive Load** during this phase (e.g., eliminating all non-essential meetings, enforcing strict **Notification Annihilation**) to conserve the limited EF reserves you have.

2. Defeating Shame through Knowledge and Self-Compassion

Perhaps the greatest payoff of understanding cycle-dependent efficacy is the liberation from shame. For years, the woman blamed her own effort when her focus collapsed.

- **The Factual Response to the Inner Critic:** Knowledge transforms the internal conversation. When symptoms worsen, the self-talk shifts from, *"I'm useless; I can't focus"* to, *"My estrogen support has dipped; this is a predictable neurochemical reality. I am being strategic by adjusting my demands and relying on my schedule."*
- **Sustainable Self-Efficacy:** By taking proactive, informed control over her treatment, the woman builds a profound sense of **self-efficacy** and agency. She replaces the cycle of frustration and failure with a system of compassionate, effective management, moving toward genuine self-acceptance.

Conclusion: Committing to Dynamic, Personalized Care

The journey through this chapter marks the shift to personalized, dynamic care that honors your unique neurobiology. You have moved beyond the static, one-size-fits-all model of treatment and armed yourself with the data and knowledge necessary to command an optimized plan.

By combining the rigor of cycle tracking with the external scaffolding of your Time Blocks and the willingness to advocate for appropriate pharmacological support, you stabilize your neurochemistry across the entire month. This stability is the vital bridge to mastering emotional resilience and building lasting, healthy relationships in the final books of this guide.

Chapter 3 Workbook: Advocate for Adjustment: Discuss Cycle Dosing of Stimulants with Your Doctor

Objective: To prepare objective data and strategic communication points to advocate for a personalized medication approach (Cycle Dosing) with a healthcare professional.

Scientific Anchor: Clinical data suggests that psychostimulant efficacy can diminish during the low-estrogen luteal phase. Proactive, temporary dose adjustments may help compensate for the premenstrual worsening of cognitive and emotional symptoms.

Activity 3.1: Data Consolidation for Advocacy

Instructions: Based on your Symptom Log (Chapter 1), consolidate the objective data needed to make your case.

1. **My Vulnerability Window:** Identify the exact days your symptoms peak (Luteal Phase).

   From Cycle Day: ____

   To Day: ____

2. **Quantify Functional Impairment:** Calculate the average change in your focus and medication efficacy during this window.

   Average Inattention / Focus Score (Peak Window): _____ (e.g., 4 or 5)

   Average Medication Efficacy Score (Peak Window) :_____ (e.g., 1=Effective, 5=Ineffective)

3. **Specific Behavioral Impairment:** Name one high-leverage task you consistently struggle to complete or initiate during this window (e.g., financial administrative tasks, deep work, or managing conflict).

Impaired Task: ____

____

____

____

Activity 3.2: The Advocacy Script Preparation

Instructions: Craft a concise, professional script to initiate the conversation with your doctor, using factual data rather than subjective complaints.

1. **Opening Statement (Factual):** State the correlation between your cycle and your function.

   Script: "Doctor, I've been tracking my ADHD symptoms and medication response over the last months, and my data shows a clear pattern." ____
2. **The Solution Proposal (Informed Request):** Propose the evidence-based strategy you wish to explore.

   Script: "Given this predictable decline, I would like to explore the potential benefit of a monitored, temporary dose increase during Cycle Days _____ to _____to prevent the premenstrual worsening of my symptoms, as supported by current guidance on cycle dosing."
3. **Holistic Context:** Briefly mention the non-pharmacological buffers you already have in place to show commitment to self-management.

   Buffer: "I am proactively managing my schedule by using **Time Blocking** and **Body Doubling** during this phase."

Reflection 3.3: Partnering with Your Care Team

Instructions: Reflect on the emotional significance of this act of advocacy.

1. **Defeating the Gender Gap:** How does bringing objective data to your appointment help you overcome the historical tendency of the medical system to dismiss or misattribute female symptom fluctuations?

   Benefit: ____

____

____

____

____

2. **Self-Efficacy Gain:** Regardless of the immediate outcome of the discussion, how does the act of preparing this data and making a clear, informed request increase your sense of control and self-efficacy?

   Control Gained: ______________________________

   ____

   ____

   ____

   ____

3. **Midlife Preparation:** If you are approaching perimenopause or menopause, what is one question you will ask your doctor about **Hormone Replacement Therapy (HRT)** in relation to stabilizing your Executive Function?

   Question: ______________________________

   ____

   ____

   ____

   ____

CHAPTER 4

MANAGE THE TRANSITION: NAVIGATE PERIMENOPAUSE AND MENOPAUSAL BRAIN FOG

The hormonal influence on the female ADHD brain culminates in midlife, presenting what is often the most profound and challenging period of cognitive shift. While the previous chapters focused on the monthly fluctuations of the menstrual cycle, this chapter addresses the sustained, systemic decline of hormones during **perimenopause** and **menopause**. This transition is frequently the tipping point where underlying Attention-Deficit / Hyperactivity Disorder (ADHD) symptoms, which a woman may have successfully masked or compensated for over decades, become significantly and often suddenly unmanageable.

Experts refer to this phenomenon as the **"ADHD Squared"** effect: the compounding of an already dopamine-dysregulated system with the severe, sustained decline of supporting hormones. This chapter provides the strategic roadmap for understanding this crisis, managing the ensuing "brain fog," and advocating for the integrated, dynamic treatment required to stabilize Executive Function (EF) and emotional resilience during this high-risk life stage.

The goal is to provide validation that the cognitive collapse you may be experiencing is a measurable neurobiological reality, not a personal failure or a sign of premature aging, and to empower you to maintain command over your attention and well-being.

Section 1: The Neurobiological Crisis: The "ADHD Squared" Effect

Perimenopause is the transition period leading up to menopause, characterized by unpredictable and often severe fluctuations in estrogen and progesterone. Menopause is defined as twelve months after a woman's final menstrual period. This hormonal shift directly impacts the neurochemistry that supports attention, memory, and emotional control, thereby intensifying pre-existing ADHD deficits.

1. Estrogen Decline and the Collapse of Cognitive Support

The sustained decline of **Estrogen** is the primary driver of the cognitive crisis in midlife ADHD. Estrogen, as established, acts as a crucial supportive ally to the brain's **dopamine system**, enhancing dopamine synthesis and receptor sensitivity.

- **The Compounding Deficit:** Because the ADHD brain is already deficient or dysregulated in dopamine, the removal of estrogen's supportive effect creates a profound neurochemical vulnerability. The resulting sustained drop in dopamine levels exacerbates core ADHD symptoms, a compounding effect that is experienced as a major functional decline.
- **Impact on EF:** This decline, in turn, directly impacts the neurotransmitters required for attention, regulating emotions, organizational skills, and memory. For women without ADHD, this decline may manifest as mild "brain fog"; for women with ADHD, these symptoms become significantly more severe, magnifying organizational difficulties, attention lapses, and the need for specialized treatment.

2. Progesterone Loss and Emotional Volatility

The decline in **Progesterone** further compromises emotional stability and sleep quality, both of which are critical for maintaining functional EF.

- **Loss of Calming Buffer:** Progesterone is often referred to as the "calming hormone" due to its role in boosting **GABA** (gamma-aminobutyric acid), a neurotransmitter that helps reduce feelings of stress and promote relaxation. As progesterone levels decline or fluctuate erratically, this crucial inhibitory (calming) effect is lost.
- **Increased Reactivity:** For women whose emotional regulation is already vulnerable due to ADHD, the loss of this GABA-boosting buffer leads to **increased anxiety, irritability, and heightened sensitivity to stress**. This makes the woman more reactive and prone to emotional outbursts, complicating relationships and increasing the risk of burnout. The sleep disturbances associated with this phase further compound the issue, as chronic fatigue drastically impairs Working Memory and Inhibitory Control.

Section 2: The Manifestation: Navigating Menopausal Brain Fog

The physiological effects of hormonal decline translate into a crisis of Executive Function that often mirrors the worst unmanaged ADHD symptoms, leading to confusion and self-doubt.

1. Profound Working Memory Failure ("Brain Fog")

The term "brain fog" accurately describes the collapse of Working Memory (WM) and processing speed that many women experience. WM is the temporary "mental scratchpad" needed for multi-tasking, complex planning, and holding instructions in mind.

- **Impaired Multi-Tasking and Planning:** The decline in estrogen directly impairs the ability to multitask, reason, plan, and problem-solve, skills that are foundational to EF mastery. A woman who previously compensated for her ADHD by meticulously planning may suddenly find her organizational systems ineffective and her capacity for managing multiple demands severely diminished.

- **Memory Lapses and Forgetfulness:** Memory problems become more pronounced, going beyond misplaced keys to include difficulty retrieving words, forgetting recent conversations, or losing the thread of complex projects. This loss of reliable recall feeds anxiety and undermines the confidence that the woman painstakingly built through her EF strategies.

2. Worsening of Core ADHD Symptoms

The symptoms that might have been manageable in early adulthood, inattention, disorganization, and low motivation, are likely to become the dominant feature of daily life, potentially "unmasking" a previously undiagnosed condition or severely intensifying a diagnosed one.

- **Loss of Inhibitory Control:** Increased anxiety and irritability, stemming from progesterone loss, weaken **Inhibitory Control (IC)**, making it harder to pause before speaking, resist impulsive spending, or manage frustration. This can lead to increased relational friction and renewed feelings of being "out of control."
- **Diminished Medication Efficacy:** The low-dopamine environment created by low estrogen can reduce the effectiveness of stimulant medication, leading to the frustrating feeling that the dose is no longer adequate, even if the woman's body size or activity level has not changed. This requires immediate reevaluation of the treatment plan.

Section 3: The Strategic Imperative: Integrating Dynamic Treatment

Managing ADHD during this transition requires abandoning the static treatment model in favor of an integrated, dynamic approach that utilizes both pharmacological and hormonal support.

1. HRT and Stimulant Integration: Offsetting the Decline

The goal of treatment in this phase is to offset the sustained loss of estrogen and its supportive effect on the dopamine system. This often requires a combined therapeutic approach, which is considered the most helpful strategy.

- **Hormone Replacement Therapy (HRT):** HRT is a primary tool for increasing estrogen levels, which can directly mitigate the cognitive and emotional severity of the menopause transition.

HRT works synergistically with stimulant medication by restoring the supportive hormonal environment, making the ADHD medication more effective at stabilizing dopamine. Research suggests that taking HRT can improve menopausal women's memory, reasoning, multi-tasking, planning, and problem-solving, which are all critical EF skills.

- **Stimulant Adjustment:** For women already taking ADHD medication, a physician may offer an increase in dose to directly offset the effects of the changing hormone levels and the corresponding drop in dopamine. The decision to use HRT, adjust stimulants, or combine both is highly individualized and must be done under specialized medical supervision.

2. The Necessity of Coordinated Care and Self-Advocacy

Navigating midlife ADHD requires a woman to become a fierce advocate for personalized care, often coordinating treatment between specialists who understand this intersection.

- **Multidisciplinary Approach:** It is critical to work with professionals who recognize the ADHD-hormone link, typically coordinating care between a psychiatrist (for ADHD medication / dose adjustment) and a gynecologist or internist (for hormone management / HRT).
- **Demand Data-Driven Care:** A woman must continue to track her symptoms (Chapter 1) to provide objective evidence of the correlation between the hormonal transition and the severity of her EF deficits. This data is essential to validate her experience and ensure the treatment plan is tailored to her specific need for cognitive stability.

Section 4: Non-Pharmacological Buffering: Supporting the PFC

When the brain is experiencing persistent decline, the external EF strategies mastered in Book 3 become non-negotiable structural buffers that prevent total functional collapse.

1. Enforcing Structural and Memory Systems

The memory and organizational systems that were once helpful now become essential survival tools against "brain fog."

- **Offload Working Memory:** Rigorously enforce the externalization of all instructions and schedules. Use fixed **Checklists** and **Templates** (Chapter 4, Book 3) for all multi-step processes, ensuring that unreliable WM is not the keeper of essential information.
- **Simplify Decisions:** Combat decision fatigue (Chapter 5, Book 3) by automating choices (e.g., automated bill pay, fixed meal plans) and strictly adhering to the **Constraint Principle** (limiting options). This conserves the highly limited EF reserves for critical thinking.
- **Routines as Anchors:** Maintain rigorous **fixed routines** (e.g., Nightly Offload, Time Blocking) to provide a predictable structure that the vulnerable PFC can rely on, minimizing the stress and cognitive effort associated with uncertainty.

2. Proactive Self-Care for Mood and Focus

The physical and emotional well-being factors that support the PFC must be aggressively prioritized during this phase to mitigate the severity of symptom worsening.

- **Prioritize Rest and Recovery:** Schedule mandatory, non-negotiable **recovery blocks** into the Time Block schedule. Recognizing and honoring the profound **mental fatigue** that accompanies this transition is essential for preventing burnout.
- **Movement and Neurochemistry:** Regular physical exercise remains a potent tool to stimulate dopamine release and improve mood, directly buffering the negative effects of the hormonal decline.
- **Emotional Support:** Given the heightened emotional volatility and anxiety caused by progesterone loss, actively use **mindfulness and grounding techniques** (Chapter 1, Book 4) to manage stress and prevent emotional escalations. Maintaining a low stress baseline is crucial, as stress further impairs EF function.

Conclusion: A New Era of Self-Acceptance

The journey through perimenopause and menopause can feel like a profound test of self-control and identity, especially for the woman with ADHD. However, armed with scientific knowledge, this transition becomes a predictable phase that can be strategically managed.

The mastery gained here allows you to move beyond the shame of cognitive decline, replacing self-criticism with **radical acceptance** and a focused, data-driven approach. You are commanding an integrated system, combining pharmacological and hormonal support with the rigorous structural management of your EF toolkit, to maintain your cognitive stability and emotional resilience during this complex, powerful era of change. This ability to navigate the shifting sands of your neurobiology with informed grace is the ultimate expression of self-mastery.

Chapter 4 Workbook: Manage the Transition: Navigate Perimenopause and Menopausal Brain Fog

Objective: To create a personalized, proactive plan for managing the sustained cognitive and emotional dips associated with the perimenopausal / menopausal transition, using data to inform self-advocacy.

Scientific Anchor: ADHD symptoms worsen due to the decline of estrogen / progesterone. Strategic management involves integrated treatment (HRT / medication) and rigid EF scaffolding to buffer WM / IC deficits.

Activity 4.1: The Midlife Symptom Audit

Instructions: Identify the three cognitive and emotional symptoms that have become most problematic *since* starting perimenopause (or in the last two years), as these represent the "ADHD Squared" effect.

1. **Symptom 1 (Cognitive / WM Collapse):** (e.g., Forgetting words, losing items, difficulty multitasking / planning)

   Symptom: ____

   ____

   ____

2. **Symptom 2 (Emotional / Anxiety):** (e.g., Increased anxiety, low patience, irritability / snapping)

   Symptom: ____

   ____

   ____

3. **Symptom 3 (Functional / Initiation):** (e.g., Severe task paralysis, constant fatigue / brain fog)

   Symptom: ____

   ____

   ____

Activity 4.2: Integrated Treatment Advocacy Plan

Instructions: Prepare a strategic statement for your healthcare provider regarding integrated treatment options, based on evidence.

1. **Data Point:** My most prominent cognitive deficit is ___ (*Symptom 1*).
2. **HRT Question:** To address this decline in Executive Function, I would like to discuss whether **Hormone Replacement Therapy (HRT)** could stabilize the hormonal support for my attention.

   Commitment: I will schedule an appointment with a gynecologist or internist to discuss HRT options.
3. **Medication Adjustment Proposal:** If you are taking stimulants, draft the question you will ask your psychiatrist about offsetting the sustained decline.

   Question: "Given the sustained hormonal decline, is an increase in my **stimulant dosage** a possible strategy to offset the loss of estrogen's neurochemical support, or should we consider an alternative medication to support cognitive function?"

Reflection 4.3: Buffering the Brain Fog

Instructions: Reflect on how the structured EF strategies from Book 3 act as a non-pharmacological buffer against the worsening symptoms of this transition.

1. **WM Offload Strategy:** When you are experiencing severe "brain fog" (Symptom 1), what single **external system** (e.g., a specific checklist, writing everything down immediately, using a visible timer) will you rely on most heavily to ensure you complete tasks?

   External System: ______________________________________

   ____

   ____

   ____

   ____

2. **Self-Compassion and Acceptance:** When you find yourself forgetting something critical, the inner critic often attacks. How will the knowledge that your struggles are due to a predictable, documented **sustained hormonal change** help you replace self-criticism with self-compassion?

   Compassionate Reframe: _________________________________

   ____

   ____

   ____

   ____

3. **Stress Buffer:** Given that anxiety and irritability (Symptom 2) worsen due to progesterone loss, what **physiological reset** (e.g., 10 minutes of walking, deep breathing) will you commit to scheduling daily to mitigate stress and conserve your vulnerable EF?

   Scheduled Buffer: ______________________________________

   ____

   ____

   ____

   ____

CHAPTER 5

BUILD YOUR BUFFER: PRIORITIZE SLEEP AND NUTRITION TO STABILIZE MOOD

You have achieved the essential structural and advocacy goals of this book: objective tracking of your hormonal cycle (Chapter 1), strategic alignment of your workflow (Chapter 2), and informed advocacy for optimizing medication during hormonal dips (Chapter 3) and midlife transitions (Chapter 4). This foundation of knowledge and external support is vital, but sustainable stability requires integrating this strategy with your basic physiology.

This chapter addresses the final, non-negotiable pillar of hormonal harmony: building a resilient **physiological buffer** against volatility. For the woman with Attention-Deficit / Hyperactivity Disorder (ADHD), who already struggles with neurochemical stability, insufficient **sleep**, poor **nutrition**, and chronic **stress** act as direct hormonal disruptors.

These factors not only exacerbate ADHD symptoms but actively impair Executive Functions (EFs) and undermine emotional regulation, especially during the low-estrogen phases.

The goal here is to transform foundational self-care into a strategic, evidence-based tool for stability. By prioritizing consistent sleep hygiene and steady, brain-supporting fuel, you proactively regulate the nervous system, conserve vital EF reserves, and build a buffer of emotional resilience that is resistant to both hormonal shifts and the daily friction of life.

Section 1: Sleep Hygiene: The Non-Negotiable Foundation of Executive Function

For anyone, quality sleep is crucial, but for the woman with ADHD, sleep consistency is the bedrock of sustained focus, emotional control, and Working Memory (WM). Disruptions to sleep directly impair the prefrontal cortex (PFC), the brain's command center for EF.

1. The Neurobiological Cost of Sleep Deprivation

Research shows that sleep problems are highly prevalent in adults with ADHD, with studies indicating that sleep deprivation in this population can be as functionally impairing as the core ADHD symptoms themselves. Sleep problems are often linked to both the hyperactivity / restlessness symptoms and the difficulties with consistent routine required for good sleep hygiene.

- **EF Impairment:** During sleep, the brain restores the PFC's capacity. Lack of sleep directly depletes **Working Memory** and weakens **Inhibitory Control (IC)**, the ability to resist impulses and regulate emotions. This results in pronounced "brain fog," forgetfulness, and lowered patience, making task completion and emotional regulation significantly harder the following day.
- **Exacerbating Emotional Volatility:** Sleep deprivation increases emotional reactivity. When tired, the amygdala (the brain's emotional accelerator) becomes more reactive, while the PFC (the emotional "brakes") is less effective. This increases the likelihood of a minor trigger escalating into a disproportionate emotional outburst, particularly during the high-risk, low-progesterone phases of the hormonal cycle.

2. Strategic Sleep Hygiene for the ADHD Brain

Since the ADHD brain struggles with consistent routines and shutting down an active mind, sleep hygiene must be treated as a structured, intentional ritual.

- **The Fixed Bedtime Anchor:** Establish a consistent **bedtime and wake-up time**, even on weekends. The human body, and especially the neurodiverse brain, thrives on regularity (circadian rhythm). This consistency helps anchor the brain's neurochemistry and regulates its sleep-wake cycle, minimizing difficulties with falling asleep.
- **The Nightly Offload Ritual:** To combat a racing mind and rumination (internal noise), commit to the **Nightly Offload Ritual** (introduced in Book 3). Before bed, write out your **To-Do List** for the next day, capturing all "open loops" (tasks and worries) that consume WM. This externalizes the cognitive burden, signaling to the brain that the day's tasks are secured on the schedule, allowing the mind to quiet down and transition smoothly toward rest.
- **Avoid the Final Dopamine Hit:** In the hour before sleep, avoid screens (blue light interferes with melatonin), caffeine, sugar, and stimulating work projects that can trigger **hyperfocus**. Use this time for low-stimulation activities that signal relaxation, such as listening to a calming audiobook or music, or taking a warm bath.

Section 2: Nutrition and Hydration: Fueling the Neurochemical System

The PFC's capacity for focus and regulation requires stable, high-quality fuel. Erratic energy supply, through poor nutrition or dehydration, mimics and exacerbates ADHD symptoms, directly undermining the efficacy of optimized treatment.

1. Stabilizing Blood Sugar for Consistent Focus

The ADHD brain is highly susceptible to energy spikes and crashes caused by erratic blood sugar levels. These crashes amplify inattention, irritability, and mental fatigue, directly opposing the effort to build EF resilience.

- **Protein and Complex Carbs:** Focus on balanced meals that combine **lean protein** (for amino acids needed to build neurotransmitters like dopamine) and **complex carbohydrates** (for sustained energy release) at every meal. This prevents the rapid energy peaks from simple sugars that are inevitably followed by a crash, which exacerbates impulsivity and mood instability.
- **The Morning Focus Fuel:** Never skip breakfast. The morning meal should be rich in protein and fiber to anchor stable blood sugar, supporting sustained attention through the challenging first work blocks of the day.

2. Essential Neuro-Nutrients: Omega-3s and Magnesium

Specific nutrients are crucial building blocks for the brain structures and neurochemistry that support EF. Prioritizing these nutrients acts as a direct buffer against neurochemical volatility.

- **Omega-3 Fatty Acids:** Omega-3s (especially EPA and DHA) are essential for brain health, supporting cell membranes and neurotransmitter function. Research has linked low omega-3 levels to ADHD symptoms, including learning difficulties and emotional regulation problems. Supplementation, or dietary focus on fatty fish (salmon, sardines), can improve mood, reduce hyperactivity, and potentially enhance **Working Memory**.
- **Hydration:** Dehydration, even mild, can impair cognitive function, mood, and mental clarity, often mimicking or worsening the "brain fog" associated with ADHD and hormonal decline. Consistent, intentional hydration throughout the day is a simple, high-leverage strategy to maintain optimal brain performance.

Section 3: Stress Management:
The Circuit-Breaker for Emotional Storms

High stress levels are a major hormonal disruptor, increasing cortisol production which, over time, depletes dopamine and serotonin and directly impairs EF function. Stress also magnifies emotional dysregulation, creating a vicious cycle of chaos. Managing stress is the final, essential buffer against hormonal and emotional volatility.

1. Proactive Grounding Techniques

When stress or anxiety levels rise, the nervous system enters a state of physiological arousal ("fight or flight"). Grounding techniques are immediate circuit-breakers that shift the body back to the calm, restorative state (parasympathetic nervous system).

- **Deep Breathing Exercises:** Practicing paced, deep breathing (e.g., inhaling for 4 counts, holding for 2, exhaling for 6 counts) immediately calms the nervous system and reduces heart rate, mitigating the physical effects of stress.
- **Sensory Reset (Grounding):** Use the 5-4-3-2-1 grounding technique (focusing on 5 things you see, 4 things you feel, etc.) to pull attention away from overwhelming internal thoughts and anchor it to the immediate, external reality. This simple redirection of focus utilizes your attentional skills (Book 3) to calm the emotional system.
- **Movement as Release:** Physical movement is a direct and healthy way to discharge the pent-up energy of frustration and anxiety. Utilize the mandatory breaks from the Pomodoro Technique (Book 3) for short bursts of intense movement (e.g., brisk walking, stretching) to act as a physiological "reset button," preventing emotional escalation.

2. Mindfulness and Psychological Buffering

Sustaining a calm baseline requires the intentional practice of mindfulness to manage intrusive thoughts and emotional reactivity.

- **Mindful Awareness:** Mindfulness, the practice of paying attention to the present moment without judgment, is crucial for supporting **Emotional Regulation** (the focus of Book 5). It strengthens the ability to observe a racing thought or an intense emotion without immediately reacting, creating the crucial "pause" that allows IC to engage.
- **Stress as Data:** Instead of reacting impulsively to stress, use the EF skills of reflection and analysis: *What caused this spike? Am I hungry? Did I skip my rest block?* Framing stress as valuable data allows you to apply a strategic solution (e.g., eating a protein-rich snack, taking a rest block) rather than engaging in self-blame.

Section 4: The Integration: A Stable Internal Ecosystem

The work of Book 4 is not about fighting hormones; it is about establishing a robust, stable internal ecosystem that supports the neurobiology of the ADHD brain against all forms of volatility, monthly, lifelong, and environmental.

1. The Synergistic Buffer

The EF resilience gained in Book 3 works synergistically with the physiological buffers established here:

- **Sleep / Nutrition** restores the PFC, maximizing **EF capacity** (Working Memory, Inhibitory Control).
- **Stress Management** lowers the baseline anxiety, minimizing **Emotional Reactivity** (Anger, Irritability).
- **EF Strategies** (Time Blocking, Milestones) prevent environmental chaos, minimizing the **Stress Triggers** that disrupt the hormonal and cognitive systems.

This continuous positive feedback loop ensures that when the inevitable low-estrogen dip occurs, your system is not depleted, but ready to rely on the robust reserves you have built.

2. The Bridge to Emotional Mastery

The physiological stability achieved in this chapter is the essential precursor to the emotional work of Book 5. A brain that is well-rested, well-fed, and less stressed is a brain that is capable of deep introspection, self-compassion, and intentional emotional regulation. You have built the stable neurological and physiological platform needed to successfully navigate the intense emotional landscape of ADHD.

Chapter 5 Workbook: Build Your Buffer: Prioritize Sleep and Nutrition to Stabilize Mood

Objective: To implement consistent, strategic physiological routines (Sleep and Nutrition) to build a robust buffer against hormonal volatility and mental fatigue.

Scientific Anchor: Quality sleep and stable blood sugar are essential for restoring the Prefrontal Cortex and maintaining Inhibitory Control, which are highly vulnerable to stress and hormonal decline.

Activity 5.1: The Sleep Hygiene Offload Ritual

Instructions: Create a fixed, low-stimulation ritual for the **60 minutes before bed** to signal rest and offload working memory (WM).

1. **Fixed Bedtime Commitment:** My committed bedtime is:

   ____

   ____

   ____

2. **The 60-Minute Wind-Down Sequence:** Detail the three non-negotiable steps you will take to close out the day, avoiding all screens / caffeine.

Time Slot	Activity	Neuro-Benefit (WM / IC Protection)
(Example: -60 to -45 min)	Read a physical book / Take a bath.	Low stimulation; avoids blue light / dopamine hit.
(Example: -45 to -30 min)	**Nightly Offload Ritual (Write List)**	**Externalizes open loops / worries from WM.**
(Example: -30 to 0 min)	Gentle stretching / Deep breathing.	Activates parasympathetic nervous system (calm).

Activity 5.2: The Neuro-Nutrient Focus Plan

Instructions: Plan two meals tomorrow to maximize focus and stability by ensuring adequate protein / fiber and hydration.

1. **Morning Focus Fuel:** Detail your breakfast, ensuring it contains **protein and fiber** to anchor stable blood sugar for the first work block.

   Breakfast Plan: ____

2. **Hydration Commitment:** Set a reminder to track your water intake during your peak focus block (e.g., 9:00 AM–1:00 PM).

   Hydration Reminder Text: ______________________________

Reflection 5.3: The Stress and Buffer Analysis

Instructions: Reflect on how proactive physiological care impacts your stress and emotional regulation.

1. **Stress as Data:** Identify one specific moment this week where you felt an intense emotional surge (e.g., snapping at someone, feeling sudden anxiety). If you had immediately applied a **Deep Breathing / Grounding Technique**, how might the intensity of that moment have been reduced?

   Intensity Reduction: ______________________________

   ____

   ____

   ____

2. **EF Conservation:** How does the intentional scheduling of a **Morning Focus Fuel** (protein / fiber) breakfast support your **Inhibitory Control** (your ability to resist distractions or impulsive spending) compared to starting the day with high sugar or skipping the meal entirely?

   IC / Impulsivity Benefit: ______________________________

   ____

   ____

   ____

3. **Hormonal Buffer:** During your next **Vulnerability Window** (low-estrogen phase), what single self-care activity (e.g., 15-min walk, early bedtime) will you commit to prioritizing to serve as your non-negotiable **Emotional Buffer**?

   Committed Buffer: ______________________________

   ____

   ____

   ____

CHAPTER 6

REFLECT AND INTEGRATE: YOUR HORMONAL HARMONY JOURNEY SO FAR

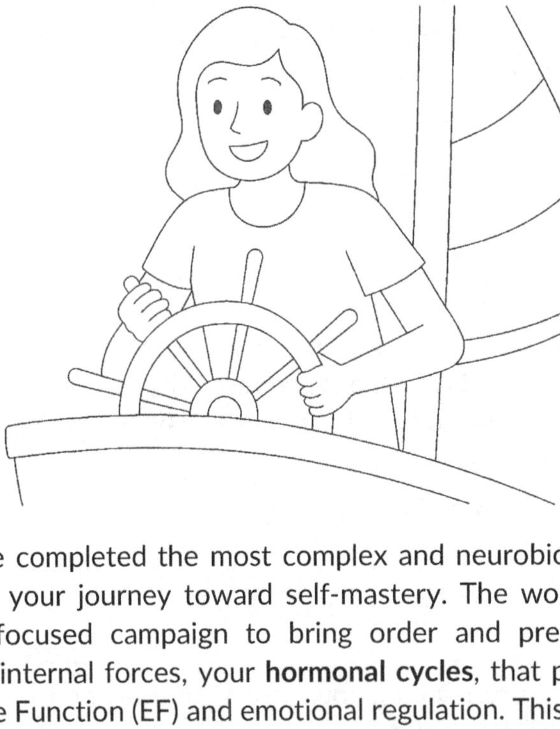

You have completed the most complex and neurobiologically intricate phase of your journey toward self-mastery. The work of Book 4 has been a focused campaign to bring order and predictability to the dynamic internal forces, your **hormonal cycles**, that profoundly impact Executive Function (EF) and emotional regulation. This is the integration chapter, a dedicated space to reflect upon the profound cognitive, physiological, and emotional gains achieved by challenging the historical notion of static treatment and embracing your unique, dynamic neurobiology.

The core achievement of this book is the replacement of unpredictable, chaotic symptom spikes with a predictable, manageable rhythm. You have learned that your struggles with focus and emotional volatility were never random failures; they were **measurable,**

neurochemical events driven by the ebb and flow of estrogen and progesterone. By acquiring this scientific knowledge and the data to back it up, you have transformed from a passive victim of hormonal chaos to a strategic manager of your own physiology. This is the ultimate victory of **self-advocacy** and **self-compassion**.

The stability cultivated here, the reliable synchronization of your internal body clock with your external structural supports (from Book 3), is the essential, stable base required to successfully embark on the challenging work of emotional mastery (Book 5).

Section 1: The Victory of Validation: Defeating the Gender Health Gap

The first, and arguably most important, victory of this book is the emotional and psychological liberation that comes with **scientific validation**. For years, women's reports of fluctuating focus and mood were dismissed as subjective or moodiness, a reality stemming from the **gender health gap** in ADHD research.

1. From Subjective Anecdote to Objective Data

You systematically gathered objective data that provided undeniable evidence of a cycle-symptom correlation (Chapter 1).

- **Quantifying the Dip:** By tracking the decline of estrogen in the **Luteal Phase** against functional symptoms (inattention, poor WM, and emotional volatility), you quantified your unique **Vulnerability Window**. This data moves the conversation with providers from subjective complaints to objective facts: "My data shows a 40% drop in focus during Cycle Days X-Y, correlating with low estrogen, which requires a strategic intervention."
- **Empowering Advocacy:** This data provided the necessary fuel for informed **self-advocacy** regarding **Cycle Dosing** (Chapter 3) and navigating the compounded challenges of **Perimenopause / Menopause** (Chapter 4). You now understand that when medication efficacy dips, it is not the fault of the dose or your effort; it is a neurochemical reality that demands a dynamic, tailored pharmacological solution to offset the loss of estrogen's supportive effect on dopamine.

2. Neutralizing Shame with Self-Compassion

The knowledge that your symptoms worsen during your Vulnerability Window is the ultimate antidote to the shame that accompanies unmanaged ADHD.

- **Radical Acceptance:** You replaced the harsh self-judgment, *"I'm falling apart; I can't handle this routine"*, with the compassionate, factual statement: *"My body is following a predictable hormonal rhythm. My system needs intentional buffering today."* This act of **radical acceptance** stops the cascade of stress and self-criticism, which would otherwise consume the limited emotional bandwidth required for resilience.
- **Managing the "ADHD Squared" Effect:** For those navigating midlife, the knowledge that "brain fog" and cognitive decline are often the predictable **"ADHD Squared"** effect (compounding low estrogen and low dopamine) provides crucial psychological safety, preventing the spiral into fear of premature cognitive decline.

Section 2: The Command Over Flow: Strategic Integration

The true power of this book lies in the integration of hormonal knowledge with the structural EF strategies mastered in Book 3. This synthesis ensures that your management plan is flexible enough to withstand internal volatility.

1. Cycle Syncing as an EF Strategy

You learned to use the **Cycle Syncing Framework** (Chapter 2) to proactively match **task demand** with **neurochemical supply**.

- **Strategic Allocation:** You maximize efficiency by scheduling cognitively complex tasks (planning, analysis, deep work) during the **High-Estrogen Follicular Phase** (Peak Focus) and reserving low-stakes, routine tasks (filing, maintenance, passive learning) for the **Low-Estrogen Luteal Phase** (Strategic Conservation). This prevents the highly taxing effort of trying to force focus when the brain is neurochemically unsupported.

- **EF Buffering:** During the low-energy Luteal Phase, you learned to rigidly adapt your scheduling parameters, including **increasing the Time Buffer** to 50% extra time and **contracting the Pomodoro work sprints** (e.g., 20 / 10 cycle) to prevent burnout and compensate for slower Working Memory and harder transitions. The external structure acts as the resilient scaffolding when the internal cognitive mechanisms are compromised.

2. The Power of the Physiological Buffer

The disciplined prioritization of foundational self-care (Chapter 5) transformed sleep, nutrition, and stress management into strategic tools for neurochemical stability.

- **Restoring the PFC:** Consistent **sleep hygiene** and the **Nightly Offload Ritual** were established as non-negotiable foundations for restoring the Prefrontal Cortex (PFC) and maximizing **EF capacity** (WM, IC) for the following day.
- **Neuro-Nutritional Support:** Stable blood sugar (protein / complex carbs) and essential nutrients (Omega-3s) were integrated to provide consistent fuel, mitigating the energy crashes that exacerbate impulsivity and emotional volatility during low-hormone periods.
- **Stress Management and IC:** You integrated **Grounding Techniques** and **Movement** into your routine as immediate **circuit-breakers** (Chapter 5), effectively engaging the parasympathetic nervous system to reduce stress arousal and protect your already vulnerable **Inhibitory Control** from emotional overload.

Section 3: The Bridge to Emotional Mastery (Book 5)

The stability achieved in this book is the essential prerequisite for navigating the intense emotional landscape of Book 5 (Tame Intense Emotions). A system that is constantly being hijacked by hormonal or physiological stress lacks the bandwidth for deep psychological work.

1. Stabilizing the Emotional Baseline

The primary outcome of Book 4 is the profound reduction in **chaotic input** that triggers emotional flares.

- **Reducing Reactivity:** By managing stress, prioritizing sleep, and buffering the low-estrogen dip, you stabilize the emotional baseline, making the brain less reactive and preventing minor triggers from escalating into a disproportionate emotional storm (the "green-to-red" phenomenon).
- **Conserving Emotional Bandwidth:** The conserved EF resources and reduced physiological stress are now available for **emotional labor**, the challenging work of introspection, cognitive reframing, and intentional response that defines emotional regulation.

2. The Foundation for DBT Skills

The structural stability provided by this book supports the efficacy of the therapeutic tools explored in the next book.

- **IC as Emotional Brake:** The **Inhibitory Control** trained through EF practice is the very same muscle required for **emotional regulation**, the ability to pause between stimulus and response.
- **Mindfulness Prerequisite:** A body that is well-rested and neurochemically stable is better equipped to engage in sustained attention, which is the necessary prerequisite for effective **Mindfulness** (the core skill of DBT / CBT), allowing for greater self-awareness and non-judgmental observation of intense feelings.

Conclusion: Committing to Dynamic, Personalized Care

The journey through Book 4 is the definitive step in achieving dynamic, personalized self-mastery. You have moved beyond feeling powerless against internal chaos to commanding a truly holistic system that honors the unique intersection of your neurobiology and your physiology.

Your ongoing commitment must be to **consistency in self-advocacy** and **self-compassion**. By maintaining your tracking data, adhering to your structural buffers, and refusing to succumb to the shame of neurobiological differences, you ensure that the stability you have fought for is sustained. This resilient foundation now fully equips you to tackle the crucial final phase: achieving emotional mastery and building robust, resilient connections with others.

Chapter 6 Workbook: Reflect and Integrate: Your Hormonal Harmony Journey So Far

Objective: To synthesize the cognitive and emotional gains achieved in Book 4, solidifying the shift from reliance on static treatment to dynamic, data-driven hormonal management.

Scientific Anchor: Reflective practice and self-compassion reduce the impact of stress on Executive Functions. Synthesis of tracking data ensures proactive buffering against neurobiological shifts (low estrogen / dopamine dips).

Activity 6.1: The Hormonal Harmony Scorecard

Instructions: Rate the severity of your challenges **before** Book 4 (Initial) and **now** (Current), focusing on the impact of hormonal stability. (Scale: 1 = Minimal Challenge, 5 = Severe Challenge)

Challenge Area	Before Book 4 (Initial)	After Book 4 (Current)	Reflection: The Tool That Helped Most
Inattention / Focus Dip (Pre-Menses)			(Example: Cycle Syncing / Time Blocking)
Anxiety / Irritability (Hormonal)			(Example: Progesterone Buffer / Deep Breathing)
Brain Fog / Working Memory Collapse			(Example: Sleep Hygiene / Nutritional Support)

Sense of Control Over Symptoms			(Example: Tracking Data / Advocacy)

Reflection 6.2: Shifting from Shame to Strategy

Instructions: Use this space to integrate the core concept that symptoms are neurobiological consequences, not moral failures, and assess your progress in building self-advocacy.

1. **The Crisis to Strategy Shift:** Recall a moment this week when a hormonal or stress dip made you feel overwhelmed. How did the ability to identify your **Vulnerability Window** (Chapter 1) or your **Physiological Buffer** (Chapter 5) prevent you from escalating to a full emotional crisis?

   The Intervention: ____

   ____

   ____

   ____

   ____

   ____

2. **The Antidote to the Inner Critic:** Identify one self-critical thought you had about your performance during a low-energy moment. Rephrase this thought using the compassionate, neurobiological reality you learned (e.g., "My brain is low on estrogen support today; this dip is predictable. I choose to prioritize rest to restore my PFC.")

   New, Empowered Narrative: ______________________________

   ____

   ____

   ____

   ____

   ____

   ____

3. **Self-Advocacy Gain:** In one sentence, summarize the most important piece of data you now possess (quantified symptom dip or medication fluctuation) that empowers you to demand personalized care from a medical professional.

   Data for Advocacy: ______________________________________

   ____

   ____

   ____

Activity 6.3: Bridge to Emotional Mastery (Book 5 Prep)

Instructions: The EF and physiological stability achieved here are the foundation for emotional regulation. Prepare your system for the challenging emotional work ahead.

1. **EF Buffer Check:** Emotional dysregulation (Book 5) is often fueled by external chaos. Name one specific, low-friction EF tool (e.g., Time Blocking, Nightly Offload) you will rigorously maintain, even during periods of high stress, to ensure you have maximum **emotional bandwidth**.

   EF Tool Commitment: ____________________________________

   ____

   ____

   ____

   ____

2. **IC and the Emotional Brake:** The first step in emotional regulation is creating a **pause**. What single **Grounding / Sensory Technique** (e.g., deep breathing, 5-4-3-2-1) will you commit to practicing daily, even when you feel calm, to strengthen your ability to deploy your Inhibitory Control when an emotional surge hits?

   Daily IC Practice: ____

   ____

   ____

   ____

   ____

CHAPTER 7

PRACTICE AND APPLY: YOUR HORMONAL HARMONY ACTION TOOLKIT

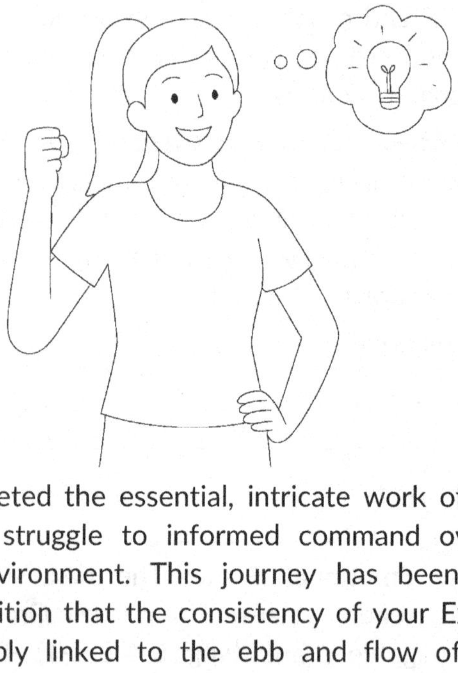

You have completed the essential, intricate work of Book 4, moving from anecdotal struggle to informed command over your internal physiological environment. This journey has been defined by the profound recognition that the consistency of your Executive Function (EF) is inextricably linked to the ebb and flow of your hormones, particularly the supportive presence of **Estrogen** and the regulatory effects of **Progesterone**. The primary achievement is the transformation of unpredictable, chaotic symptom spikes into a predictable, manageable pattern through objective tracking.

This final chapter provides the comprehensive **Action Toolkit**, designed to translate the neurobiological knowledge mastered in Chapters 1 through 5 into a seamless, resilient system of daily self-management. The goal is to integrate your data, scheduling skills (from Book 3), and physiological buffers into a cohesive framework that ensures the stability of your neurochemistry, and thus, your focus and emotional regulation, across the entire month and throughout life transitions.

The power of this toolkit lies in its synergistic effect: consistency in applying these tools minimizes the **Cognitive Load (CL)** and **stress** that deplete EF, ensuring that when the inevitable low-estrogen dip occurs, your system is buffered and ready. This is the final step in moving beyond reactive coping to a life defined by dynamic, personalized, and proactive hormonal harmony.

Section 1: Toolkit 1: The Cycle Syncing Command Protocol

Objective: To leverage your monthly tracking data to proactively schedule and adjust your Executive Function demands, thereby conserving limited neurochemical energy during the Vulnerability Window.

Scientific Anchor: Symptoms worsen due to low estrogen support for dopamine pathways during the Luteal Phase. Strategic scheduling (Cycle Syncing) ensures high-leverage tasks are performed during the high-estrogen Follicular Phase, conserving finite EF resources during the neurochemically unsupported Low-Energy Phase.

Activity 7.1: Creating the Luteal Phase Protection Plan (LPPP)

Instructions: Based on your completed cycle tracker (Chapter 1), design a non-negotiable plan for your 7-day **Vulnerability Window** (e.g., Cycle Days 22–28) that proactively adjusts your cognitive workload using EF tools (Book 3).

1. **Define the Conservation Window:**

   My Vulnerability Window (Days): ____ to ____

2. **Strategic Task De-Allocation (The "Q2 Freeze"):** Identify the high-leverage tasks (Q2 work) that require peak planning, creativity, and Working Memory. These tasks must be **moved out** of the LPPP.

   Complex Task to AVOID: ________________________________

   Routine Task to PRIORITIZE: ____________________________

   (e.g., Simple filing, routine chores, email triage)

3. **EF Buffer Augmentation (Schedule Adjustment):** Detail how your scheduling parameters (Book 3) must be augmented during this week to compensate for fatigue and WM collapse.

EF Strategy	Standard Follicular Phase (Baseline)	Luteal / Vulnerability Phase (Augmented Buffer)
Time Buffer (Chapter 3, Book 3)	25% extra time	**50% extra time** for every task (compensates for slow processing).
Pomodoro Cycle (Chapter 3, Book 3)	45 min Work / 5 min Rest	Contract to **20 min Work / 10 min Rest** (Finitude is shorter; rest is longer to prevent fatigue).
Cognitive Load Annihilation	Enforced 9 AM-11 AM	**All day enforcement** (Strict Notification Annihilation to conserve limited WM).

Commitment: I commit to viewing any work outside this LPPP structure during my Vulnerability Window as an act of **self-sabotage**, not productivity.

Section 2: Toolkit 2: The Treatment Optimization and Advocacy Audit

Objective: To systematically compile objective, measurable evidence for a dynamic treatment plan, empowering self-advocacy for hormonal support and medication adjustment.

Scientific Anchor: The decline in estrogen / progesterone during the luteal phase (menstrual cycle) and menopause exacerbates ADHD symptoms and may diminish stimulant efficacy. Objective data on this correlation is required to discuss "cycle dosing" or integrated HRT support with medical professionals.

Activity 7.2: The Efficacy Data Log Compilation

Instructions: Consolidate your tracking data (Chapter 1) and midlife symptoms (Chapter 4) into a factual summary that provides measurable evidence for your physician.

1. **Quantifying the Monthly Dip (Menstruating Women):** Summarize the functional decline based on your tracking log.
   - *During Cycle Days ____ to ____my Inattention / Focus score increased by ____ % (e.g., from 2 / 5 to 4 / 5).*
   - *During this same window, my self-rated* ***Medication Efficacy*** *consistently dropped, aligning with guidance that low estrogen can impair dopamine response.*
2. **The Midlife Symptom Inventory (Perimenopausal / Menopausal Women):** Identify the key cognitive deficits resulting from the "ADHD Squared" effect (sustained low estrogen / progesterone).

   Symptom 1 (Working Memory): ________________________

   ____

   ____

   (e.g., Word retrieval failure, losing train of thought)

   Symptom 2 (Emotional Volatility): ______________________

   ____

   ____

   (e.g., Sudden irritability, increased anxiety)
3. **Developing the Informed Advocacy Script:** Draft a concise, factual script to initiate the conversation, using data to frame the problem as a neurobiological imbalance, not a personal failing.
   - *Script (Cycle Dosing):* "Doctor, my data shows a quantifiable EF decline during my Luteal Phase. I am seeking to explore the clinical approach of **cycle dosing**, a small, monitored dose increase during my high-risk days, to stabilize my dopamine baseline, as research suggests stimulant efficacy is diminished by low estrogen."

- *Script (Midlife / HRT):* "Since my Executive Function (WM, planning) has significantly worsened during perimenopause, I would like to discuss the integration of **Hormone Replacement Therapy (HRT)** with my current ADHD treatment, as combining them has been shown to support cognitive function in this transition."

Section 3: Toolkit 3: The Physiological Resilience Builder

Objective: To automate essential self-care practices (Sleep, Nutrition, Stress Management) that act as a physiological buffer, conserving EF reserves and minimizing the impact of stress hormones (cortisol) on the PFC.

Scientific Anchor: Stress, poor sleep, and blood sugar instability directly impair EF skills (WM / IC). Prioritizing these foundational needs minimizes their negative impact, maximizing cognitive resilience against hormonal dips.

Activity 7.3: The Nightly Hormone Reset Checklist

Instructions: Create a non-negotiable 60-minute wind-down ritual that targets WM offload and physiological calming, ensuring restorative sleep for PFC recovery.

1. **Time Commitment:** My fixed bedtime is ______.

   I start this ritual 60 minutes prior.

2. **The Nightly Offload Sequence (The Final 60 Minutes):**

Time Slot	Action	Neuro-Benefit (WM / IC Protection)
-60 to -45 min	**Physical Disconnect / Offload:** (Example: Write out tomorrow's **Rule of Three** tasks, turn off all screens.)	Closes "open loops" to conserve WM; prevents blue light interference with sleep.
-45 to -30 min	**Routine Body Care / Low-Stimulation:** (Example: Take warm bath / shower, read physical book.)	Signals safety and promotes the physiological shift to rest mode.

-30 to 0 min	**Sensory Calming:** (Example: 5 minutes of paced, deep breathing or gentle stretching.)	Engages the parasympathetic nervous system, strengthening Inhibitory Control against ruminating thoughts.

Activity 7.4: The Stress-to-Calm IC Protocol

Instructions: Practice deploying immediate **Inhibitory Control (IC)** and **Grounding** as a circuit-breaker when stress or intense emotion hits, preventing escalation.

1. **The Trigger Identification:** My most common emotional trigger during the Luteal Phase is ________________________________

   (e.g., unexpected loud noise, partner criticism, task failure).

2. **The IC Circuit-Breaker:** When the trigger hits, commit to deploying the following **STOP** sequence before speaking or reacting impulsively. This is IC in action.
   - **S:** Stop (Freeze all physical action).
   - **T:** Take a breath (3 deep, paced breaths).
   - **O:** Observe (Acknowledge the emotion without judgment: "I observe that I feel intense frustration.").
   - **P:** Proceed with Opposite Action / Plan (E.g., Walk away for 10 minutes, or use a specific coping skill).

3. **Nutritional Anchor:** What single action will I take tomorrow (e.g., eat a protein-rich snack, drink a glass of water) when I feel the first sign of **Mental Fatigue** to stabilize my blood sugar and prevent an EF crash?

   Fatigue Action: ____

   ____

   ____

   ____

   ____

   ____

   ____

Section 4: Integration and Long-Term Resilience (Reflective Summary)

The culmination of Book 4 is the creation of a dynamic, interconnected system that ensures the structural gains of your EF mastery (Book 3) are not derailed by internal physiological volatility.

1. The Synergistic Buffer

The power of this toolkit lies in how the components support each other: **Tracking** informs **Scheduling**, and **Physiological Buffers** protect **EF Capacity**. You are moving beyond the frantic, low-energy cycle of coping to a sustainable rhythm where your body and schedule work in harmony. This sustained effort conserves the necessary **emotional bandwidth** required to manage the inevitable conflicts and intense feelings that define the emotional mastery journey of Book 5.

2. The Final Step to Emotional Mastery

The physiological and cognitive stability achieved here is the essential precursor to the emotional work of Book 5: Tame Intense Emotions. A brain that is well-rested, regulated by stable blood sugar, and buffered against hormonal chaos is a brain fully capable of engaging in the challenging work of **cognitive reframing** and **assertive communication** (DBT skills) that leads to profound self-acceptance and resilient relationships. You are ready to transform internal turmoil into intentional action.

CONCLUSION

SUMMARY: A HOLISTIC APPROACH TO HORMONAL HARMONY

You have completed the intensive, intricate work of Book 4, moving from anecdotal struggle to informed command over your internal physiological environment. This journey has been a focused campaign to bring order and predictability to the dynamic internal forces, your **hormonal cycles**, that profoundly impact Executive Function (EF) and emotional regulation.

The core achievement of this book is the replacement of unpredictable, chaotic symptom spikes with a predictable, manageable rhythm. You have learned that your struggles with focus, organization, and emotional volatility were never random failures; they were **measurable, neurochemical events** driven by the predictable ebb and flow of estrogen and progesterone. By acquiring this scientific knowledge and the data to back it up, you have transformed from a passive victim of hormonal chaos to a strategic manager of your own physiology. This is the ultimate victory of **self-advocacy** and **self-compassion**.

The stability cultivated here—the reliable synchronization of your internal body clock with your external structural supports (from Book

3)—is the essential, stable base required to successfully embark on the challenging work of emotional mastery (Book 5).

Section 1: The Victory of Validation and Data-Driven Care

The first and most crucial victory of this book is the emotional and psychological liberation that comes with **scientific validation**. By challenging the historical **gender health gap** (Chapter 1), you have equipped yourself with the tools to demand personalized, dynamic care.

1. Quantifying the Neurochemical Dip

You systematically gathered objective data (Chapter 1) that provided undeniable evidence of a cycle-symptom correlation.

- **Luteal Collapse:** You quantified your unique **Vulnerability Window**, the high-risk days characterized by low estrogen and a corresponding dip in dopamine support that exacerbates inattention and disorganization. This knowledge neutralizes the shame and anxiety that accompanies the sudden, overwhelming dips in performance, allowing for **radical acceptance**.
- **Targeted Advocacy:** This data provided the necessary fuel for informed **self-advocacy** regarding **Cycle Dosing** (Chapter 3), a dynamic strategy to offset the loss of estrogen's supportive effect on dopamine by monitoring a temporary dose adjustment of stimulants during the low-estrogen phase.

2. Mastering the Lifespan Transitions

You prepared for the most complex hormonal shifts, recognizing that the symptoms of midlife are often the result of the **"ADHD Squared"** effect (Chapter 4).

- **Perimenopausal Buffer:** The knowledge that cognitive decline, "brain fog," and severe anxiety during perimenopause are predictable consequences of sustained low estrogen empowers you to advocate for integrated pharmacological support, such as the strategic use of **Hormone Replacement Therapy (HRT)** combined with stimulants, to stabilize Working Memory and emotional regulation.

Section 2: Strategic Integration: Building the Physiological Buffer

The true power of this book lies in the strategic integration of hormonal knowledge with the structural strategies you have already mastered. This ensures that your management plan is flexible enough to withstand internal volatility.

1. Cycle Syncing as an EF Strategy

You learned to use the **Cycle Syncing Framework** (Chapter 2) to proactively match **task demand** with **neurochemical supply**, conserving limited cognitive energy.

- **Strategic Allocation:** You maximize efficiency by scheduling cognitively complex tasks (planning, analysis, deep work) during the **High-Estrogen Follicular Phase** (Peak Focus) and reserving low-stakes, routine tasks (filing, maintenance) for the **Low-Estrogen Luteal Phase** (Strategic Conservation).
- **Augmented Buffering:** During the **Vulnerability Window**, you learned to rigidly adapt your scheduling parameters by **increasing Time Buffers** and **contracting Pomodoro work sprints** (e.g., 20 / 10 cycle) to compensate for slower Working Memory and mitigate the high cognitive cost of context switching.

2. The Non-Negotiable Physiological Buffer

You established essential physiological practices (Chapter 5) that act as a crucial buffer against volatility, conserving EF reserves and regulating the nervous system.

- **Sleep and EF Restoration:** Consistent **sleep hygiene** and the **Nightly Offload Ritual** were established as non-negotiable foundations for restoring the **Prefrontal Cortex (PFC)** and maximizing **EF capacity** (WM, IC) for the following day.
- **Stress and Mood Stabilization:** You committed to using **Neuro-Nutritional Support** (protein, complex carbs) to stabilize blood sugar and prevent energy crashes. Furthermore, you learned to deploy immediate stress management techniques (Grounding, Deep Breathing) to act as a **Circuit-Breaker**, preventing stress arousal from further impairing your vulnerable **Inhibitory Control (IC)**.

Section 3: The Bridge to Emotional Mastery

The physiological and emotional stability achieved in this book is the essential precursor to the emotional mastery work of Book 5. A brain that is well-rested, regulated, and buffered against hormonal chaos has the emotional bandwidth necessary for deep psychological growth.

- **EF for Emotional Control:** The structural stability of your external systems reduces the chronic input that triggers emotional flares. The disciplined practice of **IC** (Chapter 5) is the very muscle required for **emotional regulation**, the ability to pause between stimulus and response, preparing you for the application of advanced behavioral therapies (DBT / CBT) in the next book.
- **Sustaining the Buffer:** Your ongoing commitment must be to **consistency in self-advocacy** and **self-compassion**. By maintaining your tracking data, adhering to your structural buffers, and refusing to succumb to the shame of neurobiological differences, you ensure that the stability you have fought for is sustained, equipping you for the profound work of Taming Intense Emotions (Book 5).

BOOK FIVE

TAME EMOTIONS AND STRENGTHEN RELATIONSHIPS IN WOMEN WITH ADHD

INTRODUCTION

You have successfully established the three foundational pillars of stability: external organization (Book 1), cognitive command (Book 3), and physiological resilience against hormonal volatility (Book 4). This comprehensive structural work has conserved the mental energy necessary for consistent follow-through and reduced the systemic chaos that fuels overwhelm. Now, the final volume addresses the challenges that define integrated success in adulthood: **Taming Emotions** and navigating the high-stakes friction points of **Relationships** and **Financial Management**.

For the woman with Attention-Deficit / Hyperactivity Disorder (ADHD), these two domains, money and love, are not merely areas of life; they are mirrors reflecting her deepest struggles with Executive Function (EF), emotional regulation, and self-worth. Both require consistent planning, impulse control, and active communication, all skills that are profoundly compromised by core ADHD symptoms. The result is often a persistent feeling of inadequacy and a chronic struggle to manage finances and nurture relationships in a way that feels effortless to a neurotypical individual.

This book provides the final, essential bridge, empowering you to translate structural stability into authentic connection and tangible financial health. We will confront the debilitating pain of **Rejection Sensitive Dysphoria (RSD)** and the heavy emotional burden of **shame**, while building proactive systems for assertive communication and financial control. The ultimate goal is to move beyond merely coping with adult responsibilities to achieving genuine integration, building a life defined by financial security, profound emotional resilience, and deep, lasting connection.

Section 1: The Emotional Core: RSD and the Cost of Internalization

For many women with ADHD, the journey of self-mastery is defined by the unique challenge of **Emotional Dysregulation**, the difficulty in managing and appropriately expressing emotions. This is not a character flaw, but a core symptom rooted in a neurological disconnect between the brain's emotional accelerator (the amygdala) and its inhibitory "brakes" (the frontal cortex, or PFC). This volatility leads to disproportionate emotional responses and intense frustration.

1. The Debilitating Pain of Rejection Sensitive Dysphoria (RSD)

A particularly painful and pervasive manifestation of this dysregulation, highly common in women with ADHD, is **Rejection Sensitive Dysphoria (RSD)**, an extreme emotional responsiveness and intense pain in anticipation of, or response to, **perceived** criticism or rejection.

- **Neurobiological Amplification:** The pain of RSD is more than hurt feelings; it is an immediate, overwhelming emotional pain that can feel physically agonizing, often described as being punched in the gut. This profound hypersensitivity is fueled by a lifetime of internalizing struggles and the fear that their "perceived failures" will be discovered.
- **The Shame Cycle:** For women, RSD fuels a deep sense of shame and inadequacy, driving compensatory behaviors like **perfectionism** and **people-pleasing** in an attempt to avoid any potential criticism. This painful feedback loop, where emotional dysregulation leads to RSD, and RSD feeds shame, creates a devastating barrier to authentic connection and self-

acceptance, often leading to co-occurring anxiety and depression.

2. Healing Through Skills-Based Intervention

The solution lies not in suppressing emotions, but in building a robust, evidence-based toolkit that provides a crucial **pause** between stimulus and impulsive response. This book draws heavily on the therapeutic principles of **Dialectical Behavior Therapy (DBT)** and **Cognitive Behavioral Therapy (CBT)**, which are highly effective for managing the anxiety, emotional intensity, and interpersonal friction associated with ADHD.

The toolkit focuses on:

- **Mindfulness and Distress Tolerance:** Creating immediate behavioral interventions (e.g., grounding, deep breathing) to calm the activated nervous system when a storm hits, allowing the PFC time to re-engage.
- **Cognitive Reframing:** Identifying and challenging the irrational thought patterns (e.g., catastrophizing, mind reading) that amplify emotional pain, replacing self-criticism with strategic, compassionate alternatives.

Section 2: The Relational Toll: Communication and Shared Responsibility

The emotional intensity and EF challenges inherent in ADHD often create significant friction in close relationships, which require consistent communication, follow-through, and empathy.

1. Communication Challenges: Attention and Interruptions

One of the most common sources of conflict is difficulty with **active listening** and **impulsivity**. A woman's mind may wander or "zone out" during a conversation (inattention), leading her partner to feel unheard. Conversely, she may impulsively interrupt or blurt out her thoughts (impulsivity) because she fears her thought will be lost due to compromised Working Memory.

The solution is structural: utilizing tools of **Interpersonal Effectiveness** (a core skill of DBT) to build trust. This includes using techniques like:

- **Mirroring and Validation:** Restating what the partner said ("Mirroring") to confirm understanding and acknowledging their feelings ("Validation") to boost their sense of being heard. This is a direct strategy to counteract the appearance of inattention.
- **"I" Statements:** Employing assertive communication that focuses on one's own feelings ("I feel overwhelmed...") rather than the other person's actions ("You never help...") to de-escalate conflict and prevent defensiveness.

2. Navigating the Parent-Child Dynamic

Unmanaged EF deficits often lead to a dysfunctional **"parent-child" dynamic** in neurodiverse couples. The neurotypical partner may unintentionally take on the role of a **taskmaster** or reminder for household chores or finances, leaving the ADHD partner feeling like a scolded child, which triggers shame and avoidance.

The solution is collaboration and externalization:

- **External Systems:** Offload shared responsibilities from the neurotypical partner's memory onto neutral, external systems (e.g., shared digital calendars, whiteboard chore charts). This shifts accountability from the person to the system.
- **Collaborative Planning:** Schedule brief, dedicated **weekly check-ins** to discuss logistics and tasks in a calm environment, building a routine of open dialogue and shared problem-solving rather than reactive arguments.

Section 3: The Financial Drain: Conquering the ADHD Tax

The financial challenges faced by women with ADHD are a direct, measurable consequence of core EF deficits—impulsivity, time blindness, and poor organization, that lead to the **"Financial ADHD Tax."**

- **The Cost:** Studies show that adults with a history of ADHD exhibit substantially worse financial outcomes, earning significantly less and having 66% less money in savings by age 30 compared to their peers. This disparity is due to chronic issues like:

    - **Impulsive Buying:** Driven by the search for immediate dopamine reward, leading to spontaneous purchases and debt.
    - **Time Blindness Penalties:** Chronic forgetfulness regarding deadlines leads to late fees, fines, and interest accrual.
- **The Solution: Automation and Boundaries:** Financial stability is achieved by bypassing compromised EF with strict external structures. This includes automating all bill payments and savings transfers to eliminate the need for memory and manual initiation (Chapter 5, Book 3), and creating clear **financial boundaries** (e.g., using specific accounts, implementing a mandatory "pause" before spending) to protect savings from impulse decisions.

Conclusion: Your Integrated Success

This book culminates the entire journey of self-mastery. You have moved beyond structural and cognitive stability to address the highest-stakes areas of life: your inner emotional world and your connections with others. By integrating the resilience gained from EF mastery and hormonal stability, you are now equipped to navigate conflict with intention, manage profound emotional pain with self-compassion, and build a financially secure, authentically connected life.

The final act of self-mastery is the commitment to this integrated system, moving from the shadow of shame into the light of self-acceptance and a truly fulfilling existence.

CHAPTER 1

GROUND YOURSELF: APPLY SENSORY TECHNIQUES TO INTERRUPT ACUTE DISTRESS

You have successfully built the robust external and cognitive structures necessary for stability (Books 1–4), conserving the mental energy required for sustained follow-through. Now, this book addresses the final, most vulnerable area of the ADHD experience: **Emotional Dysregulation**, the pervasive difficulty in managing and appropriately expressing intense feelings. For the woman with Attention-Deficit / Hyperactivity Disorder (ADHD), the onset of a profound emotional surge, whether anger, anxiety, or the overwhelming pain of Rejection Sensitive Dysphoria (RSD), often feels like a traffic light that skips yellow, flipping instantly from calm ("green") to crisis ("red").

This surge, rooted in a neurobiological disconnect between the emotional accelerator (amygdala) and the cognitive "brakes" (prefrontal cortex), compromises the ability to think rationally or employ learned strategies. This chapter provides the immediate, evidence-based toolkit to address these moments of acute distress using **Sensory Grounding Techniques**. These techniques serve as a crucial **physiological circuit-breaker**, actively calming the activated nervous system and creating the essential "pause" that allows your Executive Function (EF) skills, honed in Book 3, to re-engage and prevent a spiral into meltdown or impulsive action.

The goal is to shift your focus from overwhelming internal chaos to anchoring in the immediate, external reality, transforming emotional volatility into a manageable process.

Section 1: The Neurobiology of the Emotional Surge

To effectively interrupt acute distress, you must understand that the "emotional storm" is a real, physiological event driven by the brain's threat system.

1. The Amygdala-PFC Disconnect

Emotional dysregulation in ADHD is not a character flaw; it is a neurological vulnerability. When a strong trigger occurs (internal stress, external conflict, or perceived rejection):

- **The Accelerator (Amygdala) Overreacts:** The brain's threat system is highly sensitive, leading to an immediate, intense, and disproportionate emotional response. Emotions feel "all or nothing."
- **The Brakes (PFC) Fail:** The prefrontal cortex (PFC), responsible for **Inhibitory Control (IC)**, thinking before acting, is often less active in the ADHD brain. This diminished IC makes it difficult to suppress the automatic, intense reaction.

The result is a rapid, often unpredictable escalation of feelings that compromises the ability to judge, think, and make decisions, leading directly to mental or emotional paralysis.

2. Distress Tolerance vs. Emotional Change

This chapter introduces **Distress Tolerance** (a core skill of Dialectical Behavior Therapy, or DBT), which is the strategic skill of managing a crisis without making it worse.

- **Crisis Management:** When an emotion is at peak intensity ("red light"), it is physically impossible to use complex cognitive strategies (like challenging a thought). Distress Tolerance skills are immediate, physiological interventions designed to endure the intense, painful emotion long enough for the intensity to naturally subside—without resorting to impulsive, unhelpful behaviors (e.g., self-harm, yelling, avoidance).
- **Creating the Pause:** The goal of grounding is to activate the **Parasympathetic Nervous System** ("rest and digest") and force the attention to the external environment. This provides the necessary **physiological pause** that allows the PFC time to return online and deploy the cognitive and interpersonal skills mastered later in this book.

Section 2: Immediate Physiological Circuit-Breakers (TIPP)

The most effective distress tolerance skills are those that provide a rapid, intense sensory shock to the system, overriding the emotional alarm in the amygdala. The DBT toolkit utilizes the **TIPP** skills for this purpose.

1. Temperature (The Cold Shock Reset)

Using cold temperature is a rapid way to activate the body's **mammalian dive reflex**, which immediately slows the heart rate and calms the nervous system, forcing the body to transition from fight-or-flight to rest-and-digest.

- **Action:** Splash cold water on your face, or hold a frozen compress or a bag of ice on the back of your neck or wrists for 30–60 seconds.
- **Neuro-Benefit:** This intense, sudden sensory input provides a powerful distraction and rapidly shifts the body's physiological state, overriding the stress response and reducing the intensity of the emotional surge.

2. Intense Exercise (The Energy Discharge)

Intense physical movement provides a direct, healthy outlet for discharging the pent-up emotional energy that fuels anger, anxiety, or internal restlessness.

- **Action:** Engage in brief, intense physical activity, such as sprinting in place, rapid walking up and down a set of stairs, or performing 20 jumping jacks. The movement must be sufficient to trigger a change in heart rate and breathing.
- **Neuro-Benefit:** This burst of activity uses the physical energy of the stress response, preventing it from spiraling into a mental or emotional meltdown.

3. Paced Breathing (The Nervous System Anchor)

Slow, intentional breathing directly impacts the nervous system, shifting it from a high-arousal stress state to a calmer, more controlled state.

- **Action:** Practice paced, deep breathing, such as inhaling slowly for **four counts**, holding briefly, and exhaling slowly for **six counts**. This focuses attention on the rhythm and sensation of the breath.
- **Neuro-Benefit:** The extended exhale signals to the brain that the danger has passed, activating the restorative parasympathetic nervous system and reducing heart rate and blood pressure, which physically counteracts the panic response.

Section 3: The 5-4-3-2-1 Sensory Grounding Technique

When a woman is experiencing a rapid emotional surge or feels trapped in a cycle of rumination and intrusive thoughts, her mind is fixated on the overwhelming **internal chaos**. Sensory Grounding shifts attention immediately to the safe, neutral reality of the **external environment**.

1. Anchoring Attention to External Reality

The 5-4-3-2-1 method forces the mind, which struggles with internal filtering, to perform a sequential, structured task focused entirely on sensory input. This process utilizes the cultivated attentional skills (Book 3) to create a distraction that is constructive and calming.

- **5 Things You Can See:** Look around and name five distinct things, focusing on color, texture, or shape. *This forces visual attention.*
- **4 Things You Can Feel:** Notice four distinct physical sensations (e.g., the pressure of your feet on the floor, the texture of your shirt, the air temperature, the warmth of your hands). *This anchors physical reality.*
- **3 Things You Can Hear:** Listen for three distinct sounds (e.g., distant traffic, your own breathing, the hum of a computer). *This shifts auditory focus from internal noise to external sound.*
- **2 Things You Can Smell:** Notice two distinct scents (even if faint).
- **1 Thing You Can Taste:** Notice one taste in your mouth (e.g., mint, coffee residue, water).

2. Integrating Grounding with Self-Compassion

Once the acute emotional peak has subsided (after using TIPP or 5-4-3-2-1), the crisis is over, but the residual distress remains. This is the moment to engage the skills of **self-compassion** (Chapter 5) to prevent the distress from spiraling into shame and self-criticism.

- **Affirmation Anchor:** Pair the grounding technique with a compassionate, non-judgmental phrase. After the 5-4-3-2-1 sequence is complete, take a deep breath and repeat: *"This is a moment of suffering, and it is okay. I am here for myself. I am safe."* This reinforces self-kindness, which research shows helps deactivate the brain's threat-defense system.
- **Journaling as Offload:** If the emotional surge was triggered by overwhelming thoughts (e.g., a massive to-do list, a fear of failure), immediately write down those weighty thoughts in a journal (the **Brain Dump**). This externalizes the internal chaos, helping to contain the distress and prevent further rumination, which consumes valuable WM and emotional energy.

Section 4: The Emotional Payoff: Creating Space for Intentional Response

Mastering immediate distress tolerance is the single most important action a woman with ADHD can take to improve her emotional well-being and relationships.

1. Protecting Executive Function and Relationships

By preventing the emotional surge from spiraling into a meltdown, you protect your vital EF reserves and your relational bonds.

- **IC Conservation:** When a sensory shock (TIPP) or distraction (Grounding) creates a crucial pause, it allows the Inhibitory Control (IC) to return online and prevent the impulsive verbal reaction (e.g., snapping at a partner, sending an angry email) that leads to profound regret and relational damage (Book 5).
- **Reducing Shame:** Successfully navigating a crisis without making it worse, without resorting to impulsive, destructive behaviors, provides powerful **evidence of competence** and follow-through, actively dismantling the shame and feeling of inadequacy that accompany unmanaged emotional outbursts.

2. The Bridge to Emotional Mastery (DBT / CBT)

Grounding is merely the first step. The stability gained here is the bridge to the complex cognitive and behavioral work that follows in this book.

- **Readying the Mind:** Once the intensity of the emotion has dropped from "red" to "yellow," the mind is calm enough to engage in rational thought. You are now prepared for the work of **Challenging Thoughts** (Chapter 2) and applying **Opposite Action** (Chapter 3), the crucial, high-leverage steps that actually change long-term emotional response patterns.

Chapter 1 Workbook: Ground Yourself: Apply Sensory Techniques to Interrupt Acute Distress

Objective: To practice immediate, sensory-based techniques to interrupt acute emotional distress (anxiety, anger, RSD pain) and activate the calming Parasympathetic Nervous System.

Scientific Anchor: Grounding and sensory shock (TIPP) provide rapid physiological interventions that override the emotional alarm system (amygdala), creating the necessary pause for Inhibitory Control to re-engage.

Activity 1.1: The TIPP Circuit-Breaker Plan

Instructions: Create a clear, pre-planned sequence of physiological action for when an intense emotional surge hits.

1. **The Trigger:** Identify a frequent trigger that leads to rapid emotional escalation (e.g., Partner criticism, unexpected task failure, social rejection).

   My Trigger: ____

   ____

   ____

2. **The TIPP Sequence (The "Immediate Action" Plan):** Commit to these three low-friction, rapid interventions.

DBT Skill	Action (Must be pre-planned)	Time / Duration	Neuro-Benefit
T: Temperature	(Example: Splash cold water on face / hold ice pack on wrists.)	30 seconds	Activates the dive reflex / calms heart rate.
I: Intense Exercise	(Example: 20 jumping jacks / brisk walk to mailbox.)	1 minute	Discharges physical energy of stress response.
P: Paced Breathing	(Example: 4-count inhale, 6-count exhale.)	3 cycles	Engages parasympathetic nervous system.

Activity 1.2: The 5-4-3-2-1 Grounding Practice

Instructions: Practice the 5-4-3-2-1 technique now, deliberately slowing down and forcing your focus onto external cues. This trains your attention muscle for crisis situations.

1. **5:** List five things you see in your immediate environment:

   ----

2. **4:** List four things you can feel (e.g., temperature, texture of clothing, chair pressure):

   ----

3. **3:** List three things you can hear (external sounds):

   ----

4. **2:** List two things you can smell:

   ----

5. **1:** List one thing you can taste:

Reflective Commitment: If my mind is racing with shame or anger, I commit to performing this full sequence to achieve the **pause.**

Reflection 1.3: Analyzing the Gain in Control

Instructions: Reflect on the functional benefit of distress tolerance skills.

1. **The Crisis Pause:** If a small trigger (e.g., a partner's tone of voice) leads to a rapid emotional surge, how does the deliberate act of performing **Intense Exercise** (Action 1.1) provide the necessary physical and cognitive **interruption** to prevent you from immediately spiraling or shouting?

Interruption Mechanism: ______________________________

____

____

____

____

2. **IC Protection:** By successfully calming the intensity of the emotion using **Grounding**, you protect your **Inhibitory Control**. How does this conserved IC benefit your relationship in that moment (e.g., prevents you from sending an angry text, prevents an impulsive apology)?

   IC / Relational Benefit: ______________________________

   ____

   ____

   ____

   ____

3. **The Bridge to Cognition:** Once the emotion drops from an intensity of 8 / 10 to 4 / 10, what is the first, small **cognitive task** you are now able to perform (e.g., pick up your journal, apply a rational thought) that was impossible before grounding?

   Cognitive Regain: ______________________________

   ____

   ____

   ____

   ____

CHAPTER 2

CHALLENGE THE CRITIC: IDENTIFY AND REFRAME UNHELPFUL, SHAME-BASED THOUGHTS

In Chapter 1, you learned the crucial first response to acute emotional distress: grounding your body and mind using sensory techniques to create a **physiological circuit-breaker**. That essential pause successfully dropped your emotion from a crisis "red light" to a manageable "yellow light." Now, this chapter introduces the second, transformative step in achieving emotional mastery: engaging the cognitive brain to challenge the destructive, shame-based narratives that fuel emotional volatility.

For the woman with Attention-Deficit / Hyperactivity Disorder (ADHD), emotional dysregulation is rarely just about the feeling; it is amplified by the automatic, pervasive presence of a harsh **Inner Critic**. This voice, fed by a lifetime of internalizing struggles and feeling inadequate, converts minor setbacks into massive personal failures, often through the mechanism of **cognitive distortions** (unhelpful thinking traps).

This chapter equips you with the toolkit of **Cognitive Behavioral Therapy (CBT)**, an evidence-based approach proven highly effective for managing the anxiety, emotional intensity, and chronic shame associated with ADHD. You will learn to become a detective of your own mind, systematically identifying, challenging, and reframing the irrational thought patterns that compromise your Executive Function (EF) and sabotage your self-worth. The goal is to dismantle the source of internalized blame and replace the inner critic with a powerful, compassionate inner ally.

Section 1: The Neurobiological Bridge: Thoughts, Feelings, and Actions

To conquer the inner critic, we must first understand the powerful, instantaneous link between thoughts, feelings, and actions, particularly as it functions in a neurobiologically vulnerable system.

1. The Disconnect: Amygdala Amplification and PFC Failure

The intense, unpredictable nature of ADHD emotions stems from a fundamental disconnect: the **Amygdala** (the brain's emotional accelerator) is often highly sensitive, leading to a quick trigger for strong emotions, while the **Prefrontal Cortex (PFC)** (the cognitive "brakes") is less effective at inhibiting or modulating that intense reaction.

- **Thoughts as Triggers:** In this sensitive neurobiological context, a fleeting negative thought, unexamined and unchallenged, can immediately be amplified by the overactive amygdala, leading to a full-blown emotional storm, a phenomenon far more likely in the context of emotional dysregulation.
- **The Shame Loop:** Because the woman with ADHD is prone to interpreting her symptoms (forgetfulness, disorganization) as moral failings, her automatic thoughts often center on deep inadequacy (e.g., "I'm useless," "I'll never succeed"). This self-blaming thought acts as a **stress trigger**, increasing cortisol and anxiety, which further impairs the function of the PFC, making it even harder to think clearly and regulate the emotion, a destructive shame loop.

2. CBT's Core Principle: Thoughts are Interpretations, Not Facts

The fundamental premise of CBT is that events do not cause feelings; your **interpretation** of events causes your feelings and subsequent actions. By identifying and challenging the automatic thought, you interrupt the emotional chain reaction.

- **Intervention Point:** CBT focuses on creating a cognitive intervention point in the "yellow light" phase of the emotional surge (after grounding has calmed the initial physical alarm). This pause allows the woman to use her cognitive skills to challenge the thought before it fully dictates her emotional and behavioral response.
- **Building the Cognitive Buffer:** Through consistent practice, the CBT approach empowers the individual to develop a systematic framework for mental processing, effectively training the PFC to engage and override the automatic, unhelpful thoughts that often lead to emotional dysregulation and impulsivity.

Section 2: Unmasking Common Cognitive Distortions

Cognitive distortions are irrational or exaggerated thought patterns that reinforce negative thinking, undermine self-esteem, and exacerbate emotional distress. Recognizing these "thinking traps" is the crucial first step toward challenging them.

1. Distortions Amplified by Emotional Intensity

These distortions are common, but they become particularly damaging for the ADHD brain due to the intensity of its emotional regulation and its history of masking and shame.

- **Catastrophizing:** This involves exaggerating the negative consequences of an event, jumping to the worst possible conclusion, even when it's highly unlikely.
    - *ADHD Example:* "I missed that deadline by one hour. Now my boss will think I'm incompetent, I'll be fired, and I'll never find another job." This distortion turns a small mistake into an apocalyptic scenario, fueling intense anxiety and shame.

- **All-or-Nothing Thinking (Black-and-White Thinking):** Seeing things only in extremes, with no middle ground. Everything is either a complete success or an utter failure.
    - *ADHD Example:* "I didn't finish everything on my to-do list today, so the day was a total waste, and I'm a complete failure." This distortion ignores partial progress and effort, reinforcing the shame of imperfection.
- **Mind Reading:** Assuming you know what others are thinking or feeling, usually negatively, without any actual evidence. This is especially painful for those with Rejection Sensitive Dysphoria (RSD).
    - *ADHD Example:* "My partner gave me a curt reply. He must be disappointed in me and thinks I'm a mess." This jumps to rejection-based conclusions, triggering intense emotional pain without factual basis.
- **"Should" Statements:** Holding rigid, often unrealistic, expectations for yourself that often ignore the neurobiological reality of ADHD.
    - *ADHD Example:* "I should be able to focus for three hours without checking my phone, just like my colleagues." When this unrealistic expectation is not met, it leads to intense guilt, shame, and self-punishment.

2. Shame-Based Distortions (Internalization)

The distortions of **Personalization** and **Emotional Reasoning** are directly linked to the shame felt by women who internalize their struggles.

- **Personalization:** Blaming yourself for external events or taking things personally that are not your fault.
    - *ADHD Example:* "Our team project failed because I didn't push hard enough on my part," even when multiple factors were involved. This ties into the deep-seated belief that one's inadequacy is the root of all problems.
- **Emotional Reasoning:** Believing something is true solely because you feel it strongly, treating intense feelings as definitive evidence of reality.

- *ADHD Example:* "I feel like a lazy, unproductive person today, so I must be lazy and incapable." The intensity of ADHD emotions makes this distortion particularly compelling and difficult to challenge.

Section 3: The Practice: Becoming a Thought Detective

The key to breaking free from the grip of distorted thoughts is to become a detective of your own mind. This is an active, structured process of observation, questioning, and re-framing, a strategic application of your cognitive skills.

Step 1: Catch the Thought (The "Pause and Observe")

When you feel a sudden surge of a strong negative emotion (anger, shame, intense anxiety), use the **Grounding Techniques** (Chapter 1) to create a physiological pause. Once the intensity has dropped, engage your cognitive self.

- **Identify the Trigger:** Ask: "What just happened?" (The external event).
- **Catch the Narrative:** Ask: "What thought just went through my mind right before I felt this intense emotion?" Write the exact thought down immediately. The act of externalizing the thought helps you gain crucial distance from it, allowing you to view it as an object of analysis rather than an undeniable truth.

Step 2: Challenge the Thought (The "Courtroom Test")

Once you have externalized the thought, put it on trial. Imagine you are a neutral judge or lawyer, rigorously examining the evidence for and against the thought.

- **Test the Evidence:** What is the **concrete, factual evidence** that this thought is 100% true? (Focus only on facts, not feelings or past assumptions). What are the **facts against** the thought (e.g., "I finished 80% of the project," "My partner used a neutral tone of voice")?
- **Name the Distortion:** Am I falling into a specific thinking trap? Naming the distortion (e.g., "This is Catastrophizing") helps you depersonalize the thought and strip it of its power.

- **Practice Perspective-Taking:** What would I tell a friend in this exact situation? Use the self-compassion skills you have trained to apply rationality to the situation.

Step 3: Reframe and Replace (The "Constructive Alternative")

Based on your rigorous questioning, formulate a more balanced, realistic, and ultimately more helpful thought. This is not about forced positive affirmations; it is about finding a more accurate, nuanced, and empowering perspective that reflects reality more fully.

Original Distorted Thought (Shameful)	Reframed, Balanced Thought (Strategic / Compassionate)
"I'm a total failure for messing up that small task; I can't do anything right."	**Reframe:** "I made a mistake, which is human. I finished three Milestones today, and that's solid progress. The mistake is fixable; it does not define my worth."
"My boss ignored me. I'm sure she thinks I'm incompetent (Mind Reading / RSD)."	**Reframe:** "I observed a neutral behavior (she was busy). I'm feeling fear of rejection, which is RSD. I will gather factual evidence later by checking in about the report."
"Since I procrastinated, the whole project is ruined, and there's no point in starting (All-or-Nothing / Paralysis)."	**Reframe:** "The project is not ruined. I can allocate 25 minutes now to the first micro-step, and that momentum is better than paralysis."

Section 4: The Emotional Payoff: Healing Shame and Building Resilience

The consistent practice of identifying and challenging distorted thoughts yields profound emotional and psychological liberation, reinforcing self-worth and increasing resilience.

1. Healing from Shame and RSD

The single greatest payoff is the active dismantling of the Inner Critic, which is the relentless source of shame for the woman with ADHD.

- **Dismantling the Narrative:** By rigorously testing and replacing shame-based thoughts, you systematically dismantle a lifetime of internalized narratives about inadequacy and failure. This builds a robust, internal foundation of self-worth that is resistant to external criticism and the debilitating pain of RSD.
- **Building Self-Acceptance:** The commitment to approaching your own suffering with kindness and rational inquiry is a powerful act of **self-compassion** (Chapter 5), creating a psychological buffer that allows you to learn from mistakes without being crippled by them.

2. Protecting Executive Function and Relationships

Challenging thoughts directly protects the EF skills you have mastered and improves relational outcomes.

- **Conserving IC:** By interrupting the cascade of anxiety and anger that a distorted thought triggers, you conserve vital **Inhibitory Control (IC)** resources. This preserved IC is necessary to engage the behavioral skills (like Opposite Action) that prevent impulsive shouting or emotional outbursts.
- **Reducing Relational Friction:** Since strong emotional reactions often spiral from distorted, fear-based thoughts (e.g., Mind Reading / Catastrophizing), challenging these thoughts reduces the intensity of the feeling, allowing you to approach difficult conversations with clarity and calm. This promotes constructive communication and prevents the friction that damages relationships (Book 5).

Conclusion: Your Cognitive Command

You have achieved cognitive command over the inner critic. By consistently applying the CBT framework, you transform your mind from a source of perpetual self-criticism and shame into a reliable engine for self-compassion and intentional action. This mastery of your thought patterns is the essential cognitive anchor that supports the intense behavioral and interpersonal work that follows in this book, allowing you to use your emotions as information, not as masters.

Chapter 2 Workbook: Challenge the Critic: Identify and Reframe Unhelpful, Shame-Based Thoughts

Objective: To practice identifying common cognitive distortions that fuel shame and emotional dysregulation, and to systematically challenge and reframe them using the CBT method.

Scientific Anchor: Identifying and challenging cognitive distortions is a cornerstone of CBT, helping to interrupt the thought-emotion-action cycle that compromises emotional regulation and drives self-criticism.

Activity 2.1: The Thought Detective Audit (Catch & Name)

Instructions: Identify a recent moment when you felt a sudden, strong negative emotion (e.g., shame, anger, overwhelming anxiety). Use the framework to catch and name the distortion.

1. **The Trigger Event:** Briefly describe the objective event (e.g., "I forgot to send an important work email this morning").

   Event: ____

   ____

   ____

2. **The Automatic Thought (The Inner Critic's Voice):** Write the exact thought that immediately followed the event.

   Thought: ____

   ____

   ____

3. **Name the Distortion:** Which thinking trap best describes that thought? (Catastrophizing, All-or-Nothing, Mind Reading, Emotional Reasoning, "Should" Statements, Personalization).

   Distortion: ____

   ____

   ____

Activity 2.2: The Courtroom Test (Challenge & Evidence)

Instructions: Put your automatic thought from Activity 2.1 on trial. You are the lawyer testing the evidence.

1. **Evidence FOR the Thought:** What is the factual evidence supporting the thought? (Focus on facts, not feelings).

   Factual Evidence: ____

   ____

   ____

2. **Evidence AGAINST the Thought:** What facts contradict the thought? (e.g., "I met three Milestones this week," "The email is only one hour late," "My boss sent a neutral email earlier").

   Contradictory Evidence: ___________________________________

   ____

   ____

3. **The Verdict:** Based on the evidence, is the original thought 100% true? ____

Reflection 2.3: Reframe and Empower

Instructions: Formulate a compassionate, strategic reframe for your thought, using the evidence you collected.

1. **The Balanced Reframe:** Write a new, realistic, and compassionate statement that acknowledges the mistake but rejects the shame.

   Reframed Thought: ____

   ____

   ____

2. **RSD Healing:** If the thought was related to fear of rejection or shame (RSD), how does having a **factual list of evidence against** the thought help reduce the intense, physical pain associated with RSD?

   RSD Benefit: ____

   ____

   ____

3. **IC Conservation:** How does the act of stopping to **Challenge** the thought (Step 2) conserve the **Inhibitory Control (IC)** you need to manage your emotions, rather than letting the anger / shame immediately fuel an impulsive reaction?

   IC Conservation: ____

   ____

   ____

   ____

CHAPTER 3

CHANGE THE SCRIPT: USE "OPPOSITE ACTION" TO INTERRUPT EMOTIONAL IMPULSES

In the journey toward emotional mastery, you have secured the crucial foundations: grounding the body during crisis (Chapter 1) and challenging the destructive narratives of the inner critic (Chapter 2). However, cognitive insight alone is often insufficient when faced with the raw, intense force of an emotional surge. For the woman with Attention-Deficit / Hyperactivity Disorder (ADHD), the urge to act on an intense emotion, to yell, to withdraw, or to lash out, is powerful and immediate, driven by deficits in Inhibitory Control (IC).

This chapter introduces the essential behavioral skill for managing these moments: **Opposite Action**. This core principle of **Dialectical Behavior Therapy (DBT)** provides a structured, actionable framework for interrupting the destructive emotional cycle. Opposite Action mandates that when an intense emotion leads to an unhelpful or destructive urge, you must intentionally execute the **opposite** behavioral response.

This is a powerful, strategic intervention that bypasses compromised IC by using intentional behavior to change the emotional trajectory itself. You move from passively enduring an emotion to actively changing the internal script, transforming automatic, regrettable reactions into thoughtful, intentional responses that build long-term emotional resilience and strengthen relationships.

Section 1: The Neurobiology of the Impulsive Urge

To effectively deploy Opposite Action, you must understand that the destructive urge is a neurological event rooted in the ADHD brain's structural deficits, not a failure of character.

1. The Amygdala-PFC Disconnect and IC Failure

Emotional dysregulation in ADHD is defined by a disconnect between the emotional accelerator (the amygdala) and the cognitive brakes (the prefrontal cortex, or PFC).

- **Disproportionate Urges:** When a trigger occurs, the amygdala fires, creating an immediate, intense urge (e.g., anger, despair). Because the PFC's Inhibitory Control (IC) is inconsistent, the urge translates quickly into an impulsive action (yelling, snapping, avoiding) before the logical brain can assess the situation.
- **Emotions vs. Action:** The intense emotion is real, but the action it urges is often disproportionate or unhelpful to the situation. For instance, sadness over a minor setback is real, but the urge to isolate for three days (the action) is unhelpful because it only increases despair and shame.
- **The Behavioral Solution:** Opposite Action recognizes that if you change the destructive behavior, the emotion that fueled it will eventually change too. This behavioral intervention is often faster and more effective in the moment of crisis than trying to force a cognitive change (e.g., trying to convince yourself to *not* be angry).

2. The Unhelpful Nature of Emotional Responses

Opposite Action is deployed only when the emotion or its associated urge is **unjustified** by the facts of the situation, or when the emotion is **justified but the resulting action is unhelpful** (i.e., makes the situation worse).

Emotion	Urge (Action)	When Opposite Action is Needed
Anger / Irritation	Attack, yell, criticize, lash out.	When the situation is minor (e.g., spilled coffee) or the action will lead to negative relational consequences (Book 5).
Shame / Guilt	Hide, isolate, avoid communication, apologize excessively.	When the urge to isolate perpetuates sadness, or when avoidance guarantees task failure (Task Paralysis).
Fear / Anxiety	Avoid the situation, procrastinate, run away, seek constant reassurance.	When the avoidance is disproportionate to the actual threat (e.g., avoiding a necessary phone call), increasing anxiety in the long term.

Section 2: The Opposite Action Framework in Practice

Applying Opposite Action requires a swift, methodical three-step sequence, utilizing the **Pause** created by grounding (Chapter 1) to deploy intentional action.

Step 1: Identify the Emotion and the Urge

Use the tools of mindfulness (Chapter 3) to label the feeling and the subsequent urge. You must separate the emotion (the feeling) from the impulse (the behavior).

- *Example:* **Emotion:** Intense Anger. **Urge:** To interrupt my partner and shout that I am overwhelmed.
- *Example:* **Emotion:** Shame / RSD pain. **Urge:** To immediately send a long text message apologizing for a minor mistake and withdraw from social interaction.

Step 2: Determine Justification and Impact

Rigorously test the emotion (using CBT skills from Chapter 2). Is the emotion justified by the facts, or is the resulting urge helpful?

- *Anger Scenario:* Is my partner's neutral comment truly a massive attack (justification)? No. Is yelling at them helpful (impact)? No, it will only increase conflict and shame. *Conclusion: Opposite Action is required.*
- *Shame Scenario:* Is my minor mistake (unpaid bill) a complete and total catastrophe that warrants three days of self-isolation (impact)? No. *Conclusion: Opposite Action is required.*

Step 3: Execute the Opposite Behavior

Immediately engage in a behavior that is completely contrary to the destructive urge. The action must be immediate, visible, and sustained for a period long enough to allow the emotional intensity to subside.

Unhelpful Urge (ADHD Impulse)	Opposite Action (DBT Strategy)	Neurobiological Effect
Urge to Attack / Yell (Anger / Irritability)	**Use a Gentle Voice / Avoid Aggression.** Avoid eye contact, relax facial muscles, use "I" statements, or implement a pre-planned **Time Out** (walk away for 10 min).	Deactivates the physiological fight-or-flight response, allowing the PFC to re-engage Inhibitory Control.
Urge to Avoid / Isolate (Shame / RSD / Paralysis)	**Engage Socially / Approach Task.** Force yourself to initiate a micro-step of the avoided task (Paralysis), or call a supportive friend (Isolation).	Displaces the unhelpful emotional energy with productive, non-shaming action, building momentum.

Unhelpful Urge (ADHD Impulse)	Opposite Action (DBT Strategy)	Neurobiological Effect
Urge to Ruminate / Worry (Anxiety)	**Focus on External Reality.** Use **5-4-3-2-1 Grounding** (Chapter 1), engage in intense physical exercise (Intense Exercise TIPP skill), or switch focus to a neutral, absorbing task.	Diverts Working Memory from the anxious thought loop to an external anchor, disrupting the spiral.
Urge to Withdraw / Give Up (Despair / Sadness)	**Increase Activity.** Force yourself to engage in gentle, positive activity (e.g., listen to music, go outside, walk briskly), even if you don't feel like it.	Increases positive affect, which is the opposite of the despairing urge.

Section 3: Applying Opposite Action to Relationship and Task Friction

Opposite Action is a powerful tool for women with ADHD because it targets the precise behavioral consequences that most damage self-worth and relationships.

1. Managing Anger and Relational Conflict

Anger and irritability are highly prevalent ADHD symptoms that profoundly damage close relationships, often leading to arguments over seemingly trivial issues.

- **The Gentle Communication Script:** When Anger flares, the urge is to attack or criticize (e.g., "You never listen!"). The opposite action is to immediately shift the physical posture (relaxed hands, slow speech) and use **"I" statements** (Chapter 5, Book 5) to express the need without attacking the partner's character. For example, replace "You never listen!" with, "I feel unheard when you look at your phone while I'm talking."

- **The Time Out Protocol:** If the emotional surge is too high (high "red light"), the opposite action is to take a pre-agreed **Time Out** (e.g., "I need 10 minutes to cool down, I will return at 7:30 PM"). This is crucial IC in action, physically removing the threat of an impulsive outburst that would cause lasting damage.

2. Defeating Shame, RSD, and Task Paralysis

Shame and RSD often manifest as the paralyzing urge to hide or avoid tasks that carry the risk of failure (Task Paralysis).

- **Opposite Action for Avoidance:** If the urge is to stay paralyzed and avoid starting a daunting project (e.g., filing taxes), the opposite action is **immediate, non-judgmental initiation of a micro-step** (Chapter 1, Book 3). For example, if the urge is to zone out on the couch, the opposite action is to force yourself to walk to the desk and simply open the file folder. This breaks the shame / paralysis cycle with momentum.
- **Opposite Action for Shame / RSD:** When RSD strikes (urge to apologize profusely or withdraw after a perceived snub), the opposite action is to **engage socially** or **assert self-respect**. Instead of withdrawing, force yourself to make brief social contact. Instead of collapsing into excessive apologies, make a short, factual apology and then engage in self-compassionate thought-reframing (Chapter 2).

Section 4: The Behavioral Chain Analysis (BCA): Proactive Intervention

Opposite Action is best used proactively. The **Behavioral Chain Analysis (BCA)** is a DBT skill that helps you analyze a past regretted action to pinpoint the precise environmental and internal triggers that occurred *before* the impulsive urge, allowing for strategic future intervention.

1. Analyzing the Sequence of Events

BCA recognizes that impulsive behavior is the end of a long chain of smaller, often unnoticed, events. Analyzing this chain reveals where your EF and emotional regulation broke down.

- **The Regretted Action:** Start with the impulsive behavior (e.g., snapping at your child, making a massive impulsive purchase).

- **The Chain:** Work backward, identifying the precise sequence:
    1. **Vulnerability:** What made me vulnerable? (e.g., Low sleep, skipped meal, low-estrogen Luteal Phase).
    2. **Trigger:** What was the final external event? (e.g., Child asked for help while I was hyperfocused).
    3. **Thought / Feeling:** What was the immediate thought / emotion? (e.g., "I can't take this interruption, I'm going to fail!" -> Intense Anger / Frustration).
    4. **Action / Urge:** What was the resulting urge? (e.g., Urge to yell).

2. Strategic Intervention Points

BCA allows you to identify *where* to apply the Opposite Action skill before the urge hits.

- **Proactive Buffer:** The optimal point for intervention is at the vulnerability and trigger stage (Step 1 / 2). (e.g., Schedule a **Meal / Rest Block** in the Time Block to reduce hunger vulnerability).
- **Immediate Action:** The immediate application of Opposite Action occurs between Step 3 (Thought / Feeling) and Step 4 (Action / Urge). This pause and subsequent opposite action prevents the chain from culminating in the regretted behavior.

Conclusion: Your Internal Command

Mastering **Opposite Action** is the definitive behavioral step in achieving emotional regulation. You have moved from merely reacting to intense feelings to actively changing the emotional script through intentional behavior.

By integrating this skill with your EF mastery (IC / Attention) and your cognitive skills (Challenging Thoughts), you transform emotional turmoil from a source of chaos into a signal for strategic action. This disciplined approach builds profound self-efficacy and is the foundational pillar for building resilient, empathetic, and fulfilling relationships (Chapter 4 and 5). You are now in command of your inner world.

Chapter 3 Workbook: Change the Script: Use "Opposite Action" to Interrupt Emotional Impulses

Objective: To practice identifying unhelpful emotional urges (impulsive behavior) and defining a strategic, contrary action to interrupt the emotional spiral.

Scientific Anchor: Opposite Action is a core DBT skill used to interrupt and eventually change the destructive link between intense, disproportionate emotions and unhelpful behavioral urges, strengthening Inhibitory Control (IC).

Activity 3.1: The Unhelpful Urge Audit

Instructions: Recall a recent instance of intense, regrettable emotional behavior. Identify the emotion, the unhelpful urge it produced, and the strategic opposite action required.

1. **Emotion (e.g., Anger, Shame, Despair):**
2. **The Unhelpful Urge (The Impulse):** What did you want to do impulsively? (e.g., Yell, apologize excessively, isolate, procrastinate).

   Urge: ____

   ____
3. **The Opposite Action (The Strategy):** What is the exact behavioral opposite you should have done? (e.g., Speak softly, engage socially, initiate a micro-step of the task).

   Strategic Opposite Action: ______________________________

   ____

Activity 3.2: The Anti-Anger Protocol (Relational)

Instructions: Create a **relational circuit-breaker** for when anger or irritability flares up with a partner or loved one, using communication and physical boundaries.

1. **Anger Trigger:** (Example: Partner interrupts your hyperfocus block).

   Trigger: ____
2. **The Urge to Attack:** (Example: Shout, use sarcasm, criticize).

   Urge: ____

3. **Opposite Action Commitment:** Commit to two immediate, non-aggressive actions:

   Action A (Physical): (Example: Take a pre-agreed 5-minute time out / walk away).

   Action B (Verbal): (Example: Use a soft voice to state, "I am feeling overwhelmed right now and need 10 minutes to reset").

Reflection 3.3: Analyzing the Gain in Emotional Command

Instructions: Reflect on how deliberately applying the opposite behavior conserves EF and builds self-efficacy.

1. **IC Conservation:** When you successfully execute **Action A (Time Out)** in Activity 3.2, how does that physical removal of yourself from the argument conserve the **Inhibitory Control** (IC) you need to manage your emotions, compared to staying in the fight?

   IC Benefit: --

   ----

2. **Defeating Paralysis:** If the urge is to avoid and procrastinate on a massive project (shame / fear), how does the Opposite Action of completing a **single micro-step** (Chapter 1, Book 3) transform the emotional state from despair to momentum?

   Momentum Gain: ---

   ----

3. **Self-Efficacy:** When you choose the **Opposite Action** (e.g., engage socially instead of hiding), you are consciously overriding a powerful impulse. How does this successful choice provide **tangible evidence of self-command** that directly counters the inner critic's narrative that you are "out of control?"

   Evidence of Command: -----------------------------------

CHAPTER 4

CONNECT THROUGH LISTENING: EMPLOY MIRRORING AND VALIDATION FOR DEEPER COMMUNICATION

You have mastered the foundational work of emotional mastery: creating the crucial pause during crisis (Chapter 1) and challenging the Inner Critic (Chapter 2) through cognitive reframing. This work provides internal stability. Now, the journey shifts to the external sphere: applying this control to the most fragile and high-friction aspect of neurodiverse relationships, **communication**.

For the woman with Attention-Deficit / Hyperactivity Disorder (ADHD), communication is often compromised by core symptoms: **inattention** (mind-wandering during conversation) and **impulsivity** (interrupting due to fear of forgetting a thought). These behaviors, while rooted in compromised Executive Function (EF), frequently lead a partner to feel unheard, ignored, or unprioritized, leading to resentment and emotional isolation, a major cause of relationship stress.

This chapter provides the strategic toolkit of **Interpersonal Effectiveness** (a core skill of Dialectical Behavior Therapy, or DBT) to bridge this communication gap. By mastering the techniques of **Mirroring, Validation, and Empathy**, you actively counteract the perception of inattention, foster genuine understanding, and build the foundation of trust necessary to transform daily friction into collaborative partnership. The goal is to move from defensiveness and misunderstanding to deep, empathetic connection.

Section 1: The Neurobiological Barrier to Active Listening

Effective communication relies on sustained, mindful listening, which directly engages EF skills that are often inconsistent in the ADHD brain.

1. Inattention and the Fragmentation of Listening

The ADHD brain's difficulty with sustained attention and its impaired filtering mechanism make deep listening challenging.

- **Mind-Wandering:** During a partner's conversation, the woman's attention may fragment, pulled away by an external distraction (visual / auditory noise) or internal stimuli (racing thoughts, new ideas). This mind-wandering leads to missed details, difficulty retaining instructions, and the appearance of disinterest, even when the woman is genuinely trying to engage.
- **The Working Memory Sieve:** Active listening requires holding the speaker's points in **Working Memory (WM)** while processing their meaning and formulating a response. Because WM is easily overloaded, the woman may lose the thread of the conversation, making it difficult to accurately summarize or respond coherently, leading the partner to feel unheard.

2. Impulsivity and the Interruptive Urge

Impulsivity, a deficit in **Inhibitory Control (IC)**, creates the painful urge to interrupt or blurt out thoughts, further compromising communication.

- **Fear of Loss:** The urge to interrupt is often driven by the fear that a fleeting thought or insight will be lost forever due to compromised WM if the woman waits for her turn. This impulsive behavior, while rooted in a memory deficit, is often perceived by the non-ADHD partner as rudeness, self-centeredness, or lack of respect.

The DBT communication strategies provided here recognize that the brain must be given a **structured task** to anchor its focus, simultaneously reinforcing IC and WM during vulnerable relational moments.

Section 2: The Interpersonal Effectiveness Toolkit (Mirror, Validate, Empathize)

The core strategy for repairing communication deficits is the active, intentional use of three techniques that provide immediate, tangible proof to the partner that they have been heard and understood, bypassing the negative interpretations caused by past inattention.

1. Mirroring: Anchoring Attention and Ensuring Accuracy

Mirroring (or paraphrasing) is the act of restating or summarizing what your partner said *before* offering your own thoughts or response. This technique anchors your attention and serves as a check for accuracy.

- **Action:** When your partner finishes speaking, pause, take a breath (IC in action), and begin your response with a mirroring phrase: "So, let me make sure I understood: you feel frustrated that the chores haven't been divided fairly, and you specifically need the laundry offloaded from your plate."
- **Neuro-Benefit:** This forces the ADHD brain to engage in **Working Memory retrieval** and sustained attention, ensuring that the critical information is captured and processed. For the partner, it provides immediate, irrefutable evidence that their message was received, directly counteracting the perception of inattention or mind-wandering.

2. Validation: Acknowledging the Emotional Reality

Validation is the act of acknowledging your partner's feelings as real, understandable, and legitimate, even if you do not agree with their perspective or interpretation of the facts.

- **Action:** Connect with your partner's emotional state using a validating phrase: *"That makes complete sense. Given how much you're handling at work, I understand why you feel overwhelmed by the additional mental load of the chores."*
- **Neuro-Benefit:** Validation de-escalates emotional intensity, which is critical for the ADHD partner, who often struggles with heightened emotional reactivity themselves. By showing you are engaged and present, you boost the partner's self-confidence and foster a sense of mutual respect, which is essential for conflict resolution.

3. Empathy: Demonstrating Understanding and Care

Empathy moves beyond simply acknowledging feelings to expressing genuine understanding for your partner's experience.

- **Action:** Use statements that reflect true understanding and remove barriers of distrust: *"I see how you feel. I understand that the pattern of me forgetting things makes you feel unsafe about relying on me."*
- **Neuro-Benefit:** This powerful act of connection reduces the partner's feeling of isolation and resentment, fostering empathy that helps **repair disconnections** caused by previous ADHD-related failures (e.g., missed appointments, impulsive reactions).

Section 3: Structural Communication: Creating Predictability

Communication cannot rely on spontaneous emotional energy alone. For neurodiverse couples, intentional structure and predictability are necessary to prevent issues from escalating into intense emotional conflict.

1. Scheduling the "Relationship Roundtable"

Emotional conversations are difficult for the ADHD brain to navigate on impulse. The solution is to schedule important discussions when both partners are rested and prepared.

- **Fixed Appointments:** Schedule brief, dedicated **weekly check-ins** to discuss logistics, shared responsibilities, and emotional temperature. This creates a routine of open dialogue, preventing issues from compounding and exploding later in a reactive moment.

- **The "Pause Rule":** For spontaneous, emotionally charged conversations, establish a pre-agreed "Pause Rule." Either partner can call a **Time Out** (Chapter 3, Book 5), agreeing to disengage and return to the topic after 20 minutes when both have calmed down. This enforces Inhibitory Control and prevents the conversation from being hijacked by the impulsive emotional surge.

2. Assertiveness through "I" Statements

When communication turns to complaints or requests for change, the most effective tool for preventing defensiveness and promoting clear action is the **"I" Statement**.

- **Focus on Self, Not Blame:** An "I" statement focuses on your own feelings and needs, rather than attacking the partner's character or actions (e.g., replacing "You never listen!" with "I feel frustrated when I am talking and you are looking at your phone"). This de-escalates conflict by removing the immediate trigger for defensiveness, opening the door for collaborative problem-solving.
- **Problem-Solving Focus:** As research suggests, couples are more likely to stay constructively engaged if they look for **common ground** and focus on solutions. Redirecting the argument toward a shared goal ("We both agree that it's important for the kids to get enough sleep, so what might help us achieve the 9 PM bedtime?") reframes the discussion into a collaborative effort.

Section 4: The Emotional and Relational Payoff

Mastering active listening and validation is essential for moving past the shame and friction that define neurodiverse relationship struggles.

1. Reducing Relational Friction and the Parent-Child Dynamic

Poor communication, coupled with organizational deficits, is a major factor in the destructive **"parent-child" dynamic**, where the non-ADHD partner becomes the taskmaster.

- **Shifting Accountability:** By using **Mirroring** and **Validation** when the partner expresses frustration, you demonstrate that you are engaged, you understand the emotional impact of your symptoms, and you are taking responsibility for the problem. This rebuilds trust and reduces the partner's need to constantly remind or police, shifting the dynamic back toward a balanced, respectful partnership.

2. Healing Shame and RSD

The consistent practice of effective communication is a powerful antidote to the shame and chronic anxiety fueled by **Rejection Sensitive Dysphoria (RSD)**.

- **Evidence of Worthiness:** RSD is rooted in the fear of being perceived as unworthy or inadequate. When a woman consistently engages in open, validating communication, especially during conflict, she creates **tangible evidence of her competence and commitment** to the relationship. This steady stream of positive feedback counters the inner critic's negative narrative, strengthening self-worth.
- **Repair Attempts:** After a conflict or impulsive reaction, the ability to offer a sincere apology and validate the partner's experience (e.g., *"I was wrong to snap at you; I understand you feel hurt, and I am committed to using my Pause Rule next time."*) provides an **"olive branch"** that actively repairs disconnections, preventing small arguments from causing lasting emotional damage.

Conclusion: The Bedrock of Connection

Mastering active listening and validation is the essential bedrock of resilient relationships. You have learned to bypass the neurobiological barriers of inattention and impulsivity by using structured communication techniques that build trust and empathy.

By moving from passive coping to intentional engagement, you transform your relationships from a source of high friction and shame into a vital source of support and self-acceptance. This relational competence is the final skill set needed to complete the journey of self-mastery, preparing you to integrate your focus, emotions, and connections into a fully empowered life.

Chapter 4 Workbook: Connect Through Listening: Employ Mirroring and Validation for Deeper Communication

Objective: To practice structured communication techniques (Mirroring and Validation) that actively anchor attention, counteract the perception of inattention, and build relational trust.

Scientific Anchor: Mirroring forces active listening (engaging WM), and validation de-escalates emotional intensity, both crucial for managing high-friction conversations common in neurodiverse couples.

Activity 4.1: The Mirroring and Validation Practice

Instructions: Practice using mirroring and validation on a low-stakes conversation with your partner or a friend this week (e.g., discussing their day, a movie, or a minor logistical issue).

1. **The Scenario:** (Describe the topic of the conversation).
2. **Mirroring Commitment:** After your partner finishes a point, commit to restating the essence of what they said before responding.

   Partner's Statement (Simplified): ____________________________

   Your Mirroring Response: "So, what I hear you saying is that you feel because of ________________________. Did I get that right?"
3. **Validation Commitment:** Find a way to validate their feeling, even if you don't agree with the cause.

   Your Validation Response: "I understand why that would make you feel _______________________ That frustration makes sense."

Activity 4.2: The Impulsivity Circuit-Breaker

Instructions: Plan for a high-risk communication moment when you typically struggle with impulsive interruption. This is IC in action.

1. **The High-Risk Scenario:** (e.g., A weekly planning session, discussing finances, or a time when you are tired).
2. **The Interruptive Urge:** What thought triggers your urge to interrupt? (e.g., "If I don't say this now, I'll forget it!").

   Urge Thought: ____

   ____

   ____

   ____

3. **The IC Intervention:** When the urge hits, commit to two steps:

   Step 1 (Grounding): Deploy 3 seconds of paced breathing (Chapter 1) to create the pause.

   Step 2 (Offload): Immediately write down the thought on a notepad to offload it from WM. This reduces the fear of forgetting and allows you to return to listening.

Reflection 4.3: Analyzing Relational Gain

Instructions: Reflect on how intentional communication impacts relational trust and emotional stability.

1. **Counteracting Inattention:** How did using the **Mirroring** technique (Activity 4.1) help to anchor your attention, preventing your mind from wandering and ensuring you captured the important details of the conversation?

   Attention Anchor: ____

   ____

   ____

2. **Building Trust:** When you used **Validation** (acknowledging your partner's feelings), how did they react? How does validating their emotional reality help **rebuild trust** that may have been damaged by past impulsive or inattentive episodes?

   Trust Rebuilding: ____

   ____

   ____

3. **RSD Mitigation:** RSD is often triggered by perceived rejection during conflict. How does the practice of **Empathy** (Chapter 4, Section 2) reduce the likelihood that a neutral tone of voice from your partner will be misinterpreted through the "lens of rejection?"

   RSD Buffer: ____

   ____

   ____

CHAPTER 5

FIGHT FAIR: USE 'I' STATEMENTS AND REPAIR ATTEMPTS TO RESOLVE CONFLICT

You have established internal control by creating a crucial emotional pause (Chapter 1) and replacing self-criticism with cognitive reframing (Chapter 2). You have also mastered tools for active, validating communication (Chapter 4). This foundation of internal and interpersonal skills is vital, but relationships are dynamic and inevitably involve conflict. For the neurodiverse couple, unmanaged conflict, fueled by emotional intensity and deficits in Inhibitory Control (IC), is a major cause of relationship strain and breakdown.

This chapter addresses the highest-stakes scenario in relationships: **constructive conflict resolution.** You will learn how to apply your hard-won Executive Function (EF) skills (IC, Working Memory) and emotional strategies (Distress Tolerance) to engage in conflict without causing lasting damage. By mastering the use of **"I" Statements** to assert needs and practicing timely **Repair Attempts**, you transform arguments from destructive emotional explosions into opportunities for collaborative problem-solving, ensuring your relationship remains resilient and trust-based.

The goal is to move beyond the dysfunctional "parent-child" dynamic and the pain of impulsive reactions, learning to "fight fair" as equal, empathetic partners committed to a shared future.

Section 1: The Neurobiological Crisis of Conflict

Conflict is often disproportionately difficult for the neurodiverse couple because the core symptoms of ADHD, impulsivity, intense emotionality, and low frustration tolerance, are amplified under stress.

1. Impulsive Escalation and Inhibitory Control (IC)

Arguments are highly triggering because they activate the brain's threat system, demanding that the Prefrontal Cortex (PFC) maintain control while emotions run high.

- **IC Failure under Stress:** The core problem is that stress and high emotions compromise **Inhibitory Control** (the emotional "brakes"), making the woman with ADHD more likely to lash out, interrupt, or say regrettable things during a disagreement. These impulsive verbal actions are often perceived by the partner as unfair attacks or a failure to respect boundaries, which quickly escalates the argument.
- **The Vicious Cycle:** Arguments frequently revolve around ADHD-related deficits: the non-ADHD partner criticizes a lack of follow-through ("You never finished the laundry"), which triggers the ADHD partner's **Shame / RSD** (Chapter 2), leading to an intense, defensive, and disproportionate emotional outburst (e.g., yelling, storming off). This emotional reaction validates the partner's feeling of being in a "parent-child" dynamic, escalating the resentment.

2. Conflict as an Amorphous Problem

For the ADHD brain, which struggles with ambiguity (Chapter 2, Book 3), conflict can feel like an amorphous, unsolvable problem.

- **Focus on the Past vs. Future:** Arguments often get stuck ruminating on past failures ("You missed the deadline last month, too!"), rather than focusing the Executive Function on the present task: *solving the problem and establishing a future plan.*
- **Need for Structure:** Just as you broke down deadlines into manageable Milestones (Chapter 1, Book 3), conflict requires external structure to remain contained and solution-focused. Without boundaries, the argument feels infinite and leads to emotional exhaustion.

Section 2: Assertive Communication: The Power of "I" Statements

The most foundational strategy for productive conflict is shifting the language of the argument from blame to personal need. This is achieved through the disciplined use of **"I" Statements**.

1. Shifting from Blame to Need

"You" statements (e.g., "You never listen," "You always interrupt") are aggressive, accusatory, and immediately trigger defensiveness, making rational problem-solving impossible.

- **The "I" Statement Structure:** The "I" Statement refocuses the conversation on your own feelings, needs, and the factual impact of the behavior, allowing the other person to receive the information without feeling attacked.
  - Example: Replace "You always leave the dishes in the sink, you don't care about the shared space!"
  - With: **"I feel overwhelmed and unsupported when I see the dishes piled up, because it makes me worry that the Daily Reset routine is going to collapse."**
- **Neuro-Benefit:** This approach reduces the stress hormones associated with defensiveness, allowing both partners to stay "constructively engaged" by focusing on the shared concern (the integrity of the routine / the feeling of overwhelm), rather than character assassination.

2. Asserting Needs with DEAR MAN

For high-stakes conflicts, the DBT skill of **DEAR MAN** provides a structured framework for assertive communication, ensuring you express your needs clearly while maintaining self-respect and the relationship.

- **Describe:** Describe the situation objectively (facts only). *"The past two weeks, the bill-pay checklist wasn't completed by Tuesday night."*
- **Express:** Express your feelings using "I" statements. *"I feel anxious and worried about accruing late fees."*
- **Assert:** Clearly and respectfully assert your need. *"I need you to commit to completing the Bill-Pay block on Tuesday night."*
- **Reinforce:** Explain the positive outcome. *"If we can do this, it will save us late fees and reduce my anxiety significantly."*
- **Mindful:** Stay mindful of your goal (getting the bill paid, not blaming the partner).
- **Appear Confident:** Maintain respectful body language and a calm tone (IC in action).
- **Negotiate:** Be willing to negotiate a compromise (e.g., changing the chore to a different day / time block).

Section 3: The Circuit-Breaker: Time-Outs and De-escalation

For the conflict to remain constructive, both partners must have clear, pre-agreed methods for de-escalation when one or both become emotionally "flooded" (overwhelmed by strong physiological arousal).

1. Implementing the Time Out Protocol

The ability to call a **Time Out** is an essential act of **Distress Tolerance** (Chapter 1) and **Inhibitory Control** (Chapter 3). It physically removes the threat of an impulsive emotional outburst.

- **Pre-Agreed Signal:** Establish a clear, non-confrontational signal (e.g., a hand gesture, or a simple phrase like, "I need a 10-minute reset"). This signal must be honored immediately by the receiving partner without argument.

- **The Cool-Down Commitment:** The person calling the time out commits to:
    1. **Immediate Disengagement:** Physically leaving the room and engaging in a **Grounding Technique** (Chapter 1) or a physiological reset (TIPP) to calm the nervous system.
    2. **Fixed Return Time:** Committing to a fixed return time (e.g., "I will return at 7:45 PM") to ensure the pause is for regulation, not avoidance.
- **Neuro-Benefit:** This pause allows the amygdala's alarm to subside and the logical PFC to return online, preserving IC and preventing the conversation from spiraling out of control due to impulsive words or actions.

2. Finding Common Ground and Shared Goals

Conflict resolution is most successful when the focus shifts from **winning** to **problem-solving** the system, using EF skills to find a mutual solution.

- **Redirect to the Goal:** When an argument gets stuck on blame, redirect the focus to the shared goal. *"We might disagree on the details of how to schedule the chores, but at least we're finally in agreement that the gutters need fixing this year!"* or *"We both agree that it's important to get to bed by 10, so what might help us do that?"* This frames both partners as collaborators on the same team, rather than adversaries.
- **Objective Analysis:** Use the skills of **Working Memory** and **Planning** (Book 3) to analyze the problem objectively. Treat the argument not as a character flaw, but as a system failure. (E.g., "The system for keys failed because the bowl isn't intuitive enough; let's find a hook").

Section 4: Repair Attempts: Rebuilding Trust and Connection

Conflict causes damage. The final, critical step in conflict resolution is the intentional act of **repair**, which rebuilds trust and intimacy damaged by emotional outbursts or conflict fatigue.

1. Making the Sincere Apology

A sincere apology is not just saying "sorry"; it must validate the partner's experience and include a commitment to future action.

- **Validate the Impact:** Acknowledge the emotional impact of your action, without qualifying it with an excuse. (e.g., *"I am sorry I snapped at you; my frustration overwhelmed me, and I understand that my tone made you feel attacked."*)
- **Commit to the System:** Commit to using your EF and emotional toolkit next time. (e.g., *"Next time I feel overwhelmed, I will use my Time Out signal immediately."*) This provides tangible assurance that you are actively working on the problem, rebuilding the trust that you are a reliable partner.

2. The Power of Olive Branches and Appreciation

Repair attempts can be small, non-verbal gestures that signal reconciliation and connection.

- **Olive Branches:** During or immediately after a conflict, offer an "olive branch", a small, non-verbal signal of care (e.g., a kind touch, a drink of water, or simply acknowledging their pain). These acts mitigate the relational damage caused by the preceding emotional storm.
- **Show Appreciation:** Demonstrate appreciation for your partner's efforts, especially in areas where they provide scaffolding for your ADHD symptoms. *"I love that you have followed through on starting to exercise,"* or *"I appreciate that you checked the shared calendar this morning."* This reinforces positive behavior and shifts the focus away from chronic deficiencies, nourishing the relationship's core strength.

Conclusion: Conflict as a Catalyst for Growth

By mastering the strategies of **"I" Statements**, **Time Out Protocols**, and **Repair Attempts**, you transform conflict from a destructive, shame-inducing event into a valuable catalyst for relationship growth. You are actively using the emotional regulation and Inhibitory Control skills gained in this book to protect your relationship's integrity.

This relational competence is the definitive step toward building a fulfilling life. You have moved beyond surviving arguments to collaboratively problem-solving, ensuring that your most important connections are resilient, empathetic, and stable, thereby completing the emotional mastery pillar of your self-management journey.

Chapter 5 Workbook: Fight Fair: Use 'I' Statements and Repair Attempts to Resolve Conflict

Objective: To practice assertive communication and de-escalation techniques that replace impulsive reactions with thoughtful, solution-oriented responses.

Scientific Anchor: "I" Statements reduce defensiveness, and Time Out protocols utilize Inhibitory Control to prevent the emotional flooding that leads to destructive impulsive actions in conflict.

Activity 5.1: The "I" Statement Conversion

Instructions: Take three common relationship complaints (which typically start with "You never...") and convert them into constructive **"I" Statements** that focus on your feelings and needs.

1. **Complaint (Blame):** You never help me plan social events; I always have to do it alone.

   "I" Statement (Need): "I feel overwhelmed and alone in planning social events. I need you to commit to taking the lead on one specific step this week."

2. **Complaint (Blame):** You always interrupt me; you don't care about what I'm saying.

   "I" Statement (Need): ______________________________________

   ____

   ____

   ____

3. **Complaint (Blame):** You are so micromanaging about the finances!

   "I" Statement (Need): ______________________________________

   ____

   ____

   ____

Activity 5.2: The Time Out Protocol and IC Practice

Instructions: Plan for a high-risk conflict moment (e.g., when tired or hungry) by establishing a non-negotiable **Time Out** protocol.

1. **The Trigger:** (Example: Partner asks about the utility bill that was due).

   Trigger: ____

   ____

   ____

   ____

2. **The Time Out Signal:** What is the non-confrontational signal you will use to stop the argument immediately?

   Signal (Verbal / Non-Verbal): ______________________________

   ____

   ____

   ____

   ____

   ____

3. **The IC Commitment:** When you call the Time Out, you commit to two actions:

   Action A (Grounding): I will immediately engage in _________ (e.g., a TIPP skill from Chapter 1).

   Action B (Time Frame): I will return to the conversation at____ (Fixed time).

Reflection 5.3: Analyzing the Gain in Trust

Instructions: Reflect on how strategic conflict management heals relational damage and builds trust.

1. **Relational Damage:** How does a moment where you impulsively yell at your partner compromise the relationship's sense of **safety** and **trust**?

   Compromise: ____

   ____

   ____

   ____

   ____

   ____

2. **Repair and Trust:** If you successfully apply the **Time Out** (Activity 5.2) and return with a sincere apology that includes a commitment to use the system next time (a **Repair Attempt**), how does this action actively **rebuild** the trust that your impulsive action damaged?

   Trust Rebuilt: ____

   ____

   ____

   ____

3. **Shame Reduction:** Conflict often triggers shame. By successfully mastering a difficult conversation using **"I" Statements**, how does this successful use of EF skills provide tangible evidence that counters the inner critic's belief that you are "out of control" in relationships?

   Evidence of Control: ___________________________________

   ____

   ____

   ____

CHAPTER 6

REFLECT AND INTEGRATE: YOUR EMOTIONAL MASTERY JOURNEY SO FAR

You have completed the intensive emotional mastery work of Book 5, successfully navigating the turbulent landscape of emotional dysregulation, chronic shame, and relational friction. This journey has been a campaign to stabilize your inner world, transforming intense, automatic reactions into thoughtful, intentional responses that honor both your feelings and your commitment to others.

This chapter is a dedicated moment of pause, a time to **reflect and integrate** the profound psychological and behavioral gains achieved through the disciplined practice of the therapeutic strategies you have mastered: **Sensory Grounding, Cognitive Reframing (CBT)**, and **Opposite Action (DBT)**. The aim is to solidify the crucial shift from a life dictated by **emotional overwhelm** to a state of **calm, effective self-command.**

The core achievement of this emotional work is the consistent creation of the **"Pause"**, the critical time lag between an intense emotional stimulus (like perceived rejection or criticism) and your subsequent impulsive reaction. This pause allows your conserved Executive Function (EF) skills, honed in Book 3, to engage, making it possible to choose strategic action over automatic, regrettable behavior. You have moved beyond mere coping to building a robust, resilient foundation for genuine self-acceptance and lasting connection.

Section 1: The Victory Over Internal Chaos: Cognitive and Behavioral Synthesis

The most significant outcome of mastering the emotional strategies in this book is the mitigation of the destructive cycle where intense emotion fuels shame and shame compromises focus.

1. Grounding the Surge: The Physiological Circuit-Breaker

You learned to use immediate, sensory interventions to manage acute emotional distress, thereby preventing the emotional surge from escalating into a full meltdown.

- **TIPP and Sensory Anchors:** By practicing **Sensory Grounding Techniques** (TIPP: Temperature, Intense Exercise, Paced Breathing), you acquired the physical tools to actively calm the activated nervous system. This physiological intervention serves as the essential **circuit-breaker** that immediately drops the emotional intensity from a crisis "red light" to a manageable "yellow light."
- **IC Conservation:** This initial grounding phase is crucial because it provides the necessary time for **Inhibitory Control (IC)** to return online, preventing the impulsive verbal or physical reactions (yelling, isolating, self-harm) that cause profound regret and relational damage.

2. Dismantling the Inner Critic: Cognitive Reframing

Once the emotion is manageable, you moved to dismantle the harsh, automatic self-criticism that is the internal source of shame for women with ADHD.

- **Challenging Distortions:** You mastered the toolkit of **Cognitive Behavioral Therapy (CBT)**, systematically identifying and challenging destructive **cognitive distortions** (e.g.,

Catastrophizing, All-or-Nothing Thinking) that convert minor setbacks into massive failures.

- **The Reframe:** By rigorously testing the evidence for and against these thoughts, you learned to replace the harsh narrative with a **balanced, compassionate reframe**. This cognitive work strengthens the PFC's ability to engage rational thought, actively dismantling the internalized shame that is a primary driver of anxiety and depression in the female ADHD experience.

3. Interrupting Impulses: Behavioral Change

You learned to apply the ultimate behavioral defense against destructive urges: **Opposite Action**.

- **Opposite Action as Strategy:** This core **DBT** skill mandates that when an emotion leads to an unhelpful urge (e.g., Sadness -> urge to isolate), you must intentionally execute the **opposite behavior** (e.g., engage socially). This action directly changes the emotional trajectory, transforming automatic, regrettable reactions into thoughtful, intentional responses.
- **Analyzing the Chain:** You used the **Behavioral Chain Analysis (BCA)** framework to identify the precise internal and external triggers that lead to impulsive action, allowing you to proactively apply your coping skills before the crisis hits.

Section 2: The Relational Dividend: Building Trust and Safety

The internal mastery achieved in this book yields tangible, profound benefits in close relationships, moving the dynamic from chronic friction to collaborative partnership.

1. Constructive Conflict and Trust Repair

You mastered essential **Interpersonal Effectiveness** skills to navigate conflict without triggering defensiveness or causing lasting damage.

- **Active Listening:** By consistently practicing **Mirroring and Validation** (Chapter 4), you actively anchored your attention during conversations, counteracting the perception of inattention and providing irrefutable evidence to your partner that their message and feelings were received and understood.
- **Fighting Fair:** You learned to use **"I" Statements** (Chapter 5) to

express your feelings and needs without blaming your partner's character ("I feel overwhelmed when..." vs. "You never...") and implemented the **Time Out Protocol** to ensure that arguments are paused and regulated before IC collapses.

- **Repair Attempts:** Crucially, you understood that after conflict, sincere **Repair Attempts** (validating the partner's impact, apologizing, and committing to use the system next time) are essential "olive branches" that actively rebuild the trust compromised by past impulsive reactions.

2. Healing Shame and RSD

The consistent use of these skills is the most powerful antidote to the debilitating pain of **Rejection Sensitive Dysphoria (RSD)**.

- **Evidence of Worthiness:** RSD is fueled by the fear of being seen as unworthy. When a woman consistently engages in open, validating communication, especially during conflict, she creates **tangible evidence of her competence and commitment** to the relationship. This steady stream of positive feedback counters the inner critic's negative narrative, strengthening self-worth.
- **Creating Safety:** By demonstrating that you have a proactive plan for managing your impulsivity (e.g., the Time Out signal), you create a sense of **safety and predictability** for your partner, reducing their need to act as a **taskmaster** and thereby dissolving the dysfunctional "parent-child" dynamic that fuels friction.

Section 3: The Integration: Emotional Fuel for Future Success

The mastery of emotions is the final, essential pillar that integrates all previous books, ensuring sustainable success across your life's domains.

1. EF Mastery and Emotional Bandwidth

The EF skills you conserved in Book 3 are the very resources you now deploy for emotional mastery.

- **Conserved CL:** The reduction in **Cognitive Load (CL)** from organizational and scheduling systems ensures that your brain has the necessary bandwidth to engage in the emotionally demanding work of IC and cognitive reframing. A less cluttered mind is a less reactive mind.

- **IC as a Universal Skill:** The **Inhibitory Control** trained through emotional regulation is a universal skill that supports all high-leverage EF demands: resisting the urge to check a notification (Book 3), resisting the urge to impulsively spend (Book 5), and resisting the urge to lash out (Book 5).

2. The Final Step to Integrated Success

You have successfully moved beyond the reactive struggle to a state of internal and relational command. The stability and emotional bandwidth achieved in this book are the essential prerequisites for tackling the final phase of integrating complex adult responsibilities, Relationships and Financial Management, into a harmonious system (Book 5).

The powerful new narrative forged here is one of self-acceptance: recognizing that your emotional intensity is a neurobiological reality that, with strategy and self-compassion, can be managed and harnessed for profound connection and resilience.

Chapter 6 Workbook: Reflect and Integrate: Your Emotional Mastery Journey So Far

Objective: To synthesize the cognitive and behavioral gains achieved in Book 5, assessing the shift from emotional reactivity to self-command and self-acceptance.

Scientific Anchor: Consistent practice of DBT skills strengthens the PFC's Inhibitory Control, creating resilience against emotional flooding and reducing the physiological impact of shame and stress.

Activity 6.1: The Emotional Command Scorecard

Instructions: Rate the severity of your emotional challenges **before** this book and **now**, focusing on the gain in your ability to pause and regulate. (Scale: 1 = Minimal Challenge, 5 = Severe Challenge)

Challenge Area	Before Book 5 (Initial)	After Book 5 (Current)	Reflection: The Tool That Helped Most
Impulse Control (Snapping / Yelling)			(Example: Opposite Action / Time Out)
Intensity of Shame / Self-Criticism			(Example: Cognitive Reframing / Self-Compassion)
Relational Friction / Misunderstanding			(Example: Mirroring / Validation)
Severity of Emotional Meltdowns			(Example: Sensory Grounding / TIPP)

Reflection 6.2: Analyzing the Power of the "Pause"

Instructions: The single greatest gain is the ability to choose a response rather than react impulsively.

1. **The Trigger and the Intervention:** Recall a moment this week when you felt an intense emotional surge. What **Distress Tolerance Skill** (e.g., TIPP, Grounding) did you use to interrupt the feeling, and how long did that intervention last?

   Intervention: ____

   ____

   ____

   Duration of Pause: ____

   ____

   ____

   ____

   ____

2. **IC Success:** How did that pause (even if short) prevent your **Inhibitory Control (IC)** from collapsing, allowing you to avoid the destructive action you were tempted to take?

   IC Protection: ____

   ____

   ____

   ____

   ____

   ____

3. **The Inner Ally:** The Inner Critic often reinforces the pain of RSD. How has the practice of **Self-Compassion** (treating yourself like a friend) helped to neutralize the sting of a perceived rejection this week?

   RSD Mitigation: ____

   ____

   ____

   ____

   ____

Activity 6.3: Bridge to Relationships and Financial Health (Book 5 Prep)

Instructions: Prepare to integrate your emotional skills into the final, practical domains of life, relationships and financial health, by identifying vulnerable areas.

1. **Conflict Strategy:** Name one specific conflict that frequently recurs with a partner or family member. Which tool (**"I" Statement** or **Time Out**) will you commit to using first the next time this conflict arises?

   Conflict & Tool: ____

   ____

   ____

   ____

   ____

   ____

2. **Impulsivity Protection:** Financial chaos is often fueled by emotional impulses. Name one specific, high-stakes impulse (e.g., buying a non-essential item, starting a new project) that you will now manage using the **Opposite Action** strategy.

   Impulse & Opposite Action: ______________________________

   ____

   ____

   ____

   ____

   ____

CHAPTER 7

PRACTICE AND APPLY: YOUR EMOTIONAL MASTERY ACTION TOOLKIT

You have completed the entire emotional mastery curriculum, moving from crisis management to cognitive reframing and strategic relationship building. This final chapter provides the comprehensive **Action Toolkit**, designed to translate the therapeutic knowledge of this book into a seamless, resilient system of daily emotional command.

The power of this toolkit lies in its synergistic effect: the **grounding and cognitive skills** (DBT / CBT) create the essential **"Pause,"** which allows your conserved Executive Function (EF) resources to choose intentional action over automatic, regrettable reaction. Consistency in applying these tools is the key to minimizing the intensity of emotional dysregulation, healing shame, and building lasting relational trust.

Section 1: Toolkit 1: Crisis and Distress Tolerance Protocol

Objective: To implement immediate, sensory-based techniques to interrupt acute emotional distress (Red Light), thereby activating the calming Parasympathetic Nervous System and creating the crucial "Pause" for IC to re-engage (Chapter 1).

Scientific Anchor: Sensory shock (TIPP) and focused grounding provide rapid physiological intervention to override the emotional alarm system (amygdala), creating the necessary time lag for Inhibitory Control (IC) to deploy.

Activity 7.1: The Immediate Circuit-Breaker Plan

Instructions: Create a clear, pre-planned sequence of physiological action for when an intense emotional surge (e.g., intense RSD pain, anger, anxiety) hits.

1. **Identify the High-Risk Trigger:** What is the most common trigger that leads to rapid emotional escalation?

   My Trigger: ____

   ____

   ____

   ____

   ____

2. **The TIPP Sequence (The "Immediate Action" Plan):** Commit to this low-friction, rapid intervention when the trigger occurs.

DBT Skill	Action (Must be pre-planned)	Duration	Neuro-Benefit
T: Temperature	(Example: Hold ice cube on wrist, splash cold water on face.)	30 seconds	Activates the dive reflex / calms heart rate.
I: Intense Exercise	(Example: 20 jumping jacks or wall push-ups.)	1 minute	Discharges physical energy of stress response.

P: Paced Breathing	(Example: 4-count inhale, 6-count exhale.)	3 cycles	Engages parasympathetic nervous system.

3. **The Grounding Anchor:** Immediately follow the TIPP sequence with the 5-4-3-2-1 Sensory Grounding Technique to pull attention away from internal chaos and anchor it to external reality.

   Commitment: I will find 5 things I see, 4 things I feel, 3 things I hear, 2 things I smell, and 1 thing I taste.

Section 2: Toolkit 2: Cognitive and Behavioral Interruption

Objective: To use thought-challenging frameworks (CBT) and intentional behavior (Opposite Action) to change the emotional trajectory and reduce shame (Chapters 2 & 3).

Scientific Anchor: Challenging cognitive distortions interrupts the thought-emotion-action cycle. Opposite Action changes the emotion by changing the unhelpful behavior, strengthening IC.

Activity 7.2: The Thought-Action Reframe Protocol

Instructions: Practice applying the Cognitive Behavioral and Opposite Action protocols to a common emotional struggle (e.g., shame, anger, avoidance).

1. **The Automatic Reaction (Anger / Relational Conflict):** Recall a moment when intense anger led to the urge to **yell / attack**.

   The Urge: ____

   Opposite Action (Commitment): __________________________

   ____

   ____

   ____

   (e.g., Use a gentle voice and an "I" statement, or call a Time Out).

2. **The Shame-Based Distortion (RSD / Avoidance):** Recall a moment when fear of failure led to the urge to **isolate / procrastinate**.

The Distorted Thought: ________________________________

____

____

____

(e.g., "I'm a complete failure for missing that.")

Cognitive Challenge (Reframe): __________________________

____

____

____

(e.g., "This is just Catastrophizing. I made a mistake, which is human. I will start one micro-step now.")

3. **Behavioral Chain Analysis (BCA) Intervention:** Identify a common point of **Vulnerability** that precedes an emotional failure (e.g., low sleep, hunger, high Luteal Phase stress).

   Vulnerability: _____________________________________

   ____

   ____

   Proactive Intervention (Action): I will proactively schedule a ______ minute rest block / snack break today to prevent this vulnerability from leading to a crisis.

Toolkit 3: Relational Trust and Repair Protocol

Objective: To apply communication skills (Mirroring / Validation) and conflict strategies (Repair Attempts) to reduce relational friction and rebuild trust damaged by impulsive actions (Chapters 4 & 5).

Scientific Anchor: Mirroring anchors attention (reducing perception of inattention). Validation de-escalates conflict. Repair attempts rebuild trust and safety in the relationship, essential for resilience.

Activity 7.3: The Trust-Building Communication Sequence

Instructions: Practice using active listening and repair attempts in your next necessary conversation with a close partner or family member.

1. **Active Listening Commitment:** During the conversation, commit to using **Mirroring** once to confirm you correctly understood the core message.

Mirroring Script: "So, what I hear you saying is that you feel _____________ because of _________."

2. **Validation Commitment:** Commit to using **Validation** once to acknowledge the legitimacy of your partner's emotion.

   Validation Script: "That makes complete sense. I understand why you would feel ____________________________________ ."

3. **The Assertiveness Script (Fighting Fair):** When expressing a need for change, commit to using an "I" Statement to avoid blame.

   "I" Statement Script:_____________________________________

   ____

   (Focus on *your* feeling, e.g., "I feel frustrated when _________

   ____")

4. **Repair Commitment:** Following any conflict (even a small, regulated one), commit to offering a **Repair Attempt**—a small action to rebuild safety and connection.

   Repair Action: (Example: A sincere apology and commitment to use a Time Out next time, or a physical gesture of connection / appreciation).

   ____

   ____

   ____

Section 4: Integration and Long-Term Resilience

The EF skills conserved in Book 3 are the resources you now deploy for emotional mastery. This integrated approach ensures sustainable, resilient self-command.

1. The Universal Skill of Inhibitory Control

The **Inhibitory Control (IC)** you trained to stop checking notifications and resist the urge to procrastinate is the universal EF muscle required for emotional mastery. Every time you choose **Opposite Action** (e.g., speaking softly instead of yelling), you are successfully deploying IC under stress. This consistency builds the psychological capital necessary to navigate conflict without lasting damage.

2. The Final Step to Self-Acceptance

By consistently applying these tools, you transform the emotional struggle from a source of shame into a source of **self-efficacy**. You prove to yourself, through repeated, intentional actions, that you are capable of managing intensity, navigating complexity, and building trust. This evidence of competence is the foundation for genuine self-acceptance, moving you beyond the lifetime of internalized inadequacy. You are now fully equipped for the final pillar of integrated success.

CONCLUSION

SUMMARY: YOUR EMOTIONAL STRENGTH

You have completed the intensive, transformative work of Book 5, successfully navigating the turbulent landscape of emotional dysregulation, chronic shame, and relational friction. This final book represents the culmination of your journey toward internal stability, leveraging the structural and cognitive foundations built in the previous volumes (organization, focus, and hormonal synchronization) to master your emotional world and strengthen your most vital connections.

The core achievement of this book is the replacement of automatic, intense reactions with thoughtful, intentional responses. You have learned that your emotional struggles, from sudden anger to the debilitating pain of **Rejection Sensitive Dysphoria (RSD)**, are not signs of a character flaw, but neurobiological realities that can be strategically managed.

This stability, achieved through dedicated practice of therapeutic skills, is the final, essential pillar for realizing integrated success, enabling you to move from a life defined by emotional chaos to one rooted in calm, resilient self-command.

Section 1: The Victory Over Emotional Chaos: The Power of the Pause

The most significant outcome of mastering the strategies in this book is the ability to consistently create the **"Pause"**, the critical time lag between an intense emotional stimulus and a regrettable, impulsive reaction.

1. The Physiological Circuit-Breaker

You gained immediate command over acute distress by learning **Distress Tolerance** techniques (Chapter 1).

- **Grounding and TIPP Skills:** By deploying **Sensory Grounding** and physiological interventions (TIPP: Temperature, Intense Exercise, Paced Breathing), you acquired the capacity to actively calm the activated nervous system and reduce emotional intensity from a crisis "red light" to a manageable "yellow light."
- **IC Conservation:** This physiological pause is crucial because it allows your conserved **Inhibitory Control (IC)**, your brain's emotional "brakes", to re-engage, preventing the impulsive verbal or physical reactions (yelling, withdrawal) that cause profound regret and relational damage.

2. Dismantling Shame and the Inner Critic

Once grounded, you engaged the cognitive brain to dismantle the internal source of shame (Chapter 2).

- **Cognitive Reframing (CBT):** You learned to become a detective of your own mind, systematically identifying and challenging destructive **cognitive distortions** (e.g., Catastrophizing, All-or-Nothing Thinking) that fuel RSD and anxiety.
- **Opposite Action:** You implemented the definitive behavioral intervention, **Opposite Action** (Chapter 3), intentionally choosing to execute the behavior contrary to an unhelpful urge (e.g., engaging socially instead of isolating; speaking softly instead of yelling). This practice systematically changes the emotional script, transforming automatic reactions into thoughtful responses and building resilience against emotional volatility.

Section 2: The Relational Dividend: Building Resilient Connections

The internal mastery achieved is the foundation for navigating the high-stakes friction points of close relationships, moving the dynamic from chronic struggle to collaborative partnership.

1. Mastering Communication and Trust Repair

You mastered essential **Interpersonal Effectiveness** skills (DBT) to bridge communication gaps caused by attention deficits and impulsivity (Chapter 4).

- **Active Listening:** By consistently practicing **Mirroring and Validation**, you actively anchored your attention, counteracting the perception of inattention and providing irrefutable evidence that your partner's message and feelings were understood.
- **Constructive Conflict:** You learned to "fight fair" (Chapter 5) by using **"I" Statements** to express needs without blame, and you implemented the **Time Out Protocol** to ensure arguments are paused and regulated before IC collapses, reducing relational damage.
- **Repair Attempts:** Crucially, you committed to using sincere **Repair Attempts** (validating impact, apologizing, and committing to use the system next time) to actively rebuild the trust damaged by past impulsive reactions, ensuring that conflicts lead to growth, not erosion.

2. The Universal Antidote to Shame

The consistent use of these relational skills is the most powerful antidote to **RSD** and the chronic feeling of inadequacy that defines the female ADHD experience.

- **Evidence of Worthiness:** By successfully managing conflict with intentionality, you create a steady stream of **tangible evidence of your competence and commitment** to the relationship. This positive feedback systematically counters the inner critic's negative narrative, strengthening self-worth and self-acceptance.

- **Dissolving the Dynamic:** You gained the tools to dissolve the dysfunctional **"parent-child" dynamic**, ensuring that accountability for tasks and responsibilities shifts from the personal (blame) to the neutral (the system), fostering equality and respect within your partnership.

Section 3: Final Integration: The Holistic Whole

The journey through the five books culminates in the realization that integrated success requires all pillars to operate in harmony.

- **System Synergy:** The **IC and Working Memory** strengthened in Book 3 are the universal cognitive resources that enable the emotional **Pause** (Book 5) and the necessary **Impulse Control** for sustained financial health (Book 5). The structural predictability of Book 1 reduces the systemic stress that would otherwise compromise this entire emotional ecosystem.
- **The Empowered Narrative:** You have successfully moved beyond the lifetime of shame and self-blame, recognizing your emotional intensity and cognitive complexity as a neurobiological reality to be managed with strategy and self-compassion. The reward is a life defined by self-acceptance and competence.

You are no longer merely coping with ADHD; you are actively crafting a resilient, fulfilling life, commanding your focus, taming your emotions, and building the enduring connections that define genuine integrated success.

OVERALL CONCLUSION

THE EMPOWERED WOMAN WITH ADHD

The journey through this five-book series has been an intensive, strategic campaign against the systemic chaos and internalized shame that define unmanaged Attention-Deficit / Hyperactivity Disorder (ADHD) in women. This process has not been about finding a cure for ADHD; it has been about recognizing the profound truth that your brain is not broken, but is instead a unique operating system that demands a customized, intentional approach to thrive.

You have successfully moved beyond the reactive struggle, where your energy was a victim of distraction, procrastination, and hormonal chaos, to a state of **integrated self-mastery**.

Section 1: Synthesis of the Five Pillars: The Integrated System

The stability you have achieved is the result of strategically connecting five distinct, yet interdependent, pillars of self-management. The true power of this journey lies in recognizing how the structural, cognitive, and emotional components work synergistically to create resilient neurobiological support.

1. The Foundational Command (Book 1 & Book 3)

The journey began by establishing external and internal structural command, addressing the core deficits in Executive Function (EF) that fuel chaos.

- **External Order (Book 1):** You dismantled **Task Paralysis** and eliminated the anxiety-inducing friction of disorganization by implementing **functional organization** (designated homes, micro-steps). This work successfully reduced **Cognitive Load (CL)**, clearing the runway for cognitive work.
- **Cognitive Command (Book 3):** You conquered **Time Blindness** by making time concrete and visible, utilizing **Milestone Planning** and **Time Blocking** to enforce finite, manageable action. This disciplined approach systematically mitigated the **Estimation Deficit** and fragmentation of attention, conserving precious mental energy.

2. **The Physiological Buffer (Book 4)**

You introduced the non-negotiable science of hormonal synchronization, recognizing that the female EF system is dynamically influenced by neurochemical volatility.

- **Data and Advocacy:** By mastering **Cycle Tracking**, you transformed subjective experience into objective data, quantifying the decline in focus and organization during **low-estrogen phases** (e.g., the luteal phase).
- **Resilience:** You established a holistic physiological buffer—prioritizing sleep hygiene, nutrition, and stress reduction—to protect your vulnerable Executive Functions, ensuring that internal hormonal dips do not lead to external, functional collapse.

3. **Emotional and Relational Mastery (Book 5)**

The structural stability of the previous books provided the necessary bandwidth to tackle the deepest challenges: intense emotionality and external friction.

- **Emotional Circuit-Breakers:** You gained internal control by mastering **Distress Tolerance** (grounding, TIPP) and **Cognitive Reframing (CBT)**, consistently creating the crucial "Pause" between emotional stimulus and impulsive reaction. This work directly strengthens **Inhibitory Control (IC)**, providing the essential "brake" needed to manage intense feelings, including **RSD** (Rejection Sensitive Dysphoria).
- **Relational Resilience:** You utilized **Interpersonal Effectiveness** skills (**Mirroring, Validation, "I" Statements**) to reduce conflict and rebuild trust, actively dissolving the dysfunctional "parent-child" dynamic that plagues many neurodiverse relationships.
- **Financial Security:** You mitigated the long-term **Financial ADHD Tax** by implementing external systems to bypass compromised EF—automating high-stakes payments and simplifying decision points to combat impulsivity and time blindness.

Section 2: The Final Triumph: Defeating Shame and Building Self-Efficacy

The true success of this journey is measured not just in productivity, but in the internal shift from shame to self-acceptance.

1. The Antidote to the Inner Critic

For a woman who has spent a lifetime internalizing her struggles and masking her symptoms, the greatest liberation is the knowledge that her difficulties were neurobiological, not moral. By consistently replacing self-blame with strategic, compassionate action, you have systematically dismantled the Inner Critic. The accumulation of small, visible successes—meeting Milestones, honoring a Pomodoro sprint, successfully navigating a conflict without yelling—provides **tangible evidence of competence** that builds profound **self-efficacy** and self-worth.

2. Reclaiming Your Narrative

You are no longer a passive participant in the cycle of overwhelm. You are now equipped with the vocabulary and the data to advocate for your needs in the world, commanding the necessary support from both partners and medical professionals. This knowledge allows you to embrace your unique neurodiversity not as a deficit, but as an operating system with specific needs that, when met with strategy and self-compassion, can achieve extraordinary results.

Section 3: The Empowered Commitment

The journey of the Empowered Woman with ADHD is a continuous practice, not a destination. There will be setbacks—missed resets, moments of overwhelm, and emotional flares. The true strength of your mastery lies in your ability to consistently return to your toolkit, treat the setback as valuable **data**, and choose strategic recovery over self-criticism.

You are now equipped with the ultimate toolkit:

- **A Clear Mind:** Focused, with distractions filtered, and time managed by external systems.
- **A Stable Body:** Hormonally buffered, well-rested, and regulated by physical self-care.

- **A Resilient Heart:** Capable of pausing during crisis, choosing love over impulse, and engaging the world from a place of genuine self-acceptance.

This integrated success, the harmony between your neurobiology, your environment, and your relationships, is the most powerful foundation for living the intentional, fulfilling life you deserve.

If you enjoyed this book, I'd greatly appreciate a review on Amazon because it helps me to create more books that people want. It would mean a lot to hear from you.

To leave a review:

1. Open your camera app.
2. Point your mobile device at the QR code.
3. The review page will appear in your web browser.

HERE'S ANOTHER BOOK BY VIVIAN WHITMORE THAT YOU MIGHT LIKE

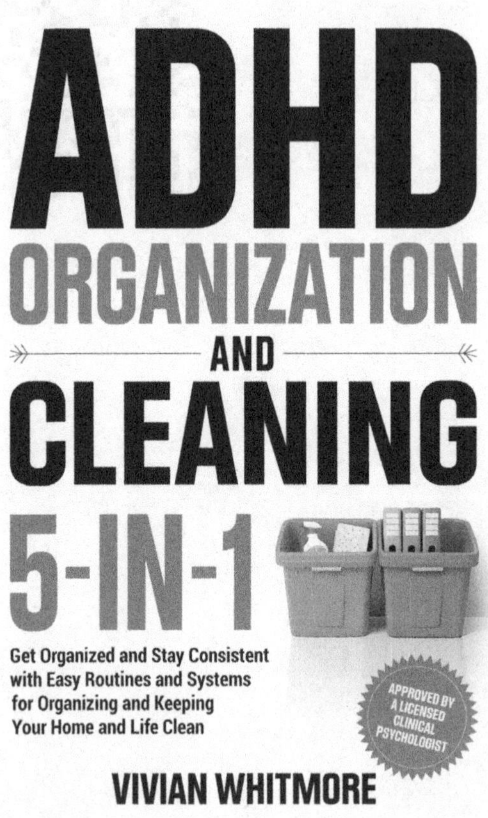

Claim Your Free Bonus

As a thank you for reading, I've put together a powerful digital bonus pack to help you apply what you've learned — even if you only have a few minutes a day.

Inside you'll find:

- ✓ Quick-access emotional reset tools
- ✓ A printable clarity map for focus and purpose
- ✓ 30 powerful journaling prompts
- ✓ Daily progress & reflection trackers
- ✓ A mini affirmation deck for calm and confidence

Access below to download your full bonus pack:

https://livetolearn.lpages.co/vivian-withmore-women-with-adult-adhd-10-in-1-paperback/

Or, scan the QR code

REFERENCES

Part 1: Women with ADHD 5-in-1

1. Par, Inc. "The Relationship Between Adult ADHD and Executive Function Deficits." https://www.parinc.com/learning-center/par-blog/detail/blog/2025/03/11/the-relationship-between-adult-adhd-and-executive-function-deficits
2. CHADD. "Why ADHD Is More Challenging for Women." https://chadd.org/attention-article/why-adhd-is-more-challenging-for-women/
3. Frontiers in Psychology. "ADHD and Sex Hormones in Females: A Systematic Review." https://www.frontiersin.org/journals/global-womens-health/articles/10.3389/fgwh.2025.1549028/full
4. PubMed Central. "Cognitive and perceptual load have opposing effects on brain network efficiency and behavioral variability in ADHD." https://pmc.ncbi.nlm.nih.gov/articles/PMC10727773/
5. Medical News Today. "ADHD and organization: Strategies to improve organization." https://www.medicalnewstoday.com/articles/adhd-and-organization
6. PubMed Central. "Learning and Memory Impairments With Attention-Deficit/Hyperactivity Disorder." https://pmc.ncbi.nlm.nih.gov/articles/PMC11081185/
7. ADD.org. "Executive Function Disorder & ADHD." https://add.org/executive-function-disorder/
8. Verywell Mind. "Multitasking." https://www.verywellmind.com/multitasking-2795003
9. Frontiers in Human Neuroscience. "The Effects of Working Memory Load on Auditory Distraction in Adults With Attention Deficit Hyperactivity Disorder." https://www.frontiersin.org/journals/human-neuroscience/articles/10.3389/fnhum.2021.771711/full

10. ADDitude Magazine. "ADHD, Masking, and Impostor Syndrome." https://www.additudemag.com/adhd-masking-signs-consequences-solutions/
11. Additude. "Why ADHD Is More Challenging for Women." https://www.additudemag.com/gender-differences-in-adhd-women-vs-men/
12. Medical News Today. "ADHD and organization: Strategies to improve organization." https://www.medicalnewstoday.com/articles/adhd-and-organization
13. LearningRx Brain Training. "Why Is Organization So Hard for People with ADHD?" https://www.learningrx.com/reston/why-organization-is-so-hard-adhd/
14. Psychiatrist.com. "3 Ways ADHD Makes Romantic Relationships More Challenging." https://www.psychiatrist.com/news/3-ways-adhd-makes-romantic-relationships-more-challenging/
15. Additude. "Hormonal Changes in Women with ADHD: 4 Gaping Holes in Research." https://www.additudemag.com/hormonal-changes-in-women-adhd-research/
16. The ADHD Centre for Women. "ADHD and Hormones in Women: Understanding the Link." https://adhdcentreforwomen.com/elementor-3748/
17. Monash University. "How hormones and the menstrual cycle can affect women with ADHD: 5 common questions." https://www.monash.edu/medicine/news/latest/2023-articles/how-hormones-and-the-menstrual-cycle-can-affect-women-with-adhd-5-common-questions
18. ADDitude Magazine. "PMS and ADHD: How the Menstrual Cycle Intensifies Symptoms." https://www.additudemag.com/adhd-and-periods-menstrual-cycle-hormones/
19. Grantome. "R01-MH119119-01A1." https://grantome.com/grant/NIH/R01-MH119119-01A1
20. ADD.org. "PMDD and ADHD." https://add.org/pmdd-and-adhd/

21. Healthline. "ADHD and Hormonal Changes in Women." https://www.healthline.com/health/adhd/adhd-and-hormonal-changes-in-women
22. CHADD.org. "Frenzied, Frazzled, and Overwhelmed: The Interaction of Hormones and ADHD in Women in Midlife." https://chadd.org/adhd-news/adhd-news-adults/frenzied-frazzled-and-overwhelmed-the-interaction-of-hormones-and-adhd-in-women-in-midlife/
23. Everynow.com. "Brain Fog or ADHD: How Perimenopause Can Make Symptoms Worse." https://www.evernow.com/learn/brain-fog-or-adhd-how-perimenopause-can-make-symptoms-worse
24. Pauz Health. "Estrogen, Executive Function & ADHD: The Untold Story of Women's Brains." https://pauz.health/blog/estrogen-executive-function-adhd-the-untold-story-of-womens-brains
25. YouTube. "ADHD & Hormones: The Impact on Women's Brains and Lives with Dr. David Chapman." https://www.youtube.com/watch?v=oCltf1A0DDA
26. Trinity Health Michigan. "Ask a Doc: Females, ADHD and Perimenopause/Menopause." https://www.trinityhealthmichigan.org/blog-articles/ask-doc-females-adhd-perimenopausemenopause
27. Relational Psych. "ADHD and Hormones in Women." https://www.relationalpsych.group/articles/adhd-and-hormones-in-women
28. PubMed. "DAT1 and DRD4 genes involved in key dimensions of adult ADHD." https://pubmed.ncbi.nlm.nih.gov/25555995/
29. Growing Therapy. "What Is Self-Compassion." https://growtherapy.com/blog/what-is-self-compassion/
30. The Center for ADHD. "The ADHD Burnout Cycle: Understanding Symptoms, Causes, and Recovery." https://www.usa.edu/blog/adhd-burnout-understanding-symptoms-and-recovery-methods/

31. Simply Psychology. "Rejection Sensitivity In ADHD Relationships." https://www.simplypsychology.org/rejection-sensitive-dysphoria-relationships.html
32. The ADHD Centre. "Emotional Dysregulation in ADHD." https://add.org/emotional-dysregulation-adhd/
33. The ADHD Centre. "DBT for ADHD." https://www.charliehealth.com/treatment-modalities/dialectical-behavior-therapy/dbt-for-adhd
34. The ADHD Centre. "ADHD and Self-Compassion." https://chadd.org/attention-article/adhd-and-self-compassion/
35. The ADHD Centre. "The Five Pillars of Self-Compassion." https://self-compassion.org/what-is-self-compassion/
36. Mi-Psych. "The Benefits of Self-Compassion." https://mi-psych.com.au/the-benefits-of-self-compassion/
37. True Peace Center. "The Surprising Science Behind Self-Compassion." https://www.truepeacecenter.com/news/the-surprising-science-behind-self-compassion-and-why-it-actually-works
38. ADHD BC. "The Impact of ADHD on Adult Life." https://adhdbc.ca/blog/the-impact-of-adhd-on-adult-life-navigating-work-relationships-and-self-care
39. Gallup News. "Women Still Handle Main Household Tasks in U.S." https://news.gallup.com/poll/283979/women-handle-main-household-tasks.aspx
40. BYU ScholarsArchive. "Household Labor, Gender Roles, and Family Satisfaction." https://scholarsarchive.byu.edu/context/facpub/article/4865/viewcontent/Household_Labor__Gender_Roles__and_Family_Satisfaction.pdf
41. United Way NCA. "Gender Norms." https://unitedwaynca.org/blog/gender-norms/
42. Cleveland Clinic. "Executive Dysfunction." https://my.clevelandclinic.org/health/symptoms/23224-executive-dysfunction

43. ResearchGate. "The Neurobiological Profile of Girls with ADHD." https://www.researchgate.net/publication/390030819_Exploring_the_Experiences_of_Women_with_ADHD_in_Professional_Settings_A_Qualitative_Study
44. Investopedia. "The Financial Challenges of ADHD—And How To Overcome Them." https://www.investopedia.com/financial-challenges-of-adhd-11775648
45. ADD.org. "ADHD Money Management: Financial Success And Stability." https://add.org/adhd-friendly-financial-management-yes-and-its-not-what-you-think/
46. ADDitude Magazine. "Rejection Sensitivity Dysphoria." https://www.additudemag.com/rejection-sensitivity-women-adhd/
47. WebMD. "Rejection Sensitive Dysphoria." https://www.webmd.com/add-adhd/rejection-sensitive-dysphoria
48. ADDitude Magazine. "Women with ADHD: Mental Fatigue, Internal Hyperactivity, Emotional Dysregulation." https://www.additudemag.com/women-with-adhd-mental-fatigue-internal-hyperactivity-emotional-dysregulation/
49. ADDitude Magazine. "The Link Between ADHD and Hormones." https://www.additudemag.com/gender-differences-in-adhd-women-vs-men/
50. PMC. "The Neurobiological Profile of Girls with ADHD." https://pmc.ncbi.nlm.nih.gov/articles/PMC3534724/
51. Johns Hopkins University. "The Neurobiological Profile of Girls with ADHD." https://pure.johnshopkins.edu/en/publications/the-neurobiological-profile-of-girls-with-adhd-4
52. The ADHD Centre for Women. "ADHD and Hormones: Understanding the Link." https://adhdcentreforwomen.com/elementor-3748/

53. "ADHD and organization | Proven strategies to simplify your life" https://www.tiimoapp.com/resource-hub/adhd-at-work-how-to-get-organized

Part 2: ADHD Workbook for Women 5-in-1

Introduction

1. https://advancedpsychiatryassociates.com/resources/blog/strategies-for-adults-living-with-adhd
2. https://lifeskillsadvocate.com/blog/pomodoro-technique-for-adhd/
3. https://add.org/adhd-paralysis/
4. https://www.sarahwest-adhd.com/blog/adhd-perimenopause-progesterone
5. https://www.zrtlab.com/blog/archive/supporting-teens-with-adhd-navigating-hormonal-changes-during-puberty/
6. https://add.org/emotional-dysregulation-adhd/
7. https://scholars.uky.edu/en/projects/estrogen-effects-on-adhd-and-cognition
8. https://pmc.ncbi.nlm.nih.gov/articles/PMC12145478/
9. https://www.additudemag.com/making-peace-with-your-clutter/
10. https://adhdandautismclinic.co.uk/unleashing-productivity-the-pomodoro-technique-for-adhd-management/
11. https://pubmed.ncbi.nlm.nih.gov/38039899/
12. https://lifeskillsadvocate.com/blog/time-blocking-for-adhd/
13. https://pmc.ncbi.nlm.nih.gov/articles/PMC10751335/
14. https://www.berkshirehealthcare.nhs.uk/media/109514308/4-adhd-guide-menopause.pdf
15. https://womensmentalhealth.org/posts/should-we-adjust-stimulant-dosage-premenstrually/
16. https://www.additudemag.com/adhd-and-periods-menstrual-cycle-hormones/

17. https://www.additudemag.com/how-to-improve-executive-function-adhd/
18. https://shahincarrigan.com/improving-communication-between-adhd-and-non-adhd-partners/
19. https://www.additudemag.com/dbt-skills-for-adhd-emotions-rsd/
20. https://www.simplypsychology.org/dialectical-behavior-therapy-for-adhd.html
21. https://chadd.org/attention-article/how-can-couples-with-adhd-keep-a-strong-relationship/
22. https://www.newportinstitute.com/resources/empowering-young-adults/body-doubling/
23. https://www.medicalnewstoday.com/articles/body-doubling-adhd

Book 1

1. https://www.helpguide.org/mental-health/adhd/managing-adult-adhd
2. https://add.org/executive-function-disorder/
3. https://add.org/adhd-paralysis/
4. https://advancedpsychiatryassociates.com/resources/blog/strategies-for-adults-living-with-adhd
5. https://www.additudemag.com/making-peace-with-your-clutter/
6. https://www.medicalnewstoday.com/articles/body-doubling-adhd
7. https://www.newportinstitute.com/resources/empowering-young-adults/body-doubling/
8. https://lifeskillsadvocate.com/blog/pomodoro-technique-for-adhd/
9. https://lifeskillsadvocate.com/blog/time-blocking-for-adhd/
10. https://www.iterateadhd.com/blog/the-adhd-tax
11. https://www.additudemag.com/how-to-improve-executive-function-adhd/

12. https://www.additudemag.com/how-to-calm-down-destress-techniques-adhd/
13. https://www.addrc.org/managing-rejection-sensitive-dysphoria-7-evidence-based-strategies-for-emotional-resilience/
14. https://psychiatry-psychopharmacology.com/en/marital-impact-of-adult-attention-deficit-hyperactivity-disorder-131265
15. https://shahincarrigan.com/improving-communication-between-adhd-and-non-adhd-partners/
16. https://chadd.org/attention-article/how-can-couples-with-adhd-keep-a-strong-relationship/
17. https://adhdandautismclinic.co.uk/unleashing-productivity-the-pomodoro-technique-for-adhd-management/

Book 2

1. https://lifeskillsadvocate.com/blog/pomodoro-technique-for-adhd/
2. https://lifeskillsadvocate.com/blog/time-blocking-for-adhd/
3. https://www.additudemag.com/how-to-improve-executive-function-adhd/
4. https://womensmentalhealth.org/posts/should-we-adjust-stimulant-dosage-premenstrually/
5. https://pmc.ncbi.nlm.nih.gov/articles/PMC6940517/
6. https://www.jmcp.org/doi/10.18553/jmcp.2021.21290
7. https://www.iterateadhd.com/blog/the-adhd-tax
8. https://pmc.ncbi.nlm.nih.gov/articles/PMC12145478/
9. https://scholars.uky.edu/en/projects/estrogen-effects-on-adhd-and-cognition
10. https://pubmed.ncbi.nlm.nih.gov/38039899/
11. https://www.additudemag.com/low-estrogen-adhd-hormones-theory/
12. https://pubmed.ncbi.nlm.nih.gov/39837362/

13. https://www.sarahwest-adhd.com/blog/adhd-perimenopause-progesterone
14. https://pmc.ncbi.nlm.nih.gov/articles/PMC10751335/
15. https://www.simplypsychology.org/dialectical-behavior-therapy-for-adhd.html
16. https://add.org/adhd-paralysis/
17. https://www.addrc.org/managing-rejection-sensitive-dysphoria-7-evidence-based-strategies-for-emotional-resilience/
18. https://shahincarrigan.com/improving-communication-between-adhd-and-non-adhd-partners/
19. https://www.medicalnewstoday.com/articles/body-doubling-adhd
20. https://adhdandautismclinic.co.uk/unleashing-productivity-the-pomodoro-technique-for-adhd-management/
21. https://www.berkshirehealthcare.nhs.uk/media/109514308/4-adhd-guide-menopause.pdf
22. https://add.org/executive-function-disorder/
23. https://www.newportinstitute.com/resources/empowering-young-adults/body-doubling/
24. https://add.org/executive-function-disorder/
25. https://www.additudemag.com/adhd-and-periods-menstrual-cycle-hormones/

Book 3

1. https://add.org/executive-function-disorder/
2. https://adhdandautismclinic.co.uk/unleashing-productivity-the-pomodoro-technique-for-adhd-management/
3. https://add.org/adhd-paralysis/
4. https://www.additudemag.com/how-to-improve-executive-function-adhd/
5. https://www.verywellmind.com/the-financial-toll-of-living-with-adhd-6744610

6. https://lifeskillsadvocate.com/blog/pomodoro-technique-for-adhd/
7. https://advancedpsychiatryassociates.com/resources/blog/strategies-for-adults-living-with-adhd
8. https://pmc.ncbi.nlm.nih.gov/articles/PMC6406620/
9. https://add.org/emotional-dysregulation-adhd/
10. https://www.additudemag.com/adhd-and-periods-menstrual-cycle-hormones/
11. https://chadd.org/attention-article/how-can-couples-with-adhd-keep-a-strong-relationship/
12. https://www.iterateadhd.com/blog/the-adhd-tax
13. https://lifeskillsadvocate.com/blog/time-blocking-for-adhd/

Book 4

1. https://pmc.ncbi.nlm.nih.gov/articles/PMC12145478/
2. https://pubmed.ncbi.nlm.nih.gov/38039899/
3. https://lifeskillsadvocate.com/blog/pomodoro-technique-for-adhd/
4. https://www.additudemag.com/low-estrogen-adhd-hormones-theory/
5. https://pmc.ncbi.nlm.nih.gov/articles/PMC10751335/
6. https://womensmentalhealth.org/posts/should-we-adjust-stimulant-dosage-premenstrually/
7. https://www.additudemag.com/adhd-and-periods-menstrual-cycle-hormones/
8. https://www.additudemag.com/how-to-calm-down-destress-techniques-adhd/
9. https://www.additudemag.com/dbt-skills-for-adhd-emotions-rsd/
10. https://www.additudemag.com/how-to-improve-executive-function-adhd/
11. https://www.ovid.com/journals/pnpbp/fulltext/10.1016/j.pnpbp.2025.111261~the-effects-of-psychostimulants-in-menstruating-women-with

12. https://www.sarahwest-adhd.com/blog/adhd-perimenopause-progesterone
13. https://add.org/executive-function-disorder/
14. https://add.org/emotional-dysregulation-adhd/
15. https://adhdandautismclinic.co.uk/unleashing-productivity-the-pomodoro-technique-for-adhd-management/
16. https://www.berkshirehealthcare.nhs.uk/media/109514308/4-adhd-guide-menopause.pdf

Book 5

1. https://add.org/executive-function-disorder/
2. https://add.org/adhd-paralysis/
3. https://www.additudemag.com/dbt-skills-for-adhd-emotions-rsd/
4. https://www.simplypsychology.org/dialectical-behavior-therapy-for-adhd.html
5. https://chadd.org/attention-article/how-can-couples-with-adhd-keep-a-strong-relationship/
6. https://www.additudemag.com/how-to-calm-down-destress-techniques-adhd/
7. https://www.additudemag.com/how-to-improve-executive-function-adhd/
8. https://add.org/emotional-dysregulation-adhd/
9. https://pmc.ncbi.nlm.nih.gov/articles/PMC10751335/
10. https://www.addrc.org/managing-rejection-sensitive-dysphoria-7-evidence-based-strategies-for-emotional-resilience/
11. https://www.additudemag.com/marriage-communication-adhd-spouses/
12. https://psychiatry-psychopharmacology.com/en/marital-impact-of-adult-attention-deficit-hyperactivity-disorder-131265
13. https://neurodivergentinsights.com/how-to-deal-with-rejection-sensitive-dysphoria/

14. https://www.sarahwest-adhd.com/blog/adhd-perimenopause-progesterone
15. https://pubmed.ncbi.nlm.nih.gov/39837362/
16. https://womensmentalhealth.org/posts/should-we-adjust-stimulant-dosage-premenstrually/
17. https://pmc.ncbi.nlm.nih.gov/articles/PMC12145478/
18. https://pubmed.ncbi.nlm.nih.gov/38039899/
19. https://www.additudemag.com/women-hormones-and-adhd/
20. https://www.verywellmind.com/the-financial-toll-of-living-with-adhd-6744610

Overall Conclusion

1. https://psychiatry-psychopharmacology.com/en/marital-impact-of-adult-attention-deficit-hyperactivity-disorder-131265
2. https://pmc.ncbi.nlm.nih.gov/articles/PMC6940517/
3. https://pmc.ncbi.nlm.nih.gov/articles/PMC12145478/
4. https://www.jmcp.org/doi/10.18553/jmcp.2021.21290
5. https://www.helpguide.org/mental-health/adhd/managing-adult-adhd
6. https://pmc.ncbi.nlm.nih.gov/articles/PMC10751335/
7. https://pubmed.ncbi.nlm.nih.gov/39837362/
8. https://www.additudemag.com/how-to-improve-executive-function-adhd/
9. https://www.simplypsychology.org/dialectical-behavior-therapy-for-adhd.html
10. https://www.verywellmind.com/the-financial-toll-of-living-with-adhd-6744610
11. https://chadd.org/attention-article/how-can-couples-with-adhd-keep-a-strong-relationship/
12. https://add.org/emotional-dysregulation-adhd/
13. https://www.iterateadhd.com/blog/the-adhd-tax
14. https://lifeskillsadvocate.com/blog/time-blocking-for-adhd/

15. https://www.addrc.org/managing-rejection-sensitive-dysphoria-7-evidence-based-strategies-for-emotional-resilience/
16. https://www.sarahwest-adhd.com/blog/adhd-perimenopause-progesterone
17. https://www.psychologytools.com/resource/mastering-your-adult-adhd-a-cognitive-behavioral-treatment-program-workbook

Made in United States
Orlando, FL
10 September 2026

87552076R00361